D1557163

CONSTITUTIONALISM

NOMOS

XX

N O M O S

Lieber-Alberton, Publishers

New York University Press

NOMOS XX

Yearbook of the American Society for Political and Legal Philosophy

CONSTITUTIONALISM

Edited by

J. Roland Pennock, *Swarthmore College*

and

John W. Chapman, *University of Pittsburgh*

New York: New York University Press · 1979

Constitutionalism: Nomos XX
edited by J. Roland Pennock and John W. Chapman

Copyright © 1979 by New York University

Library of Congress Cataloging in Publication Data
Main Entry under title:

Constitutionalism.

  (Nomos 20)
  Includes bibliographical references and index.
  1. Constitutional law—Addresses, essays, lectures.
2. Constitutional law—Interpretation and construction
—Addresses, essays, lectures. I. Pennock, James Ro-
land. II. Chapman, John William, 1923-
III. Series.
K3165.C6   342.02′9   78-58843
ISBN 0-8147-6573-4

Printed in the United States of America

K5
4-26

PREFACE

Among the living authors whose names are outstanding in the literature of constitutionalism, none outshines that of Carl Joachim Friedrich. After the members of the American Society for Political and Legal Philosophy voted to make this subject the topic for the 1975 meetings of the Society, it was an easy decision to make this event a celebration of Friedrich's career and of his contribution to constitutionalism, both in theory and in practice. Unfortunately, ill health prevented him from attending the meetings, which were held in San Francisco in conjunction with those of the American Political Science Association. In recognition of Friedrich's scholarly work, as well as of his founding and years-long leadership of this Society, two of his former students, Dante Germino and Paul Sigmund, presented papers. They appear as the opening pieces in this volume—which the editors are pleased to dedicate to their friend, Carl.

The program of the meetings, arranged by a committee under the chairmanship of Gordon Schochet, provided much of the meat of this volume. As usual, some of the chapters are revisions of papers presented at the meetings; others are expanded (sometimes transformed!) comments of program commentators; others grew out of

impromptu remarks called forth by the papers; and still others—
those of Keohane and Mojekwu—were arranged for subsequent to
the meetings. While the resulting volume makes no pretense to
being a treatise on constitutionalism, nor even to dealing with all of
its central issues, we believe that anyone interested in the subject
will find in these pages much to enlighten, to intrigue, and to
provoke.

A brief preview will give some guidance to the selective reader,
without stealing the thunder of the contributors. Appropriately,
Gordon Schochet provides a general introduction. Among the
papers that follow, some are historical and comparative, some
philosophical and jurisprudential, and some deal with constitutional interpretation. For the most part, barring the Introduction
and the Epilogue, they do not deal in a general way with the
broadest issues of constitutionalism, being more specialized. The
first two papers following the Introduction comprise our celebration
of the work of Carl Friedrich, as presented by Germino and
Sigmund.

The historical-comparative section opens with a paper by Nannerl Keohane that deals with constitutionalism in pre-Reformation
France, more specifically with the work of Claude de Seyssel. It
provides an example of traditional, extralegal constitutionalism.
The two succeeding papers comprise a discourse on the establishment of democratic constitutionalism in America, as exemplified in
the drafting of three of the original state constitutions, by Cecelia
Kenyon, and an account of James Madison's views on the value of
bills of rights, especially with reference to our own Constitution, by
Wilfrid Rumble. The last paper in this section, by Christopher
Mojekwu, demonstrates the problems of fitting a Western-style
constitution to the needs of an emerging nation, Nigeria, in which
the problems of tribalism are still acute.

The philosophical-jurisprudential section is introduced by
Thomas Grey's paper, which provides a careful conceptual analysis
and classification of the various aspects of constitutionalism. It is
followed by two papers sparked, almost accidentally as it now
appears, by Cecelia Kenyon's contribution. In her original paper,
she made certain remarks suggesting that a written constitution, as
a set of forms and procedures, is morally neutral. It is fortunate that
she did—although she now indicates that the remarks did not repre-

sent her true meaning—because they evoked very useful responses in the form of the papers by William Bennett and George Kateb, each of whom, in quite different ways, takes issue with that position. The other two papers in this section deal with the work of John Rawls. Ronald Moore, pointing out that little if any of the "Rawls industry" has dealt with the second of Rawls's four stages, the constitution-making stage, concentrates his attention upon certain aspects of that stage, in which he finds serious "inherent difficulties." Richard Parker discusses the usefulness of Rawls's work for the law school teacher of jurisprudence, believing that it will provide the entering wedge for ethical argumentation into the law.

The next three papers deal with the subject of constitutional interpretation. George Fletcher is concerned to show that utilitarianism does not provide an adequate foundation for the allocation of powers among branches of government and, more specifically, that the attempts of courts to do so in particular areas have not succeeded. Stephanie Lewis, while agreeing with his antiutilitarian stance, contends that Fletcher's arguments do not prove his point and that a different mode of approach is required. Arthur Miller's contribution is less philosophical, and more attuned to current controversy in the law, than the other papers in this and the preceding section. His is a defense of judicial activism and an attack on Nathan Glazer's neoconservatism. In judicial activism he sees a "final, even desperate hope of a crumbling system of American constitutionalism."

Finally, in an Epilogue, one of the editors reverts to the general theme of the nature and prospects of constitutionalism, especially with reference to the United States.

To Gordon Schochet for arranging the program for the meetings, and to all the contributors to this volume, as well as to our editorial assistant, Eleanor Greitzer, the editors are indeed grateful.

J.R.P.
J.W.C.

CONTENTS

PART II

PART III

PART IV

CONTRIBUTORS

WILLIAM J. BENNETT
Philosophy and Law, National Humanities Center

GEORGE P. FLETCHER
Law, University of California, Los Angeles

DANTE GERMINO
Government, University of Virginia

THOMAS C. GREY
Law, Stanford University

GEORGE KATEB
Political Science, Amherst College

CECELIA M. KENYON
Government, Smith College

NANNERL O. KEOHANE
Political Science, Stanford University

STEPHANIE R. LEWIS
Philosophy, Princeton University

ARTHUR S. MILLER
Law, George Washington University

CHRISTOPHER C. MOJEKWU
Politics, Lake Forest College

RONALD MOORE
Philosophy, University of Washington

RICHARD B. PARKER
Law, Rutgers University—Newark

J. ROLAND PENNOCK
Political Science, Swarthmore College

WILFRID E. RUMBLE
Political Science, Vassar College

GORDON J. SCHOCHET
Political Science, Livingston College

PAUL SIGMUND
Politics, Princeton University

1

INTRODUCTION: CONSTITUTIONALISM, LIBERALISM, AND THE STUDY OF POLITICS

GORDON J. SCHOCHET *

I

The veneration of "constitutionalism" is among the enduring and probably justified vanities of liberal democratic theory. Struggles for personal freedoms and for escape from arbitary political rule have been among the conspicuous features of the history of Western Europe and America since the sixteenth century. Constitutional-ism's fundamental principles of limited government and the rule of law (that governments exist only to serve specified ends and properly function only according to specified rules) emerged as the operative ideals of these struggles.

The *tradition* of constitutionalism is much older, extending through the Middle Ages to antiquity. Among the central tasks of

* This essay is a considerable revision and elaboration of my introductory remarks at the first session of the 1975 meeting of the American Society for Political and Legal Philosophy. The research out of which this paper grew has enjoyed the support of the National Endowment for the Humanities and the Research Council of Rutgers University. I am especially grateful to Louise Haberman of Princeton University for her very helpful criticisms and suggestions.

political thought is to establish criteria for distinguishing between valid and illegitimate political action. The "constitution"—in all its historical forms—has always been a standard of legitimacy, for it has been seen as embodying the defining character of its civil society. Classically, the concept had to do with the components or *constituents* of a society and could be used in a purely descriptive sense. Civil institutions were to function in accordance with the constitutional ordering of their society. This doctrine was related to conceptions of human nature, for the constitution can never be divorced from human capacities, needs, and deficiencies.

In addition to human capacities, constitutional limitations included the accumulated traditions, folkways, and practices of a people as well as the overarching dictates of nature and/or divinity. There is a slippery quality to standards such as these, for unless their requirements are codified they may be unclear or contradictory. More important, the problem of enforcement remains even after that of interpretation has been settled. The classical solution to this problem was expansive participation. It was presumed that having the entire citizenry take part in politics—or when that proved impossible, having such "representative" institutions as the Roman Senate act in its stead—would insure that the requirements of the constitution were met. The participatory institutions of Athens and the later representative bodies of Rome were in some sense the protectors and defenders of unwritten constitutional limitations. Their histories are marked by frequent though not always successful assertions of the constitution against the designs of institutionally independent and despotic rulers.

Still, a strain of traditional constitutionalism appears to have been compatible with independent rulers. The enforcement of constitutional limits ultimately depended upon the good will of public officials, for traditional constitutionalism was external to the institutions it limited. Constitutionalism could not, by itself and in a way that was internal to the polity, guarantee that its requirements were met. When good will failed, there was nothing other than the coercive ability of various social agencies to enforce constitutionalism.[1] The legal ability of governors to ignore constitutional standards was insurmountable, and thus the presumption that constitutionalism actually existed before the early modern period is something of a fiction. The problem for traditional constitutional doctrines was that of effectively and consistently imposing limits on the political order.

A pair of political phenomena in the two centuries following the Reformation effected the transformation of traditional constitutionalism and thereby resolved this dilemma. They were the emergence of the secular (and eventually liberal) state and the rise of popular sovereignty. The secular state, not bound by the restraints that had limited the medieval polity, developed its own ethic, an ethic that was peculiarly political and potentially free of the more expansive aspects of constitutional limits. The earliest versions of that ethic were embodied in the theory of absolute sovereignty and the practices of absolutism in seventeenth-century France and England. Thus, the theoretical conflict between governors and constitutional rules was initially resolved in favor of the sovereign. By the end of the eighteenth century, popular sovereignty had supplanted absolutism as the political standard and carried with it the notion that the state was the consciously contrived creature of the people. So conceived, the state was subject to whatever limitations the people imposed. The process by which absolutist rule was gradually subjected to the restraints of popular sovereignty is excellently described in John Locke's account of the growth of limitation on prerogative. Lock's story contains the germ of the modern theory of constitutionalism.

It is easie to conceive, that in the Infancy of Governments, when Commonwealths differed little from Families in number of People, they differ'd from them too but little in number of Laws: And the Governours, being as the Fathers of them, watching over them for their good, the Government was almost all Prerogative. A few establish'd Laws served the turn, and the discretion and care of the Ruler supply'd the rest. But when mistake, or flattery prevailed with weak Princes to make use of this Power, for private ends of their own, and not for the publick good, the People were fain by express Laws to get Prerogative determin'd, in those points, wherein they found disadvantage from it: And thus declared limitations of Prerogative were by the People found necessary in Cases, which

they and their Ancestors had left, in the utmost latitude, to the
Wisdom of those Princes, who made no other but a right use of
it, that is, for the good of their People.[2]

Once established, these limitations on the prerogative were
presumed to be permanently binding.[3] Indeed, the hallmark of
modern constitutionalism is its reliance upon formal limitations on
political power that are directly tied to popular sovereignty.[4] Since
the seventeenth century, constitutionalists have sought institutional
means of imposing popularly originated limits on governments.

The transition from traditional to modern constitutionalism
involved something of a persuasive redefinition [5] of the term. It
seems self-evidently true that a society's constitution (taking the
term in its traditional sense) should define its political institutions
and processes and establish standards for their evaluation. What is
not self-evident is the assertion that those defining standards should
be the formally enacted expression of the will of the people. By
calling the latter, modern doctrine "constitutionalism," its proponents were able to capture for it the force of the tradition.

Modern constitutionalism, with the emerging liberalism whose
ideology it shares, predicates naturally free, apolitical, and rights-
bearing individuals who *need* and therefore establish governments
that they can, may, and should control. The control is necessary
because, as historical experiences have shown, there is an almost
natural tendency for governments and governors to become arbitrary and oppressive, a tendency that may be due to human frailty
or to the irresistible push of institutions.[6] The modern doctrine
appears to be quite different from traditional constitutionalism, but
that difference is largely due to a narrowing of the meaning of
politics and its place in the social order. Where classical theories saw
the state and society as coextensive, modern conceptions distinguish
between them. Many of the limits on the modern constitutional
state spring directly from the distinction and from our determination to maintain the separation of the social and the private from
the political and the public.

II

Reliance upon formal constitutional embodiments of governing principles is nearly universal today. Written constitutions, which originated as protections against arbitrary, authoritarian, and absolute rule, traditionally signaled the desire for (if not always the existence of) limited, responsible government. Today, however, a "constitution" in this sense merely identifies a set of *formal* political institutions rather than an ideology. The social, economic, technological, military, and even political exigencies of contemporary society have encouraged the rapid expansion of governments throughout the world. Shifting political, moral, and economic belief systems have justified the process; and the simple persistence of authoritarian impulses continues to challenge the ideal of limited government without weakening the resort to written constitutions.

It is no wonder, then, that "constitutionalism," once part of the standard vocabulary of the student of politics, is now seldom encountered, having fallen into apparent intellectual disrepute. The word itself has something of a strange, old-fashioned, or perhaps even irrelevant sound to the modern political ear.[7]

The disappearance of "constitutionalism" from recent scholarship is due to shifting academic fashions and new political realities to which they have been in part a response. The political factors are (1) the virtually universal resort to written constitutions and (2) the growing inadequacy of limited government to modern problems. The academic factors include (3) behavioralism and (4) a multifaceted critique of liberalism.[8]

1. As I have already suggested, there is a sense in which constitutionalism is irrelevant or trivialized because of the nearly worldwide appeal to formal constitutions and to constitutional principles to justify partisan politics. There is hardly a modern state that does not have a formal constitution that purportedly establishes and defines its governmental institutions. Thus, there is little point in discussing constitutionalism as a significant and distinct political concept; its apparent universality has rendered it vacuous. Under the rubric of "constitutionalism" construed in this narrowly formal and descriptive sense can be found an array of polities that includes traditional "constitutional democracies" of the West,

autocratic and single-party states, communist political systems, and the racially oppressive regimes of South Africa and Rhodesia. Indeed, it is clear that an international collection of state constitutions—of the kind that could be found on library shelves in relative abundance in the 1950s—would not be an adequate guide to actual political practices.

2. Many of the urgent problems of modern society have arisen long after the heyday of constitutionalism and require more decisive and resolute action than limited constitutional government can provide. Expanding population coupled with growing economic disparities, the need to conserve natural resources, and the regulation of deadly technologies provide only the most conspicuous examples. I shall discuss the theoretical counterpart to this practical condition in the analysis of the critique of liberalism.

3. In political science, constitutionalism was among the unnoticed victims of the "behavioral revolution" of the 1950s. For most of its history, the discipline had been dominated by institutional, historical, and normative concerns. Part of the achievement of behavioralism was to turn attention from institutions to behavior, from laws and formal structures to systems and social settings, and from normative philosophy to "scientific" and "value-free" theoretical generalizations.[9] The discipline that emerged from the 1950s had little room for political philosophy or its history; constitutionalism had its roots and many of its branches in both fields.

The term and its related concepts have functioned normatively in political and academic debates.[10] Probably because of its status as the barrier to authoritarianism, constitutionalism had been one of those justifying concepts that people fought to possess.[11] The debates raging between Great Britain and the American colonies in the 1760s and 1770s over the meaning of the British constitution and whose claims it sanctioned provide an excellent case in point; the issue here is not who was right but that each side was equally persuaded that its interpretation was correct.[12] Eventually, a concept that functions so loosely must be abandoned by a discipline that aims at scientific rigor.

4. Current and widespread dissatisfaction with liberalism further contributes to the neglect of constitutionalism.[13] The principles and practices that engendered the individualism, the welfare economics and even some aspects of the social democracy that are integral to

liberalism depend upon constitutionalism. In its modern form, constitutionalism was a major accomplishment of the individualist attack on European absolutism. The establishment of constitutional protections for individual rights was a crucial step in the development of liberal politics, and criticisms of individualism and its concomitant theory of rights must also entail criticisms of constitutionalism.

The relevant aspects of the critique of liberalism are (a) the rejection of the negative state in the name of civic virtue and leadership, and (b) the attack on rule formalism and proceduralism.

a. Historically, the general political view of which modern constitutionalism is an expression has treated government as a kind of necessary evil. Political institutions, while making substantial contributions to human well-being, present great opportunities for tyranny and abuse, against which strong safeguards must be provided. The most important of these safeguards is the limitations and restraints contained in constitutional protections. The negative constitutional state cannot act either positively or creatively; its functions are largely restricted to the removal of irrelevant public obstacles to citizens' enjoyment of their rights. The liberal state rests upon the presumption of a fundamental and unbridgeable gap between public and private existence; its functions are restricted to the public realm, for in their private lives, people are regarded as self-sufficient. This state—the constitutional, liberal state—is prohibited from participating in the moral life of the citizen, is unable to assist in the pursuit of "virtue," and can never function as a "civic educator." [14]

The recent, reawakened interest in "civic virtue" has consequently condemned the minimal state. Liberalism has emptied citizenship of its meaning and reduced participation to voting. The instrumentalities of political participation have become ends in themselves, to the exclusion of more genuine forms of participation in the life of the polity. Contemporary politics is characterized by cynicism and indifference that are the inescapable results of our beliefs and practices. Instead of emphasizing the limitations on the political order and instead of conceiving the political relation in terms of public power, individual rights and freedoms, and voluntarily assumed obligation, we must learn to deal with citizen responsibility and leadership. In our quest for a restored politics of "civic virtue," we shall have to abandon liberalism and constitutionalism as well.

b. Finally, there is a growing dissatisfaction with the procedural and voluntaristic conceptions of politics that are presupposed by constitutionalism and by the claim that political institutions are created and manipulated simply to serve various public ends. Conformity to established procedures, rather than results, is the major criterion of "constitutionality." Therefore, constitutionalism supports a rule formalism that maintains the status quo, leaves no room for political discretion, is incapable of sanctioning resolute responses to emergencies and radically new situations, and is indifferent to political substances. The ends of the constitutional state are at best contingent and false abstractions from the social world.

While there are absurdities in the extremes of some of these claims as I have overstated them (in the hope of making them clear), there are recognizable truths in each of them. The relatively simple point I have wanted to make is that collectively the effect of these contentions has been to hinder the study of constitutionalism, in part by misconstruing its nature and significance.

It is not possible to develop responses to these criticisms without launching a defense of liberalism itself. Even that would not be fully satisfactory, for it would not be an answer so much as the assertion of a rival conception of politics. Nonetheless, we can suggest in broad outline that such an assertion would rest upon the desirability of the irreducible *value* pluralism in liberal democratic society [15] and would emphasize the importance of formal constitutional rules in preserving that pluralism. Further points would include a defense of privacy from politics, an emphasis upon the essentially nonpublic nature of virtue in the context of value pluralism, and a recognition of the importance of personal liberty to the achievement of virtue.[16] The essential difficulty with substantive and "civic-virtue" critiques of liberal constitutionalism is that the capacity for doing public good and engaging in civic education that they would bestow upon political institutions is, as such classical "liberals" as John Locke and John Stuart Mill realized, equally the capacity for doing public evil.

It should also be noted that much of the contemporary discussion of liberalism and its roots has omitted the possibility of relying upon constitutional structures and practices to assure that the state will perform its positive functions of *improving* its citizens and facilitating their achievement of virtue. A sense of this possible relation of liberal constitutionalism to civic virtue can be found in many eighteenth-century republican theories (to which attention has been drawn by the recent work of J.G.A. Pocock and Bernard Bailyn); [17] it is present in James Harrington's dependence in *Oceana* upon constitutional arrangements to create a virtuous citizenry; and the same sentiment pervades John Rawls's reliance upon formal institutions in *A Theory of Justice* to encourage and support the "moral development" of citizens in his just society. Indeed, if it were possible to recapture this aspect of eighteenth-century republicanism with its union of virtue and liberalism, we might also again see the vitality and value of constitutionalism.[18]

III

Recent events, it would seem, have spurred a renewed academic interest in constitutionalism. The observation of the Bicentennial of American independence has inspired a number of studies of the nation's constitutional tradition as well as of the Constitution itself. The "constitutional crisis" that led to Richard Nixon's resignation generated new analyses of the doctrine of the separation of powers and the constitutional problem of impeachment. Finally, John Rawls devoted nearly one-third of his *Theory of Justice* to analyses of the constitutional structure of his just society.[19] One result of all this attention could be an updated and reinvigorated theory of constitutionalism.

To my knowledge, no rigorously comprehensive conceptual study of constitutionalism has been published; work on the subject has been primarily historical and political. What follows is intended as the beginnings of a preface to a proper conceptual analysis.

Let me begin from James Madison's words in *Federalist* 51:

> But what is government itself but the greatest of all reflections on human nature? If men were angels, no government would be necessary. If angels were to govern men, neither external nor internal controls on government would be necessary. In framing a government which is to be administered by

men over men, the great difficulty lies in this: you must first
enable the government to control the governed; and in the next
place oblige it to control itself. A dependence on the people is,
no doubt, the primary control on the government; but
experience has taught mankind the necessity of auxiliary
precautions.

This passage captures the heart of constitutionalism. The essence
of Madison's contention is that political authority ought to consist
in determinate and relatively clearly specifiable powers and that
proper government is therefore limited rather than omnicompetent.
The principles of governmental specificity are necessarily external
and logically prior to the operation of the system, are positive or
human (perhaps "conventional") rather than natural, and establish
criteria of validity for the system. This set of strictures distinguishes
constitutionalism as a conception of political limits from classical
appeals to natural law and to the cosmic order as sources of political
limits. (These latter appeals, with considerable warrant but I think
ultimately incorrectly, are labeled ancient or medieval constitutionalism.)

Three corollaries follow from this reading of Madison.

1. The *validity* of the constitutional rules of governmental
specificity must be independent of the system. In a formal sense,
these rules are at least contingent if not somewhat arbitrary from
the internal perspective of the system, even though they may be,
and in fact usually are, fully consonant with the system's own,
internal sense of purpose and validity. I do not now wish to analyze
the relationship between these constitutionalist rules of specificity
and the internal operation and ideology of the system to which they
pertain and the political-legal functions they superintended; I
should simply note the obvious fact that the constitution and its
rules grow out of an ideology which they then support and tend to
confirm, thereby helping to slow the pace of ideological change.
Conversely, when such changes do occur—and however they may be
caused—if they are permanent and sufficiently important, they will
condition and perhaps alter the constitutional rules.

2. In order to be effective, the constitutional rules of specificity
must be knowable and known. In principle, they must be *clearly*
knowable, but in practice, their application must be "open tex-

tured" unless a political-legal system is static. The effective operation of a body of constitutional rules over a long period requires a level of abstractness sufficient for its application to new and possibly unanticipated circumstances. Indeed, the exercise of judgment and political wisdom that is necessary for such extensions of constitutional rules, and is necessarily built into the practice of constitutionalism, weakens the complaint that constitutionalism is apolitical and indifferent toward leadership. The existence of these knowable rules provides an important check on the activities of governing officials. Where their interpretations of constitutional permissibility are questioned, there exists a public standard to which to refer.

3. Since the rules are positive, human contrivances, they can be altered as general perceptions of societal purpose and political efficacy vary. Accordingly, what is reasonable, desirable, and constitutionally valid at one time can be deemed invalid at another. Similarly, no one set of political arrangements is uniquely required by constitutionalism; the separation of powers, for instance, is not entailed by constitutionalism as a means of limiting government.[20]

I shall conclude with two additional conceptual points. There is a closeness between constitutionalism per se and the having of a constitution, a closeness that is behind the easy and frequent slippage from one to the other. This closeness is both conceptual and political. In seventeenth-century England, the philosophically inconclusive debates over the fundamental law led quite easily to such *political* devices as the Agreements of the People, the Instrument of Government, and the great volume of formal, constitutional proposals offered in 1659-60 for altering and revivifying the old Commonwealth even as the details of Charles II's return were being worked out in France. Little more than a century later, similar debates and unhappy political experiences lay behind the universal resort to written constitutions in Revolutionary America. The American view, in effect, seems to have been that the best way to insure that the principles of constitutionalism would be observed was through formal constitutions.

Second, whatever its historical and political status may be, there is something logically incoherent about the modern doctrine of constitutionalism; for it places a limit on supreme political authority without denying its existence. This conceptual difficulty was well expressed more than three hundred years ago by Sir Robert

Filmer, Royalist defender of Charles I and posthumous opponent of John Locke, who insisted:

> There never was, nor ever can be any people governed without a power of making laws, and every power of making laws must be arbitrary: for to make a law according to law, is *contradictio in adjecto*.[21]

It is precisely that contradiction of limited supreme power that is at the heart of constitutionalism's rejection of the traditional doctrine of absolute sovereignty. Both the theory and practice of constitutionalism ignore the logical niceties of absolutism, opting instead for the contradictions of popular sovereignty and revealing how far from philosophy politics can be.

NOTES

1. When persuasion failed, the standard means of acting in defense of the constitution were revolution and regicide.
2. John Locke, *Two Treatises of Government* (1690), ed. Peter Laslett (Cambridge, 1960), II, 162. See also sections 163-165.
3. Political debates in seventeenth-century England were precisely about the legitimacy of imposing binding limits on the sovereign. See, for instance, J. W. Gough, *Fundamental Law in English Constitutional History* (Oxford, 1955); Margaret A. Judson, *The Crisis of the Constitution* (New Brunswick, N.J., 1949); J. G. A. Pocock, *The Ancient Constitution and the Feudal Law* (Cambridge, 1957); and Gordon J. Schochet, *Patriarchalism and Political Thought* (Oxford, 1975).
4. See Julian H. Franklin, "Constitutionalism in the Sixteenth Century: The Monarchomachs," *Political Theory and Social Change,* ed. David Spitz (New York, 1967), pp. 117-132, esp. pp. 117-120. See also Franklin's introductory essay in his *Constitutionalism and Resistance in the Sixteenth Century: Three Treatises by Hotman, Beza, and Mornay* (New York, 1969). Also relevant is Francis D. Wormuth, *The Origins of Modern Constitutionalism* (New York, 1949); cf. Charles H. McIlwain, *Constitutionalism: Ancient and Modern,* rev. ed., paperbound reprint (Ithaca, 1958), for the claim that traditional and modern constitutionalism are continuous. For discussion of this issue, see Harvey Wheeler, "Constitutionalism," *Handbook of Political Science,* vol. 5: *Governmental Institutions and Processes,* ed. Fred I. Greenstein and Nelson W. Polsby (Reading, Mass., 1975), pp. 1-91, esp. pp. 28-37.

5. I am using the term "persuasive definition" in its philosophic sense. See Charles L. Stevenson, *Ethics and Language* (New Haven, 1944), ch. 9.

6. The United States Constitution and its historical context provide an excellent illustration. Contemporary Americans, proud heirs to the British constitutional tradition which our forebears claimed and began to transform in the late eighteenth century, see in the constitutional limits on our government the preservation of democratic freedoms and rights. The American constitutional formula was designed to avoid both the tyranny of a George III and the tyranny of governmental powerlessness. It was a formula that had virtually defined the nation's recently ended colonial past and that owed as much to skepticism about human nature as it did to the scientific rationalism of the Enlightenment. Only by recognizing that the government is to be administered, not by angels but by "men over men," Madison reasoned in *Federalist* 51, and by building a set of "auxiliary precautions" into the system itself, could America escape the potential of tyranny. This reliance upon a written constitution as the surest means of guaranteeing limited government and the rule of law is the most conspicuous attribute of modern constitutionalism and represents one of America's major political contributions to Western culture.

7. "Constitutional law," of course, is of major importance to lawyers and political scientists (but in the latter discipline the field is often now broadened into "public law," has become increasingly oriented toward "policy" and "impact," and is less concerned with normative and institutional analyses). The evolution of the Constitution of 1789 remains a central issue to historians of the post-Revolutionary period. Legal and political philosophers continue to be interested in questions about the validity, interpretation, and change of law, questions that at base must refer to "fundamental" or constitutional law and to the *principles* of constitutionalism. But through it all, "constitutionalism" is a word scarely uttered. In fact the significance that remains to the concept is almost purely historical, for it suggests the names of Charles Howard McIlwain, Edward S. Corwin, and Carl J. Friedrich and serves largely to remind us of the kinds of questions that exercised our academic progenitors.

8. In the discussion that follows, most of the examples are taken from seventeenth- and eighteenth-century English and American history, my normal academic bailiwick and the context to which modern constitutionalism traces its origins.

9. As Robert Dahl wrote in his influential *Preface to Democratic Theory* (Chicago, 1956), p. 83, "The first and crucial variables to which

political scientists must direct their attention are social and not
constitutional." See also pp. 134-135; cf. M. J. C. Vile, *Constitutionalism
and the Separation of Powers* (Oxford, 1967), ch. 9, esp. pp. 303-313.

10. Charles Howard McIlwain, for instance, often failed to distinguish
between constitutionalism as a concept and as a political standard.
See his *Constitutionalism and the Changing World* (Cambridge, 1939), pp.
85 and 266-273 and the whole of ch. 4, in which he insisted that
"Whig sovereignty," that is, the theory of unlimited (legislative)
sovereignty, is equivalent to the doctrines of Hobbes and Hitler!

11. See W. B. Gallie, "Essentially Contested Concepts," originally published in 1956 and reprinted as ch. 8 of his *Philosophy and the Historical
Understanding*, 2d ed. (New York, 1968). Constitutionalism is not
general enough to fit Gallie's notion of an "essentially contested
concept," but it seems to qualify in every other respect.

12. See Randolph G. Adams, *Political Ideas of the American Revolution*, 3d ed.
(New York, 1958), pp. 135-149, and Charles Howard McIlwain, *The
American Revolution: A Constitutional Interpretation*, paperbound reprint
(Ithaca, 1958).

13. In political philosophy, the earliest sustained statements of this attack
are to be found, in different forms and resting on different premises, in
Sheldon Wolin's *Politics and Vision* (Boston, 1960) and C. B. Macpherson's *Political Theory of Possessive Individualism* (Oxford, 1962). Wolin's
attack on the liberal devaluation of political philosophy and Macpherson's critique of the "bourgeois" character of liberal ideologies of
seventeenth-century England were supplemented in the academy by
wholesale rejections of the tacit but undeniably liberal and status quo
biases of much scholarship and teaching that claimed to be value
neutral. (Interestingly, political science behavioralism was attacked on
precisely this ground.) These criticisms go beyond ideology and reach
the institutions and practices of modern society. Liberalism, it is
claimed, works in support of the interests of a particular segment of
society at the expense of other, less privileged groups.

14. See Wolin, *Politics and Vision*, pp. 388-393, esp. p. 390: "What is
significant about these tendencies in modern constitutional theory lies
not merely in what was said but in what was omitted. We look in vain
for any theory of political education, of political leadership, or, until
recently, of social consensus."

15. See Judith N. Shklar, "Facing Up to Intellectual Pluralism," *Political
Theory*, ed. Spitz, ch. 12.

16. Precisely this argument has been made by Herman Belz, "New Left
Reverberations in the Academy: The Antipluralist Critique of Constitutionalism," *Review of Politics*, 38, no. 2 (April 1974), 265-283. I should
note, however, that while I have substantial reservations about current

attacks on traditional doctrines of individual rights and the value of privacy, I do not endorse Belz's formulation or his conclusions.

17. Bernard Bailyn, *The Ideological Origins of the American Revolution* (Cambridge, Mass., 1965), and J.G.A. Pocock, *The Machiavellian Moment* (Princeton, 1975).

18. For attempts to introduce a more positive and creative role for the state into constitutionalist theory, see Charles E. Wyzanski, Jr., "Constitutionalism: Limitation and Affirmation," *Government Under Law*, ed. Arthur E. Sutherland (Cambridge, Mass., 1956), pp. 473-490, esp. pp. 487 and 490; and Douglas Sturm, "Constitutionalism: A Critical Appreciation and Extension of the Political Theory of C. H. McIlwain," *Minnesota Law Review*, 54, no. 2 (December 1969), 215-244, esp. 240-244. Neither Wyzanski nor Sturm seems aware of the eighteenth-century flavor of his position; nor does either author provide safeguards against the potential absolutism inherent in his theory.

19. The best sources for preliminary bibliographies on the first two of these subjects are the volumes of the *Index to Legal Periodicals* published since 1973. For the Bicentennial consult the heading "Constitutional History"; for the Nixon "constitutional crisis," see "Executive Disclosure," "Impeachment," and "Separation of Powers." For Rawls, see the following bibliographies: J. H. Wellbank, "John Rawls' Theory of Justice: A Bibliography," *Philosophy Research Archives*, 2 (1976), unpaginated (microcard); and Robert K. Fullinwider, "A Chronological Bibliography of Works of John Rawls' Theory of Justice," *Political Theory*, 5, no. 4 (November 1977), 561-570. (So far, there has been surprisingly little literature on Rawls's theory of the "just constitution.")

20. The arguments in the three previous paragraphs owe much to H.L.A. Hart, *The Concept of Law* (Oxford, 1961), and Peter Winch, "Understanding a Primitive Society," *American Philosophical Quarterly*, 1 (1964), 307-324.

21. Sir Robert Filmer, *The Anarchy of a Limited or Mixed Monarchy* (1648), reprinted in his *Patriarcha and Other Political Works*, ed. Peter Laslett (Oxford, 1949), p. 277. Cf. McIlwain, *Constitutionalism and the Changing World*, ch. 4, who insists against this argument of Filmer's upon the *historical* validity of limited sovereignty without ever coming to grips with the *conceptual* difficulties.

PART I

2

CARL J. FRIEDRICH ON CONSTITUTIONALISM AND THE "GREAT TRADITION" OF POLITICAL THEORY

DANTE GERMINO *

In rereading the works of Carl Friedrich, one is struck by the central importance of tradition in his teaching. This may be somewhat surprising, for Friedrich is not generally regarded as a "traditionalist," and his *magnum opus, Man and His Government,* was hailed by Karl Deutsch and Leroy Rieselbach, who are usually thought of as among our more innovative political scientists, as "the most important work of its kind to appear during the last several decades." [1] Yet, there it is, in one volume after another: his admiration for Aquinas, Hooker, and Burke; his disdain for abstract "rationalism" in politics, his fascination with myth and symbol, his insistence on his indebtedness to previous scholarship and his generous recognition of the same, and his conception of political philosophy as the continuation of a great conversation begun with the Greeks. Thus, in the Introduction to his *Philosophy of Law in Historical Perspective* he writes:

the historical chapters of this book are actually an integral part of the philosophical and systematic approach; for unlike the historicists and the positivists, I believe that history, and

* I wish to thank the Guggenheim Foundation for the award of a fellowship during which this paper was written.

especially intellectual history, exhibits design and that successive philosophies of law embody progressive insights, parts of
the truth we seek. . . . One's search for the novel is tempered by
a realization of "the old truth" which Goethe counseled his
romantic contemporaries to grasp. [*"Das alte Wahre, fass es an,"*
Goethe wrote.] Most of the so-called novelties are old errors in
new linguistic garb.[2]

Not that Freidrich conceives of tradition as a body of dogma to
be followed unquestioningly by succeeding generations. On the
contrary, he rightly emphasizes that one of the key responsibilities
of contemporary political scientists is the provision of fresh perspectives and insights for expressing the vital core of truth in the
traditional or perennial philosophy. But the values of our Western
constitutional tradition are to be treated with respect. The so-called
detached or "value-free" approach to political science, he has
written, is, in fact, a position based upon the "valuational judgment
that the community's values are irrelevant to the role of the
researcher. . . . We are as political scientists cast in the role of
guardians, whether we like it or not. Our endeavors are bound to
affect the community's values. . . . We cannot close our eyes to such
responsibility." [3]

As Carl Friedrich notes many times in *Man and His Government,* his
approach to political analysis "stresses values and beliefs alongside
of interests." Such an approach, he continues, "is bound to be
concerned with tradition. For such values and beliefs must be
transmitted in order to be fully operative. Any strictly temporary
belief or value is bound to be of limited impact, except in periods of
revolutionary upheaval." [4] And, of course, a concern for tradition
militates against the overemphasis upon the merely contemporary
which one encounters in too much of our political science and in our
culture generally. Exclusive preoccupation with the "now" phenomena, with what at the moment is considered trendy and "with
it," is caustically rejected by Friedrich; he calls it the "frog's
perspective."

In a particularly important chapter in *Man and His Government,*
Friedrich distinguishes between tradition and ideology, going so far
as to call the former the "antithesis" of the latter.[5] He indicates that
human societies are kept alive through the transmission of an

"image of what man ought to be like—an idealized projection of all relevant aspirations. The Greek *kalos k'agathos* and the English gentleman embody such aspirational images." [6] Education, both formal and informal, has the task of transmitting the tradition embodying this image of the paradigmatic human type, and this moral education is more important than technical training in giving a community "cohesion and consensus" and a "sense of direction." [7] A tradition is handed on informally by the family and the intimate association; its influence, by cultural osmosis, as it were, on formal education is great; but while the state can prescribe an ideology it can never dictate a tradition, authentically conceived. For a tradition is the work of many minds and many generations. An ideology, on the other hand, is an attempt to promote a substitute tradition or plastic myth through formally organized methods. With the triumph of ideology, we witness the "perversion of education into propaganda." [8]

In so arguing, Friedrich appears to be on the same intellectual frequency as was the literary critic Philip Wheelwright, who himself was affiliated with the traditionalist "Fugitive" group at Vanderbilt University. Wheelright distinguished sharply between the "community mind" and the "mass mind." Whereas the community mind creates myths which have a transcendent reference and which express the interests of the group as a cooperative organism, the mass mind creates ideologies expressing the "interests of each member of the group reflected and repeated in each other member. . . . A mass cannot create myths, for it has no real history. Myths are the expression of a community mind which has enjoyed a long natural growth, so that the sense of togetherness becomes patterned and semantically significant." [9]

In a book significantly entitled *Transcendent Justice: The Religious Dimension of Constitutionalism,* published by Duke University Press in 1964, Friedrich emphasized the importance of a "belief in a constitutional order based on transcendent justice" [10] as the foundation for the development of Western constitutionalism. This stress on the moral foundation of constitutional government in *Transcendent Justice* has seemed to some scholars to be at variance with, and a welcome corrective to, his memorable "definition," first advanced in 1937 in *Constitutional Government and Politics,* of constitutionalism as the "technique of establishing and maintaining effective restraints on political and government action." [11] Thus, John Hallowell of Duke University, at whose invitation Friedrich gave the lectures that were published as *Transcendent Justice,* had written a decade earlier:

> Professor Friedrich has defined a constitution as a system of effective, regularized restraints upon governmental action. This is satisfactory as far as it goes, but it leaves unanswered the question "restraints in terms of what?" ... Constitutional government is a kind of self-restraint which the people in a democracy impose upon themselves; and, whether we have institutions of judicial review or not, its continued existence depends less upon the institutional checks provided than upon the commonly shared knowledge that there are restraints and upon willingness of individuals voluntarily to submit to those restraints.[12]

Whether, by emphasizing more pronouncedly the moral basis of constitutionalism in his later works, Friedrich was responding constructively to Hallowell's criticism—and it has always been one of Friedrich's strengths that he learns much from scholarly dialogue and criticism—or whether he was merely developing more fully a theme already implicit in his earlier works, is a matter of interpretation with which we need not concern ourselves here. Certainly there is no abrupt break; one is not properly entitled, I think, to distinguish between an "early" Friedrich preoccupied with technique and a "late" Friedrich concerned with "belief" in the study of constitutionalism. Thus, at least as early as 1950, with the publication of the revised edition of *Constitutional Government and Democracy,* one can detect in Friedrich's writings an increasing emphasis on the substantive and philosophical dimensions of constitutionalism, without, of course, his neglecting its procedural and institutional manifestations. Already in 1950, Friedrich was writing that "the governments of Western civilization [have] tended toward the constitutional pattern. This tendency may justly be attributed to the *Christian* concern for the individual and his personal salvation. Attempts by nationalist historians to claim that Germanic folk traditions or English national character are responsible for it are unconvincing. For the tendency is universal throughout Christian lands, though continually under pressure from one quarter or another." [13]

Thus, for Friedrich, behind the techniques and methods for restraining power which characterize constitutional government as an institutional complex, there is the *idea* that government should be restrained, that its power should not be wielded arbitrarily, that even the king should be *sub deo et lege*. There are, he tells us, "two important roots to the idea of restraints" underlying the development of modern constitutionalism. The first of these is the "medieval heritage of natural-law doctrine." This notion of a higher moral law, knowable by right reason, of course, antedates Christianity, and Friedrich writes with appreciation of the contribution of Greek philosophy, Stoicism, and the Roman law; [14] yet, he finds, it was only by commingling with the Judeo-Christian religiousness, with its emphasis on the innate worth of each individual human being as made in the image of God and being called to obey God's law, that the idea of natural law became an effective source of modern constitutionalism.

It is on the second, or religious, root of the idea of restraints that Friedrich focuses particular attention in numerous writings. Thus, in both *Transcendent Justice* (1964) and in his most recent treatment of constitutionalism, *Limited Government: A Comparison* (1974), he concludes that the most plausible explanation of why constitutional government developed first and remains most strongly entrenched in the West is the influence of Christianity. The following excerpt from the former work summarizes his position:

> The constitution is meant to protect the *self* in its dignity and worth; for the self is believed to be primary and of penultimate value. This preoccupation with the self, rooted in Christian beliefs ... eventually gave rise to the notion of rights which were thought to be natural. Hence the function of the constitution may also be stated as that of defining and maintaining human rights. Among these rights that of each person's religious conviction was and is as crucial in the spiritual sphere as the right of private property was and remains in the material sphere. ... [W]hat has persisted throughout the history of Western constitutionalism is the notion that the individual human being is of paramount worth

and should be protected against the interference of his ruler, be he a prince, party, or a popular majority.[15]

Thus, constitutional government presupposes the idea of restraints, and the idea of restraint grows out of the experience of an order of moral reality symbolized concretely in the West through Greek and Stoic philosophy and through the Judeo-Christian religious tradition. It is in a philosopher-theologian like Richard Hooker, writing in the sixteenth century and summarizing two thousand years of Western intellectual and spiritual development, that Friedrich finds the most complete expression of constitutionalism's philosophical underpinning.

Hooker's importance for the development of constitutionalism in the English-speaking world is rarely given sufficient attention.[16] His defense of reason as reflected in, rather than antithetical to, tradition; and his insistence, following Bracton, that the law makes the king rather than the king the law directly influences Sir Edward Coke, who studied under Hooker, then Master of the Temple.[17] In *Transcendent Justice* Friedrich does much to correct this neglect of Hooker by devoting considerable attention to his contribution. He shows how, in his theory of law, Hooker relates the restraints of the constitutional order to the "law of reason," or higher moral law, which men by the "light of their natural reason" may apprehend, and then places that law (otherwise known as the natural law) in the context of Christian theology in such a way as to defend it from the Puritan's "disparagement of reason" and tradition. Man, for Hooker as for Plato, inhabits the realm of the Between; while part of his being is bound by the laws of material nature, in his mind and spirit he is free. He may abuse this freedom, but he may, when conforming to his true nature, choose to follow his reason in shaping human law consonant with the moral order of God. Constitutions are human laws, or particular determinations for a particular people based on the principles of the higher law of reason. Hooker, Friedrich concludes, erects his "theory of the constitutional order" on the basis of his understanding of man as a rational and cooperative creature, participating in an order of moral reality whose source is God, in whose image man was fashioned.

The constitutional order, which is compounded of both custom and statute, with statutes often simply ratifying what the common law required, may not be rightfully resisted but rather serves as a restraint upon all who live within it. Its laws are evident to reason and grounded on consent—not necessarily the expressly declared consent of the present generation, represented in parliament, but more generally "that which hath been received long sithence and is by custom established," and which is therefore ordinarily to be accorded greater deference than momentary choice. Thus, an established order may be assumed to have a basis in consent unless it is explicitly revoked. And it should not be revoked out of some idiosyncratic fancy, private demand, or giddy choice, but should reflect the common reason and common deliberations of the best and wisest men, seeking to apply the principles of the law of reason.

As Friedrich indicates, for Richard Hooker it was inconceivable that a constitutional order—or "polity," as he called it—could exist without a religious foundation. As he has summarized Hooker's teaching: "Hence the 'religious verities' supported the polity in its essential order, and the transcendence of the faith provided a lasting underpinning for the prevalent ideas on justice and law. Ultimately, their authority rests on their consonance with reason, the divine spark in man. In this he followed Aquinas and opposed the Puritan's preoccupation with the word [Scripture]." [18]

Hooker's defense of an "ecclesiastical polity" failed, as it had to fail, with the disappearance of religious unity among Christians and with the increasing recognition that the principle of the inviolable dignity of the individual person entailed freedom of conscience for all, regardless of faith. The problem of articulating a moral foundation for constitutionalism scarcely disappeared with that polity, however; rather, Friedrich contends, it came to be expressed in a new key: the language of Locke and Kant and Mill, of natural rights and "utility" comprehensively conceived; in sum, in the language of liberalism.

There are some—and they have had very great influence among scholars in the humanities and social sciences—who argue that the language of Locke, Kant, and Mill constitutes a decisive, qualitative advance for human freedom over that of Plato, Aristotle, Aquinas, and Hooker. They may even go so far as to contend that these great political philosophers and others are "enemies" of the kind of "open society" which constitutional democracy aspires to be, and they may argue that fascist totalitarianism is the offspring of the "authoritarian," "essentialist," and "historicist" features of Platonic, Aristotelian, and Thomistic philosophy. Thus, in a recent book on fascism, Paul Hayes of Oxford announced his intention to "undermine" Carl Friedrich's well-known position that fascism is a historically unique phenomenon.[19] From Hayes we learn that "National socialism in particular, and fascism in general, derived important political concepts from a very ancient political tradition, reading back into the distant past for support and intellectual justification—to Plato and Heraclitus."[20] After Heraclitus and Plato, the enemies' list of fascist precursors includes Aristotle (in whose writings there "may also be discerned some basic characteristics of totalitarianism"); Machiavelli (who had "little respect for the benevolence of human nature or for the notion of the invincibility of reason" and who in the *"Discorsi* captured the essence of the totalitarian outlook"); Bodin (who anticipated Rosenberg's concept of the *Ordenstaat);* Hobbes (who "justified the utilitarian power of the sovereign state"); and archenemy Hegel (who serves as the "vital link" in the "chain" of totalitarian thought by synthesizing into a "strange and incoherent" philosophy such elements as "mysticism, universalism, aristocracy, anti-democracy and utilitarianism"). From Hegel we move in this imaginative account to such philosophers as Jaspers, Husserl, and Max Scheler.[21] Against these obscurantist proponents of the "closed," that is, "totalitarian" society were and are rallied, we are told, the enlightened friends of the "open society," these being the "rationalists," including Locke, Voltaire, Hume, Spinoza, Rousseau, and Karl Popper.[22]

Obviously, the above argument is derived, in an admittedly gross and clumsy way, from Sir Karl Popper's hugely influential book, *The Open Society and its Enemies,* first published in 1945.[23] For Popper, the intellectual history of the West reduces itself to a struggle between the advocates of closure (Heraclitus, Plato, Aristotle, Aquinas, Hegel, Marx, contemporary "essentialists") and the champions of "openness," including the sophists, Socrates, the Epicureans, the Cynics, Lucretius, Locke, the French Enlightenment in general, Kant, Mill, Bertrand Russell, and presumably Sir Karl himself.

Now Carl Friedrich yields to no man in his devotion to constitutional democracy and to the "open society," properly understood. He also has been critical of certain features of the political thought of Plato, Aristotle, and Hegel, features which need revising in the light of our further experience with, and reflection on, constitutional government. But Friedrich has never been tempted to indulge in the kind of conspiratorial construction one encounters in Popper. By contrast with those of Popper, Friedrich's interpretations of Plato and Hegel are judicious and balanced. Only by willfully ignoring the liberal elements in Hegel could one force him into the mold of fascist precursor, he has indicated.[24] As for Plato, about whose political thought he has always had important reservations, note this judgment in *Man and His Government* and reflect on how much they are at variance in spirit and content with the vehement denunciations of Popper:

> This challenge has given rise to the view that Plato was a "totalitarian." He was not, unless the term "totalitarian" is defined so broadly that even the monastery must be classed as totalitarian. But he was authoritarian and hence rejected completely the notion of personal freedom of independence as a necessary part of a well-ordered community. It is important to remember that in taking this view he had. a good deal of human experience on his side, as there have been many political orders which lack such a personal sphere.[25]

Friedrich's interpretations of individual thinkers are based on the most careful and conscientious examination of the original sources and upon his truly voracious reading of the interpretive literature; he cites that literature generously, because he has always regarded himself very much as a member of a *community* of scholars. From his career of teaching and writing about the history of political theory and about constitutional government, he has come to the conclusion that a "great tradition" of Western thought—extending, yes, from poor old Heraclitus and Plato—does exist, and that, despite criticisms and necessary revisions of certain specific features of the thought of the individuals who make it up, a vital core supportive of constitutional government may be detected in this *"perennial* philosophy." Indeed, I submit, Friedrich would go farther and argue that not only is the "great tradition"—called "great" both because it is made up of thinkers of the first rank and because it asks the "great questions" about human life in society—*compatible* with constitu-

tionalism; it is its *conditio sine qua non*. The great tradition is necessary
for constitutionalism in two respects: (1) because, historically, the
rise of limited governemnt would be unintelligible without the
moral and intellectual foundations of the idea of restraint which is
the essence of such government, the roots of that idea being, as he
has attempted to show, in Christianity and natural law; and (2)
because without a vital core of belief in the worth and dignity of the
person, it is impossible to conceive of the long-term survival of this
all-too-uncommon form of government.

For Friedrich, the great tradition, or perennial philosophy,
extends from the Greeks through Locke and Kant and Mill and
even Hegel (!) to our own time, when it falls to us to keep the
conversation going. Thus, for the man whom we honor tonight,
there is no abrupt, Popperian-style break between Aquinas and
Hooker on the one hand and Locke, Kant, and Mill on the other.
The following passage from *Transcendent Justice* makes clear how
interdependent, for Friedrich, were constitutionalism and the
natural-law tradition:

> in Locke and indeed in Kant, the distinctive feature of modern
> constitutionalism, the recognition and protection of a sphere of
> independence, receives open recognition: freedom is not only
> the freedom of participation, but also that of independence.
> God's law, which is the law of reason and of nature, indicated
> it: for unless men can retain a measure of independence, they
> cannot reason freely, and if they cannot reason freely, they
> become slaves. This sphere of independence is essentially
> compounded of two primary aspects: the right of free religious
> conviction and that of property (in the broadest sense).[26]

Indeed, one of Carl Friedrich's most distinguished students, who
also served as president of our Society, the late Frederick Watkins,
perfectly captured the flavor of Friedrich's approach to the history
of political theory as a great tradition supportive of constitutionalism when he wrote a book on the development of modern liberalism
and entitled it *The Political Tradition of the West*.[27]

It may well be true, of course, that, despite its considerable
strengths, today, with our additional experience and increasing
knowledge of the sources of our intellectual and spiritual past, and

with the development of new philosophical principles for interpreting them, the Friedrichian approach to our intellectual history will need revision. If so, we would continue to be working in the spirit of this most intellectually generous of men, who wrote:

> For no matter how hard we try, political theory is not certain and final; it deals with reality, the most fateful reality which confronts man, namely himself in politics, where man is at his best and his worst. That is why the political theorist is always in transition, more so than any other theorist. The reality with which he deals is the most kaleidoscopic part of man's experience.[28]

If the kind of viewpoint represented in the works of Carl Friedrich—with its ecumenical spirit and its minimizing of intellectual differences between the ancients and the moderns—is to undergo revision, it is probable, I submit, that three of its cardinal principles will be retained against all attempts at an ahistorical, Popperian-style "critical rationalist" reconstruction: (1) the understanding that constitutionalism is more than a set of techniques and has a moral foundation; (2) the need to hold fast to the "old truth" in the Western philosophical and religious tradition, even as we struggle to apply its principles to new historical developments; and (3) the recognition that reason and tradition, rather than being antithetical, complement, illumine, and correct each other.

NOTES

1. Karl W. Deutsch and Leroy N. Rieselbach, "Recent Trends in Political Theory and Political Philosophy," *The Annals of the American Academy of Political and Social Science,* 360 (July 1965), 139-162 at p. 145.
2. C.J. Friedrich, *The Philosophy of Law in Historical Perspective,* 2d ed. (Chicago: University of Chicago Press, 1963), p. 7.
3. Friedrich, *Man and His Government* (New York: McGraw-Hill, 1963), pp. 67-68.
4. *Ibid.,* p. 613.
5. *Ibid.,* p. 614.
6. *Ibid.,* p. 617.
7. *Ibid.*
8. *Ibid.,* p. 618.

30 DANTE GERMINO

9. Philip Wheelwright, "Poetry, Myth, and Reality," in G. and M. Goldberg, eds., *The Modern Critical Spectrum* (Englewood Cliffs, N.J.: Prentice-Hall, 1962), pp. 306-320 at p. 310. Wheelwright's essay was originally published in 1942. Friedrich's analysis is also reminiscent of Frederick Juenger's account of the "invasion of ideologies" in modern industrialized societies. Man in such a society tends to be increasingly "mobile," and this physical mobility has an uprooting effect on traditional mental beliefs. He then becomes "wide open" to ideologies, which are plastic myths, or "vulgarizations of faith and knowledge." Men become prey to ideologies because technique, apparatus, and organization are "not enough, because they do not satisfy the human need for moral support and spiritual comfort without which a man cannot exist." In fact, "the efforts of the technician" by uprooting traditional values intensify the "spiritual vacuum" and "feeling of emptiness" so characteristic of modern life. Frederick Juenger, *The Failure of Technology* (Hinsdale, Ill.: Regnery, 1949), pp. 128, 133.

10. Friedrich, *Transcendent Justice: The Religious Dimension of Constitutionalism* (Durham, N.C.: Duke University Press, 1964), p. 56.

11. Friedrich, *Constitutional Government and Politics* (New York: Harper & Row, 1937), p. 101. This definition is repeated in successive editions of this well-known work, sometimes with the inclusion of "regularized" before "restraints." Also "action" is sometimes rendered as "power."

12. John H. Hallowell, *The Moral Foundation of Democracy* (Chicago, 1954), pp. 63-64.

13. Friedrich, *Constitutional Government and Democracy*, 2d ed., rev. (Boston: Ginn & Co., 1950), p. 126.

14. Friedrich, *Philosophy of Law*, chs. 2-4.

15. Friedrich, *Transcendent Justice*, p. 17. See also, Friedrich, *Limited Government: A Comparison* (Englewood Cliffs, N.J.: Prentice-Hall, 1974), p. 14, and *Transcendent Justice*, p. 3.

16. See, as a refreshing exception to this rule, John S. Marshall, "Richard Hooker and the Origins of American Constitutionalism," in Arthur L. Harding, ed., *Origins of the Natural Law Tradition* (Dallas: Southern Methodist University Press, 1954), pp. 49-68. Alexander Passerin d'Entreves published a book on Hooker in Italian in 1932, but references to it are rare.

17. *Ibid.*, p. 55.

18. Friedrich, *Transcendent Justice*, pp. 55-56. For the whole section on Hooker, see pp. 48 ff.

19. Paul M. Hayes, *Fascism* (New York: The Free Press, 1973), p. 12.

20. *Ibid.*, p. 40.

21. Quotations are from chapter form of *ibid.,* pp. 41-42, 42-43, 43, 40, 45, 47.

22. *Ibid.,* p. 44.

23. I have used the Fifth Edition, Revised (2 vols., Princeton University Press, 1966). For a brief discussion of my views of the defects of Popper's interpretation of the idea of the open society, see my article, "Preliminary Reflections on the Open Society: Bergson, Popper, Voegelin," in Dante Germino and Klaus von Beyme, eds., *The Open Society in Theory and Practice* (The Hague: M. Nijhoff, 1974), pp. 1-25, at pp. 12-20. Popper's evaluation of tradition differs radically from that of Friedrich. Whereas Friedrich extols a moral consensus as the bond which unites a constitutional order and relates consent to consensus, Popper relates such a consensus to tribalism and the closed society (see especially *The Open Society and Its Enemies,* I, 174-175, on the "organic society"). Popper does later speak of a "faith" of the open society, but it rests on procedural rather than substantive agreement: i.e., on an agreement about the supremacy of what from his scientific epistemology Popper holds to be the method of "critical rationalism." Popper's notion of reason amounts to a severe contraction of that of Plato, Aristotle, Aquinas, Hooker, and Leibniz—i.e., of leading representatives of the "great tradition." The question of the open society will be explored at length in a book which I am now writing, to be entitled *Toward a Theory of the Open Society.*

    For Friedrich's own conception of reason, which also differs significantly from that of Popper, see, *inter alia, Man and His Government,* pp. 40, 217. In the latter passage, Friedrich contends *(contra* Popper) that the Enlightenment substituted another form of authority "for the authority of church and monarchy." That is, we cannot say that the eighteenth century was *tout court* the "age of reason" as distinct from the "obscurantist" Middle Ages, as Popper tends to do.

24. See the Introduction to *The Philosophy of Hegel,* edited by Friedrich (New York: Modern library, 1953).

25. Friedrich, *Man and His Government,* p. 359. Elsewhere *(Philosophy of Law,* p. 196, n.), Friedrich describes Popper's view that Plato was a totalitarian "amazing . . . considering Plato's bitter hostility toward tyranny."

26. Friedrich, *Transcendent Justice,* p. 75.

27. Cambridge, Mass.: Harvard University Press, 1948, 1967.

28. Friedrich, *Man and His Government,* p. 23.

3

CARL FRIEDRICH'S CONTRIBUTION TO THE THEORY OF CONSTITUTIONALISM-COMPARATIVE GOVERNMENT

PAUL SIGMUND

To sum up in a few pages a scholarly career spanning a half a century which has resulted in the publication of over fifty books and hundreds of articles is a difficult task. When the range of interests of that career has extended to every area of political science and indeed has seemed to anticipate in a remarkable way the direction in which that profession is moving, it is even more difficult. Can the work of a scholar whose publications include works on the Swiss civil service, the control of advertising, U.S. foreign policy, and the age of the baroque be discussed in the space of a few pages? I think it can—if we focus our discussion on Carl Friedrich's contribution to the subject of this year's meeting: constitutionalism. As one of the Society's founding fathers, its first president, and the editor of *Nomos* for many years, it is appropriate that we dedicate one of our sessions exclusively to his work, because constitutionalism has been a central theme of his scholarly interests, from his first published book, a scholarly edition of the work of Johannes Althusius (1932), to *Limited Government: A Comparison,* published in 1974. His best-known book, *Constitutional Government and Democracy,* has appeared in four editions and been translated into at least five foreign languages, and the profession has recognized that he is the preeminent authority in this field when he was chosen to write the article on "Constitutions and Constitutionalism" for the *International Encyclopedia of the Social Sciences,* published in 1968.

Friedrich's background and special qualifications for the study of constitutionalism are well known. Born in Germany in 1901, he came to this country as an exchange student at Harvard after World War I and after completing his doctorate at Heidelberg returned in the mid-1920s to begin a Harvard teaching career that lasted nearly fifty years, until his retirement in 1971. He continued to maintain close touch with European higher education, teaching for many years at Heidelberg and as a visiting professor or lecturer at universities in France and Italy. During World War II he helped train Americans for the occupation of Germany, and after the war he served as a consultant there, devoting special attention to the establishment of the institutions of constitutional democracy. He was also involved in advising on the creation of the special links between Puerto Rico and the United States when it acquired commonwealth status, was consultant on the Virgin Islands constitution, and has maintained a continuing active interest in the promotion of closer links among the countries of Europe. All of this activity has taken place at the same time that he was publishing one or more books a year, many of them devoted to themes related to his consulting and advisory activities.

Professor Germino has concerned himself with the relation of Carl Friedrich's analysis of constitutionalism to his general views on the history of political theory—the area in which both of us worked with him at Harvard. My own work, like that of both Germino and Friedrich, has also included substantial research and publication in the field of comparative government—both historical and contemporary—and it is from this point of view that I would like to examine what I consider to be his particular contributions to the study of comparative constitutionalism. I would like to divide my consideration into three sections: (1) an evaluation of Friedrich's contribution to a greater precision in the definition of constitutionalism; (2) a review of his work on the conditions for the rise and maintenance of constitutionalism; and (3) a discussion of his special contribution to the practice of constitutionalism in the area of federalism.

THE DEFINITION OF CONSTITUTIONALISM

Carl Friedrich's writings on the subject of constitutionalism may be seen both as constituting a continuation of earlier analyses of the subject and as an important shift of emphasis in its understanding. We can see this best, perhaps, by contrasting his work with that of his predecessor as teacher of the history of political theory at Harvard, Charles McIlwain. Both McIlwain and Friedrich describe constitutionalism as centrally concerned with the limitation of government action and contrast *constitutional* government with *arbitrary* government power, and both are also interested in the historical phenomena associated with the rise of constitutionalism. However, where McIlwain tended to concentrate his interests primarily if not exclusively on the *historical* and *legal* aspects of constitutionalism, Friedrich has taken a much broader approach, stressing the *political* aspects and viewing constitutionalism more as a dynamic process than, as it sometimes appeared in McIlwain, simply another name for the rule of law, especially of fundamental law.[1] Friedrich's concern also goes beyond the preoccupation with functional relations within the government, especially the separation of powers and mutual checks, which has characterized other writers on constitutionalism such as Wormuth, Vile, and Gwyn.[2] Although both the rule of law and some partial separation of functions form part of his constitutionalist theory, Friedrich recognizes that it is a much broader phenomenon than that discussed by most other writers on the subject.

1. The classic "Friedrichian" definition of constitutionalism as it appears in slightly different forms in various publications is "an institutionalized system of effective regularized restraints on governmental action" (1963, p. 271). As early as the first (1937) edition of *Constitutional Government and Democracy* (then entitled *Constitutional Government and Politics*), Friedrich observed that these restraints may be extralegal as well as legal (pp. 103-6), as, for example, regular and effective criticism and possible opposition by political parties, the press, or pressure groups. It was also in the 1937 edition (pp. 16-18) that Friedrich recognized that an important aspect of constitutionalism was its internalization in those who exercise governmental power, describing this process in his "Rule of Anticipated Reac-

tion"—the expectation by those in power that there were certain types of action which the public or organized groups within it would not stand for.

In his most recent work on the subject, he also emphasizes what he calls the "experimental" character of constitutionalism—that every constitution is continually changing and that the making of a constitution is a continuous process. Yet at the same time he asserts that an effective constitutionalism is *institutionalized;* it does prescribe certain regularized limits on conduct; and it has an effect on behavior, even if its component elements are undergoing substantial alterations over time (1974, p. 11; see also the bibliographical essay in 1968, pp. 601 ff.). Thus, Friedrich seems to go part of the way toward meeting the behavioralist criticism of the static legalism of earlier constitutionalist theories (he is particularly critical of Hans Kelsen on this point [1968, p. 602]), while insisting on the centrality of constitutions and the belief in governmental action on a constitutional basis as a *political* reality of central importance ("Constitutions and Constitutionalism," 1968c).

2. Friedrich's rejection of excessive legalism but acceptance of the basic core of good sense in earlier theories also is evident in his discussion of the separation of powers. He admits that the traditional threefold division into legislature, executive, and judiciary as three separate departments is artificial and misleading, yet he asserts that there is an important analytic distinction between individual decision (measure-taking), the establishment of general rules, and the applications of those rules to disputes, although one must be aware that these kinds of actions may be taken by different government organs than those to which they have been traditionally assigned, and that in modern pluralistic societies the division of functions has been accompanied by an increasing tendency toward their mutual interaction and checking (1968, ch. 10).

3. The mention of checks suggests another aspect of Friedrich's approach to constitutionalism—his awareness that constitutionalism considered as effective regularized restraint on government requires first that there be a government to restrain. This emphasis on the importance of effective government for constitutionalism runs through all of Friedrich's work on the subject. His continuing interest in the analysis of bureaucracy is partially attributable to the

influence of Max Weber, but his admirable treatments of this subject (e.g., 1968, ch. 2) are also related to a recognition that a constitutional government must first govern; and he is aware that one of the most effective instruments of modern government has been the development of specialized bureaucratic instruments. The bureaucratic phenomenon is also seen as an aspect of a more general phenomenon—the rationalization of government—which has contributed to the development of constitutionalism, involving as it does an analysis of the relation between institutional means and the ends of government.

4. The problem of the maintenance of some restraints on government even in periods of emergency when very wide scope is given to governmental action is a recurrent concern in Friedrich's writings. He saw the perversion of emergency powers by the Nazis lead to the overthrow of the Weimar Republic, yet he was also aware that throughout history allowance has had to be made for an area of discretionary government power with minimal limitations when the survival of the constitutional order is at stake. The analysis of the various forms this has taken in theory and practice and the ways in which constitutional rights can be limited without destroying constitutionalism is the principal concern of Friedrich's book, *Constitutional Reason of State* (1957). Here as elsewhere, he treats constitutional restraints as located on a continuum between the "unreal limits" of no restraint and of complete restraint (1968, p. 127).

Summarizing, then—Friedrich's contribution to our understanding of constitutionalism may be seen as an effort to transcend the narrowly legalistic and formal approaches which had hitherto prevailed and to see it as essentially a political phenomenon, dynamic and processual in character but also institutionalized in one way or another, and dependent for its initial emergence and continued existence on the ability of constitutional governments to govern effectively.

UNDERLYING VALUES AND CONSTITUTIONALISM

I do not wish to encroach on Professor Germino's area of concern, but I would like to single out three theoretical concerns in Friedrich's writings on constitutionalism that relate to a comparative treatment of constitutionalism—the questions of the religious conditions associated with its emergence in the West, the necessity of a basic value consensus, and the relation between constitutionalism and democracy.

1. As one surveys his work one finds an increasing emphasis in Friedrich's writings on the religious bases for the constitutionalist values of individual rights, the higher law, and the dignity as well as the corruptibility of man (1963, p, 271). His book, *Transcendent Justice—The Religious Basis of Constitutionalism* (1964), is devoted entirely to this topic, and there aré frequent references to it in his other works. The question that thése references suggest is how decisive or central is the Judeo-Christian religious tradition, first in the emergence of constitutionalism in the West, and second, for its continued existence in an increasingly secularized world and its extension to other parts of the world that do not share the same religious traditions. Friedrich seems correct in relating the theory of natural law closely to the development of Christianity even though its origins are classical, and to see the transformation of the theory into one of natural rights as intimately connected with the development of religious pluralism in the West after the Reformation. He does not attempt, however, to relate the religious factor to other explanations—for example, economic, social, political, and military—and he is somewhat pessimistic as to whether other cultures can support a constitutional order effectively (1968, pp. 584-85; 1974, p. 9). In the specific case of India, he is moderately optimistic, but he does not give the reasons for his optimism—in terms either of the influence of the Western tradition or of the existence of societal conditions which promote both the unity and diversity that make a constitutional order possible or desirable.

2. The question of the basic values upon which constitutionalism rests is given divergent answers by Friedrich at different points in his writings. In the initial edition of *Constitutional Government and Politics* he asserted that there must be an agreement on fundamentals in order for a constitutional system to work—although he did not specify what those fundamentals were (1937, p. 136). Five years later, in the midst of World War II, he published *The New Belief in the Common Man* (1942), an entire chapter of which was devoted to the importance of dissent. In that chapter he in effect retracted his earlier views and asserted that the only agreement necessary was "the agreement to disagree" (p. 156) and emphasized the danger of

insisting on further fundamental beliefs as a precondition for
constitutional government. This view was also reflected in the
preface to the second edition of *Constitutional Government* (1941). In
1950, at the height of the cold war, he reverted to his earlier position
when in the Preface to the third edition of *Constitutional Government
and Democracy* he asserted that "there are limits beyond which no
community can allow rights and freedoms to go" and that "lack of
agreement on all fundamentals except on these basic procedures of
the democratic process itself, entails risks which may prove fatal in
the face of a determined and totalitarian opponent" (1950, p.v).
Finally, in his *magnum opus* on politics, *Man and His Government,*
published in 1963, he seemed to arrive at a kind of intermediate
position which saw a basic consensus in the society as making
possible a minimum of formal agreement on basic rules, while
deeper divisions entailed formal adherence to a broader range of
fundamental values (1963, p. 146). The question is an important
one, and Friedrich continually recurs to it; but he does not seem to
have given it as thorough an analysis or as systematic a discussion as
it deserves.

3. As was noted above, the title of Friedrich's best-known work on
constitutionalism was changed from *Constitutional Government and
Politics* in 1937 to *Constitutional Government and Democracy* in 1941. This
was accompanied by a substantial expansion of the content of the
text but not of its principal topics, since the first edition had already
contained chapters on electoral and party systems as well as on
interest groups and the instrumentalities of direct democracy.
Friedrich is aware, as any native of Germany would be, that a
system can be constitutional without being democratic. He even
gives an example of a dictatorship that provided itself with a
working constitution—Cromwell and *The Instrument of Government*
(1937, p. 146). Yet as a naturalized American, Friedrich was also
concerned to explore the theoretical basis for the most common
form of constitutionalism—constitutional democracy. During World
War II he published *The New Belief in the Common Man* (1942), a
ringing defense of the superiority in the long run of the judgment of
the common man concerning the needs of the community and an
attack on the elitisms of earlier rationalist and modern irrationalist
theories. He restated this view twenty years later in the first chapter
of *Man and His Government,* where, beginning from a conception of

man as adaptable, purposive, self-aware, and community-oriented, he argued that although all men are fallible the capacity to make "common judgments about common needs" is not concentrated in a rational elite but rather requires a quality of "character," a personality trait which is not directly related to intellectual ability and which indeed may even be threatened by the intellectual's capacity to "rationalize" his conduct (1963, ch. 1). Like most constitutionalists, however, Friedrich combines his support for democratic participation with a distrust of "absolute democracy," or straight majoritarianism, and asserts that universal suffrage is not itself a sufficient limit on power to guarantee the protection of individual freedom, which is the overall purpose of constitutionalism. Here as elsewhere, however, the point is not systematically developed, and his theory of the relationship of constitutionalism and democracy must be elicited out of individual statements in several works.

FEDERALISM

The particular aspect of constitutionalism with which Friedrich has been especially concerned is what he calls in his *International Encyclopedia of the Social Sciences* article the "spatial" division of political power—federalism. From his early interest in the subject as the distinctive contribution of the political theory of Johannes Althusius down to his 1968 list of the six hypotheses concerning the relationship of federalism to the realization of constitutional democracy, constitutionalism has been a central concern of his work as a political scientist (1931; 1968, p. 208). Particularly significant contributions on the subject include a massive collection of *Studies in Federalism* published in 1954 and a summary of federal theory and practice, *Trends of Federalism,* published in 1968.

As important as, and contributing to, his considerable writing on the subject has been his advice as a consultant to governments engaged in the development of federal relationships. The German Federal Republic's Basic Law is an authentically German product, but American advisers, including Friedrich, contributed to its development. The movement toward European integration has been studied and assisted by Friedrich since its inception after World War II. He is perhaps proudest of his role in the development of the

status of Puerto Rico as a free associated state, and his 1959 book on
the subject was reprinted in 1975. Its third chapter concerning the
ambiguities of the complex new relationship but defending it as "a
realistic compromise" which is likely to possess "enduring strength
while simpler and more radical solutions fail" seems thus far to have
been borne out by succeeding events (1954-75, p. 77; also 1968, p.
639). What has not been borne out so far has been his hope for the
emergence of world federalism which was expressed in *Inevitable
Peace* (1948), his book on Immanuel Kant's theories of the progressive development of a worldwide federal union to achieve *Perpetual
Peace* on the basis of republican government.

Federalism recommended itself particularly to a German-Amer-
ican scholar. It had been studied by Otto von Gierke in the
nineteenth century, and the undermining of German federalism was
one of the ways in which the Weimar Republic was prepared for the
Nazi takeover. More important, the American experiment in
federalism was a model for all other subsequent experiences; and in
Friedrich's judgment it is the particular aspect of American
constitutionalism that has had the most decisive impact upon other
countries (1967). It, too, has undergone an evolution since its
inception, which defies a strictly formalistic or legal analysis—and
like constitutionalism in general it attempts to combine stability,
democracy, and freedom in the fragile synthesis to which Carl
Friedrich has dedicated the bulk of his scholarly career.

CRITICISM

This would not be a scholarly treatment of Friedrich's work if it
did not contain some critical remarks, and I have already made a
few relatively minor comments of a critical nature. Only two
additional points might be added from someone who has conducted
graduate seminars for several years on the subject of constitutionalism. I do not think that Friedrich's writings on the subject have
given sufficient attention either to the contemporary critics of
constitutionalism or to the reasons why there are so few constitutional governments in the world today.

On the first point, I think that more explicit attention should
have been given to the behavioralist and to the Marxist criticisms of
constitutionalist theory. It was not until the publication in 1967 of

Constitutionalism and the Separation of Powers by a British scholar, M.J.C. Vile, that the fallacies were pointed out in Robert Dahl's influential critique of Madisonian constitutionalism in *A Preface to Democratic Theory*, published in 1956. Friedrich might have done so sooner—particularly given the importance of behavioralism in the profession during the period.[3] Similarly, a scholar in touch as Friedrich has been for so much of his life with intellectual currents in other countries should perhaps have devoted more attention to the Marxist-influenced criticism of constitutionalism and federalism as instruments in the hands of conservative economic elites to prevent or impede social and economic change. Marxism in Friedrich's writings is viewed primarily as the ideology of a totalitarian system rather than as an influential and important criticism of liberalism and capitalism. It might have been well to note more explicitly that constitutionalism *does* tend to have conservative tendencies in practice but that this is a price modern constitutionalists are willing to pay in the interests of stability and freedom. In an era in which a broadening recognition of the necessity of common action to solve problems that are national and in some cases worldwide is combined with a post-Watergate suspicion of abuse of government power, it is well for the constitutionalist to be explicit about the value priorities that are involved in one's adherence to a belief in the slower but more certain processes of constitutionalism.

It is well, too, to examine, possibly more systematically than Friedrich has done, the reasons why there are so few constitutional systems in the contemporary world. As has been noted, his work does give us some clues to answering this question. The importance of the Western religious and humanistic tradition would certainly be emphasized by a student of his writings, but perhaps more important would be another point which he stressed earlier—the need for *effective* government. The demands on government in the Third World are so great and the divisions as to the course which it should take so deep that it is difficult to make a constitutional system work. The incomplete discussion in Friedrich's works concerning the necessity of agreement on fundamentals is relevant here, since the basic consensus on constitutional procedures seems to be lacking or so fragile that when government effectiveness declines, as it so often does after independence, the immediate result has been the abandonment of constitutionalism. In states with more deeply rooted constitutional traditions such as Chile oı India, the undermining of constitutionalism has taken longer, but sadly, the costs to human freedom of the overthrow of constitutionalism are evident in those countries as well today. Friedrich deals with the problem of developing nations in a brief new chapter added to the most recent edition of *Constitutional Government* (1968), and his work on the decline of constitutionalism in Europe is also relevant; but he never drew together his earlier insights to develop a systematic theory on the preconditions of constitutionalism that might be useful in explaining the plight of constitutionalism today.

CONCLUSION

Pessimistic as the outlook for the adherent of federalist constitutionalism appears today, Friedrich, like his mentor, Kant, continues to assert his faith in its eventual triumph. While noting that there is nothing inevitable about the development and extension of constitutional democracy in the contemporary world, he concludes the most recent edition of *Constitutional Government and Democracy* with the observation that the emergence in recent years of wider cultural communities seems to be producing a "growing insight into the interdependence of men everywhere" which by "the conscious effort of goal-oriented actual persons" may lead ultimately to "a world community which embraces them all" (p. 598). This faith in the future of constitutionalism provides a common element of moral concern and commitment that infuses Carl Friedrich's lifelong scholarly interest in constitutionalism and federalism and his substantial contribution to their study and implementation.

NOTES

1. See Charles H. McIlwain, *Constitutionalism, Ancient and Modern* (Ithaca, N.Y.: Cornell University Press, 1940; rev. ed., 1947); *Constitutionalism in a Changing World,* (Cambridge University Press, 1939).
2. Francis D. Wormuth, *The Origins of Modern Constitutionalism* (New York: Harper, 1949); M. J. C. Vile, *Constitutionalism and the Separation of Powers* (London: Oxford University Press, 1967); W. B. Gwyn, *The*

Meaning of the Separation of Powers (New Orleans: Tulane University Press, 1965).

3. In the notes to ch. 1 of the 1968 edition of *Constitutional Government* Friedrich alludes to the controversies engendered by the behavioral approach but asserts only that "more tried and traditional methods give greater promise of a satisfactory answer" (p. 604).

Bibliography of Works on Constitutionalism by Carl J. Friedrich

Constitutional Government and Democracy. Boston: Little, Brown, 1941, 1946; Boston: Ginn, 1950; Waltham, Mass.: Blaisdell, 1968.

Constitutional Government and Politics. New York: Harper, 1937.

Constitutional Reason of State. Providence, R.I.: Brown University Press, 1957.

"Constitutions and Constitutionalism," *International Encyclopedia of the Social Sciences,* vol 3. New York: Macmillan, 1968. Pp. 318-326.

From the Declaration of Independence to the Constitution, coeditor. New York: Liberal Arts, 1954b.

The Impact of American Constitutionalism Abroad. Boston: Boston University Press, 1967.

Inevitable Peace. (Cambridge, Mass.: Harvard University Press, 1948; reprinted, Westport, Conn.: Greenwood Press, 1970.

Limited Government: A Comparison. Englewood Cliffs, N.J.: Prentice-Hall, 1974.

Man and His Government. New York: McGraw-Hill, 1963.

The New Belief in the Common Man. Boston: Little, Brown, 1942; rev. ed., *The New Image of the Common Man.* Brown: Beacon Press, 1950.

The Philosophy of Law in Historical Perspective Chicago: University of Chicago Press, 1958, 1963b.

Politica Methodice Digesta of Johannes Althusius, ed. Cambridge, Mass.: Harvard University Press, 1932.

Puerto Rico, Middle Road to Freedom. New York: Rinehart, 1959; reprinted, New York: Arno Press, 1975.

Studies in Federalism, coeditor. Boston: Little, Brown, 1954.

Transcendent Justice: The Religious Dimension of Constitutionalism. Durham, N.C.: Duke University Press, 1964.

Trends of Federalism in Theory and Practice. New York: Praeger, 1968b.

PART II

4

CLAUDE DE SEYSSEL AND SIXTEENTH-CENTURY CONSTITUTIONALISM IN FRANCE

NANNERL O. KEOHANE

André Lemaire begins his pioneering study of *Les lois fondamentales de la monarchie française* by asking "Did France under the *ancien régime* have a constitution?" There was, of course, no written constitution until 1791, and partly for this reason it has sometimes been taken for granted that the Old Regime had none at all. But the familiar English example reminds us that whatever may be essential to a constitution, it is not the writing down and labeling it as such; and indeed an English observer of the French in their new-found constitutional glory in 1792 remarked with disapproval on their use of the term, "as if a constitution was a pudding to be made by a receipt." [1] Some of the *cahiers* in 1789 asserted that France had always had a constitution, "for how could it be that a State which has flourished for 1300 years was never constituted?" [2] By this claim they meant something more than the commonsense notion that states, like other complex entities, must necessarily have regular patterns of action, and at least a minimum of authoritative form. As their proud reference to France's long flourishing makes clear, they assumed that their country had always had a distinct political structure that was the basis for its health and longevity.

One good piece of evidence for the notion that the French had always had a constitution is that they had constitutional disputes with great regularity throughout *l'ancien régime,* and the disputants tended to agree roughly on what it was that they were arguing about. The word "constitution" was rarely given political significance in France until the late seventeenth century and was commonly used in this sense only after 1748.[3] But questions about "la régime et gouvernement du monarchie," and "les lois fondamentales" dominated French political discourse long before that. Especially from the mid-sixteenth century onward, innumerable treatises were written with the intention of staking out authoritatively the precise provisions of the elusive constitution of the polity. Legists and publicists, administrators and priests, poets and polemicists took part in the effort to determine the true origin and extent of political authority in France.[4]

At the center of French constitutional discourse was the figure of the king. The most accurate device for picturing debate about the constitution in the sixteenth and seventeenth centuries is surely a solar system, in which all participants are subject to the centripetal force of the monarch, to a greater or lesser degree. Adulatory admirers, Budé or Priézac, or even Bossuet, circulate close at hand like Mercury; advocates of corporate and community liberties, Hotman and the author of the *Soupirs de la France esclave,* have their orbits in the cold Plutonic regions. Most thinkers are somewhere between—Seyssel, Bodin, Richelieu, Retz, Joly, Pascal, La Bruyère, Fénelon, Vauban, and all the rest stake out their orbits round the throne. But all are part of a system dominated by the monarch. All arguments are defined with reference to him, in support or opposition, or with whatever distinctive modifications a particular theorist has to offer in the prevailing dogma of monarchism.

Most French theorists began with the assumption that their king possessed a *puissance absolue.* This was true even of those theorists, like Seyssel, who went on to describe a complex set of limits and restraints upon the king's power. French theorists worked in serene confidence that they could have their absolute monarch and eat their constitutional cake as well, by showing how the king, though formally *délié,* and possessing undivided sovereignty, was nonetheless bound by the *lois fondamentales,* and required to work in harmony with other institutions in the state and to obey his own laws as well, if he wished to govern France. Much of the peculiar fascination and frustration experienced by students of French constitutionalism arises because of this apparently paradoxical assumption that power can be both absolute and limited.

By ascribing to their monarch a *puissance absolue,* French theorists conveyed the sense that he was not subject to the authority of any human will inside or outside his realm. The thrust of the concept was originally defensive, against potential interference by pope and emperor. French constitutional theorists were Gallican almost to a man. But it was generally assumed as well that the king was subject to no authority within his realm—that neither the Estates General nor the "sovereign" courts of law, the two major potential contenders for a measure of autonomous authority, could rightfully claim superiority to, or even equality with, the king. Yet these same theorists insisted that French government was not despotic or arbitrary. They agreed that the king was subject to natural and divine law and to the elusive *lois fondamentales.* Some of them insisted that he was also subject to the traditional customary law of the kingdom and to the positive law made by the kings, including his own laws. The difficulty with the notion of subjection to all these sorts of law was that there was no universally acknowledged human sanction which could be brought to bear against a king who behaved in ways that contravened them. French theorists, with very few exceptions, were convinced that there was a great gulf between their absolute monarchy and the tyrannical regimes of Turkey or Persia. This widespread belief may well have had political value of its own as a sanction against despotism; but the institutional support for it was vague and invited recurrent dispute.

One of the most important reasons Frenchmen had trouble identifying firm institutional obstacles to abuses of the royal power was that they found the notion of a divided sovereign power profoundly uncongenial. Even before Bodin asserted clearly that sovereignty by definition cannot be divided, sixteenth-century Frenchmen took for granted that authority must have some specific unitary locus in the state. Most of them also took for granted that this locus must be in the king. During the religious wars, some argued that the locus ought instead to continue in the people; but arguments for popular sovereignty were very much in the minority in France. The disinclination to think in terms of a division of

authority marked French theorists until the late seventeenth
century and was not seriously challenged until publication of the
Spirit of the Laws.

Despite this deep-seated aversion in French theory to the notion
of divided power, there was an equally deep-seated attachment to
the notion of fundamental law. Even if no clear-cut human
sanctions for this law could be agreed upon there was agreement
about what the *lois fondamentales* were supposed to provide: a
statement of conditions for accession to the throne of France, and of
the legitimate extent and proper uses of power in the state. The
ancient constitution of France, like that of England, supposedly
determined the pattern of succession to the monarchy and regulated
the relationships between the king and all his subjects, setting out
rights and obligations on both sides. But while the French
constitution possessed rather more precision than the English about
the former subject, it did much less well at setting out clear limits on
authority and obligation.

The *loi Salique,* which set out the conditions for monarchical
succession, was the nucleus of the fundamental law. Its provisions
were universally understood and had sufficient sanctity that they
were virtually unassailable. One royal publicist under Henry IV,
Jerome Bignon, spoke of this law as "engraved on the heart of
Frenchmen," not written down on paper but "born with us, not
invented by us, but drawn out of nature herself, who taught it to us
as an instinct." [5] The instinct, if such it be, was given a name only
in the fourteenth century when an ancient law governing the
disposition of private property was put to use to exclude Edward III
of England from the throne of France; and several provisions of the
Salic law still excited controversy when Henry of Navarre, a
Protestant, was heir to the throne.[6] Nonetheless, the basic rules for
accession to the French monarchy were almost universally
acknowledged.

But France had nothing comparable to the Magna Carta; and it
was in the vexed area of the proper uses and extent of the royal
power that constitutional disputes were joined. The juridical basis
for a *puissance absolue* had been laid at the very foundation of the
monarchy, even during the period when the customary restraints
were obvious to all. Recurrent interregnums and civil wars made
Frenchmen long for stability and treasure firm monarchical au-

thority. A succession of strong leaders developed the power of the crown after each period of weakness, a tendency that was accelerated in the seventeenth century. Theory kept pace with practice and was sometimes well in advance of it, as treatises were written including ever bolder claims for the royal power. There was no clear set of institutional limits standing against this developing absolutism, to protect the traditional liberties of the people against encroachment by the crown. For a variety of complex reasons, at no period in French history did opposition to growing absolutism crystallize around a single institution or provide a widely accepted justification for organized resistance to the crown. Many Frenchmen felt the need for better protection for ancient liberties and attempted to show that such protection was provided by one or another aspect of the ancient constitution. But the imprecision and pliancy of the *lois fondamentales* in this area made it hard to agree on firm bulwarks against the crown, even among men who agreed that such were needed.

In French constitutional theory major steps in argument are often based on barely perceptible nuances in interpretation of familiar phrases, and impassioned disagreements are founded on differences so subtle that they hardly appear to be worth bothering about. In such a complex and peculiarly homogeneous intellectual universe it is difficult to distinguish sharply among sets of theorists for purposes of analysis. Nonetheless, historians have commonly discovered that two fairly distinct intellectual tendencies can be discerned in arguments about the French polity, which I have called the "absolutist" and the "constitutionalist"—on the one hand, those whom Mousnier speaks of as "du côté du roi," who bent their efforts to defending a broad interpretation of the scope of monarchical authority and belittled or ignored other institutions in the state, which they described as firmly subordinate to the king, agents and instruments of his governance; and on the other hand, those who stressed the role of other institutions in the government of France and described the way in which the king's power depended on them and was circumscribed by them.[7] From the early sixteenth until the late seventeenth century the absolutist theorists gradually became more confident and more numerous, vying with one another to carry adulation of the sovereign to unequaled heights. However, a durable strain of constitutionalism was established firmly in the sixteenth century and provided the basis for periodic restatements of theories of limitation in later years.

Constitutionalists describe a complex state; absolutists, a unitary one, in which all power is focused in the prince and all authority flows directly from him. The best indications of constitutionalist as opposed to absolutist strains in a treatise are references to the social order at the basis of the state, to the role of prescription and custom in the legal order, and to institutions which have some claim to participation in the lawmaking, administrative or judicial order along with the king, particularly the parlements, the provincial estates, and the Estates-General. References to the king as a God on earth mark absolutist theorists; constitutionalists are more likely to speak of the king as a paternal figure, or as *primus inter pares,* or even as the servant of the people. Absolutists in the early stages of the argument tended to rely more heavily upon Roman law and abstract divine law, constitutionalists upon traditional customs and practices of the French people; but this distinction became blurred later on, and by the early eighteenth century proponents of the *thèse royale* as well as the *thèse nobiliâire* relied upon historical arguments and natural-law arguments alike.

Among constitutionalists themselves, two different basic types can be discerned. On the one hand, there are loyal monarchists like Claude de Seyssel and Etienne de Pasquier, jurists, historians, and administrators who take for granted the *puissance absolue* of the monarch and depict a close harmony among all the laws and institutions of his kingdom. On the other hand, there are polemicists who are opponents of absolute royal power, Huguenots like Hotman or the members of the Catholic League who stress the primary authority of popular institutions and argue for strict limits on the king. Hotman's arguments, as well as those of Buchanan and the author of the *Vindiciae contra tyrannos,* have attracted the attention of students of political thought because of their sharp polemical edge. Monarchomach arguments for resistance to tyranny during the French religious wars have become central in our own interpretation of the development of liberal political thought. Yet Seyssel's more moderate arguments were much more important in shaping French political thought in the sixteenth and seventeenth centuries, and more representative of the ideas of his countrymen.[8] They also have an inherent subtlety and interest at least equal to the ideas of the monarchomachs; therefore, they deserve closer attention from students of political ideas than they have in fact received.

CLAUDE DE SEYSSEL

Claude de Seyssel was a diplomat, jurist, and churchman active in the service of Charles VIII and Louis XII. By birth a Savoyard, by training a legal scholar, and by reason of his proven usefulness to the French king a negotiator and ambassador in several European countries, Seyssel combined a thorough acquaintance with the law with a broad experience in contemporary politics. When Louis died in 1515, Seyssel retired to his bishopric at Marseilles to take up his episcopal duties actively for the first time; but before he left Paris, he wrote a political testament called *La monarchie de France* which he presented to his new sovereign, Francis I. The treatise was published in 1519 under the more ambitious title *La Grant Monarchie de France,* and was reissued periodically thereafter.[9]

Seyssel has often been compared with Machiavelli, for several reasons. Both wrote on the basis of long and similar experience of actual politics, to give advice to princes who had newly taken up their office and who bid fair to be strong and aggressive rulers, directing their thoughts pragmatically to the specific kinds of problems and opportunities such princes would face. Both were committed patriots as well as realists; they explicitly denied the usefulness of traditional encomia and moralistic patterns for kingship and went out of their way to ridicule and subvert such practices. Some scholars have assumed a link between them, searching for ways in which Seyssel might have read Machiavelli's *Prince* before he wrote his *Monarchie,* or even taking for granted that he must have done so.[10] But a search for explicit indebtedness seems misdirected; *La Monarchie* is in many ways more like *The Discourses* than *The Prince,* and *The Discourses* were not written until after Seyssel finished his own work. Whatever the explanation for the similarities between them, the comparison between them is a fruitful one.

There are also differences, of course. Although *La Monarchie* was composed as hastily as *The Prince,* Seyssel was not interested in coming back to power and had no intention of using his little

treatise to gain the prince's favor. His concern is with the realm
itself, and with the qualities of leadership required to maintain its
strengths and heal its imperfections. There is more admonition and
exhortation in *La Monarchie* than the *The Prince,* and more attention
to other bodies in the state. Most significantly, there is also a theory
of a complex sociopolitical order, a quasi-idealized picture of what
the French polity could easily become, based closely upon what it
was in fact. For this reason, J. H. Hexter, in a penetrating study of
Renaissance political ideas, places Seyssel between Machiavelli and
Thomas More as the exemplar of a "constitutional" mode of
thought that shares some aspects both of Machiavelli's "predatory"
mode and of the "utopian" mode of More.[11]

In writing about *La Monarchie de France,* Seyssel brought to his task
not only his training as a jurist and his political experiences and
observations but also extensive familiarity with ancient history. He
had translated several classic histories for the king's use, including
those of Xenophon, Justin, Diodorus, Eusebius, Thucydides, and
Appian Alexandrin. These translations were later published, and
Seyssel's observations in the preface to one of them—the *Histoire
d'Appien*—were as familar to later Frenchmen as the argument of his
Monarchie.

In his "Prohème" to the translation of Appian Alexandrin,
Seyssel sketches a paradigm shared by French constitutionalists
until the Revolution. He takes for granted that because of "the
imbecility and imperfection of the human condition" all regimes
will develop through cycles of birth, growth, decadence, and finally
"ruin and total mutation." But the best-governed monarchical
regimes have achieved exceptional stability and longevity

> because they have been and are governed and ruled more
> justly, more equally, and more virtuously; their heads are more
> in consonance with their members, [*les chefs se sont mieux accordés
> avecques les membres*] the members with one another, and all
> together with their heads; which cannot be the case except
> when each individual is protected in his preeminence and his
> *raison* according to his condition [*état*], and when the head is
> regulated [*réglé*] by good laws and civil customs, for the good of
> the whole, as far as can possibly be achieved; in order to ensure

that his royal and legitimate power does not convert itself into tyranny and willful domination.[12]

There are a number of things about this rich passage which should be noticed: the consonance between all parts of the state; the maintenance of each individual member of the whole in his particular condition and proportion; the regulation by law and custom to prevent deformation of royal power into tyranny, defined as domination by pure will. There is a subtle blend of equality amidst diversity, of particularity within unity, that characterizes French constitutionalism throughout the old regime.

Seyssel continues this passage by describing the French regime as "si raisonnable et si politique qu'elle est toute alienée de la Tyrannie." This use of *raison*, like that in the long passage quoted just above, defies translation and requires close attention; it bespeaks proportion, order, regularity, rationality in a sense more generous than our ordinary usage of the word "reason" can convey. Similarly, the term *politique* is not "political" in a familiar sense, but has overtones of medieval Aristotelianism, as in the "dominium politicum" of Fortescue. The best translation, surely, is "constitutional," in the sense of Aristotle's *politeia*. Though he does not use the term itself, Seyssel describes a regime with a strong constitutional structure, in which the uses of royal power and the political condition of each member of the state are carefully established and protected by custom and law.

It is significant that Seyssel asserts in this same passage that "à bien prendre le totaige de cet empire français, il participe de toutes trois les voies du gouvernement politique," in other words, that the French regime overall has elements of all three political forms. Seyssel did not repeat this assertion in *La Monarchie,* but it was identified as part of his argument by later publicists who often took strong issue with it. At first glance the assertion sounds like the familiar tribute to mixed government, uncommon only in its reference to France. If we look more closely, however, it is apparent that Seyssel has a peculiar mixture in mind, one which is not quite reducible to familiar assertions about mixed government; for it is not conceived in terms of mechanical checks and balances but of a pliant and subtle interdependency of mutually limiting spheres of authority, all combining harmoniously to work together in the government of France, encompassing every official down to the merest parish clerk. It is not, in other words, a fundamentally different picture from the system of "bridles" on the *puissance absolue* of the French monarch in *La Monarchie de France,* even though Seyssel did not use the concept of three different forms of government to express his meaning in that treatise.

In his description of the French constitution in the "Prohème," Seyssel does not specify particular institutions in the state which play aristocratic or democratic roles. Instead, he begins by focusing on the monarch, then widens his perspective slowly to encompass first those officers closest to the king, then finally to take in all politically active subjects, in a complex pyramid of function and protection. In this he reflects, perhaps, the fact of patronage and clientelage in contemporary politics, and he sketches out a participatory hierarchy which was to reappear in later French theory in different guises, in the work of La Boétie, of Fénelon, of Montesquieu.

Seyssel refers to the French monarch as having "all power and authority to command and do what he wishes" but holds that "this great and sovereign liberty is so well regulated and limited by good laws and ordinances, and by the multitude and great authority of officers who are near his person and in the several parts of his Kingdom," that a king can hardly manage to act violently or against the good of his subjects. Surrounded by counselors, exercising his justice through a great number of officers, the king finds himself hedged in on all sides by those persons and institutions whom he and his predecessors have established to help in governance, most notably by the parlements. Seyssel compares the parlements with "a true Roman Senate," a comparison which was to be used often in the sixteenth century, again during the Fronde, and in the conflict between Louis XV and his parlements in the eighteenth century. He speaks next of the royal administrative officers and ordinances which effectively restrain "la volonté desordonée d'un Prince volontaire," providing time and means to block the exercise of a "commandement déraisonnable" until the king is brought to change his opinion, or to repair the damage that occurs. He stresses that the forms and procedures of these officers are so hallowed in the kingdom that any prince, however depraved, would be ashamed to break them, and that it is because of them that his majesty is "plus décorée, plus aimée et mieux obéié" than a majesty which uses "un volonté désordonnée." This notion that the king's power is increased rather than diminished by effective restraints upon its use recurs as the keynote of *La Monarchie de France.* Finally, Seyssel asserts that the members of each of the estates of the realm have offices and dignities open to them appropriate to their situation.

> And in this way, the goods and honors, charges and admin-istration of *la Chose publique* being divided and distributed among all the estates proportionately, according to their condition, and each individual in those estates maintained in his preeminence and equality, there follows a harmony and consonance which is the cause of the conservation and augmen-tation of this Monarchy. And the affairs of the kingdom prosper to the extent to which the kings (who are the fountain and the source from which emanate and flow all the streams of good *polices* and justice) are attentive in upholding this union and correspondance, like true and natural Princes who are concerned primarily with the common Good of the kingdom, which they identify with their own.[13]

The major lesson to be learned from Appian's history, to which this paean forms a prologue, is the effect of civil dissension and mutiny in Rome. Appian shows how sedition, ambition, and civil conflict in a poorly regulated polity destroyed the Roman state. Machiavelli's focus upon Livy and the origins of Rome is paralleled by Seyssel's interest in Appian and its demise, as a way of showing what must be avoided if the French kingdom is to continue to flourish: the encroachment of overly ambitious people or princes on other parts of the complex social organism, an encroachment which threatens the mutual dependence that sustains the whole.

LA MONARCHIE DE FRANCE: THE ORDER OF THE REALM

Seyssel's major treatise, like Machiavelli's, is clearly and deliber-ately distinguished from traditional political theory at the very outset. *La Monarchie* begins with a reflection on the great number of wise men who have disputed and dogmatized about the best form of government and composed huge volumes on the subject, tiresome to look at and hard to understand. Yet the imperfection of humankind is so great that men like those depicted in such treatises—wise, virtuous, and prudent—have never been discovered in reality; nor has any "cité ou chose publique" ever been regulated entirely by "la raison morale et politique." For a new monarch, such treatises are almost useless; what he needs are shrewd nuggets of practical advice, and information about the strengths and weaknesses of his own kingdom. *La Monarchie* is intended to provide such advice and information, based on a novel fusion of material: the political experience and lifelong observations of a high officer of the crown, selected and ordered for immediate utility, consonant with "political reason, approved authority and the example of authentic history." [14]

Accordingly, the first section of *La Monarchie* includes a set of comparative reflections on Rome and Venice, most excellent among popular and aristocratic states, respectively. Seyssel's interest in these polities is principally with their value as object lessons and as foils for his analysis of the French monarchy. The discussion of Venice also gives him the opportunity to present a general theory of society, rich in Renaissance images and metaphors, which warrants close attention. The theory includes cyclical and organic themes familiar since antiquity but has a new and striking element: a stress upon the clashing desires and wills that make up a state and threaten its health and stability. Seyssel's whole theory of politics is based on this conception of the social order composed of energetic, discordant social wills and purposes.

All things that come into being are necessarily impermanent, in this vision of the world; "les corps mystiques," political communities, like human bodies, must decay. The four humors that make up a human body are contrary to one another and compete for dominance; in the long run one gains excessive prominence in the body and destroys it. So the "mystical body of human society," having been "assembled by a civil and political union," must in the end, because it is "composed of multiple judgments and discordant wills repugnant to one another," decline and fall into nothingness. [15] The image is extended by the description of five ages of societies,

like individuals—birth/beginning, youth/augmentation, maturity/
state, age/decline, decrepitude/dissolution. The use of the fluid
word *état* as a synonym for maturity is worth remarking. But the
major interest of this theory is its insistence upon pluralistic conflict
as the essential feature of political society, the notion that each part
of the society will attempt to gain dominance over all the others,
and that unless this unhealthy monopoly can somehow be fore-
stalled the state is necessarily destroyed. Seyssel assumes that the
development of states is naturally toward an increasingly particularistic pluralism that threatens to destroy them; this assumption parallels similar themes in Machiavelli's *Discourses* and finds
clear echoes in later French constitutionalists such as Domat and
Montesquieu.

The lesson of Venice for France is that an aristocracy is more
vulnerable to such destruction than a well-ordered monarchy. Envy
and encroaching appetite by each part of the state, each desiring a
plenitude of control and none content with its own place, each
"having more regard to their particular passions than to the public
good"—all these tendencies gravely endanger the health of the
Venetian society. An aristocracy, in Seyyssel's eyes, has no real
protection against these "mauvaises humeurs de ce corps mystiques" as they become more numerous and more corrupt. But the
great advantage of monarchy is that it provides a single strong will
above the fray that can regulate conflict, forestall the process of
envy and encroachment, and ward off the day of doom.

> For a single Head and Monarch can remedy and obviate all
> these dangers and inconveniences much more successfully than
> an assembly of men elected or chosen to govern, wno are
> nonetheless subject to those whom they govern; and such a
> Head is always better obeyed, more revered, feared and
> esteemed than a Community (whether large or small) or a
> temporary and changing Head who does not have complete
> authority.[16]

This justification for monarchy is central to the French constitutional tradition. At the same time and afterward, other defenses
were also being offered—that monarchy is rightful because the king
is God's image on earth, his counterpart on the political plane of the

great chain of being; that monarchy is superior to other forms of
government because of its efficiency and rapidity in decision-
making. But Seyssel's defense proved particularly attractive to later
French theorists, and the two elements of his argument can
regularly be found in later thought: that monarchy is superior
because only a single leader enjoying complete authority can
control the complex and active forces that make up a political
system, keep order among them, and prevent the fatal tendency to
encroach on one another; and that an hereditary monarch has a
clear psychological advantage over any other ruler in commanding
obedience, reverence, and esteem among his subjects.

Until the eighteenth century Frenchmen took for granted the
nucleus of Seyssel's claim: that only a royal will obviously superior
to all partial wills within the realm, unlimited by any of those wills,
can prevent petty tyranny within the state. Rousseau's political
philosophy, at first sight so far removed from Seyssel's Renaissance
monarchy, retains this nucleus in the *volonté générale*. The notion that
it is a grave disadvantage for government to be subject to the partial
wills of those who are governed, that such subjection is not a source
of liberty but of chaos and destruction, distinguishes French theory
from the beginning of the sixteenth century and sets it apart from
Anglo-Saxon modes of thought. The second part of Seyssel's claim—
the psychological advantage of hereditary monarchy, the symbolic
power of ancient kingship to elicit awe and obedience among
ordinary men—was also accepted by many later theorists, including
men like Montaigne and Pascal, who were more fascinated by the
effect of the royal spell on other men than subject to it.

Seyssel did not write as a pure apologist for monarchy, however,
and this was not the sole source of his influence. The other side of
his argument in *La Monarchie* must immediately be brought to bear
on his defense of the superiority of kingship. For if it is true that
only a single will can control the complex social forces in the state, it
is also true, in Seyssel's eyes, that these forces themselves provide
both the restraints and the limits on the monarch's power, and also
the effective basis for the exercise of his authority. Seyssel had no
illusions about the excellence of kings; he knew that the personal
vices and imperfections of monarchs are the Achilles' heel of this
form of government. But he was convinced that, at least in France,
this weak point had been effectively secured by a constitution

sufficiently pliable to make room for the active will of a talented and vigorous monarch bent upon working for his people's good, yet strong enough to restrain the disordered will of a depraved or imbecilic successor and prevent him from destroying the kingdom while it awaits a better king. Seyssel asserts that the French monarchy is "governed by a much better order" than any other. In defining that constitutional order he made his most famous and fruitful contribution to French thought: the theory of the three bridles on the monarchy of France.

The image of the bridles was a happy choice to express Seyssel's meaning. Unlike brakes or obstacles, bridles regulate and direct energy as well as restraining it. This was the sense Seyssel wished to capture in his argument. Bridles are flexible and sensitive, not mechanical and automatic; they can restrain the headlong energy of a runaway monarch, and then be relaxed to move in gentle harmony with a well-intentioned king, subtly informing his direction yet setting no obstacles in the way of his productive energy. This image of a flexible and durable constitution, responding in different ways to different monarchs for the long-run benefit of the French polity dominated French constitutional argument until the middle of the eighteenth century. The specific image of the bridles was not often used in later thought, but the corresponding verb— *refréner*—was quite common. The insight that supported the image— of the subtle connections between psychology and social forces, symbols and institutions—gave French thought its distinctive character.

The first bridle named by Seyssel is *la religion.* The functioning of this bridle depends on beliefs held by the prince and by the people too. Long indoctrination in religion shapes the psychology of French kings and deters them from tyrannical behavior, since the patterns of Christian morality instilled in them from birth provide a sufficient guarantee against tyranny for princes who have been taught to heed them. But Seyssel has no intention of resting his case primarily on the traditional tutelage of princes, or the vague precepts of natural and divine law which they are always exhorted to obey. The crucial thing about this bridle is not what the prince believes but what the people believe about his religion, based on his overt behavior. Like Machiavelli, Seyssel uses the career of Numa Pompilius as an example of the benefit that accrues to leaders who have the "color and appearance of religion and of having God on their side." [17] The French people are notably devout. They obey their kings because they regard them as instruments of the divine will, and they will be reluctant to follow the commands of a king who is obviously impious. The royal power will in such cases actually be diminished by this withdrawal of allegiance and support. Thus, even a king who has little personal respect for Christian ethics cannot afford to deviate too much from their dictates if he wishes to retain the enthusiastic obedience of his people. And there is also an institutional aspect to this bridle; any priest, however lowly, can condemn a prince in his pulpit for falling away from his religious obligations, and draw attention to his sin. In such a case, says Seyssel, the king dare not silence him because of the outcry that would result.

In discussing *la justice,* the second bridle on the prince, Seyssel focuses on one institution—the parlements—which insure, in his eyes, that justice is better protected and established in France than anywhere else in the world. He believes that the parlements were originally instituted by the kings themselves to provide justice and to guarantee the *civilité* of the laws and institutions of the kingdom. Because of their number and their status as respected personages, the members of the parlements have been able to establish their authority so firmly that "Kings have, so far as distributive Justice is concerned, always been subject to them." [18] They assure that justice is fairly and equally done to all subjects, and by passing judgment on the king's own laws and ordinances, they effectively "restrain the absolute power our kings desire to use." Seyssel recognizes that these courts are more pliant to the royal will than they ought to be if they are to exercise a firm check upon that will. But he is confident that they are so well established in authority that at least they cannot be completely broken by any king. His confidence as well as his reservations about these institutions were borne out in subsequent experience. The parlements recurrently provided the focal point for opposition to the monarchy, yet never managed to become an independent check upon the king's authority.

La police is the third of Seyssel's bridles. This is a term which is difficult to translate satisfactorily, since Seyssel applies it very broadly. He uses it initially to refer to those ordinances set up by kings themselves, legitimated and confirmed by time and usage, which provide the procedural patterns for the government of the realm. Here, as in the case of the parlements, Seyssel assumes that all authority in the French polity flows from the king. Institutions that now act as checks on his power derive their legitimacy from that same royal authority that was originally responsible for instituting them. Royal ordinances have established a complex administrative structure which is the basis for the king's government, and yet the several parts of that structure limit and direct the king's authority in the very act of governing—as, for example, the Chambre des Comptes in matters of finance.

The royal ordinances are not the only component of *la police,* however. Seyssel discusses "another order and form of living in this kingdom that tends to the same end," that is, the exercise of well-tempered power. This is a reference to the other part of the "corps mystique" in addition to its head: the body of the nation, the three estates of the people themselves, "bien réglés et entretenus" with their own patterns and consonances. This is a primary source of the constitutional order that Seyssel finds in France: not only is there a single head to govern the "mystical body," but that body is itself well ordered in its several estates and conditions, so that the energies and ambitions of each part of the body are controlled and checked internally, in addition to providing checks upon the king who governs them. Seyssel here follows a well-established tradition in France, gradually eroded in the next few centuries—the tradition that the nation as a body possessed coherent customary rights and privileges, distinct from those enjoyed by the monarch and not subject to his dictates. His description of the king's power as *absolue,* like that of most of his contemporaries, must therefore be understood to refer only to a certain sphere of action appropriate to a king; outside this sphere, over against it, in harmony with it but not completely subject to its control, there was another sphere of legal right and established usage, another part of *la police* of France.[19]

This elusive term, therefore, like Aristotle's *politeia,* refers to the whole sociopolitical structure of a community. Seyssel sometimes uses it to refer to economic patterns of merchandise and trade, the way people make their living, the material abundance that sustains them. The term is gradually extended in the course of his treatise, as it is in Aristotle's *Politics.* At first it refers to the structure of offices, the ways of allocating and exercising power; but in the end it encompasses "the way of life of a citizen body," a constitution in the largest sense.[20]

Seyssel's discussion of *la police* of the mystical body itself is noteworthy on several counts. He describes this order in terms of three estates, but these do not correspond exactly to the traditional ones in France. Seyssel distinguishes between the *peuple gras* and the *peuple menu* as the two lower orders, and gives first place to the nobility. The clergy is an estate "common to all the others," whose members are drawn from throughout society. This way of dividing up the world allows Seyssel to make some interesting observations on the relations among these different socioeconomic strata. As in the "Prohème" to Appian Alexandrin, Seyssel specifies that each estate has "its rights and preeminences according to its quality," with offices and dignities, opportunities for specific types of political participation, open to each order. But his most novel contribution is a theory of social mobility, an unexpected theme in a theorist of his time and status.

The *peuple menu* are introduced to Seyssel's readers with the traditional expressions of fear of the masses, of the dangers to be expected if these folk are given too much liberty and disproportionate wealth, or excited into action, because of their great number and natural envy of their betters. But then Seyssel asserts promptly that this same envy and energy can be a source of health in the social body when it is properly regulated, as it is in France. A member of the *peuple gras* who provides important services for the common good can be ennobled by his prince, and even more easily, a member of the *peuple menu* can rise to the middle class (and hope to rise even higher) because of his merit and industry alone. The church provides another route by which an ordinary Frenchman can hope to "parvenir à grand et digne degré." Seyssel asserts that such things happen every day in France and remarks on this as a great source of social stability and vigor. For the hope of rising in this way

> ensures that each individual [*un chacun*] is content with his estate and has no occasion to conspire against the others, knowing that by good and licit means he can rise higher, and that he puts himself in danger if he attempts to do so in any other way. If there were no hope of rising, or if it were too

difficult to do so, those who had too great a spirit could induce others in their own Estate to conspire against the other two.[21]

Seyssel was probably exaggerating the ease of social mobility and the frequency of its occurrence in his time; but the importance of his argument does not depend on its accuracy as a sociological generalization. It is notable that, rather than assuming that the social order requires that each man keep to his own station, Seyssel shows Aristotelian subtlety in recognizing that social stability often depends on outlets for energy instead of on repression. The individualism of Seyssel's theory is also worth attending to, here and elsewhere in his treatise; he thinks of each Frenchman as a member of an estate, but significantly considers "un chacun" both as protected in his own dignities and rights as a member, and also as having the capacity and desire to change his status and improve his lot. Seyssel specifies that the king ought actively to encourage such mobility, not only to prevent dissatisfaction, but also to encourage industry and the use of talent in the state. By this means commerce, science, literature, and military discipline will all be enriched, and each Frenchman will be encouraged by the success of his neighbors to devote himself to similar pursuits. This healthy and productive emulation is "the true spur which makes all sorts of men run in the course of virtue. And a single man raised by such a means leads ten thousand others to take up the effort, as we see every day." [22] Such confidence in the political and social value of emulation became a marked characteristic of later utilitarian thought in France, finding its most systematic expression in the ideas of Saint-Pierre.

LA MONARCHIE DE FRANCE: THE ROYAL WILL

The theory of social mobility in Seyssel's *Monarchie,* like his image of the bridles, rests on a delicate interplay of scope and limits. The social orders locate each individual, providing a definite and limited socioeconomic base for his endeavors. Yet they are also pliable, giving scope to vigorous socially useful action which transcends their limits, and restraining efforts at antisocial conspiracy. In the same way, the three bridles that limit the action of the king also provide the stuff and substance of his power, extending its rightful scope rather than mechanically constraining it. It is significant that Seyssel first discusses how the bridles limit power, and then, in the second section of *La Monarchie,* argues that it is in the king's own interest to cultivate and maintain these bridles instead of always attempting to evade or resist them. He describes the second section as much more difficult to write but also much more useful than the first; it is in this section that he deals with the faults and imperfections of the monarchy. It is clear that Seyssel believes the major imperfections arise because monarchs have not understood the subtle connections between the bases of their power and the limits on its use, and in attempting to contravene those limits they have undercut their own authority.

Since a large part of the king's authority and legitimacy comes from his status as Most Christian King, French kings ought not only "to endure and submit sweetly" to the first bridle but also "fortify it with their power." Since the French king is traditionally recognized first of all as the source and embodiment of justice, he ought to "study well how he can maintain and augment it." And as for *la police,* it is by means of the "laws, ordinances and admirable customs" of the kingdom that the prince prospers; not only is he bound by his coronation oath to honor them, but if he does not, he "enfeebles his strength and thereby diminishes his glory and his own renown." [23] Seyssel insists that "this moderation and bridling of the absolute power of Kings is to their own great honor and profit" and urges kings to recognize the dependence of their own authority on the very factors that constrain its use. He uses an analogy which recurs often in later French theory, asserting that if the king's power

> were ampler and more absolute it would be worse and more imperfect; just as the power of God is not thought to be the less because he cannot sin or do evil, but is thereby the more perfect. And in the same way, Kings are to be praised and prized much more when they choose in their great authority and power to be subject to their own laws and live according to them, though they could at will make use of their absolute power. [24]

Thus, Seyssel is well aware that the effectiveness of the bridles depends finally on the voluntary submission of the king himself. To show the great advantages of such submission, for king as well as kingdom, is his major purpose in writing *La Monarchie.*

The central constitutional distinction in Seyssel's treatise is between an ordered and a disordered will. His theory of decision-making recognizes that royal decisions are not simply formal moments of pure disposition of *volonté* but are shaped by advice and information and depend heavily on the quality of the counselors of the king. A disordered will operates hastily and erratically, on the basis of poor, unsystematic information; an ordered will operates smoothly and regularly, on the basis of a good system of advice and counsel. An ordered decision is the reflection of sober deliberation by a number of men in cooperation with the king. Seyssel, unlike later monarchical apologists, saw realistically that it is "impossible that a single man or even a small number, however accomplished they may be, could understand and manage all the affairs of a large kingdom." Later apologists were fond of the image of the farseeing monarch raised high above his people, enabled by his peculiar perch to encompass the whole kingdom in his vision. Seyssel's approach was much more commonsensical than this; he referred rather to the "obfuscation of understanding" that afflicts a monarch who tries to do everything himself.[25]

In Seyssel's view, the best ordering of the royal will depends on the use of a variety of councils. He discusses four, to be convened for different purposes. The reasoning behind this set of councils has much to do with merit, something to do with a type of representation which rests on clientelage rather than consent, and nothing at all to do with popular participation. Seyssel believes good counselors are rare, and large assemblies move him to contempt. Considerations of blood, rank, and dignity are irrelevant in determining a man's excellence as a royal adviser, though they are relevant to the matter of counsel on other grounds. The king should hear information and opinion from a wide range of people but rely most heavily upon a small group of trusted advisers who have demonstrated their zeal for "le Bien public du Roi et du royaume."

The king should depend first upon a cabinet of ten or twelve men, chosen wholly for their "vertu, expérience et prudhomie," and within this group select an inner cabinet of three or four among whom ideas can be canvassed informally and freely, particularly when some portion of the ordinary council can be expected to "have an interest" in the issue.[26] Seyssel warns the king against singling out any one of his advisers as superior to all the rest, no matter how talented, since this preeminence puts a dangerous barrier between the prince and the rest of his advisers and gives excessive power to one man. However well intentioned such a first minister might be, "it is very difficult for anyone possessing such great authority to maintain equality and use it entirely reasonably." Here once again *égalité* and *raison* crop up as Seyssel's fundamental criteria for judging the excellence of government. His entire constitutional apparatus is designed to protect these values by focusing all decision-making in one authoritative royal will, while assuring that this will is informed and ordered by deliberation and by constraint.

All great affairs of state are to be discussed not only in the cabinet but also in a "Grand Conseil," corresponding roughly to the traditional French Assemblée des Notables.[27] Ordinarily the Grand Conseil will be composed of those men resident at court or easily available who have some claim of degree, status, or office to be included in a discussion of important issues. In case of particularly grave decisions about "les lois et ordonnances générales concernants le Justice ou la Police universelle du royaume," this Great Council should be enlarged by the inclusion of a small number of men from major towns and cities of the realm, in a special Assemblée Casuelle. This is Seyssel's sole allusion to anything resembling the Estates General. There is no notion that the consent of such an assembly is constitutionally mandatory even for new taxes, which was held to be the case by a good many French jurists from Commines to Bodin. Seyssel may well have taken for granted that changes in taxes would warrant the calling of an Assemblée Casuelle; but his whole focus is on the utility of the councils in royal decision-making, and he gives them no autonomous legitimacy. In the ongoing debate among French constitutionalists between supporters of the estates and supporters of the parlements, Seyssel was firmly on the side of the latter.

The virtue of these large councils, in Seyssel's eyes, is not that they are likely to give better advice than smaller groups. Quite the contrary: the minority in such assemblies is always wiser and more farseeing than the mass, and yet there is great pressure to adopt the majority view, "la plus grande et commune opinion." [28] Therefore, such assemblies will be of little use to a wise monarch in shaping or enlightening his decision, but they will be of considerable use in matters of publicity and support. A grave decision affecting the whole kingdom is best taken in the presence, and with the advice, of powerful leaders who command the deference of numerous other Frenchmen. The agreement of the magnates is the best guarantee of obedience by their followers. There is no notion that the consent of such assemblies is necessary to legitimate the king's decision, or that most of those participating contribute anything of importance to the making of it.

In Seyssel's constitutional system, the role of the ordinary people is primarily socioeconomic. Unlike the unitary absolutist theorists, he gives the subjects a vigorous and active role. The people through their own *métiers* support the health of the *corps mystique* and are responsible for filling certain offices in that body appropriate to their rank. But they have nothing to do with the functioning of the Head of that body beyond providing support and obedience. The body of the *corps mystique* has its own order and regular activity, which in a sense puts limits on the crown; but the political action of the king as such does not depend upon any action by the members. There is no suggestion in Seyssel's treatise that the will of the members of the *corps mystique* is required to legitimate or to confirm the decision of the head. His is an intricate constitutionalism from which the notion of consent is virtually absent. Only insofar as the obedience of the people is elicited by good government, so that the king's power is diminished if he behaves in a disordered way, can one speak of popular consent.

Much of the royal business, in Seyssel's account, has to do with the maintenance of a healthy pluralistic balance in the *corps mystique,* by means of the sensitive regulation of the three orders in their relations with each other. Each estate should be protected in its own rights and dignities and prevented from encroaching on the others or swelling disproportionately in strength. Seyssel shows with great subtlety how each of the three orders can threaten the others. The nobles tend toward insolence and overmightiness and attempt to exploit and oppress the others. The middle class is likely to weaken the nobility by catering as merchants to aristocratic tastes for luxury and pomp, and by wearing them out in long judicial processes. The middle class will also attempt to dominate the *peuple menu,* who in turn threaten to upset the whole *corps* with rebellious envy if they are not kept in order. Only the king is in a position to maintain equilibrium among the orders, while encouraging useful social emulation and mobility as well. In discussing the king's responsibilities on this score, Seyssel touches on themes which were to become prominent in later French social theory: the mercantilistic notion that the king was responsible for actively encouraging and augmenting trade and commerce to enrich his kingdom; and the prescient warning that the greatest evil for the lower classes lay in excessively heavy and irrational taxation.[29]

Taking his system as a whole, it is clear that Seyssel has described a complex constitutional machinery in which the prince has a central role, but which is designed to function even if he is weak or incapacitated, through the councils and advisers to the king. In this Seyssel strikes the keynote of French constitutionalism: a constitution ought to operate in three different ways, depending upon the quality of the king in office: (1) to provide scope and support for strong creative government when the country is blessed with a true king; (2) to restrain the tyrannical impulses of an evil ruler and prevent him from doing too much damage; and (3) to govern the kingdom competently when the monarch lacks ability or energy. The royal will is the formal point of decision-making in the state, but the personal component of that will provided by the king can be expanded and contracted within the framework of the constitution.

This is true only for domestic affairs, however; and Seyssel regards the prince's responsibilities in foreign affairs as more delicate and difficult precisely because an energetic and creative royal will makes all the difference. In the diplomatic and military arenas of the Renaissance there was no substitute for personal initiative and skill on the part of the prince himself. Accordingly, Seyssel devotes three of the five sections of his treatise to questions of war, conquest, and negotiation. For our purposes these sections are less relevant than the two on internal affairs of France; but it is worth noticing that Seyssel's concerns in these chapters closely parallel those of Machiavelli. There is the same preoccupation with military discipline and fortification, with complex negotiation based often on deceit and treachery, and with the conquest and governance of new states. There is also the same basic assumption about the nature of political men: "corrupt, commonly so ambitious and lustful for dominance (even Princes and others who manage great States) that one cannot trust them."[30] The wise prince will therefore always be watchful for deceit and even occasionally engage in dissimulation himself. But Seyssel, unlike Machiavelli and later French disciples of the Florentine, insists that though the prince must act shrewdly he should always confine himself to measures that are fundamentally honest and reasonable, "keeping always to the *ordre de la charité.*"

CONCLUSIONS

In his conception of a constitution as a rich, complex sociopolitical order dominated by a royal head, Seyssel reflected and inspired themes that were characteristic of French thought throughout *l' ancien régime*. Constitutional theorists in the later sixteenth century followed him closely; even men like Bodin and Hotman who developed quite different systems of ideas acknowledged their indebtedness to Seyssel and show it in their works. The historical school of jurists centered around Du Haillan and Pasquier built on Seyssel's *La Monarchie* and helped make his ideas available to others. In the early seventeenth century, his ideas continued to be echoed in some treatises, even as the general current moved toward the refinement of theories of absolutism, divine right, and *raison d'état*. In his study of seventeenth-century constitutionalism, Mousnier quotes two passages as representative of French attitudes in that era, from Loyseau and Coquille; both are heavily laced with Seysselian motifs:

> It is necessary, that there be Order in all things, for their fitness [bienséance] and direction. . . . For we could not live together in equality of condition; some must command and others obey. Those who command are divided into several orders and ranks, so that each one of them will have Superiors. . . . By means of these multiple divisions and subdivisions, of these several Orders a general Order is composed, and of the several Estates [*Etats*] a well-regulated State [*Etat*], in which there is a beautiful harmony and consonance, and a correspondance and

rapport from the lowest to the highest part: in such a way that
finally, by means of Order, a numberless number ends in unity.

The king is the *head* and the people of the three orders are the
members, and all together make up the *mystical and political* body,
whose liaison and union is individual and inseparable, so that
one part cannot suffer ill without the rest feeling it and
sorrowing.[31]

Claude Joly during the Fronde, and Jean Domat under Louis XIV,
were influenced by *La Monarchie,* and theorists such as Fénelon and
Montesquieu show the power of Seysselian themes into the eighteenth century. His influence was not confined to political theorists
but continued to be felt by professional jurists as well. Thus, in a *lit
de justice* held in March 1776, the *avocat du roi,* Séguier, addressed
these words to Louis XVI and the Parlement de Paris:

Sire, the clergy, the nobility, the highest courts, the lower
tribunals, the officers attached to these tribunals, the universities, the academies, the financial and commercial companies,
all present, in all parts of the state, living bodies which one can
consider as links in a great chain of which the first link is in the
hands of Your Majesty, as head and highest administrator of
all that makes up the body of the nation.[32]

Seyssel's treatise must itself be seen as a crucial link in a chain of
constitutionalist thought in France, contributing to a fruitful
continuity in ideas, between the medieval concept of a corporate
community rich in custom and tradition, the Renaissance idea of
the conflict of the humors in the body of the state, and the modern
notion of pluralistic interplay between society, economy, and polity.
The notion of the bridles on the power of the king, and of power as
increased rather than diminished by right use, were central to *ancien
régime* constitutionalism. Yet however influential he may have been,
it could be argued that Seyssel's theory has major deficiencies when
compared with other constitutionalist systems; that the set of
constitutional limits he helped develop proved their impotence
against the growing absolutism of the French kings, and therefore
showed their own insufficiency in practice. We cannot, obviously,

begin to explore all the complicated reasons for the weakness of French institutions in the face of developing absolutist power, nor for the triumph and eventual downfall of the monarchy. However, it is important to look at some of the criticisms that can plausibly be leveled against Seyssel's theory itself, as a contribution to constitutionalist thought.

Seyssel's system has been criticized as static, depicting a state in which there is no provision for deliberate change in laws and institutions to deal with conflicts and crises of development.[33] On this view, Seyssel's perception of the world was shortsighted. On the eve of major changes in the French polity he expected the perpetuation of the medieval community without change. It is hardly fair to fault a man for having failed to prophesy the Reformation and the industrial revolution; but the brunt of this criticism has to do with Seyssel's inability to provide for strong legislative power in the state, compared, for instance, with Bodin's achievement on this score. There is something to this; but the criticism is not wholly accurate and does not get at the real difficulty with Seyssel's system.

It is misleading to speak of Seyssel's theory as static, since in fact it is remarkable for its recognition of dynamic energy in society and in the state. Seyssel pictures a polity in movement, with each member of each order performing an active function, yet also spurred to emulate his more successful brethren. The central authority is expected to regulate this healthy energy, to maintain the balance of equality amidst diversity, and to direct its own energies in exploits of war and conquest. The institutional structure of this polity is expected to be sufficiently pliable that it can handle such flows of energy without stifling them while providing justice and order in the state. It is true that Seyssel does not make specific provisions for regular institutional changes or for revision in the law; he takes for granted that such changes will occur smoothly in *la police* he has described. This assumption is indeed a weak point in his theory, but the weakness lies not so much in an excessively static picture of the world as in an excessively generous view of the abilities of kings and their advisers to discern what must be done and to do it.

The real trouble with Seyssel's theory, in fact, is not that it is static but that it puts too much faith in the strength of subtle bridles to direct the dynamic energy of the crown. He does not assume that men are by nature good; but he does assume that power and energy can easily be channeled into useful patterns in a polity. In common with almost all French theorists, Seyssel admires strong sovereign power and hesitates to block its ability to perform brilliant and glorious acts.

In Seyssel's defense it must be kept in mind that, except for a few memorable periods, the French monarchy until the late seventeenth century was regularly threatened by other powers in the state, particularly by ambitious princes and nobles. This goes far to explain the tendency of French constitutional thought to move very close to absolutism, to insure sufficient power for the crown to act in such a situation. And in such a situation, the real threat to the liberties and security of ordinary individuals comes, not from strong royal power, but from potential petty tyranny; so that the job of French constitutionalism until the reign of Louis XIV was not so much to protect the people from the prince as to protect the prince and the people from the ambition and particularistic oppression of other powers in the state. Mousnier puts it very well:

> There was no need to insist on the guarantee of the rights of individuals. The rights of the strong were sufficiently guaranteed by the nature of things. The rights of the others could only be guaranteed by the power of the King. It is important to focus clearly on this truth: *in such a social situation,* the true guarantee of rights was the royal sovereignty.[34]

As a theory of power and protection in sixteenth-century France, therefore, Seyssel's theory has much to recommend it. But he made more general claims for his theory; he asserted that the well-ordered monarchy of France had a constituion, which he described and analyzed, that deserved the admiration and envy (if not the imitation) of less fortunate realms. He claimed, in other words, that the constitutional order of *La Monarchie de France* should be regarded as a model of excellence in governance, not simply as a good job of adaptation in a difficult situation. Looked at from this perspective, Seyssel's constitution undoubtedly suffers from a grave deficiency: the vagueness and fluidity of all institutions except the royal will. None of the other instituions in the state, not even the parlements, has sufficient power to stand up against a king determined to abuse his authority. All authority in this polity is derived finally from the head. The energetic *corps mystique* itself has no institutional skeleton sufficiently rigid to maintain it against authoritative encroachment and oppression from above. Such a constitutionalism too easily prepares the soil for its own destruction. Yet we must remember that no French theorist before Montesquieu recognized clearly, that "pour qu'on ne puisse abuser du pouvoir, il faut que, par la disposition des choses, le pouvoir arrête le pouvoir." [35]

To shift the metaphor from the organic to the mechanical, the difficulty with Seyssel's constitutionalism is that the energy of the subjects is not well integrated into the machinery of authority in the state; the critical gears are absent. This is most striking in the case of the Estates General, which might plausibly be expected to have a central role in Seyssel's theory as the political expression of the orders in the state. It is worth noticing that when Francis Hotman revised his *Francogallia* to take into account the argument of Seyssel's *Monarchie,* he took for granted that Seyssel's discussion of the three orders in the state was designed to provide the basis for an argument for the authority of Estates General.[36] In fact, this is exactly what Seyssel's discussion does not do. The description of the three orders is quite removed from any consideration of the councils of the realm; and as we have seen there is only an offhand reference to anything resembling a gathering of the estates. The order of the kingdom has its own complex form; but it is not connected with the authority of the head. The king in governing is advised to make use of the advice of a large number of his subjects; but there is no suggestion that this is an authoritative nexus in the state.

To adapt Walter Ullmann's familiar categories, this is a purely *descending* theory of authority, in which there is no ascending authority in the people welling up to meet the royal will.[37] The patterns of activity and energy in the *corps mystique* itself do not flow upward. The only flow is from the top downward in a pyramidal fashion; the various officers in the state derive their authority finally from the king. Such a pattern is unusual among constitutionalist theorists; and indeed it might be argued that a system that makes so little room for the institutionalized expression of popular will, for independent guarantees against the abuse of centralized authority, does not even deserve the name. Seyssel's system provides for neither of the two basic sets of guarantees we are accustomed to finding in constitutionalist theories: guarantees from above the political system, in the form of a higher law considered morally binding on authority, with sanctions of divine wrath; and guarantees within the system, in the legitimation of resistance by specifically named representatives of the community against a king who contravenes such higher law, culminating, if necessary, in the use of force. Seyssel obviously believes that an impious king will incur divine disapproval and have reluctant and disobedient subjects; but he makes no references to a generally accepted divine or higher law; nor does he provide any clear institutional focus for resisting a tyrannical prince or determining that he has, in some sense, unkinged himself. In his theory, respect for God's law is defended on basically utilitarian grounds, as advantageous to the king in exercising and expanding his authority.

It might therefore appear that Seyssel's is a pure theory of monarchical authority, in which constitutionalist elements are subordinated and truncated beyond recognition. But such a dismissal would be narrow and shortsighted, betraying our own Anglo-Saxon bias about what a constitutional theory must contain. Seyssel describes a complex *politeia* reminiscent of that of Aristotle, an intricate sociopolitical system in which the arbitrariness that plagues the exercise of mortal authority is diminished, not by independent control from above or below, but by the institutional and legal instruments through which that authority itself is exercised. The strength of his theory lies in its sophisticated recognition that the exercise of political authority depends upon devising institutions and patterns, upon appointing officers and administrators, judges and tax collectors; and that in providing these instruments to make authority effective throughout a large kingdom, that same authority is necessarily limited and ordered in specific ways by all these lesser wills and by the patterns themselves. As Hexter says of the "empiricism" or "institutionalism" common to Machiavelli, More and Seyssel:

> The trait ... which differentiates them from the ordinary writers of books of advice to princes, is their common awareness

that in politics, general principles usually operate through specific institutional structures, when they operate at all.[38]

The phrase "specific institutional structures" must, however, be understood in a rather special sense, if it is to be used in discussing Seyssel. For he was not concerned with establishing well-defined rigid corporate bodies, such as the Estates General, as concrete obstacles to the power of the king. Instead, he was interested in institutions in a more fluid sense: regular patterns of behavior recognized and respected by all participants in the political process, identified with particular groups or authorities within the state—the church, the merchants, the parlements, the councils, and the monarchy itself. The regularity, the recognition, the respect, combined with the identification with specific bodies or persons, warrant the term "institutional," though "procedural" might be a better term to use in capturing the peculiar flavor of Seysselian constitutionalism.[39] Within the French tradition, the special service of such a view of the world was to provide grounds for distinguishing absolute monarchy from arbitrary tyranny, since absolute power could be "constituted" and regularized in such a fashion, and this set it apart from government by arbitrary whim and mere irrational caprice. This makes it difficult, of course, to distinguish between "absolutist" and "constitutionalist" argument in France. But theorists who (like Seyssel) stress the power and legitimacy of these inherent limitations within the monarchy itself differ in intent and rhetoric from those who ignore or minimize these regularized restraints, and this is why the distinction can normally be drawn in analysis, at least.

On of the most important contributions of Montesquieu's *Spirit of the Laws* to the French political tradition was that he was the first to state clearly that such grounds for distinguishing absolute from arbitrary power are insufficient, and that absolute power always tends toward tyranny unless more concrete "institutional structures" are devised as counterweights to the power of the king. He drew upon the Anglo-Saxon tradition to do so, of course; and after 1748, Montesquieu's constitutionalism absorbed and superseded the older arguments stemming from Seyssel's *Monarchie*. But this should

not lead us to overlook Seyssel's contributions. His message, reduced
to its simplest form, was that pure arbitrariness is impotent, and so
is abstract virtue. The exercise of authority depends on order,
regularity, and the participation of many human wills. Such
authority is increased rather than diminished when it is in accord
with the beliefs, needs, and expectations of subjects, since their
enthusiastic obedience and support is thereby elicited. The *politeia*
described by Seyssel can operate only when there is a fundamental
shared agreement about the ends of political life, and when those in
authority are not perpetually insensitive to the need for limits. Since
these conditions do not always obtain, his constitutionalism is not
sufficient in itself. But he draws attention directly to one crucial
aspect of the flow of authority, one often obscured by the more rigid
categories of Roman and Anglo-Saxon thought as well as by the
ponderous historical apparatus characteristic of later constitutionalism in France. This aspect is the subtle relationship between the
elements of political power and the limits on its use, an inherent
patterning of authority that must be present to some degree in any
polity, and which provides the basis for all constitutions.

NOTES

1. Arthur Young, quoted in Charles H. McIlwain, *Constitutionalism
   Ancient and Modern* (Ithaca, N.Y.: Cornell University Press, 1940), pp.
   3-4.
2. "Cahiers de la noblesse d'Alençon," quoted by André Lemaire, *Les
   lois fondamentales de la monarchie fransaise* (Paris 1907; reprinted, Geneva,
   1975), p. i. See also W. F. Church, "The Problem of Constitutional
   Thought in France," IXe International Congress of the Historical
   Sciences, *Etudes . . . des assemblées d'Etat* (Louvain, 1952), pp. 173-186.
3. Roland Mousnier in his essay, "Comment les Français du XVIIe siècle
   voyaient la constitution," *XVIIe siècle*, nos. 25-26 (1955), 11, follows
   Walther von Wartburg in arguing that Bossuet was the first to use the
   word "constitution" as a synonym for fundamental law. E. M. Beame,
   "Limits of Toleration in Sixteenth-century France," *Studies in the
   Renaissance*, 13 (1966), 255, finds a reference in a pamphlet of the late
   sixteenth century reprinted in 1665.
4. In addition to the work by Lemaire and Mousnier already cited, other
   important sources for French constitutionalist argument include W. F.
   Church, *Constitutional Thought in Sixteenth-Century France* (Cambridge:

Harvard University Press, 1941); R. W. Carlyle and A. J. Carlyle, *History of Medieval Political Theory in the West,* vol. 6 (Oxford, 1950); François Dumont, "Royauté Française et monarchie absolue au XVIIe siècle," *XVIIe siècle,* nos. 58-59 (1963), 3-29; and Denis Richet, *La France moderne: l'esprit des institutions* (Paris, 1973).

5. *De l'excellence des Roys et du Royaume de France* (Paris, 1610), cited by Mousnier, *op. cit.,* p. 15. Cf. David Maland, *Europe in the Sixteenth Century* (Macmillan, 1973), 128: "Civil war might be a constant feature of French history; but from 987-1794 no king was ever deposed nor did anyone succeed to the throne in defiance of the Salic law."

6. Richet, *op. cit.,* pp. 46-54.

7. Mousnier, *op. cit.,* 18-21; this distinction corresponds roughly to that drawn in discussions of late seventeenth- and early-eighteenth-century French thought, between proponents of the *thèse royale* and the *thèse nobiliaire*—by, e.g., Albert Mathiez, "La Place de Montesquieu dans l'histoire des doctrines politiques du XVIIIe siècle," *Annales historiques de la Revolution Française,* 7 (1939), 97-112. Julian Franklin's distinction is the most concise: "The critical difference, then, between limited and absolute monarchy has to do with the presence or absence of institutional restraints." *Jean Bodin,* Verhandlungen der internationalen Bodin Tagung (Munich, 1973), discussion, pp. 451-452; see also J. H. M. Salmon's contribution to the same discussion, pp. 454-455, in which a classification of three types of sixteenth-century constitutionalism is suggested.

8. J. W. Allen, in his *History of Political Thought in the Sixteenth Century* (London and New York, 1928), p. 275, asserts that "much of the controversy that followed can be read as a commentry on or an expansion, on one side or another, of the views of Seyssel," and yet gives him much less attention than the Huguenots and their opponents. Reliable French histories of political ideas, such as Pierre Mesnard's *Essor de la philosophie politique au XVIe siècle* (Paris, 1969) or Jean Touchard's *Histoire des idées politiques,* mention him only in passing; and George Sabine's familiar *History of Political Theory,* 3d ed. (New York, 1961), which is generally weak on the French tradition, does not mention him at all.

9. For Seyssel's biography, see Jacques Poujol's Introduction to his edition of *La Monarchie de France* (Paris, 1961), which also includes a useful discussion of the various editions of the *Monarchie* and its influence.

10. Allen, *op. cit.,* p. 275, takes for granted that Seyssel read *The Prince,* ignoring the fact that it was published only after *La Monarchie* was written. Leon Gallet, "La monarchie française d'après Claude de

Seyssel," *Revue historique de Droit Française et étranger* IVe séries, nos. 1-2 (1944), argues that since Seyssel had Florentine connections, he may well have read the work in manuscript before he wrote his own treatise. Poujol, pp. 36-39, has a useful discussion of this whole question, and makes the point that the resemblance to the *Discourses* is in some ways more marked, in any case. He also draws attention to the similarities in both men's works in their judgments about the French polity.

Donald R. Kelley, in a good study of "Murd'rous Machiavel in France: a Post Mortem," *Political Science Quarterly*, 85 (1970), 550, notes that Seyssel's treatise was "closest in spirit to Machiavelli's work" among French political works of the first half of the century. He also notes, p. 553, that at least one notorious "Machiavellian" maxim during the French religious wars was in fact taken from Phillip de Commines, the "French Machiavelli." Since Seyssel was familiar with Commines's famous *Mémoires* of the French polity in the late fifteenth century, it is reasonable to suppose that this might have had something to do with his "Machiavellism" also.

11. Hexter's essay, "Claude de Seyssel and Normal Politics in the Age of Machiavelli," in Charles S. Singleton, ed., *Art, Science and History in the Renaissance* (Baltimore, 1967), pp. 389-415, is the best available discussion. It is reprinted in *The Vision of Politics on the Eve of the Reformation* (New York, 1973), which also includes some references to Seyssel in the introductory "Discourse on Method." See also J. Russell Major, "The Renaissance Monarchy as seen by Erasmus, More, Seyssel and Machiavelli," in Theodore Rabb and Jerrold Siegel, ed., *Action and Conviction in Early Modern Europe* (Princeton, N.J., 1969), pp. 17-31.

12. The "Prohème" is included in Poujol's edition of *La Monarchie de France;* this passage is from p. 79; all translations from Seyssel are my own.

13. "Prohème d'Appien," pp. 83-84; the reference to the parlements is on p. 81.

14. "Prohème" to *La Monarchie de France,* "addressant au Très-Chrétien Roy de France, François, premier de ce nom"; Poujol, 95-101.

15. *La Monarchie,* part I, section 3, p. 108; cf. Paul Archambault's useful study of "The Analogy of the 'Body' in Renaissance Political Literature," *Bibliothèque d'Humanisme et Renaissance,* 29 (1967), 21-52.

16. *Ibid.,* 1, no. 4, 110.

17. *La Monarchie,* I, 9; 117; cf. Machiavelli, *Discorsi,* I, 11; and Joseph R. Strayer, "France: the Holy Land, the Chosen People, the Most Christian King," in Rabb and Siegel, *op. cit.,* pp. 3-16.

18. *La Monarchie,* I, 10; 117; on the role of the *parlements* in the French constitution and in the works of other jurists, see Church, *op. cit.,* pp. 131-155.

19. *La Monarchie,* I, 13; 120-121; Church, pp. 77-81, refers to this "all-important doctrine" that there were "two primary spheres of legal right, those of ruler and people respectively" as a fundamental legacy from medieval to Renaissance France. Lemaire describes the same phenomenon in slightly different language when he asserts (pp. 283-284) that "L'Etat, alors *respublica,* c'était la chose publique: c'était une *chose,* et non pas une personne," a thing which signified both "l'ensemble des interêts collectifs de la nation, et l'organisme politique lui-même." Thus the republic was a body without a soul, and the soul which animated it was "la souveraineté," which was thought of as something "de *personnel,* d'intelligent et de libre," which could only appertain to a specific human person, the prince.

20. *La Monarchie,* II, 17; 154-155; and V, 9; 216-218. Cf. the various definitions of *politeia* given in Aristotle's *Politics,* esp. those at pp. 1278b, 1289a, and 1295a.

21. *La Monarchie,* I, 17; 125.

22. *Ibid.,* II, 25; 165.

23. *Ibid.,* II, 14-17, 149-155.

24. *Ibid.,* I, 12, 120, cf. II, 11; 143.

25. *Ibid.,* II, 4; 133-134. Innocent Gentillet's "Anti-Machiavel" depends heavily on Seyssel; it is interesting to notice that he argues that the three supports of the French crown are *consilia, pietas,* and *politia,* giving pride of place to council; C. E. Rathé, "Innocent Gentillet and the First "Anti-Machiavel," *Bibliothèque d'Humanisme et de Renaissance,* 27 (1965), 198.

26. *Ibid.,* II, 6-9; 136-142. This is one of the rare instances when Seyssel uses this word instead of "profit" or other more general synonyms; it is notable that he does so in the context of describing a narrow selfish stake in a decision which is a source of danger for the public good; this is one way in which the term was used in the sixteenth century in France, though it was more common to use it in the context of international affairs, as in V, 9; 216.

27. *La Monarchie,* II, 5; 135-136; on the *assemblée des notables* and other institutions of *l'ancien régime,* see François Olivier-Martin, *Histoire du droit Français des origins à la Révolution* (Paris, 1948), esp. pp. 364-392; and Pierre Goubert, *L'Ancien régime,* vol. II: *Les pouvoirs* (Paris, 1973), ch. 4.

28. *La Monarchie,* II, 4; 133-134.

29. *La Monarchie,* II, 21-24; 160-165.

30. *La Monarchie,* IV, 3; 191-192; cf. Machiavelli, *Prince,* chs. 15-17; *Discorsi,* I, 37.

31. Charles Loyseau, *Traité des Ordres,* and Guy Coquille, "Discours des Etats de France," quoted in Roland Mousnier, "Comment les Français voyaient la constitution," pp. 11-12; translations my own.

32. Quoted and translated by A. R. Myers, "The Parliaments of Europe and the Age of the Estates," *History,* 60 (1975), 11.

33. E.G., W. F. Church, *op. cit.,* pp. 40-42, 72-73. R. W. and A. J. Carlyle, in their *History of Medieval Political Theory in the West* (Oxford, 1950), VI, 225-226, place Seyssel firmly in the medieval tradition.

34. *Op. cit.,* p. 28.

35. *Esprit des lois,* in *Oeuvres complètes,* ed. Roger Caillois (Paris, Pléiade, 1951), vol. II; book XI, ch. 4. R. W. K. Hinton, in a thoughtful discussion of Seyssel, insists upon the role of force—the force of public opinion and of the institutions of *la police*—in the operation of the bridles, and thus brings Seyssel closer to Montesquieu than I have done. According to Hinton, "Seyssel is to be understood as saying in effect that the king of France is physically prevented from using his admittedly great power at his own pure will (which would be tyranny) by the corresponding and countervailing great power of the people of France." Hinton contrasts Seyssel's optimistic Renaissance realism with Bodin's pessimistic abstract legalism in his essay on "Bodin and the Retreat into Legalism," his contribution to the Bodin conference at Munich cited above, pp. 303-313. This draws attention to an interesting aspect of Seyssel's thought, but Hinton (in my view) overstates the raw power of the bridles as opposed to their subtle moral force.

36. François Hotman, *Francogallia,* ed. Ralph E. Giesey and J. H. M. Salmon (Cambridge, 1972), X, 293 (added in the second edition, 1576).

37. Walter Ullmann, *History of Political Thought in the Middle Ages* (Harmondsworth, Middlesex: Penguin Books, 1970), pp. 12-13. In Ullmann's argument the orginal point from which power descends is God himself; in Seyssel's, effectively, the king. Seyssel goes out of his way to deny that a well-ordered monarchy has any taint of aristocracy in *La Monarchie* I, 12, where he explicitly dissents from the great weight of opinion connecting political stability with mixed government.

38. *Vision of Politics on the Eve of the Reformation,* p. 15; on the next page, referring specifically to Seyssel's system, Hexter points out that "it is through the institutions of the realm, political and social, and by his relation to them, rather than by exemplifying an abstract set of virtues, that the King of France preserves and augments the monarchy of France and thereby preserves and magnifies himself."

39. This useful distinction was suggested by John Chapman, who notes the "procedural" connotations of the idea of "bridles," and also argues that "Western constitutionalism may be thought of as evolving from 'procedural' to 'institutionalist' structures. ... In this perspective, Hobbes is a 'procedurist,' Locke is an 'institutionalist.'" This is an interesting perspective, although an overly strict distinction between procedures and institutions might obscure the essentially "procedural" nature of all institutions to which contemporary theorists of organizations are now drawing our attention.

5

CONSTITUTIONALISM IN REVOLUTIONARY AMERICA

CECELIA M. KENYON

INTRODUCTION

In Book III of *The History of Florence,* Niccolò Machiavelli stated, "Nobody should start a revolution in a city in the belief that later he can stop it at will or regulate it as he likes." [1] Although no one has yet disproved the validity of Machiavelli's assumption that revolutions once initiated are likely to be uncontrollable, the American Revolution can be characterized as one that never got completely out of control and came close to realizing the hopes of the men who began it. The ideals proclaimed in the Declaration of Independence are by their very nature probably incapable of perfect realization, but the men of the Revolutionary generation achieved a remarkable degree of success in establishing political systems that have endured and have not yet failed so radically or irrevocably as to foreclose the possibility that our own and later generations of Americans can continue the work of the Founding Fathers. One of the principal causes of the relative success of the Revolution and of the remarkable control which its makers exercised over it was the degree to which a profound and pervasive spirit of, and commitment to, constitutionalism guided their thought and governed their conduct.

There were other factors that contributed to the success of the Revolution: the low ratio of population to land; the wide distribution of property and a comparatively high standard of living; the absence, with the major exception of enslaved blacks and the minor exception of Germans in Pennsylvania, of sharp ethnic or religious cleavages within the population; the generations of experience with quasi-republican politics. All these factors provided uniquely fortunate circumstances for the establishment of stable republican governments. By concentrating on constitutionalism, then, I do not mean to imply that it alone was responsible for the success of the Founding Fathers.

The era of Revolutionary constitutionalism divides itself readily into three relatively distinct chronological periods during which Americans were preoccupied with different issues, problems, and tasks. The first, beginning about 1761 and lasting until 1775-76, was triggered by British attempts to tighten administration of the colonies and to derive significant revenue from them. The colonists responded with protests that parts of the new policy were contrary to the British constitution, to their colonial charters, or to both. During the second period, 1776-80, the colonies or states framed new constitutions and launched the first large-scale modern experiment in constitutional republicanism. (Concern and discussion began in 1775, and some states changed their first constitutions or adopted new ones after 1780. But the essential work began with the Virginia constitution of 1776 and ended with the ratification of the Massachusetts constitution in 1780.) The third period was that of the framing and ratification of the federal Constitution in 1787-88, to which should be added the enactment and ratification of the first ten amendments, or the Bill of Rights.

I shall concentrate primarily on the middle period, because it is the least well known to students of politics and because experience with more than thirteen state constitutions helped shape the federal Constitution and influenced the making and revising of state constitutions in the nineteenth century. In order to understand this first great creative and experimental aspect of Revolutionary constitutionalism, it is essential to review some of the ideas and attitudes expressed when the colonies were protesting what they

believed to be policies contrary to the British constitution and/or to
their colonial charters.

THE PERIOD OF PROTEST: 1761-1775/1776

To select a specific moment and a specific quotation to designate
the beginning of the American Revolution is somewhat arbitrary. I
shall follow a reasonably well established convention and choose as
the spark that ignited the Revolution and continued to glow
throughout its duration, the two short sentences attributed to James
Otis, Jr., in his attack on the "writs of assistance" in Boston in 1761:
"An act against the constitution is void. An act against natural
equity is void." [2]

Otis's appeal to "the constitution" was not new in American
politics. As early as the 1630s, according to John Winthrop, settlers
in the Massachusetts Bay Colony had asked to have a look at the
Colony's charter; after that, again according to Winthrop, they
cited it when it supported their position and ignored it when it did
not.[3] So if Americans of 1761 appealed to "the Constitution" in
their political polemics, they did so in accordance with a tradition
that was already venerable and with a naturalness that now seemed
instinct.

If we look at the second sentence in Otis's assertion, "An act
against natural equity is void," we cannot be certain whether he
intended it to be a separate, independent argument, or whether he
meant it to be an extension of the first. In the eighteenth century the
British constitution was widely regarded as being an embodiment of
natural law and therefore necessarily of natural equity. We have
now lost this attitude, but if we are to understand the concept of
constitutionalism throughout the Revolution, we must attempt to
recapture the inclination partially to identify a proper constitution
with natural law or equity.

Perhaps the easiest way to perform this intellectual somersault is
to examine John Dickinson's exposition of happiness as a natural
right. Dickinson's logic was simple and no doubt questionable, but
it, and especially the conclusion to which he pushed it, suggest that
at least in the early years of colonial protest the concept of
constitutionalism was magnificently spacious but unfortunately
deficient in precision.

Dickinson began with the assumption that God had given man life and then reasoned that God had therefore also given man a natural *right* to life. God had also given man a desire to be happy; therefore, Dickinson reasoned further, God had given man a natural *right* to happiness. If man could not be happy without being free, he had a natural right to freedom; if he could not be free without being secure in the possession of property, he had a natural right to property. After demonstrating that man had a natural right to happiness because God gave man a natural desire for happiness, Dickinson made an enormous logical leap and suggested that the criterion for an act's constitutionality should be its tendency to make the people happy.[4] For a modern American, Dickinson's proposed criterion seems hopelessly vague. Yet the criterion and its context are worth pausing over because they reflect conveniently the curious Janus-like quality of the Revolution, its peculiar blend of old and new ideas, its protean process of transforming old ideas by adapting them to new uses and new contexts without destroying their ancient lineage.

The idea that the good of the community was the proper end or purpose of government was not new. Neither was the inclusion of happiness, properly interpreted, as an ingredient in that common good. What was new was the claim that *individual* happiness was a natural right not to be violated by government. There was implicit in this new position a profound problem: the happiness of different individuals might require different policies on the part of the government. Indeed, one of the major parts of Dickinson's argument against the British theory of virtual representation was that the interests of British subjects on the two sides of the Atlantic were not identical—were, in fact, in the matter of taxation, contradictory. Dickinson's proposal that happiness be the criterion of constitutionalism seems to reflect the old concept of the public good as a unitary entity, but his demonstration that the happiness of an *individual* is a natural right provides partial legitimacy for the individual's pursuit of his own self-interest (or happiness).

Within a few years this partial legitimization of individual self-interest would lead to two further problems for Americans of the Revolutionary era. One was the question of what degree and quality of homogeneity of individual and group opinion and interest were required for a people to live under one political roof.

Dickinson himself seemed only partly aware of the implications of his argument at the time he was developing it in the late 1760s; by 1770 some Americans, and by 1774 many Americans, had come to the conclusion that the British Empire no longer comprised a single people united by common interests. The British in Great Britain were perhaps still one people, but the British (and other white ethnic groups) in America had become a separate people. From this analysis of the political situation, American pamphleteers such as James Wilson and Thomas Jefferson drew a constitutional conclusion: the British Parliament could have no legitimate authority to legislate for the American colonies. The only link between the two peoples, then, was the British Crown. This conclusion was expressed in constitutional terms and buttressed by constitutional arguments derived from centuries of real or imaginary English history, from the original grants of colonial charters by the Crown, and from a selective account of colonial political practice.

The second problem implicit in Dickinson's thought is one that I shall mention here only briefly and return to later for a somewhat fuller examination. It was the possibility of tension or conflict between the acceptance of self-interest as at least partially legitimate and the traditional conception that virtue, whether "public" or "private," was the distinctive and requisite characteristic of republican government. If it is legitimate—indeed an inalienable natural right—for individuals to seek happiness, and if happiness involves some degree of satisfying self-interest, then the older view that public virtue included the voluntary subordination of self-interest to the public interest would seemingly be eroded or perhaps stand in need of redefinition.

The existence of different interests in society, and the inevitability of men's pursuit of them, had already been recognized by Americans and had achieved a limited legitimacy by a route different from the logical one implicit in Dickinson's justification of individual happiness as a natural right. For at least three quarters of a century, colonial Americans had been concerned with factions, or what a Massachusetts clergyman in 1694 referred to as "sinister interests." [5] These interests or factions had at first been regarded as the result of sin, and the pursuit of them as destructive of the body politic. But generations of preaching and exhortation had neither eliminated the different interests nor changed men's behavior, and factions had eventually been reluctantly accepted as an unavoidable characteristic of a society growing more complex and heterogeneous as it increased in population and developed beyond the comparative simplicity of the early settlements.

One may conjecture that this background of intracolonial factional conflict was partly responsible for the Revolutionary generation's selective acceptance and modification of John Locke's version of social contract doctrine in the *Second Treatise of Civil Government*. One of the purposes for which men entered into civil society, Locke had written, was to secure in the government an impartial judge. James Otis remarked dryly that there were few if any instances in the history of governments that had actually functioned impartially.[6]

In this statement Otis reflected the experience and opinions of his fellow Americans. For some purposes or in some respects, "the people" were regarded as a unitary whole; for others, they were known to be split into diverse groups with different opinions and interests. This dualistic perception of "the people" was both implicit and explicit during the period of constitutional protest. For purposes of refuting the British theory of "virtual" representation, colonial polemicists assumed a unity of interest among Americans that set them apart from the British in the home islands and made them a discrete "people." But the faraway British were not the sole target of these polemicists. Their newspaper articles, pamphlets, orations, and broadsides were directed to fellow colonists as well and were intended to create "a people" as well as to express opposition to the British government.

This dualism with respect to "the people"—in one sense a united whole, in another sense a collection of groups and individuals with different and sometimes conflicting interests and opinions—has been associated with a similar dualism in our attitude toward constitutions. On the one hand, we seem to have a very deep need for something above or beyond the politics of everyday life to which to refer, some firm ground on which to stand, and that "something" has been "the Constitution." On the other hand—and if John Winthrop is to be believed, we have been doing it for almost three and one half centuries—we have never completely separated the "constitutional" from the "political," and indeed have constantly jeopardized the function that we seem to want the conception of constitutionalism to perform by overloading it with indiscriminate appeals.

That there should *be* a fundamental law or constitution was assumed by the men of the Revolutionary era. It is time now to turn to them and examine their thought and action at that crucial moment when they had made the ultimate decision to break away from Great Britain and to create governments entirely their own.

THREE STATE CONSTITUTIONS OF 1776-1780

The job of drafting constitutions for the newly independent states did not come unexpectedly or without warning. As the authority and power of royal governments began to erode—in Massachusetts in 1774, in other colonies later—the absence of a recognized, legitimate government was felt by many men to be a grave problem. To some extent, the various provisional congresses, conventions, assemblies, and committees performed some functions of a regular government. Most of them possessed a limited legitimacy because their membership was constituted by popular election. But, as the Tories were quick to point out, these groups were almost all extralegal and extraconstitutional. For them to exercise power, and for their supporters to accept that exercise, was not altogether consistent or becoming, since the same groups had been and still were arguing vehemently that their resistance to British acts was justified because Parliament had enacted unconstitutional laws. After the fighting broke out at Lexington and Concord, the sense of unease among the patriots seemed to increase, and by the fall of 1775 the Continental Congress was receiving requests from various colonies for advice as to what they should do about regularizing their situation—specifically by instituting new governments. It was not a question the Congress either wanted or was prepared to answer at that time, because to advise the formal creation of new governments was tantamount to a decision for independence—and the Congress was not yet ready for that—while to advise the patriots to do nothing was to leave them with the possibility of anarchy. Congress compromised by suggesting the formation of explicitly temporary constitutions to serve until the dispute with the mother country was resolved. New Hampshire and South Carolina did attempt to regularize their situations in this manner.

On May 10, 1776, the Congress passed a resolution advising all the colonies to establish new governments of a permanent nature. This resolution amounted to an implicit decision for independence and was so understood, though the formal and official decision was not made until July 2, and the Declaration of Independence not accepted until July 4. Before the end of 1776, most of the new states had written new constitutions or revised their colonial charters. Massachusetts did not adopt a constitution until 1780, primarily because of prolonged debate over the proper means of framing and ratifying a constitution intended to serve as the fundamental law of the Commonwealth.

Before looking briefly at three of the constitutions to obtain a sense of the range of opinions on the proper structure of republican government, I should like to pause for a moment to explore the attitudes that underlay the almost instant rush to legitimize the hitherto provisional governments by written constitutions. Why did the rebels of 1776 think that the proper thing to do in the midst of revolution was to write a constitution? Why did they not wait until peace had come, and then soberly and leisurely set about the task of constructing sound foundations for their new republics?

The decisive factor appears to have been a pervasive and unusually consistent belief in the doctrines of social contract and consent—and, lest we forget, the right of revolution. There was almost a literal quality in the way these doctrines were accepted and put into practice. There was among some Americans a sense that they were in a state of nature and a belief that the new constitutions would become their social contracts. Thus, in some, but not all of the states, property qualifications for voting for delegates who would frame these constitutions were suspended for all free, adult males. Thus, too, oaths of allegiance to the new governments, which some modern Americans find antilibertarian, were then perceived as the logical corollary of social-contract doctrine: they were the means by which men gave their explicit consent to the new states. We tend to forget that it *was* a *revolution* begun by the military action at Lexington and Concord in April 1775 and officially proclaimed by the Declaration of Independence. If it is difficult for us to imagine Washington or Jefferson captured by the British and shot or hanged as traitors, it is even more difficult to remember that every member of the state assemblies or conventions that drafted constitutions was publicly committing himself to the Revolution and therefore placing his life in jeopardy should the Revolution fail in its immediate objective of gaining independence from Great Britain. The new constitutions were the means by which the new states sprung from repudiation of their colonial status would achieve the legitimacy of a fundamental law derived, at least indirectly, from the consent of the people.

It was in this context *during* the Revolution, not after its successful military conclusion, that the first state constitutions were written. All but that of Massachusetts were completed rather quickly. The story that one was written overnight in a tavern without the aid of a single book may be an exaggeration, but it illustrates the urgency that many of the Revolutionary leaders felt; it provides a clue to one of the reasons why some of the constitutions seem rather crude; it also explains why, with the exception of Massachusetts, there is no adequate documentation of this extraordinary episode in the history of modern constitutionalism.

It is impossible as well as inappropriate to attempt a complete review of more than thirteen constitutions in this paper. (The total is more than thirteen if one includes the temporary constitutions adopted before the decision for independence was made, their later replacements intended to be permanent, and the constitution of the party in Vermont which eventually emerged victorious in its efforts to free the area involved from the claims of both New York and New Hampshire and gain statehood.) I shall treat briefly the constitutions of Virginia, Pennsylvania, and Massachusetts, because these three represent reasonably well the typical as well as the atypical in both the processes of framing and adopting a constitution and in the provisions of the constitutions.[7]

The Virginia Constitution of 1776

The Virginia Convention of 1776 was not elected for the sole purpose of framing a constitution. Like its immediate predecessor, it was elected to take the place of the former royal government. At the time of its election, March 1776, opinion among the electorate was strongly in favor of independence according to contemporary accounts, and the voters probably assumed that the convention would frame a constitution and establish a regular government to replace its own *ad hoc* management of public affairs. The membership of the convention did not reflect any massive change in the voters' choice of leadership. A few former representatives, known or suspected to be Tories, were defeated; a significant number of other familiar figures were not members because they were absent with the army or were representing Virginia at the Continental Congress. The weight of power in the convention lay where it had lain for generations—with the Tidewater planters. If the constitution produced by this convention leaned toward democracy, as Richard Henry Lee thought, it did so primarily because of the opinions of the aristocracy, not because that aristocracy had been displaced by a new class of men.

The convention did not begin its work with a complete *tabula rasa.* It had its colonial charter, and it had several recent proposals. In the previous November, Lee had asked the advice of John Adams, and in January, Adams's "Thoughts on Government" was published. It proposed a bicameral legislature: a lower house to be elected directly by the people (or those of them qualified to vote); an upper house elected by the lower. The executive and his council would be elected by both houses and would have the power to veto bills passed by the legislature. Also in January, Thomas Paine published *Common Sense,* which in addition to making a powerful argument for independence, attacked the much-admired British constitution with its assumed embodiment of the principle of separation of powers, and proposed instead a simple government with power concentrated in a unicameral legislature. The convention also had available a plan prepared by Carter Braxton, a loser in the March election. The outstanding features of Braxton's plan were an upper house and governor elected for life. While the convention was sitting it received a plan from Thomas Jefferson, but too late for serious consideration.[8]

Thus as the convention began its work, its members had several models or proposals for consideration. The Constitution eventually adopted, reportedly after heated debate, was not as extreme as either Paine's or Braxton's proposals, nor did it follow closely the more moderate plan of John Adams. Its principal author is said to have been George Mason, but there are enough differences between

Mason's original draft and the document voted by the convention
to make it very clear that its members did not slavishly accept the
ideas of one of their most respected fellow planters.[9]

The constitution consisted of three principal parts: the Bill of
Rights, which was primarily the work of George Mason; the
Preamble, which, with some additions made by the convention, was
essentially Jefferson's and almost identical to the indictment of
George III and Parliament written into the Declaration of Independence; the body of the Constitution, which established the frame of
government.

With one definite major exception, and two or three possible
exceptions, the latter can be characterized as somewhat "democratic." The constitution established a bicameral legislature: the
lower house was to be elected by the voters, with each county to
have two representatives, and with provision for one representative
from existing or future cities or boroughs. The upper house was to
consist of twenty-four members, each elected directly by the voters
of the twenty-four districts into which the state was to be divided for
this purpose.

It is significant that the upper house was not differentiated from
the lower in either socioeconomic source or membership. Representation was not apportioned according to the value of taxable
property, and like the lower house, membership was restricted to
freeholders with no minimum value of the freehold specified. There
were two noneconomic differences between the lower and upper
houses: members of the latter had to be at least twenty-five years
old, and the term of office was four years, with provision for one-
fourth of the membership to be elected each year. The term of the
lower house was one year, and though not specified, the usual age of
majority, twenty-one, seems to have been assumed for both electors
and representatives. Age, tenure, and limited size thus appear as
possible means for making one house more aristocratic than the
other.

A governor and privy council of eight members were to be elected
jointly by the two houses of the legislature; the governor was to be
chosen annually, and if he served for three consecutive years, was
ineligible for the next four; the members of the council were subject
to compulsory, triennially staggered rotation. Neither the governor

alone nor the governor and council jointly could veto bills passed by the two houses of the legislature.

The suffrage qualifications remained the same as those under the colonial charter (ownership of 100 acres of vacant land, of 25 acres with a building at least 12 by 12 feet, or a town lot with the same size building, or a total estate of £25, or completion of a five-year apprenticeship in Williamsburg or Norfolk); there was no difference in the requirements for voting for the two houses.[10]

So far, the constitution looks rather democratic. The most serious exception is partly hidden under the provisions for equal representation of counties and districts. By this time, the white population of the Tidewater counties was generally less than that of the Piedmont counties, and thus by this provision alone the Tidewater aristocracy may have hoped and expected to retain its control over state politics.

One other provision in the constitution introduced an element of flexibility and ambiguity. The explicit, specific qualifications for membership in the lower house of the legislature were residence in the county and status as a freeholder. The only additional specific qualification for membership in the upper house was age—"upwards" of twenty-five years. Yet to the specifications for membership in both houses there was added the phrase, "—or duly qualified according to Law—." This phrase could theoretically enable the legislature to change either or both sets of specified qualifications. It apparently did neither; one of the criticisms Thomas Jefferson leveled against the constitution was that the two houses of the legislature were too homogeneous in membership and source of power to act as adequate checks on one another.[11]

One may also note that there were no additional property qualifications for the governorship or for membership in the council, and that for the governor the constitution specified an "adequate, but moderate salary." The absence of such qualifications is rather surprising, and the records of the convention are not complete enough to allow one to be sure of the explanation.

So, although the Virginia constitution can be characterized as slightly more democratic than the average of those adopted by the newly independent states, such characterization must be qualified. We do not know for certain what proportion of the free adult male population was excluded by the property qualifications for voting; we *do* know that the failure of the convention to reapportion the legislature in accordance with population left effective political power very largely in the hands of its traditional possessors—the Tidewater aristocracy.

Two observations are in order at this point. If one judges by the face of it only, the Virginia constitution broke the connection between the principle of separation of powers and the ancient theory of mixed government. There was no difference explicitly specified in the property qualifications for electing or holding office in the two houses of the legislature. The upper house was not economically differentiated from the lower house and was accordingly not even a pale, elective imitation of the British House of Lords. There were no property qualifications specified for the governor or his council. The provision that the governor should have an "adequate, but moderate salary" apparently reflected an intention to make that office available to men of limited wealth, but not to make it attractive for financial reasons alone. The second characteristic to note is that the framing of this constitution by a collective body broke the venerable tradition that the founding of a state or a radical change in its laws could be effected only by a single individual—a Lycurgus, a Solon, a Machiavellian prince, or a Rousseauian legislator.

Because it was the first constitution to be adopted, the form of government devised by the Virginia Convention exerted some influence in other states. Virginia's Bill of Rights had much greater influence, both in America and abroad. To the modern American scholar, this famous document seems strange and puzzling, for two reasons: (1) It consists of a mixture of fragmentary statements of political ideology, of familiar maxims, of admonitions to various civic and private virtues, of procedural rights taken over from English law, and of newer substantive rights of freedom of the press and of religion; (2) it uses the subjunctive or normative mode of key verbs about as frequently as the declarative or imperative modes. The result of these factors is that the document as a whole seems to be a statement of ideology and aspirations as much as a list of precise rights legally enforceable.

A few examples will serve as illustrations. The first article states that "all men are by nature equally free and independent, and have certain inherent rights." The article goes on to say that men cannot divest or deprive their posterity of these rights when they enter into civil society. So far so good. But the rights listed are, "the enjoyment of life and liberty, with the means of acquiring and possessing property, and pursuing and obtaining happiness and safety." This list of rights gives the reader pause. Perhaps under favorable circumstances, some governments could fulfill the right of all men to the means of *acquiring and possessing* property; it seems quite impossible that any government of any kind could insure the right of all men actually to *obtain* happiness. Articles 8, 9, and 10 pertain to criminal procedure. Article 8 uses declarative or imperative modes of verbs and thus seems to provide adequate legal underpinning for the right to trial by jury and the other rights which had come to be associated with it. But Articles 9 and 10 use the subjunctive mode: excessive bail and fines, cruel and unusual punishments "ought" not to be required, imposed, or inflicted, and general search warrants "ought" not to be granted. Even stranger, at least to ears accustomed to the language of the First Amendment to the federal Constitution, is the language of Virginia's Article 12: "That the freedom of the Press is one of the greatest bulwarks of liberty, and can never be restrained but by despotic Government." The last article in the declaration is frequently cited as embodying a significant advance in the enjoyment of freedom of religion because James Madison, who was making his debut in politics, was successful in substituting the phrase "free exercise of religion" for "toleration." Again, so far, so good. But what is the final clause in this article doing in a Declaration of Rights: "And that it is the mutual duty of all to practice Christian forbearance, love, and charity, towards each other?"

What is the explanation of these characteristics, some of which appear to be serious deficiencies, not in the sense of substantive criticisms of the form of government such as Thomas Jefferson made a few years later, but in the sense of legal craftsmanship? There is probably no single explanation, and any that are offered must be speculative. Yet it seems worthwhile to probe for an answer, because this constitution was the first in a continuing series of modern constitutions, both American and foreign.

First, it is well to recall that this constitution was not drafted in the leisure of peace and assured security from internal and external

98   CECELIA M. KENYON

threats of violence. The main theater of Revolutionary military action was still in the North, but Williamsburg did not enjoy the feeling that the war was distant. The last royal governor, Lord Dunmore, had fled the city months before, but he had not gone very far. He was in fact a few miles away on the York River with a small fleet and a motley collection of troops. There were not only rumors that he was being reinforced, but while the convention was sitting, 217 Scots Highlanders were actually brought to Williamsburg, having been captured before they could reach Lord Dunmore. Thus the convention not only worked on the constitution, to use Irving Brant's phrase, "under the shadow of an ever-present danger," but it also had to cope with that danger.[12]

In the second place, if the indictment of George III and the British Parliament seems to be out of place in a constitution, it may be because to us, the social-contract doctrine is not a real, operative force. For Virginians of 1776, the two issues of independence and a new government were inextricably linked; and if the new constitution was regarded as a new social and/or political compact, it must have seemed entirely proper to include in it a statement of the reasons for considering the old one broken by the Crown, and therefore no longer binding on the colonies.

As for the seeming peculiarities of the Bill of Rights, I think we are faced with something fundamental and more complex. Perhaps two opinions cited earlier in this paper provide hints for understanding what a constitution and constitutionalism meant to the Virginia Convention of 1776. The first opinion is the famous statement of James Otis in 1761: "An act against the constitution is void. An act against natural equity is void." The second opinion is John Dickinson's suggestion that the criterion for the constitutionality of an act should be its tendency to make the people happy. Behind both opinions, but especially the first, was the belief that the British constitution was an embodiment of natural law. If it was, then it was also an embodiment of fundamental ethical principles (though, to be sure, it also included laws, customs, and institutions peculiar to Britain and the British).

It may be that this conception of the British constitution still influenced the Virginia Convention and was responsible for the frequent use of the words "ought" and "should" in the Declaration of Rights. That part of the constitution was intended to be a statement of universal and fundamental political and ethical principles. If so, then the words "ought" and "should," which strike the modern reader as legally weak, were to its authors, both morally strong and technically accurate: they express both their idealism and their realism—neither men nor governments always do what they *ought* to do, but the concept of "ought," ought always to be present.

Nor should we overlook the obvious. There was then no agreed-upon institutional means for enforcing the provisions of the Bill of Rights or indeed of any other part of the Constitution. Within a few years the courts of Virginia and some other states would assume the practice of judicial review. But though imminent, that was still in the future for the Virginia Convention of 1776. The principal means for preserving the rights of the individual and of the people were seen to be public opinion, elections, a properly constructed constitution, and—the ultimate remedy—revolution. That being so, Section 15 of the Bill of Rights may take on new meaning: "That no free government, or the blessings of liberty, can be preserved to any people, but by firm adherence to justice, moderation, temperance, frugality, and virtue, *and by frequent recurrence to fundamental principles*" [emphasis added]. The Constitution was a repository of those "fundamental principles." It was not intended to be a document for lawyers and judges only. It was intended to express the will of the people and to inform that will. For this purpose, it was right and proper that some of those "fundamental principles" be expressed in hortatory form.

THE PENNSYLVANIA CONSTITUTION OF 1776

The Pennsylvania constitution of September 1776 has been the subject of heated controversy since the moment of its adoption. On only two points has there been general agreement among the men who supported and opposed it during the Revolution and among scholars who have studied it in the succeeding two centuries: (1) it was the most radical of all the state constitutions, and with the limited exceptions of its partial imitators—Georgia and Vermont—it was unique; (2) it was, more than any other constitution of the era, the product of new men who represented the seizure of political power by a class which had hitherto exercised limited influence in the politics of colonial Pennsylvania.

Until the French and Indian War, the government of Pennsylvania had been dominated by Quakers. Then, in order to avoid the difficult choice of either compromising their pacifist principles or leaving the colony undefended, the Quakers had voluntarily withdrawn from leadership. They were replaced by men of similar socioeconomic class, with little disturbance of the old system of upper-class domination. Events in the spring of 1776 increased support for independence among the population at large, and this factor, plus the successful tactics of political agitation and organization employed by a new group of leaders who supported both independence and a democratization of Pennsylvania politics, resulted in the defeat of the old leadership. Thus, this colony presents the strongest and clearest case for supporting the interpretation popularized by Carl Becker, that the Revolution was a contest not only over home rule versus imperial rule but also over who should rule at home. In the summer of 1776, the victors in this latter contest were the insurgents, and they proceeded to write a constitution that embodied their populist or democratic opinions.[13]

The method chosen for writing the new constitution was an elected convention, and it is at this point that one meets the first major question of the extent to which the constitution, and the movement of which it was the product, were or were not "democratic." Property qualifications were replaced by the payment of taxes; in socioeconomic terms, then, the electorate was extended. But it may have been contracted by the requirement that each voter take an oath to support independence, or "do their best to 'establish and support a government in this province on the authority of the people only.' " [14] A religious oath was also required of candidates for election. It would have excluded any person sensitive about the sanctity of oaths who did not believe in Jesus Christ as the son of God and in the divinely inspired nature of the Old and New Testaments. Similar requirements were common in most of the colonies at the time, and it is only mildly surprising to find this one in Pennsylvania. It is perhaps significant as a reminder that the *demos* is not always libertarian.

The provisions of the constitution that set the basic structure of the government can be summarized as follows.

First: Payment of taxes was substituted for ownership of property as a qualification for voting for legislative representatives, but with the discriminatory proviso that adult sons of freeholders were exempt even from this requirement.

Second: Representation in the legislature was to be apportioned according to taxable inhabitants, with the accompanying statement that this was "the only principle which can at all times secure liberty, and make the voice of the majority of the people the law of the land." No ratio of representatives to "taxable inhabitants" was specified, but reapportionment in accordance with a septennial census was required.

Third: Legislative power was vested in a unicameral assembly, with several provisions partly intended to make this assembly both responsive and accountable to the people or the voters, and partly to supply the guard against rash and hasty legislation ordinarily assumed to be one of the functions performed by a second house. All "bills of public nature" were to be published for the people's consideration before they were read, debated, and amended for the last time; furthermore, "except on occasions of sudden necessity," no bills were to be "passed into laws" until voted upon in the next session of the legislature. The constitution also provided that meetings of the legislature should be open to "all persons who behave decently," except when "the welfare of this state" might require otherwise, and that the votes and proceedings of the legislature be published weekly, with every member given the right to "insert his reasons for his vote" when the latter was taken by ballot. The term of each legislature was one year, and no man could serve more than four out of seven years. In addition to an oath promising to render faithful service to the people, each member of the legislature was required to make a religious "declaration": *"I do believe in one God, the creator and governor of the universe, the rewarder of the good and the punisher of the wicked. And I do acknowledge the Scriptures of the Old and New Testament to be given by Divine inspiration"* [emphasis in the original]. The people's representatives in Pennsylvania were to be avowedly Christian. (Virginia's constitution did not contain such an oath.)

Fourth: The constitution provided for a plural executive, a council to consist of twelve persons elected by the freemen of the various districts for a term of three years. A system of rotation was established so that every three years the council would be renewed by having a third of its membership elected either for the first time, or after a required lapse of at least four years. It was stated that this combination of election and rotation would produce "more men . . . trained to public business," provide continuity, and prevent the establishment of "an inconvenient aristocracy."

Fifth: The constitution provided for a supreme court, to be appointed by the executive council for a term of seven years and eligible for reappointment. Its members were to have fixed salaries, and apparently in addition to, or as a substitute for, liability to impeachment, were "removable for misbehavior at any time by the general assembly." Provision for lower courts was also made.

Sixth: The constitution provided for a council of censors to consist of two members from each city or county, to be elected by the freemen once every seven years. Its functions were to examine the actions of the legislature and the executive for the preceding seven years, to review the levying of taxes and the expenditure of public moneys for the same period, to "pass public censures" and "to order impeachments" if warranted, to recommend the repeal of any laws found to be contrary "to the principles of the constitution," and to call for a convention for the purposes of amending any article for the constitution which may be defective," of clarifying any provisions thought to be "not clearly expressed," and of adding any that might be necessary "for the preservation of the rights and happiness of the people." Proposals for amendment had to be promulgated at least six months before the election of the convention, "for the previous consideration of the people, that they may have an opportunity of instructing their delegates on the subject."

Seventh: The populist authors of this constitution wanted to prevent the emergence of class of professional politicians, but they were also aware that the lack of any payment at all for public service meant government by the wealthy, or at least by men with independent incomes. They feared that to fix high salaries for public office would invite "faction, contention, corruption, and disorder among the people." Their solution to the classic dilemma was "reasonable compensation," plus a directive to the legislature to reduce the income of any office which became "so profitable as to occasion many to apply for it."

Such were the major characteristics of the frame of government created by the Pennsylvania constitution of 1776.

Its most outstanding characteristics were concentration of governmental power in a unicameral legislature and provisions that the exercise of that power under normal circumstances should be constantly monitored by the people. The opening of legislative sessions to the public, the weekly publications of the legislature's proceedings, the requirements that all bills be published before their last reading, and that a bill not become law until enacted in two successive sessions of the legislature, all represented an attempt to render the legislature not only accountable but almost instantly responsive to the people.

Fear and distrust of the executive power was expressed by dividing it among twelve men, in the compulsory and staggered rotation of membership explicitly intended to prevent the growth of aristocracy, and in assigning it limited powers.

The supreme court of the state was not independent, the term being for seven years, and the members being subject to removal by the legislature at any time. Apparently lower courts were not independent either, but the constitution leaves this point unclear.

The council of censors was meant to be a sort of septennial watchdog. Perhaps because it was the most unusual and unfamiliar institution in this or any other Revolutionary state constitution, it was the object of ridicule as well as of criticism. It is slightly reminiscent of the Nocturnal Council in Plato's *Laws,* or of the *Nomosthetai* of ancient Athens. At first glance it appears as something of an excrescence, but upon reflection it appears to be an interesting invention, and with one or two exceptions, consistent with the spirit of the constitution and an institutionalization of an important aspect of early American republican theory.

In order to recover that aspect, it is necessary to turn to parts of the Pennsylvania constitution other than those that created the main institutional structure of the government.

The Declaration of Rights, which like those of the majority of other states, borrowed heavily from that of Virginia, included a concept that appears to have had the status of an accepted axiom of the science of politics: "That a frequent recurrence to fundamental principles, and a firm adherence to justice, moderation, temperance, industry, and frugality are absolutely necessary to preserve the blessings of liberty, and keep a government free." Thus far, Pennsylvania followed Virginia closely, but it then made two additions: (1) an admonition that the people should "pay particular attention to these points" in electing officers and representatives: (2) a statement that the people had a right to "exact a due and constant regard to them" from those exercising the powers of government.

That this statement in the Declaration of Rights was not merely rhetorical is indicated by several provisions in the Frame of Government, some of which suggest a significant tension between the ideals and the expectations of the authors of this constitution. Section 7 uses the imperative mode of the verb and states that the legislature "shall consist of persons most noted for wisdom and virtue." Section 32 contained provisions imposing penalties upon both the voter and the candidate who took or offered bribes. The constitution had another provision that reinforced the traditional association of republican government with a virtuous population. Section 45 provided that "Laws for the encouragement of virtue, and prevention of vice and immorality, *shall* be made and constantly kept in force, and provision *shall* be made for their due execution" [emphasis added].

The early theory of republican government now comes into sharper focus. The authors of this Pennsylvania constitution believed that one of the primary requisites of such government was virtue, and the virtue they attempted to guarantee was not merely the traditional "civic virtue" of willingness to subordinate individual interest to the public interest. One may say either that they did not distinguish between "civic" and "private" virtue, or that they believed that at least some of what we would regard as private virtues were essential to republican government. Furthermore, the constitutional imperative that laws for the "encouragement of virtue, and prevention of vice and immorality, shall be made and constantly kept in force," is comparable to James Harrington's "agrarian law" or Thomas Jefferson's belief that legislators should actively encourage a wide distribution of property. Republican government required a moral basis for its successful operation, and government itself should act to preserve that basis: there was no concept of laissez-faire with respect to morality.

The council of censors was an institutional device for securing or formally encouraging the recurrence to fundamental principles called for in the Bill of Rights. It was to "inquire whether the constitution has been preserved inviolate in every part" and to recommend repeal of any legislation believed "contrary to the principles of the constitution." With respect to the function of judging the constitutionality of laws, it would appear that the people themselves might be an indirect object of review. As we have seen earlier, the constitution made provision for them to express their opinion, and perhaps to instruct their representatives, during the time when legislative bills were pending. Thus, at least in theory, the council of censors might find unconstitutional a law which, when enacted, had had the support of the majority of the people. The council of censors' opinion that an act was unconstitutional had no legal force, however. It could only *recommend* repeal to the legislature.

Indeed, all but perhaps one of its powers were or could become effective only through the operation of public opinion on the legilature or the executive. The one possible exception was probably unintentional. In its septennial review of the state of the commonwealth, the council was to examine the constitution itself, and if it believed amendment to be necessary it was empowered to call a convention for that purpose. The constitution stated that all proposed amendments had to be promulgated at least six months before the election of the convention in order that the people might have an opportunity to express their opinions on them. Because the language used is in the passive voice, it is impossible to state categorically what body or bodies might "promulgate" proposed amendments. The context suggests—but does not explicitly state—that promulgation was the function of the censors. If so, then the council did have one potentially important independent power: *a priori* approval of all proposed changes in the constitution. Regardless of who had the power of promulgation, the requirement that all proposed amendments be published six months before election of the convention would presumably have imposed significant limitations on the power of the convention itself. In fact, the attitude of the authors of this constitution toward future amendments seems to have been one of reluctance. The council of censors was to call for a convention only if "there appear to them an *absolute necessity* of amending any article of the constitution" [emphasis added].

The council of censors did not turn out to be very practical (nor did some other parts of the constitution), and it was not included in the new constitution adopted in 1790. But it does represent an insight into the kind of constitutionalism with which Americans began their independent existence, and an attempt to solve two crucial problems ignored altogether in several of the other state constitutions. One was that of how to enforce a constitution of written fundamental law, including the bills or declarations of rights. The other was how to change a written constitution. Thus, although the council of censors was bitterly criticized and rejected as a solution to both problems, its very conception and the controversy it aroused may have accelerated the process by which Americans recognized that written constitutions are not *ipso facto* self-enforcing, that their meaning is not self-evident, and that although they may embody those "fundamental principles" to which "a frequent recurrence" is either necessary or salutary, they must also make provision for regular procedures for change— perhaps change even in those very "fundamental principles."

THE MASSACHUSETTS CONSTITUTION OF 1780

Massachusetts did not adopt a constitution and become a Commonwealth until 1780, five years after the Battles of Lexington and Concord and four years after the Declaration of Independence. The reason for the long delay was widespread insistence that a constitution should be created by some special means and not be written and proclaimed merely by an elected assembly acting as a provisional government. Massachusetts was not the only state in which there were men who believed that a constitution, being a fundamental law and in some sense a social contract, should be framed by a special body and have the explicit consent of the people.

The crucial factors that set Massachusetts on a different course from its sister states appear to have been three: the existence of *enough* men who believed that a constitution should be created in a manner radically different from mere statutory law; the existence of small groups of leaders who were highly articulate and who understood the importance of organization and agitation in securing what they wanted; the existence of the towns and town meetings as traditional and familiar institutions for the formation of public opinion and for its transmission to the colonial/state government.

It appears to have been a group of men in Berkshire County who applied the initial and sustained pressure that led eventually to the framing of a constitution by a convention elected specifically and solely for that purpose and to the submission of that constitution to voters in the separate towns for their rejection or ratification. (It is significant that the vote was taken by towns and not in a statewide referendum. Massachusetts towns had a long tradition of seeking harmony and agreement. A considerable number of the towns turned in very large majority votes, not closely divided ones. It is impossible to know what the result might have been had the referendum been by secret written ballots in a statewide referendum, but the chances are that it would have been different.) In the course of a process that extended over almost five years, many towns expressed their opinions concerning both the manner of creating a constitution and the substance of a constitution. The documents produced during this period afford the modern scholar a unique opportunity to catch glimpses of what the ordinarily inarticulate citizenry of the early republic thought about some fundamental issues of politics and government. For once, the silent majority spoke, and spoke in official documents that have had the great good fortune to be preserved.

Berkshire County is the westernmost county in the state, and at the time of the Revolution showed some of the characteristics of the frontier later emphasized by Frederick Jackson Turner. It also had a significantly large number of highly educated men, and it is the opinion of one recent scholar that the combination of frontier "democracy" and an educated elite in sympathy with this "democracy" was responsible for the role that Berkshire played, not only in Massachusetts, but ultimately for the process of constitution-making in America as a whole.[15]

In December 1775, the town of Pittsfield dispatched a memorial, petition, or manifesto to the provisional government sitting in

Watertown, protesting the proposal that Massachusetts resume its charter of 1691. The people of Pittsfield stated that they viewed themselves as living in a state of nature; asserted that it was preferable to a government under the old charter; and claimed that since the suspension of royal government they had "lived in peace, love, safety, liberty and happiness except the disorders and dissentions occasioned by the Tories." The petition did not suggest that this condition continue indefinitely but expressed the hope that a new constitution would be established with "such a broad basis of civil and religious liberty as no length of time will corrupt and which will endure as long as the Sun and Moon shall endure." [16]

Six months later, the men of Pittsfield dispatched another message eastward. This one stated what was apparently regarded as an axiom needing no demonstration, that "every Man by Nature has the seeds of Tyranny deeply implanted within him so that nothing short of Omnipotence can eradicate them . . ." and again appealed for a proper method of establishing a legitimate government that would not end in tyranny. Their sense of urgency, their belief that they stood at a critical moment is clear in the statement that "now is the only time we have reason ever to expect for securing our Liberty and the Liberties of future posterity upon a permanent foundation that no length of time can undermine." Their principles of action for this crucial moment were simple and unambiguous: no ordinary legislature had the authority to impose a constitution on the people; no constitution could be legitimate without "the Approbation of the Majority of the people." They reiterated their belief in the existence of a "strong Byass of human Nature to Tyranny and Despotism," and they assured the government on the Charles that what motivated them was "the purest and most disinterested Love of posterity and a fervent desire of transmitting to them a fundamental Constitution securing their sacred Rights and Immunities against all Tyrants that may spring up after us. . . ." [17]

Doubtless feeling the pressure not only of Berkshire County but also of other areas in the state, the provisional government passed a resolution in September 1776 requesting the towns to express their opinions as to whether the provisional legislature should frame a constitution. The returns were mixed, but the weight of opinion seemed to be negative. For example, Belchertown voted unanimously against the proposal; two of its reasons are especially interesting and significant. First, it said that the framing of constitution was "an affair of Great Importance and wants perhaps more time for Deliberation than the present Exigencies of the State will allow." Second, "Further more Great Numbers of the Inhabitants of this Town being absent in the War we thought it not adviseable to Consent to the Seting up of a Constitution at present as we Could not have their mind Concerning the Matter and we Judge it to be So in most other Towns So that their Can not be a proper Consent of the people of this State by the voice of those who Can now assemble in Town meeting." Belchertown went on to say, "We mean not to object to the haveing a Constitution, but wish and hope for a wise one in Due time, but we think it Concerns the youngerly men Especially who are in the war to have a voice in the affair which Can not now be had." [18] Similar views were expressed by other towns, and there was a widespread opinion that whoever framed a constitution, it should be submitted to the people for their acceptance or rejection.

Although a number of towns had expressed the opinion that the legislature should not itself frame a constitution, but that a special convention should be elected to do so, the two houses put on the hat of a convention in the summer of 1777 and drafted a constitution. After it was completed in February 1778, it was sent out to the towns and was overwhelmingly rejected.

Thus 1778 passed, and Massachusetts still had no constitution. The provisional government at last gave in to the idea that a special convention elected solely for the purpose of framing a constitution should be called. John Adams was among the delegates chosen in the special election, and he became the principal author of the constitution adopted by the convention and ratified by the towns. The concept of the constitution as a social contract was reflected in the suspension of property qualification for voting for delegates to the convention and for participating in the town meetings called for ratification or rejection. Thus, in the electoral base of the convention which drafted it, and in the mode of ratification, this Massachusetts constitution of 1780 was the most democratic of any. The frame of government that it established was among the most aristocratic or oligarchic of any. These two facts—popular base and quasi-oligarchic structure—have long puzzled historians. They also

illustrate the difficulty of finding proper terminology for characterizing political and constitutional positions of the era.

The Declaration of Rights followed rather closely that of
Virginia. It added "piety" to the cardinal virtues requisite for the
preservation of liberty and free government, and it contained an
unusually strong statement of the principle of separation of powers.
"In the government of this Commonwealth, the legislative department shall never exercise the executive and judicial powers, or
either of them: The executive shall never exercise the legislative and
judicial powers, or either of them: The judicial shall never exercise
the legislative and executive powers, or either of them: to the end it
may be a government of laws and not of men."

Unlike the constitution of Virginia, that of Massachusetts ad-
hered closely to the old theory of mized government and embodied
it in its bicameral legislature, its strong executive, and its property
qualifications for officeholding.

If property qualifications for voting and for holding office are a
sure index to the degree of democracy or aristocracy established in a
constitution, this constitution must be characterized as leaning
toward a moderate aristocracy, particularly with respect to the
requirements for officeholding. The case is not so clear with respect
to the qualifications for voting. The qualification for the suffrage
was the ownership of a freehold yielding an annual income of at
least £3 in Massachusetts currency or of any property valued at £60
or more. This looks like a 50 percent increase over the qualifications
under the charter, but it probably reflected the shift from British to
Massachusetts money and probably excluded only a small proportion of free adult males.[19] The requirements for major offices were
higher and undoubtedly reflected John Adams's conviction that
separation of powers *and* mixed government were essential to the
preservation of liberty and property. In order to be a member of the
lower house in the legislature, a man had to possess real estate
valued at £100 or more or a total estate valued at at least £200. In
order to be a member of the upper house of the legislature, a man
had to own real estate valued at £300 or more, or a total estate of at
least £600. In order to be governor or lieutenant governor, a man
had to be possessed of a *freehold*—that is, of real estate—valued at
£1,000 or more. Other states had similar requirements, but when
compared with the Virginia and Pennsylvania constitutions, and

especially with the federal constitution of 1787, the Massachusetts constitution stands out as unambiguously reflective of the conviction that a government purely popular could not possibly be a good government, and probably could not long endure.

It is more difficult to characterize the executive as democratic or aristocratic—disregarding for the moment the requirement that he own real estate valued at a thousand pounds or more—because of the method of election. The constitution provided for popular election in the first instance: if a man received a majority of all the votes cast, he was elected governor; if no man received a clear majority, first the lower house of the legislature was to select two candidates from the four who received the largest number of votes, and then the upper house would select one of these two. It was the clear intention of Adams to establish a strong executive, and direct, popular election was one element in implementing that intention. The other major element was to give the governor a qualified veto over bills enacted by the legislature; it could be overriden by a veto of two-thirds of both houses. Adams meant the executive to stand between the two houses of the legislature, the lower representing the common people, the upper representing the natural aristocracy, and to perform the function ideally attributed to the monarch in the classical theory of mixed government. There were safeguards against an excessively powerful governor. The constitution created an executive council of nine members plus the lieutenant governor, to be chosen by the two houses from among their own membership. The governor was subject to impeachment and was to be elected for a term of only one year. His powers were carefully defined, and of particular interest—"at this point in time"—he was explicitly prohibited from using the power to pardon *before conviction.*

The constitution also created a partially independent judiciary. Judges were to hold office during "good behaviour, excepting such concerning whom there is different provision made in this Constitution": the primary "different provision" was that justices of the peace should have a seven-year term. In addition to impeachment, judges could be removed from office by the governor with the consent of the executive council upon address of both houses of the legislature.

Among the most controversial of the constitution's provisions were those concerning religion and churches. Article 3 of the

Declaration of Rights declared that the people of the Commonwealth had a right to invest their legislature with the power to
require "the several towns, parishes, precincts, and other bodies-
politic, or religious societies" to support "public worship," and
"public Protestant teachers of piety, religion and morality, in all
cases where such provision shall not be made voluntarily." If there
were a public teacher of his own choice in his locality, a voter could
designate that his money should go to that teacher, if indeed he did
attend the latter's instruction; if not, his money should go to others.
The constitution also required that any person elected to the
legislature, council, governorship, or lieutenant governorship take
an oath that he believed in the Christian religion. A number of
towns objected to the section in the support-of-religious-instruction
article that provided that the taxes of a person who had no teacher
of his choice in his community should go for the support of other
sects. Some towns expressed the opinion that no laws of the state
should affect religion at all. There were also a number of objections
to the wording and substance of the oath required of officeholders:
that oath required profession of belief in Christianity, but it did not
specify *protestant* Christianity; a number of the people of Massachusetts thought it should.

The other issue about which there was much disagreement, the
property qualification for voting, produced some of what eighteenth-century men called "very affecting" passages of protest. The
general opinion expressed by many towns was that the payment of
taxes was sufficient indication of an individual's "stake" in the
community and that it was inconsistent to have fought Great
Britain upon the ground of "no taxation without representation,"
and then tax men who were excluded from voting for a representative to the General Court of Massachusetts. There was also reference
to the instability of the economic situation and to the possibility
that a man who met the qualifications for voting during one year
might not do so the next—through circumstances that had nothing
to do with industry, frugality, virtue, and the like.

The constitution contained a provision for amendment, though a
rather peculiar one. It provided that in 1795—fifteen years after
anticipated ratification of the proposed document—the legislature
should issue calls to the appropriate officials of the various towns
and unincorporated plantations to direct them to assemble the

voters for the purpose of ascertaining whether there was sentiment for revising the Constitution. If two-thirds of the voters did so decide, then a call should be issued for a new convention, to be elected by the towns, to meet and consider revisions to the constitution. No provision was made for other future revisions, the assumption apparently being that fifteen years of experience was sufficient time to expose whatever errors the present document contained, and that thereafter no further changes would be needed.

The constitution was declared ratified after the towns in the state had sent in their returns. It seems quite impossible to arrive at an exact conclusion as to whether that ratification was strictly in accordance with the requirement that two-thirds of the voters approve of the constitution. The basic reason is that the returns from the towns did not follow a uniform pattern. Some towns simply gave the vote on the constitution as a whole; others gave conditional approval subject to revisions of specific articles; others gave the exact votes on each article; Ashfield, with less than forty voters, turned in a very complete report with votes recorded in three columns: those in favor of the article or section; those in favor of it if amended as the town proposed; those opposed. Since this required a total of 98 separate votes (if my arithmetic is correct), with three options on some votes, it shows clearly how seriously this little town in the western hills took its responsibility in deciding the future political system of the Commonwealth.

One closes the chapter on Massachusetts with both satisfaction and regret. The long process of adopting a constitution involved a dialogue between the voters in the towns and their elected representatives. Although the towns varied in their initiatives and responses, the documentation they left behind them seems to provide a more reliable cross section of public opinion than either newspapers or pamphlets. The latter may reflect factors such as intensity of motivation, literacy, and accessibility to the press— factors that may render them less precisely representative of opinion than the reports of duly called town meetings. It is a matter of regret that Massachusetts alone provided documentation that may correct this kind of bias.

CONCLUSIONS

The American Revolutionaries made two radical decisions in 1776: first, to declare independence, break away from Great Britain, and constitute themselves a separate "people" or "peoples"; second, to create republican government for the states thus established. These decisions involved some ideas and attitudes that have survived and with which we feel very much at home, some that have been abandoned, and some that are so familiar as to obscure the vitality they had for the men of two hundred years ago.

Those men brought to their task of laying foundations for the new societies ideas drawn from different traditions of political thought and experience. First and most important was the heritage of English constitutionalism, centuries old and unwritten in the case of the mother country, generations old and written in the form of their charters in the case of the thirteen colonies. A second tradition from which the Founders drew was the cyclical theory of history, and as handed down by Machiavelli, the choice of republicanism as the preferred form of government. This tradition had two subsidiary ingredients: that a return to first principles by the people could lengthen the duration of the republican phase of the cycle, and that virtue was a requisite for a people who wished to retain republican government. A third tradition, reaching back to the Old Testament and transmitted by Reformation theorists of resistance to tyranny, was the association, not of republicanism *per se,* but of liberty and free government, with virtue among the people. The newest tradition, but an important one, was that of social-contract theory, of which the revolutionaries emphasized especially the ideas that all legitimate governments were based on consent, and that their ends were the protection of individual rights. Thus from disparate sources the revolutionaries drew materials for the construction of constitutions they hoped would secure to them and their posterity the rights and liberties they had failed to preserve within the British Empire.

It is the attitude of *founding* that is perhaps the most difficult for us to recapture, because we take our political existence for granted and have lost the sense of creating a new body politic. We speak of the "Founding Fathers," but we do not always realize that they themselves were intensely conscious of their role as Founders. The political literature of the period is replete with phrases such as "generations yet unborn," "millions yet unborn," and more simply, "posterity." The men of the Massachusetts frontier spoke for many of their generation when they expressed the hope that the constitution to be framed for the state would be one which "no length of Time will corrupt and which will endure as long as the Sun and Moon shall endure" (see p. 108) Statements such as these doubtless contain a certain degree of hyperbole, but they also reflect the conviction of the revolutionaries that fate and their own actions had brought them to a critical moment in history: what they did would influence if not determine the future for generations to come. In the act of creating new constitutions, they brought together the Machiavellian concept of the founding of a republic and the concept of the social contract as creating a new body politic.

The Virginia Bill of Rights included the dictum, "That no free government, or the blessings of liberty, can be preserved to any people, but by a firm adherence to justice, moderation, temperance, frugality, and virtue, and by frequent recurrence to fundamental principles." This theme of virtue and recurrence to fundamental principles, when considered with other elements in the political thought of the founders, seems to reflect an ambivalent attitude toward progress. The Virginia constitution did not contain any provision for amendment, a fact that may be attributed to inadvertence or inexperience. The Pennsylvania and Massachusetts constitutions both had amending clauses, but their wording suggests that their authors intended them to be used for "perfecting" purposes—that is, correcting defects in the original constitutions that might be revealed by experience—not as means to adapt the constitutions to future change, growth, or progress in the society or the people. Indeed the Founders believed that fortune had favored them by casting the moment for creation at a propitious point when the American people were unusually virtuous. Their virtue was neither inherent nor permanent; it was associated with a moderate material prosperity and would tend to become eroded when Americans were exposed to the luxurious life known to England and Europe. When that time came, the institutional structure and the principles of the constitutions might, if heeded by posterity, postpone the loss of liberty.

The idea that a return to first principles would help to put a brake on the descent to despotism underlines the self-consciousness of the Founders of themselves as Founders and their assumption that their work would shape the destiny of their descendants for generations to come. It was also congruent with the conception of the constitutions as social contracts. If the constitutions were perceived as social contracts establishing new states for peoples newly independent, it was appropriate that they should delineate the principles that partially defined the new people, those to which the people were committing themselves, and those believed to be essential to the preservation of liberty and free or republican government. It must also have seemed natural to include among these principles some aspirations and obligations not susceptible to strict legal interpretation and enforcement. Provisions that to us seem hortatory may partially reflect the Founders' attempts to insure that the constitution be enforced as fundamental law. Although both the Pennsylvania and the Massachusetts constitutions provided for some form of judicial or other review as a means of maintaining adherence to the constitution, the full implications of this could not have been foreseen at the time. The Founders apparently hoped for a more active and vigilant role for the people, and "the frequent recurrence to fundamental principles" was an important part of that role.

The institutional structures established by the three constitutions were likewise intended to provide responsible government. The differences among them reflect the spirit and attitudes of the time and also give us an intimation of other directions in which the main pattern of American government might have evolved. The general distrust of the executive power, associated as it was with its locus in king and royal governor, was reflected in the Virginia constitution, which concentrated power in a bicameral legislature and reduced the executive to an administrative figure elected annually by the legislature and deprived of the power to veto acts of the latter body. Had that pattern prevailed, the evolution of American government might have been toward a parliamentary form. What is more remarkable about the Virginia constitution is that it quietly broke the association of separation of powers with mixed government by not distinguishing the two houses of the legislature by different property qualification for either electors or members. Few of the provisions in the Pennsylvania constitution intended to subject the power of the unicameral legislature to scrutiny and action by the people have survived, but the populist spirit that lay behind these provisions has subsequently emerged repeatedly in demands for popular initiative and referendum as a part of the legislative process. The Massachusetts constitution was a classic example of the fusion of separation of powers with the theory of mixed government. The graduated property qualifications for office have long since disappeared, but the strong governor directly elected by the people helped to break down the association of the executive function with its previous monarchical locus and thus may be regarded as a major contribution to the invention of a republican executive. Equally important was the method used for framing and ratifying the fundamental law of the Commonwealth.

The authors of the first state constitutions thus attempted to make them serve the dual purpose of stating the principles of social contracts creating new political peoples and of establishing institutions that would secure the purposes for which the new governments were designed. The Founding Fathers were eclectic in their political thinking, and as a result, their ideas fit together with varying degrees of harmony and emerge with varying degrees of clarity. Their cardinal principle is absolutely clear: good government requires a written constitution to secure the liberty and welfare of the people and especially to guard against what the men of the Massachusetts hills referred to as a "strong Byass of human Nature to Tyranny and Despotism" (see p. 108). Yet human nature was also capable of virtuous behavior, and the exercise of certain virtues was also essential to good government. It was as if the constitution were an absolutely necessary tool, but one that had to be kept in good working order by the attentive care of its owners and users.

Much less clear are the Founders' concepts of virtue and self-interest and the relationship between the two. The cardinal virtues listed in the Bills of Rights were justice, moderation, temperance, frugality, and virtue—to which Massachusetts added piety. Christian love, charity, benevolence, forbearance, and social affections were also mentioned; and the Pennsylvania constitution included an imperative provision calling for laws to encourage virtue and prevent vice. On the other hand, some elements in the institutional structure of the constitutions, as well as the priority given the rights of life, liberty, property, and happiness according to social-contract doctrine, lent a degree of legitimacy to the exercise of self-interest. Decades of political experience as colonies had led to recognition and acceptance of different and conflicting economic interests as inevitable, and the notion of balancing rather than suppressing these interests also implied some degree of legitimacy. The exigencies of colonial opposition to the British theory of virtual representation had reinforced acceptance of self-interest, because Americans had argued that their interests as colonies were different not only from those of members of Parliament but also from the electoral constituencies of Parliament. Furthermore, the ancient institutions of mixed government and property qualification for voting recognized the role of self-interest in the attainment of good government. Yet the Founding Fathers regarded the unrestrained pursuit of self-interest as licentious.

It is tempting to look upon the prescriptions for virtue in the state constitutions as evidence that their authors perceived the potentially centrifugal force of natural-rights doctrine and deliberately tried to provide a centripetal counterweight. It is even more tempting to believe that the Founders perceived the extraordinary difficulty of securing justice and stability in any political system which not only vested power in the people but which, by recognizing the priority of individual rights, had logically to include satisfaction of those rights in any definition of the public good. I do not think very many of the Founders saw the problems in these terms (though Jefferson and Madison did). The linkage of virtue with liberty and free or republican government stemmed from older traditions, and they did not quite realize that they were not only establishing republican government but a *new kind* of republicanism linked with the individualism of social-contract doctrine. This new republicanism involved a value system that was inherently pluralistic and possibly contradictory. The state constitutions linked the virtue of "justice" to the preservation of liberty and in doing so followed the legacies of the past. A few years later James Madison expressed the possibility of conflict between the two. "Justice is the end of government. It is the end of civil society. It ever has been and ever will be pursued until it be obtained, or until liberty be lost in the pursuit" *(Federalist* 51).

Madison's statement helps to bring into focus the Janus-like posture of the authors of the first state constitutions. They created something new; their use of the word "experiment" indicates that they were aware of doing so. The ingredients they used were old, and what they produced was a mixture and not a compound. Unless we recognize this, we may overlook a difference in attitude between the Revolutionary generation and our own. The former assumed a greater homogeneity and consensus with respect to moral values than we do. They also seemed to assume that such homogeneity was essential to the success of republican government and that it might therefore be enforced by governmental means. As a result of the individualism secured by the liberty they established, we have become a more heterogeneous people and have come to assume that a greater heterogeneity in values is compatible with republican government. That our position depends partly on the removal from the sphere of governmental jurisdiction of much moral behavior that the Founders would have included therein seems to be indicated by the intensely emotional and divisive reactions that occur when a subject with profound ethical content, such as abortion, becomes an issue for government determination or individual choice.

The Founders looked upon constitutions as social compacts which defined the principles, including the ethical values, upon which the newly formed peoples were agreed and to which they presumably committed themselves. We have come to regard our constitutions— but not necessarily those of other political systems—more as instruments that define the means by which conflicts of values as well as other issues and interests are to be decided. It is not that we regard constitutions or the constitutional process as value-free or ethically neutral: freedom of religion, press, and speech are all values, but they are of a different order from the Christian love, charity, and forbearance enjoined by the Virginia constitution, or the benevolence, piety, and social affections enjoined by that of Massachusetts.

Perhaps it may be said that the conception of constitutions held by the Founders was closer to that of Aristotle than our own; a constitution not only defined the arrangement of offices within a *polis;* it also embodied a way of life. We have not abandoned the latter part of this concept completely, but we have perhaps narrowed it. A constitution defines a *political* way of life, but the acceptance of natural rights has created a sharper distinction between that which is "private" and that which is "political."

One aspect of our modern attitude would doubtless gratify the Founders. We do perform that "frequent recurrence to fundamental principles" they believed essential to the preservation of liberty and free government, though perhaps not in the precise way imagined by the Founders. That "the Constitution" is the final Law by which our political lives should be governed is an attitude deeply rooted in the American mind. We do not have perfect agreement as to what the Constitution means, and the "fundamental principles" to which we recur may not always be identical with those of our Revolutionary ancestors. One of them is. It was already ancient at the time of the American Revolution, and it was then and is now perceived to be both an anchor and an ideal. It was the deceptively simple principle that whatever the form of government may be, the ultimate safety of the people and of the individual lies in having a government of laws and not of men.

NOTES

1. Machiavelli: *The Chief Works and Others,* trans. Allan Gilbert. 2 vols. (Duke University Press, 1965), vol. III, p. 1154.
2. This is the version of Otis's argument that has been frequently quoted. For a note on the various records of Otis's remarks, see L. H. Butterfield, ed., *The Adams Papers.* Diary and Autobiography of John Adams (4 vol., Atheneum edition, 1964), vol. I, pp. 211-212.
3. See Edmund S. Morgan, ed., *Puritan Political Ideas* (Bobbs-Merrill, 1965), pp. 99 and 114.
4. Dickinson's development of the right of happiness is to be pieced together from a number of his writings. See especially *The Political Writings of John Dickinson* (Wilmington, 1801), vol. I, pp. 111-112, 275, 332, 395.
5. Samuel Willard, Massachusetts Election Sermon (Boston, 1694).
6. See "The Rights of the British Colonies Asserted and Proved" (1764). Reprinted in *Some Political Writings of James Otis,* collected with an Introduction by Charles F. Mullett, part I, p. 54, in *The University of Missouri Studies,* 4, no. 3 (July 1, 1929), 303-357.
7. Texts of the three constitutions are reprinted in Francis Newton Thorpe, compiler, *The Federal and State Constitution, Colonial Charters, and Other Organic Laws of the State, Territories, and Colonies Now or Heretofore Forming the United States of America.* 7 vols. (United States Congress,

1909). The Massachusetts constitution in vol. 3, pp. 1888-1923; the Pennsylvania constitution in vol. 5, pp. 3081-3092; the Virginia constitution in vol. 7, pp. 3812-3819.

8. For a concise account of the several plans available for consideration by the Virginia Convention, see the editorial note in Julian P. Boyd, ed., *The Papers of Thomas Jefferson.* (Princeton University Press, 1950), vol. I, pp. 329-337. The three drafts of Jefferson's plan, plus other notes and documents, including the constitution as adopted by the convention, are printed on pp. 337-386.

9. For a full account of George Mason's role and copies of Mason's drafts and the Declaration of Rights and Constitution as adopted, see Robert A. Rutland, ed., *The Papers of George Mason 1725-1792.* 3 vols. (University of North Carolina Press, 1970), vol. I, pp. 274-291 and 295-310.

10. See Robert E. and B. Katharine Brown, *Virginia 1705-1786: Democracy or Aristocracy* (Michigan State University Press, 1964), ch. 6 and pp. 288-290. The Browns point out that the Virginia legislature enacted laws liberalizing the suffrage in 1762 and 1769-70, but that the laws (with one minor exception) were disallowed by the British government.

11. *Notes on the State of Virginia,* Query XIII, "The Constitution of the state, and its several charters?" Reprinted in Merrill D. Peterson, ed., *The Portable Jefferson* (New York, 1975). See p. 164.

12. I have relied heavily on Irving Brant, *James Madison: The Virginia Revolution: 1751-1780.* 6 vols. (Indianapolis, 1941), vol. I. For the phrase quoted here, see pp. 210-211.

13. For Pennsylvania politics during the year 1776, I have relied heavily on David Hawke, *In the Midst of a Revolution* (University of Pennsylvania Press, 1961).

14. See Hawke, *In the Midst of a Revolution,* pp. 173-174.

15. Lisa Farrell, senior honors thesis presented to the Department of Government, Smith College, 1974.

16. Oscar and Mary Handlin, editors, *The Popular Sources of Political Authority: Documents on the Massachusetts Constitution of 1780* (Harvard University Press, 1966), pp. 61-64.

17. *Ibid.,* pp. 88-92.

18. *Ibid.,* p. 130.

19. See Robert E. Brown, *Middle-Class Democracy and the Revolution in Massachusetts, 1691-1780* (Cornell University Press, 1955), p. 394. Brown calculates that the real increase was 12.5 percent.

6

JAMES MADISON ON THE VALUE OF BILLS OF RIGHTS

WILFRID E. RUMBLE

The political philosophy of James Madison, the "father of the Constitution," was ignored by scholars for many years.[1] As recently as 1938 the author of the first book on this subject could write that it has received but "slight recognition."[2] Fortunately, this situation has changed substantially in the last three or four decades. A number of significant studies of Madison's political philosophy are now in print.[3] Yet, this body of scholarship does not include a *comprehensive* account of his analysis of the value of bills of rights. A *systematic* explanation of its relationship to his political philosophy is also unavailable.

The existence of this vacuum in the literature is almost inexplicable in light of Madison's crucial role in drafting the Bill of Rights.[4] Nonetheless, the gap exists. Its elimination is desirable for several reasons, one of which is the need to increase understanding of Madison's political philosophy. His most enduring achievement may be his explanation of how to control the abuse of governmental power. Knowledge of this contribution is incomplete without a full grasp of his analysis of bills of rights. For he concluded that these measures are one of several means for the protection of natural rights, violation of which is one definition of abuse of power.

Furthermore, the need for institutionalized safeguards for basic rights is more acute now than it was in 1791. One of the most conspicuous trends in this century is a vast expansion in the bureaucratic structure and powers of the state. The possibility that the fundamental rights of the individual will be violated has correspondingly increased. Certain recent constitutional developments reflect a belief in the efficacy of bills of rights as deterrents or remedies for such transgressions.[5] Yet, this faith may be unfounded. Respect for basic rights appears to be secure in some nations with a long democratic tradition, but no bills of rights. Great Britain and the Scandinavian countries are the most obvious examples. In other nations these constitutional mechanisms have not prevented very severe deprivations of fundamental rights. The Soviet Constitution of 1936, which elaborates such rights in great detail, is perhaps the prime illustration. This evidence at least partially explains why no less of a political scientist than Robert Dahl can argue that "in so far as there is any general protection in human society against the deprivation by one group of the freedom desired by another, it is . . . to be discovered, if at all, in extra-constitutional factors." [6] The evidence is overwhelming, Dahl believes, that "if constitutional factors are not entirely irrelevant, their significance is trivial as compared with the nonconstitutional." [7]

Madison would no doubt reject this contention. To be sure, he initially opposed the amendment of the Constitution by a national bill of rights. He also justified his opposition by arguments, some of which are quite similar to Dahl's.[8] Nevertheless, Madison eventually concluded that bills of rights are useful means to protect fundamental rights. His arguments reflect, however, an acute awareness of some of the limitations of these mechanisms. His ultimate evaluation of bills of rights is thus a *via media* between the extreme positions that these measures are of great efficacy, or none. As such, Madison's analysis has a balance which is often absent from the views of either the advocates or critics of bills of rights.

These considerations indicate why a detailed explanation and appraisal of this analysis is desirable. The purpose of this paper is to contribute to the development of such an account, by analyzing these problems. What exactly is a *bill* of rights? How did Madison conceive of the abuse of power and how did he hope to prevent it? What precisely was his attitude toward bills of rights, and how did it evolve? What content did he think these measures ought to have? How should they be enforced? How cogent is his defense of the limited utility of bills of rights? Unfortunately, resolution of some of the issues which these questions raise is beyond the scope of this study. Even so, it is both possible and desirable to explain and evaluate Madison's ideas much more fully than has been done in the past.

THE NATURE OF BILLS OF RIGHTS AND MADISON'S CONCEPT OF THE ABUSE OF POWER

The objective of bills of rights is to give special protection for rights which are felt to be of fundamental importance. This goal is achieved in numerous ways, one of which is to enumerate systematically the protected rights. A second means is to impose legal obligations on governments to respect these rights. The duties which are imposed are either negative or positive. They obligate governments either not to infringe, or to implement, the specified rights. The Bill of Rights imposes largely negative obligations, which prohibit government from doing certain things or in certain ways. More recent bills of rights tend to impose more positive duties as well. As such, these measures require *action* rather than *inaction* by government. The United Nation's Universal Declaration of Human Rights (1948) is a good illustration of the nature of these rights. To cite only a few examples, Article 22 asserts the right of every person to social security. Article 23 prescribes a right to just and favorable conditions of work and to protection against unemployment. Article 25 stipulates the right of every person to a standard of living adequate for his health and the well-being of his family.

A third means by which the objective of bills of rights is achieved is by providing for their enforcement. Since this possibility exists for any legal right, it is not distinctive of bills of rights. The fourth means is to require a more difficult process of formal change for the enumerated rights than statutory or other rights. The provisions of bills of rights need not be, however, immune to legal change. In this

respect they differ from declarations of rights. The most important
American example of the latter is no doubt the Declaration of
Independence. The rights which it declares are inalienable and,
putatively, unchangeable. The legal status of the guarantees of bills
of rights is different, for the Constitution can be amended. Yet, the
process is and was intended to be difficult.

Madison's evaluation of bills of rights reflects a particular concept
of the purpose and abuse of political power. An explanation of this
concept is necessary if his specific appraisal of these measures is to
be fully understood. The Virginian began from a basically Lockean
perspective. The *raison d'être* of government is the protection of
natural rights, which is uncertain in the absence of political power.
The word which Locke uses for these rights is "property," which he
interprets in a narrower and broader sense. At times it means only
estate or possessions, while in other places the word also denotes life
and liberty.[9]

Madison employed the same term to express his concept of the
purpose of government. In this respect he differed from his fellow
Virginian Thomas Jefferson. At least the *Declaration of Independence*
does not cite "property" as among the "unalienable Rights" with
which men are endowed. Rather, the rights which are enumerated
are "life," "liberty," and the "pursuit of happiness." According to
Madison, government is instituted to "protect property of every
sort." [10] In fact, however, this apparent difference is not as
important as this language seems to suggest. Madison sharply
distinguished between the narrower and broader meaning of
"property." The latter incorporates virtually all the natural rights in
which Jefferson believed.[11]

For Madison, "property" literally means possessions such as land,
merchandise, or money. The word in this sense denotes " 'that
domination which one man claims and exercises over the external
things of the world, in exclusion of every other individual.' " [12]
Property also has both a larger and a juster meaning. As such, it
"embraces every thing to which a man may attach a value and have
a right; and *which leaves to every one else the like advantage.*" [13] Property
in this broad sense includes the opinions of the individual; his
religious beliefs and practices; the safety and liberty of his person;
the free use of his faculties; and the free choice of the objects on
which to employ them.[14] Only that government which *"impartially*

secures to every man, whatever is his *own*" in these senses is *"just."* [15]

Since the purpose of government is to protect property, it must have whatever powers are necessary to achieve this end. Yet, this authority must not be so vast as to endanger the very rights the protection of which is the rationale of government. It must be powerful enough to elicit obedience but not so potent as to threaten tyranny. In Madison's famous words: "In framing a government which is to be administered by men over men, the great difficulty lies in this: you must first enable the government to control the governed; and in the next place oblige it to control itself." [16] A government which does not fulfill this obligation abuses its power. The likelihood of such excesses is attested to by "universal experience." [17]

This line of thought suggests how Madison conceptualized *abuse* of power, which can take several forms. One of the most obvious is unconstitutional or illegal actions. The Virginian might agree, though, that under exceptional circumstances these acts may be justified. At least his friend Thomas Jefferson expressed his approval of the maxim *salus populi suprema lex esto:*

> A strict observance of the written laws is doubtless *one* of the high duties of a good citizen, but it is not *the highest*. The laws of necessity, of self-preservation, of saving our country when in danger, are of higher obligation. To lose our country by a scrupulous adherence to written law, would be to lose the law itself, with life, liberty, property and all those who are enjoying them with us; thus absurdly sacrificing the end to the means. [18]

This statement indicates a second form of abuse of power: action by rulers contrary to the purpose of government. The essence of this kind of injustice is transgression of natural rights, security for which *is* the purpose of goverment.

THE EVOLUTION OF MADISON'S ATTITUDE TOWARD A BILL OF RIGHTS

A bill of rights seemed to many Americans in 1787 to be essential for the full protection of natural rights. Accordingly, they criticized the absence of such a measure from the Constitution. [19] Other citizens of the fledgling republic took a different point of view. The matter was discussed only briefly at the Constitutional Convention which met in Philadelphia. Five days prior to its adjournment a motion was introduced to appoint a committee to prepare a bill of rights. The proposal was defeated by the unanimous vote of ten states.[20] The vast majority of delegates apparently agreed with Roger Sherman: "The State Declarations of Rights are not repealed by this Constitution; and being in force are sufficient.... The Legislature may be safely trusted." [21] Several months later George Wilson argued that a bill of rights is also impracticable:

> For who will be bold enough to undertake to enumerate all the rights of the people?—And when the attempt ... is made, it must be remembered that if the enumeration is not complete, everything not expressly mentioned will be presumed to be purposely omitted.[22]

The classic case against the amendment of the Constitution by a bill of rights came from the pen of Alexander Hamilton. His criticisms are variations of three basic themes, one of which is that this measure is *unnecessary*. In fact, the Constitution is "in every rational sense, and to every useful purpose, a BILL OF RIGHTS." [23] Does it not establish the writ of *habeas corpus,* prohibit bills of attainder, guarantee trial by jury, and bar titles of nobility? Indeed, the fundamental charter contains *greater* securities for liberty than some state constitutions, most notably New York's. Moreover, bills of rights of the type desired by critics of the Constitution are pointless. These devices originated as means to control the power of kings and are inapplicable in republics. Since under the Constitution the people "surrender nothing; and ... retain everything they have no need of particular reservations." [24] In the second place, the incorporation of a bill of rights into the Constitution is *dangerous*. Its provisions could be interpreted as exceptions to powers which were not in fact granted. On that account, a bill of rights "would afford a colorable pretext to claim more than were granted. For why declare that things shall not be done which there is no power to do?" [25] In the third place, bills of rights are *inefficacious*. As is the case with some modern critics of constitutionalism, Hamilton argued that *attitudes* are much more important than *legal guarantees*. Liberty of the press is an example. Security for this fundamental right "must altogether depend on public opinion, and on the general spirit of the people and of the government. And here . . . must we seek *for the only solid basis of all our rights.*" (Emphasis added) [26]

Madison initially shared many of these ideas. He once claimed, of course, that he had always been in favor of a bill of rights, "provided it be so framed as not to imply powers not meant to be included in the enumeration." [27] The statement appears to be more of an afterthought than an accurate description. To be sure, Madison served on the committee which drafted Virginia's celebrated Declaration of Rights of 1776.[28] Still, in 1787 and much of 1788 he was opposed to amendment of the Constitution by a bill of rights. As such, his attitude contrasts markedly with the point of view of Jefferson. Although his response to the Constitution was on balance favorable, he expressed certain reservations. One of them was the omission of a bill of rights. Jefferson did not believe that this defect was sufficiently catastrophic to necessitate defeat of the Constitution. He did insist that the absence of a bill of rights was a major flaw in the work of the founding fathers. He wrote from Paris that the "enlightened part of Europe have given us the greatest credit for inventing the instrument of security for the rights of the people, and have been not a little surprised to see us so soon give it up." [29] The American ambassador fully shared this surprise. The Constitution should provide "clearly, and without the aid of sophism, for freedom of religion, freedom of the press, protection against standing armies, restriction of monopolies, the eternal and unremitting force of the habeas corpus laws, and trials by jury." [30] A bill which protects these rights is "what the people are entitled to against every government on earth, general or particular; and what no just government should refuse, or rest on inference." [31] Bills of rights are "fetters against doing evil, which no honest government should decline." [32]

Jefferson played no direct part in drafting or ratifying the Constitution. Madison could not have been more directly involved in the process, a fact which conditioned his evaluation of a national bill of rights. After submission of the Constitution to the states, two means of amending it were proposed.[33] One was *subsequent* amendment, the alternative which the Virginian eventually supported. The other was *previous* amendment or *conditional* ratification, to which he was unalterably opposed. He was convinced that this course of action would delay and probably prevent ratification of the Constitution.[34] A majority of the delegates in each of the state constitutional conventions apparently agreed. No state ratified the Constitution conditionally. Indeed, the first five states that approved the new charter of government recommended no amendments whatsoever. The next four state conventions that ratified the Constitution did recommend *subsequent* amendments. They included bills of rights or substantial guarantees for personal liberty. These proposals reflected the widespread belief that the Constitution provided insufficient protection for basic rights.[35] According to one historian, none of the arguments of the Anti-Federalists "proved so potent a weapon . . . as the failure to include a bill of rights . . . 'no Bill of Rights!' was the main chant of the opponents of ratification." [36]

Virginia was the tenth state to ratify the Constitution. Madison did not publicly commit himself to *subsequent* amendments until the last few days of the Convention. On June 2, 1788, he explained his position in a letter to a friend:

> The opponents [of ratification] will bring forward a bill of rights with sundry other amendments as conditions of ratification, & in case of disappointment will probably aim at an adjournment. Some apprehend a secession; but there are too many moderate and respectable characters on that side to admit such a supposition. It has been judged prudent, nevertheless, to maintain so exemplary a fairness on our part, (and even in some points to give way to unreasonable pretensions) as will withhold every pretext for so rash a step. . . . This expedient is necessary to conciliate some individuals, who are in general well affected, but have certain scruples drawn from their own reflexions, or from the temper of the constituents.[37]

Even so, Madison at this point in time could hardly be called a staunch proponent of the amendment of the Constitution by a bill or rights. His lack of enthusiasm is apparent in a letter to Jefferson, written *almost four months after the constitutional convention in Virginia.* Madison wrote that a bill of rights *"might* be of use, and if properly executed could not be of disservice." (emphasis added) [38] Still, he confessed that he never regarded its absence from the Constitution as a "material defect." Accordingly, he was not anxious to supply it by subsequent amendment "for any other reason than that it is anxiously desired by others." [39] In short, he did not view the addition of a bill of rights in an "important light." [40]

Madison justified this point of view by numerous arguments, some of which merely reiterate the logic of *Federalist* 84. In the first place, a bill of rights is unnecessary. The Constitution provides sufficient protection for basic rights, over which the federal government has no control. Its powers are delegated, and the "delegation alone warrants the exercise of any power." [41] In the second place, a bill of rights is dangerous. It provides a pretext for the argument that unenumerated rights may be restricted by the national government. The contention would be that every thing omitted is given to the general government.[42] For this reason the Constitution as it stands is the most effective protection for *natural* rights. Security for them, which is the purpose of government, will be lessened by a *bill* of rights. In the third place, bills of rights are inefficacious. Experience demonstrates that they are ineffective when most needed. Repeated violations of these paper barriers have been committed by "overbearing majorities in every State. . . . Whenever there is an interest and power to do wrong, wrong will generally be done." [43] For example, Virginia's bill of rights has been violated in every instance when it has been opposed to a "popular current." [44] In the fourth place, popular ratification of the most essential rights is unlikely to be obtained in the "requisite latitude." [45] The rights of conscience, for example, "if submitted to public definition would be narrowed much more than they are likely ever to be by an assumed power." [46]

The final reason for Madison's initial lack of enthusiasm for a national bill of rights is of special importance. This consideration not only breaks new ground in the discussion of these measures. Beyond this, it also reflects a keen insight into one limitation of constitutional safeguards for control of the abuse of power. The Virginian obviously did not regard such mechanisms as insignificant. He was, after all, a constitution-maker of the very first rank. Still, he argued that a certain sort of society is even more important. The *sine qua non* is social pluralism, which will "render an unjust combination of a majority of the whole very improbable, if not impracticable." [47] The most effective guarantee of freedom of conscience, for example, is that "multiplicity of sects, which pervades America, and which is the best and only security for religious liberty in any society." [48] The same is true of civil rights, security for which requires a "multiplicity of interests." [49] To this extent, *constitutional* protections are much less important than *social* diversity.

Nevertheless, on June 8, 1789, Madison introduced on the floor of Congress amendments to the Constitution. They included a bill of rights, which he justified on two basic grounds. To begin with, it is desirable as a means to secure the widest possible support for the Constitution.

> This House is bound by every motive of prudence, not to let the first session pass over without proposing to the State Legislatures some things to be incorporated into the constitution, that will render it as acceptable to the whole people of the United States, as it has been found acceptable to a majority of them. . . . It will be a desirable thing to extinguish from the bosom of every member of the community, any apprehensions that there are those among his countrymen who wish to deprive them of the liberty for which they valiantly fought and honorably bled. . . . We ought . . . on principles of amity and moderation, conform to their wishes, and expressly declare the great rights of mankind secured under this constitution.[50]

In addition to this, a bill of rights has genuine if limited utility. Madison confessed that he had not regarded its absence to be important enough to warrant defeat of the Constitution. Yet, he claimed to have always believed that "in a certain form, and to a certain extent, such a provision was neither improper nor altogether useless." [51] Assuming that all power is subject to abuse, "then it is possible the abuse of the powers of the General Government may be guarded against in a more secure manner than is now done." [52] At the same time, a bill of rights will not endanger the "beauty of the Government in any one important feature." [53] In short, there is "something to gain, and . . . nothing to lose" by this measure.[54]

Madison then addressed each of the major arguments by which the absence of a bill of rights from the Constitution had been

justified. Although the powers of the federal government are express
and limited, a bill of rights is not for this reason unnecessary. The
general government has some discretion, which could be abused,
about how its delegated powers are to be executed. On the basis of
the necessary-and-proper clause, for example, Congress could justify
the use of general warrants to collect revenue. Nor does the
existence of state bills of rights obviate amendment of the Constitution. Some states have no such measures, while others are either
defective or improper. The Virginian also denied that a bill of rights
is necessarily dangerous, because it implies powers not specifically
delegated. He acknowledged the plausibility of this argument but
felt that the danger it identifies can be minimized. To achieve this
end he proposed a clause, much of the substance of which was
embodied in the ninth amendment: "The exceptions here or elsewhere in the constitution, made in favor of particular rights, shall
not be so construed as to diminish the just importance of other
rights retained by the people, or as to enlarge the powers delegated
by the constitution; but either as actual limitations of such powers,
or as inserted merely for greater caution." [55]

Furthermore, Madison denied that a bill of rights would be
wholly inefficacious. It may have "to a certain degree, a salutary
effect against the abuse of power." [56] A bill of rights provides good
ground for appeal to the sense of the community if rulers subvert
liberty. The protected rights will also be enforced by courts and
guarded by state legislatures, institutions which Madison strongly
praised.[57] Finally, a bill of rights has an important educational
value. Some modern critics of constitutionalism claim that this
doctrine places far too much emphasis on *legal* guarantees rather
than *attitudes*. Since the latter determine *how* the former will be
interpreted and enforced, they are much more important. If
Madison is correct, the causal relationship is not so one-sided. In
fact, bills of rights can foster respect for fundamental rights. These
devices are somewhat efficacious means for educating public
opinion in certain "political truths." Once rights are solemnly
declared, they "acquire by degrees the character of fundamental
maxims of free Government, and as they become incorporated with
the national sentiment, counteract the impulses of interest and
passion." [58]

The most striking characteristic of this defense of the value of bills of rights is the modest character of Madison's claims. The essence of his position is that these measures have *some,* but not *very much,* utility. Since the amendment of the Constitution by a bill of rights can also do no harm, this course of action is desirable. In any event, the case which Madison made cannot be reconciled with his earlier criticisms of a national bill of rights. *Each of the arguments which he criticized on June 8, 1789, can be found in his writings or speeches prior to this date.* Assuming that he meant what he said before Congress, he must have undergone a "change of heart." Unfortunately, the "real" reasons for the development of his thought cannot be known. A number of factors could have had an impact, one of which was his desire to be elected to Congress. At the least during the campaign, the outcome of which was far from certain, Madison publicly committed himself to work for amendments.[59] A second possible contributing factor was ratification by eleven states of the Constitution. This development eliminated one cause of the Virginian's apprehension about amendments. As he wrote to George Eve on January 2, 1789:

> I freely own that I have never seen in the Constitution as it now stands those serious dangers which have alarmed many respectable Citizens. Accordingly whilst it remained unratified, and it was necessary to unite the States in some one plan, I opposed all previous alterations as calculated to throw the States into dangerous contentions, and to furnish the secret enemies of the Union with an opportunity of promoting its dissolution. *Circumstances are now changed.* [emphasis added] The Constitution is established ... and amendments, if pursued with a proper moderation and in a proper mode, will be not only safe, but may serve the double purpose of satisfying the minds of well meaning opponents, and of providding additional guards in favour of liberty.[60]

Indeed, Madison apparently believed that amendment of the Constitution would facilitate its ratification by the two "holdout" states of North Carolina and Rhode Island.[61] A third factor which could have influenced him was the arguments of the Anti-Federalists, with which he certainly was familiar. Their critique of the Federalists' defense of the omission of a bill of rights from the

Constitution was cogent.[62] It is more likely, however, that he was influenced by Jefferson.

On March 15, 1789, Jefferson wrote Madison a most important letter. The American minister to France attempted to assuage each of the doubts which his friend had expressed about a bill of rights. To begin with, Jefferson insisted that this measure *is* necessary. The Constitution does not sufficiently protect basic rights. The document "leaves some precious articles unnoticed, and raises implications against others." [63] It must for this reason be supplemented by a bill of rights which guards against the abuse of power. These safeguards also enunciate principles by means of which abuses by either the federal or state governments can be identified. Aside from this, Jefferson questioned the inference which Madison drew from the improbability of popular ratification of a sufficiently strong bill of rights. In fact, "Half a loaf is better than no bread. If we cannot secure all our rights, let us secure what we can." [64] Still further, the American ambassador to France expressed his faith in the efficacy of a bill of rights. Although it is not absolutely efficacious under all circumstances, "it is of great potency always, and rarely inefficacious. A brace the more will often keep up the building which would have fallen, with that brace the less." [65] Finally, a bill of rights could and would be enforced by the judiciary. As Jefferson wrote to Madison:

> In the arguments in favor of a delcaration of rights, you omit one which has great weight with me; the legal check which it puts into the hands of the judiciary. This is a body, which, if rendered independent and kept strictly to their own department, merits great confidence for their learning and integrity.[66]

Although the Virginian subsequently evaluated judges very differently, these were his sentiments as of 1789.[67]

Definitive proof that these arguments in fact influenced Madison is unavailable. The possibility of a significant impact does not depend, however, only on his known affection and respect for his older friend. The arguments which Madison eventually adduced for a bill of rights constitute additional evidence. Some of them are similar to Jefferson's contentions. The most notable example, probably, is Madison's strong insistence on the value of judges as guardians of a bill of rights. Whatever the explanation for the development of his thought, the conclusion which he ultimately reached is not surprising. Approbation of a national bill of rights is surely more consistent with his political philosophy as a whole than opposition to this measure. He was a staunch proponent of natural rights, protection for which he believed to be the purpose of government. He believed no less firmly in the tendency of power to be abused. From these premises it is not difficult to conclude that a bill of rights is one means to facilitate achievement of the end of government. The only question is why Madison did not draw this inference earlier. The factors discussed in this study help to explain, without fully resolving, this problem.

MADISON ON THE CONTENT OF A BILL OF RIGHTS

The provisions of the Bill of Rights are too well known to examine here. Still, a response to a number of questions about them is desirable. What are the most important similarities and differences between the first eight amendments and those which Madison proposed to Congress on June 8, 1789? What is the nature of the rights that he enumerated in his bill of rights? Did he regard them as natural rights? Is their protection absolute or less than absolute? What are these rights protection against?

The similarities between the provisions of the Bill of Rights and Madison's amendments are striking. In some cases even the precise language is the same.[68] Nonetheless, there are differences. Madison preferred the incorporation of specific rights into the body of, rather than at the end of, the Constitution.[69] Three other important differences warrant brief explanation. They indicate more completely than the first eight amendments the precise kind of bill of rights the Virginian desired.

To begin with, he wished to add to the Constitution a preface which stated the basis, purpose, and limits of government. It should stipulate that

all power is originally vested in, and consequently derived from, the people.

That Government is instituted and ought to be exercised for

the benefit of the people; which consists in the enjoyment of life
and liberty, with the right of acquiring and using property, and
generally of pursuing and obtaining happiness and safety.

That the people have an indubitable, unalienable, and
indefeasible right to reform or change their Government,
whenever it be found adverse or inadequate to the purposes of
its institution.[70]

Furthermore, Madison's initial guarantee of religious freedom
differs from the language of the first amendment. It specifies that
Congress shall pass no law "respecting an establishment of religion,
or prohibiting the free exercise thereof." Madison initially recommended this sentence: "The Civil rights of none shall be abridged
on account of religious belief or worship, nor shall any national
religion be established, nor shall the full and equal rights of
conscience be in any manner, or on any pretext, infringed." [71] His
lifelong and intense concern with the latter also explains his
proposal of an additional guarantee for religious freedom. The bill
of rights should stipulate that "no person religiously scrupulous of
bearing arms shall be compelled to render military service in
person." [72] To this extent, the Virginian wanted a stronger protection for the rights of conscience than the amendments eventually
contained.

Aside from this, Madison wished at least some rights to be
protected against invasions by *state* governments. To this degree, he
wished to erect a stronger barrier to their violation than did
Jefferson. To be sure, the latter asserted that the people are entitled
to a bill of rights against every government on earth. Nonetheless,
he appears to have believed that the Bill of Rights neither does nor
should apply to the states. At the least Leonard Levy has adduced
an imposing array of evidence to support this interpretation.[73]
Madison believed, in any event, that the states should be restricted
from violations of certain basic rights. The amendment he initially
proposed to Congress contained such a "double security" for the
rights of conscience, freedom of the press, and trial by jury in
criminal cases.[74] The House approved the proposal and added
freedom of speech, but the amendment failed to pass in the
Senate.[75] Madison himself described it as "the most valuable . . . in

the whole list. If there was any reason to restrain the Government of the United States from infringing upon these essential rights, it was equally necessary that they should be secured against the State Governments." [76]

Nevertheless, the first eight amendments are a skillful blend of rights that receive either absolute or less-than-absolute protection. One of the reasons for Madison's early doubt about the utility of a bill of rights was his dislike of unconditional prohibitions. Such restraints will never be complied with if opposed to the "decided sense of the public." [77] If these paper barriers are violated in emergencies, they will eventually lose even their ordinary efficacy. Madison gave two interesting examples, one of which is suspension of *habeas corpus*. If a rebellion or insurrection sufficiently alarmed both the people and the government, "no written prohibitions on earth would prevent the measure." [78] Prohibition of standing armies is another illustration of the same point. If a foreign power established an army in the neighborhood of the United States, "declarations on paper would have as little effect in preventing a standing force for the public safety." [79]

The kind of protection that particular rights enshrined in the Bill of Rights receive is not identical. Some are guaranteed in the most absolute and imperative terms. The first amendment specifies that Congress *shall* make *no* law "respecting an establishment of religion, or prohibiting the free exercise thereof; or abridging the freedom of speech, or of the press; or the right of the people peaceably to assemble and to petition the Government for a redress of grievances." The second amendment prescribes that the right of the people to keep and bear arms *shall* not be infringed. The third amendment stipulates that *no* soldier *shall* in time of peace be quartered in *any* house without the consent of the owner. The fifth amendment specifies that *no* person *shall* either be "subject for the same offense to be twice put in jeopardy of life or limb" or compelled in any criminal case to be a witness against himself.

To say that the protection for these rights is absolute is not to suggest that their meaning is fully known or fixed. The language of even these guarantees requires interpretation, the need for which may promote or occasion judicial disagreement. The unconditional injunction of the first amendment against abridgments of freedom of speech or the press is a good example. The meaning and extent of these safeguards was seldom discussed by the framers in any detail. Their precise intentions for many issues which courts confront are difficult, if not impossible, to determine. As Leonard Levy has correctly pointed out, "If the controversy in the states over the ratification of the Constitution without a bill of rights revealed little about the meaning and scope of freedom of speech-and-press, the debates by the First Congress . . . are even less illuminating." [80] The decisions of the Supreme Court in this century indicate that these freedoms are not in fact absolute.[81] The decisions of the Court also disclose the wide range of possible conflicting interpretations.[82] This fact is one reason for a *degree* of uncertainty about the *extent* of the protection that even these guarantees provide.

The less-than-absolute protections of other of the first eight amendments probably generate an even greater degree of uncertainty. Thus the fourth amendment protects only the right of the people to be secure against "unreasonable" searches and seizures. The fifth amendment does not prohibit deprivation of life, liberty, or property. Instead, it forbids such transactions "without due process of law." The same amendment does not rule out the taking of private property for public purposes. Rather, it forecloses such "takings" without "just" compensation. The eighth amendment forbids only "excessive" bail or fines and "cruel and unusual" punishments. The history of the Supreme Court vividly demonstrates how widely the Justices can disagree about *what* these guarantees prohibit.[83]

Madison did not specify, in any event, which of the rights protected by the Bill of Rights are natural. He did assert that some of them do not belong in this category. The important example is trial by jury, which is not a natural right. Yet, it is as "essential to secure the liberty of the people as any one of the pre-existent rights of nature." [84] The need for this bulwark of freedom indicates, thus, that a bill of rights must contain both "positive" and "natural" rights.

Madison no doubt believed that each of the rights spelled out in the Bill of Rights was important. The only question is whether he regarded some of these rights as more important than others. A number of possibilities exist, one of which is that he attached highest value to the rights of conscience. They were usually the first to be mentioned in his several enumerations of the rights to be protected by a national bill of rights.[85] Furthermore, this champion of religious freedom once implied that these rights were more important than others. In his words:

> If "all men by nature are equally free and independent," all men are to be considered as entering into society on equal conditions, as relinquishing no more, and, therefore, retaining no less, one than another, of their rights. *Above all,* they are to be considered as retaining an "equal right to the free exercise of religion, according to the dictates of conscience." (emphasis added) [86]

In addition to this, Madison may have regarded the rights of conscience and two or three other rights as of special importance. The latter include freedom of speech and the press and trial by jury in criminal cases. These are the rights, at least, which he wished to see protected from *both* federal and state restrictions.

Although these interpretations are plausible, they cannot be conclusively substantiated. Madison never explicitly ranked the various rights in the Bill of Rights. Each of these interpretations also raises its own problems. If he believed the rights of conscience to be more important than the rights of property, why did he define the purpose of government as the protection of the latter? Furthermore, he may *not* have urged a "double security" for some rights *because* they were more important than others. Rather, the reason may have been his belief that state constitutions insufficiently protected these rights.[87]

As a result, it is impossible to predict with complete certainty precisely how Madison would react to some recent constitutional controversies. The most important example, probably, is the question of whether "first amendment" freedoms have a "preferred position" over other rights.[88] Even so, a case can be made that he would support a modified version of this doctrine. For certain of his statements imply that some "first amendment" freedoms are more important than any other rights, with the exception of trial by jury.

Madison believed, in any case, that the Bill of Rights was a barrier against more than governmental actions. It was indeed intended to deter such infringements on fundamental rights. The

Virginian believed, however, that the great danger was the abuse of power by the community itself. In America the body of the people possess the "highest prerogative of power," [89] against the abuse of which the Bill of Rights can be a deterrent. Whether this same logic would require Madison today to recommend the enforcement of this mechanism against nongovernmental organizations is uncertain. Some of them obviously possess, however, a staggering amount of power that may be used to violate the basic rights of individuals.[90]

MADISON ON THE ENFORCEMENT OF A BILL OF RIGHTS

It is one thing formally to amend the Constitution by a bill of rights. It is another thing to insure in practice that these paper guarantees are in fact respected. Madison was acutely aware of the insufficiency of a mere demarcation on parchment of constitutional protections. In this respect twentieth-century proponents of realistic jurisprudence had little to teach this Founding Father. Furthermore, the existence of violations of rights is often the subject of strong disagreement. The question frequently is not so clear-cut that the proper answer to it is self-evident. This fact raises the crucial question of *who* is to decide *whether* a particular right has in fact been violated.

Unfortunately, Madison said surprisingly little about *how* a bill of rights was to be enforced. Nor did he explain in detail *who* was to resolve controversies about its violation. He did expound at considerable length on the conditions that facilitate respect for other constitutional limitations. His analysis of this general problem must therefore be explained. For it provides a solid foundation for inferring how he would probably respond to the issue of enforcing a bill of rights.

The Virginian might well begin by distinguishing between preventative and remedial measures. The purpose of the former is to deter violations of bills of rights, while the goal of the latter is to furnish remedies for transgressions. Although social pluralism is a fundamental deterrent, it is not the only one. A particular form of government, with a certain kind of structure, is of no less importance. Nothing illustrates more clearly the basis of this belief than Madison's celebrated analysis of the "violence of faction." [91]

Factions consist either of majorities or minorities of the people. The distinctive attribute of either kind of group is a common passion or interest "adverse to the rights of other citizens, or to the permanent and aggregate interests of the community." [92] Factions in this sense have been the ultimate cause of the "mortal diseases under which popular governments have everywhere perished." [93] The new republican governments of the United States are by no means immune to this malady. Many Americans of the time believed that "the 1780's . . . had become the really critical period of the entire Revolution." [94] In the words of Gordon Wood:

> The period was truly critical not solely because members of the social and economic elite felt themselves and their world threatened, but because anyone who knew anything of eighteenth-century political science could not help believing that the American republics were heading for destruction even as they were being created.[95]

Such anxiety is surely evident in the writings of James Madison.

This apprehensiveness about factions is not, of course, unique to the Sage of Montpelier. In his sense of the term most, if not all, major political philosophers have been concerned with the problems which such groups pose. The prescriptions for this malady which they have set forth may be divided into two general categories. One remedy, which theorists as different as Plato and Marx have embraced, is to exorcise the causes of faction. For Madison, this solution is both undesirable and impossible. Factions can be eliminated only by destroying liberty, which is to these groups what air is to fire. Since the protection of liberty is a major goal of political life, Madison rejected this panacea as worse than the disease. Aside from this, the seeds of faction are "sown in the nature of man." [96] Although it is possible to read *Federalist* 10 as an early version of economic determinism, any such interpretation is incorrect. Madison said, to be sure, that the most common and durable source of factions has been the various and unequal distribution of property. Still, it is neither the ultimate nor the only cause. Human fallibility, selfishness, and inequalities of potential are more fundamental sources.[97]

For these reasons Madison opted for control of the effects of factions rather than removal of their causes. The remedy for factions which are minorities is the republican principle. Through its employment the majority is able to defeat the "sinister views" of minority factions by regular vote.[98] This principle is of no use, however, if the majority is itself the faction. This kind of group poses the genuine problem confronting the American republics. The major threat to private rights is acts in which the government is the "mere instrument of the major number of the Constituents." [99] No difficulty would exist, to be sure, if all citizens had precisely the same interests and feelings. Then the interest of the majority and the minority would coincide. Differences of opinion would occur, but the "major voice would be the safest criterion." [100] In fact, however, all citizens do not have the same interests and feelings. No society ever did or could consist of so "homogeneous a mass." [101]

This argument reflects Madison's keen sensitivity to the rights of minorities. Unfortunately, even this partisan of the rights of the individual had his blinders. If anything is a violation of natural rights, it is the institution of slavery. As was the case with the other Founding Fathers the Virginian accommodated himself to this great wrong.[102] On the one hand, he fully recognized that slavery was a moral, political, and economic evil.[103] It was a "sad blot on our free Country," [104] the "greatest of our calamities." [105] Indeed, he once wrote that the magnitude of the evil was such that "no merit could be greater than that of devising a satisfactory remedy for it." [106] On the other hand, he was willing to exchange the benefits of the Union for the preservation of slavery. "Great as the evil is, a dismemberment of the union would be worse." [107]

In any event, Madison urged the people to indulge all their "precautions" and "jealousy" against the "enterprising ambition" of the legislature.[108] Numerous factors most fundamentally account for his perception of the legislature as the most dangerous branch. To begin with, he fully shared the suspicion of power that the other Founding Fathers also manifested. The ambition and lust for power are "predominant passions in the hearts of most men." [109] Power is "too intoxicating," [110] and "so alluring that few have ever been able to resist its bewitching influence." [111] Aside from this, Madison firmly believed that in republican forms of government the legislature necessarily predominates.[112] Its powers are stronger and less limitable than those of any other branch. Since lawmakers frequently act either irrationally or selfishly, their vast power is a cause of concern.

Explanation of this last crucial point requires a brief review of Madison's concept of the relationship between reason, passions, and legislation. In his eyes the reason of the public ought to control and regulate the government, which should in turn control popular passions.[113] Although the Virginian may well have been influenced by David Hume, he would never agree with the Scotchman that "reason is, and ought only to be the slave of the passions." [114] Yet, Madison was convinced that the passions frequently have a decisive impact on public opinion and legislative decisions. Both individuals and groups are all too likely to be emotional and subordinate their long-range to their immediate interest. The "mild voice of reason, pleading the cause of an enlarged and permanent interest, is but too often drowned, before public bodies as well as individuals, by the clamors of an impatient avidity for immediate and immoderate gain." [115] For this reason the people may well call for measures that they themselves will afterward be the most ready to "lament and condemn." [116] No less dangerous is the likelihood that lawmakers will use their reason as means to gratify *popular* passions. A legislature is numerous enough "to feel all the passions which actuate a multitude, yet not so numerous as to be incapable of pursuing the objects of its passions by means which reason prescribes." [117]

To a large extent, this fear of legislative gratification of popular passions explains Madison's concern with leadership. The aim of every political constitution ought to be "first to obtain for rulers men who possess most wisdom to discern, and most virtue to pursue, the common good of the society." [118] The American's observations of the behavior of state legislatures under the Articles of Confederation reinforced this belief. One student of the period has written that in the 1780's "suspicion and jealousy of political power, once concentrated almost exclusively on the Crown and its agents, was transferred to the various state legislatures. Where once the magistracy has seemed to be the sole source of tyranny, now the legislatures ... had become the institutions to be most feared." [119]

The fear is certainly apparent in the writings of James Madison, who explained its basis in a letter to Jefferson. The reason for the anxiety of the former, it is clear, is his perception of developments in the United States. According to Madison, Jefferson (who was then in France) has contemplated abuses of power from a very different quarter.[120] In America evidence of the "impetuous vortex" of the legislative department might be multiplied "without end." [121] "Vouchers in abundance" can be adduced from "the records and archives of every state in the Union." [122] The mutability and injustice of state laws "has been so frequent and so flagrant as to alarm the most stedfast friends of Republicanism." [123] The fundamental source of the problem is the failure of the founders of the American republics to remember "the danger from legislative usurpations, which, by assembling all power in the same hands, must lead to the same tyranny as is threatened by executive usurpations." [124]

To say that Madison particularly distrusted popular passions and feared the legislature is not to suggest that he despised the people. One of the great political problems is to oblige the government to control itself. The primary control is a "dependence on the people." [125] Madison insisted, however, that experience has "taught mankind the necessity of auxiliary precautions." [126] Every student of American governemnt is familiar with the additional safeguards which he felt to be necessary. They range from the separation and division of governmental powers enforced by numerous checks and balances, to social pluralism. All of these measures reflect the Virginian's conviction that "Divide et impera, the reprobated axiom of tyranny, is under certain qualifications, the only policy, by which a republic can be administered on just principles." [127]

REMEDIES FOR VIOLATIONS OF A BILL OF RIGHTS

Although a republican form of government which includes the system of checks and balances can discourage violations of constitutional rights, it cannot wholly prevent them. This fact raises the question of the remedies which Madison favored for infringements of the Bill of Rights. The remedy which the course of American history has made familiar to the world is judicial review. Although the Virginian's attitude toward this practice is not absolutely clear, the balance of his comments support it. In *The Federalist Papers* he defended the need for a federal tribunal to resolve jurisdictional conflicts between the states and the national government.[128] Besides this, in 1789 he explicitly praised the judiciary as protectors of bills of rights. Independent courts of justice "will consider themselves in a peculiar manner the guardians of those rights; they will be an impenetrable bulwark against every assumption of power in the Legislative or Executive; they will be naturally led to resist every encroachment upon rights expressly stipulated." [129] Madison subsequently wrote that the abuse of the judicial trust "does not disprove its existence" and that judges are the "surest expositor of the Constitution." [130]

This interpretation is not intended to deny that on other occasions Madison took a different position. His opposition to the Alien and Sedition Acts of 1798 is a famous, but not the only, example. The Report on the Virginia Resolutions he drafted explicitly denied that judges are the sole expositor of the Constitution in the last resort.[131] In certain *great* and *extraordinary* cases the states as parties to the compact must decide whether it has been "dangerously violated." [132] According to Madison, on "any other hypothesis, the delegation of judicial power would annul the authority delegating it." [133] The authority of constitutions over governments and of the sovereignty of the people over constitutions are "truths which are at all times necessary to be kept in mind." [134]

Statements such as these subsequently were to haunt Madison. He strenuously denied that the Virginia Resolutions contemplated nullification, which he denounced as a "preposterous & anarchical pretension." [135] Any such innovation would be "fatal" and "presents a catastrophe at which all ought to shudder." [136] Madison insisted that the Virginians had expressed only their judgment that the Alien and Sedition Acts were unconstitutional. The form of "interposition" which they desired was *not* nullification. Furthermore, some of the language of his Report supports this interpretation. This document asserted that the Resolutions "are expressions of opinion, unaccompanied with any other effect that what they may produce on opinion by exciting reflection." [137] The Report contrasted these expressions with the expositions of the judiciary, which are carried into immediate effect by force.

Nevertheless, the constitutional remedies Madison favored were not limited to judicial review. They also include attempts to change oppressive laws through such means as remonstrances, instructions, and the electoral process. The Constitution also provides for other remedies for unconstitutional actions, such as amendments or impeachment. Madison believed these measures to be particularly applicable to usurpations of power in which the Supreme Court of the United States concurs. In any event, he also insisted that *extreme* cases of oppression justify recourse to the "original right of resistance." [138] Exercise of this extraconstitutional right is the *ultima ratio* under all governments whatever their form or structure.[139] This right may be exercised in extreme circumstances by an individual state or even a "single citizen, could he effect it, if deprived of rights absolutely essential to his safety & happiness." [140] If such a person is unable to resist, he may seek relief in expatriation or voluntary exile. This last course of action "may well be deemed a reasonable privilege, or rather as a right impliedly reserved." [141]

THE COGENCY OF MADISON'S JUSTIFICATION OF BILLS OF RIGHTS

Madison's view is, thus, that bills of rights are useful if imperfect means to protect basic human rights. Unfortunately, a comprehensive appraisal of this thesis raises some issues, the resolution of which is beyond the scope of this essay. One example is the question of the truth or falsity of a basic premise of Madison's entire political philosophy. He assumed that control of the *effects* of factions, rather than elimination of their *causes,* was the only viable option. Factional conflict is inevitable and politics is a world of the second-best. The basic political problem is not to perfect man, which is impossible. Rather, it is to devise institutions which control his evil impulses without endangering the human rights governments must protect. Bills of rights are one not entirely efficacious means to achieve this end.

Although this belief in the inevitability of factional strife is plausible, it raises some serious questions. One such problem is the identification of factions, which may not be easy. In particular, disagreement is likely over which groups are acting contrary to the permanent and aggregate interests of the community. One man's faction in this sense frequently turns out to be another person's good government group. Assuming that factions can be identifed, elimination of their causes *may* be possible. For the roots of some of these groups *may* not be an unchanging human nature, but institutions that are capable of alteration or abolition. The institution of slavery is a vivid example from American history.

If this line of argument is justified, then Madison's political philosophy is somewhat flawed. His constitutionalism is an incomplete remedy that treats only the *symptoms* of social conflict. The real need may be treatment of the *causes* of the illness. The political theories of Plato and Marx symbolize two such radical prescriptions. To be sure, the differences between their respective positions are substantial.[142] Plato also believed that the ideally best solution was possible only under extraordinary circumstances, which were unlikely to emerge. The polity that he regarded as second-best exemplifies many features of constitutionalism.[143] Still, both men believed that elimination of the causes of factional conflict is possible.

Madison would no doubt criticize this belief as utopian. His writings reflect a definite pessimism about the human condition and what can be done to alleviate man's estate. Determination of the *extent to which* this attitude is justified, which is the crucial question, is immensely difficult. Still, some forms of constitutional checks on government are desirable even if Madison's concept of human nature is too pessimistic. Human behavior may be much more modifiable than he thought to be the case. Institutional changes are conceivable that may reduce, if they would not exorcise, some factional conflicts that vex modern man. Nonetheless, it is difficult to visualize a society in which some individuals do not have more power than others. Until human behavior changes almost beyond recognition, constitutional checks are necessary to control the probable abuse of this power.

A comprehensive appraisal of Madison's position also raises a second issue, resolution of which is beyond the scope of this essay. This problem is the adequacy of the philosophy of *natural rights* which underlies Madison's case for a *bill of rights*. The question is whether this philosophy, which historically was the basis for the belief in bills of rights, is a satisfactory foundation for *human rights*. Unfortunately, philosophers do not agree on the proper response to this question. From a purely logical point of view belief in the value of bills of rights does *not* presuppose the existence of natural rights. Other philosophical foundations for human rights, the existence of which is presupposed by bills of rights, are conceivable. Determination of which is presupposed by bills of rights, are conceivable. Determination of which, if any, of these alternative foundations is most satisfactory is not possible in this study.

An appraisal of the cogency of Madison's arguments also raises other issues, one of which is whether special protection for basic rights is necessary. On balance his explanation of the need for safeguards beyond purely democratic restraints seems to me to be cogent. Admittedly, the legislature may no longer be the branch of government which poses the gravest threat to fundamental rights. This dubious distinction arguably belongs to the executive branch and the numerous bureaucracies which pervade modern government. The immense growth of their power in this century would astound most, if not all, of the Founding Fathers. Still, this very development only accentuates the need for special protection for the basic rights of individuals. Moreover, these rights are capable of being enforced against executive and bureaucratic as well as legislative abuses of powers. Indeed, the scope of bills of rights may need to be extended to cover nongovernmental organizations.

Madison had a realistic awareness, in any case, of the dangers of maximizing legislative responsiveness to popular pressures. No democrat could deny that a substantial degree of responsiveness is essential, which the Virginian did not deny. He was, after all, a proponent of a republican form of government. No democrat need also deny, however, that *maximization* of responsiveness may have certain disadvantages. It would not deter, and could facilitate, laws that deprive relatively powerless or unpopular minorities of their basic rights. Despite its immense advantages, a republican form of government does not preclude deprivations of fundamental rights.

This possibility means that special protection for these rights is necessary. Recognition of this need does not necessarily imply anything, however, about the value of bills of rights. This is a separate question, the answer to which depends in large part on the efficacy of these mechanisms. The American experience indicates that bills of rights are not sufficient to deter severe deprivations of basic rights. The first eight amendments were of no value as a means to prevent slavery, the most severe such deprivation in our history. Indeed, the Bill of Rights may have been positively harmful in this respect. For the Supreme Court interpreted the fifth amendment to bar the abolition of the "peculiar institution" in the territories of the United States.[144] Nor did the enactment of the thirteenth, fourteenth and fifteenth amendments prevent very serious forms of racial discrimination.[145] Moreover, the Bill of Rights did not deter what may be the second most severe deprivation of basic rights in American history. This was the forced evacuation and internment of thousands of Japanese Americans during World War II. The Supreme Court upheld this indiscriminate denial of due process as a valid exercise of the war powers of the President and Congress.[146] The Bill of Rights also did not prevent the recent and massive infractions of constitutional rights by the FBI and the CIA.

The more interesting question is not *whether*, but *why*, the Bill of Rights has been of limited efficacy. Although an exhaustive explanation is not possible, some of the most important factors can be described. To begin with, the first eight amendments do not enumerate certain rights which are now widely perceived to be basic. The right to vote, to education, and to protection against unemployment are examples of three of these rights.[147] To be sure, their omission from the Bill of Rights is understandable. Nevertheless, it indicates an important limitation of these constitutional mechanisms. Bills of rights invariably reflect the limited perspectives of their authors, which are strongly conditioned by considerations of time and place.

In addition to this, for most of American history the Bill of Rights was a restraint only upon the actions of the federal government. In 1833 a unanimous Supreme Court established precisely this point, which prevailed for almost a century thereafter.[148] Nor did the ratification of the fourteenth amendment in 1868 quickly change this situation. Indeed, it was not used as a vehicle to extend the coverage of the Bill of Rights to state actions until the 1920s. Only then did the first eight amendments begin to be gradually and selectively applied to the states.[149]

A third factor is the spirit or attitudes of the people, the importance of which Madison very properly emphasized. These attitudes strongly condition whether governmental deprivations of basic rights of minorities will be tolerated. The historical evidence indicates that a majority of the people is perfectly willing to sanction such deprivations on at least some occasions. The lack of widespread protest against the forced evacuation and internment of Japanese Americans in 1942 is a good example.[150] Aside from this, the attitudes of the people sometimes limit who may *exercise* constitutionally protected rights. Although Alexis de Tocqueville's brilliant analysis of this problem was written almost 150 years ago, it retains considerable validity.[151] Nothing illustrates this point better than Article VI of the Constitution. It stipulates that "no religious test shall ever be required as a qualification to any office or public trust under the United States." Yet, a de facto religious test did exist for the highest political office in the land for at least 170 years. A case can be made that in practice a religious test still exists. Could a Jew be nominated or elected president of the United States?

The decisions of the Supreme Court constitute a fourth reason for the less-than-complete efficacy of the Bill of Rights. Numerous cases have sustained assertions of governmental power that have seriously limited the basic rights of some Americans. In particular, the Supreme Court has often been reluctant to invalidate such assertions of power by the federal government. As of 1955 the Court had declared only three acts of Congress to be unconstitutional violations of civil liberties.[152] In this respect, Fred Rodell contends, a majority of the Justices have been "most bumblingly bashful, most reluctant to assert the autocratic power they hold." [153] The author of a study that appeared twenty-one years later reached much the same conclusion. According to Robert Dahl, "Until recently, the Court has not made a significant contribution as protector of the rights of otherwise weak or defenseless minorities against encroachment by the federal government."[154]

A number of decisions interpreting the free speech provision of the first amendment support this evaluation. The language of this part of the Bill of Rights could not be more imperative or unconditional. Congress *shall* pass *no* law . . . abridging the freedom of speech. Still, the Supreme Court has never interpreted the first amendment to mean what it appears to say. In fact, the Justices have sustained numerous types of restraints against certain kinds of speech.[155] They include the political speech of political dissenters.

During World War I hundreds of persons were convicted for little more than criticizing the draft. The Court upheld the conviction of one such critic in a unanimous opinion written by Mr. Justice Holmes. He justified the decision on the ground that when "a nation is at war many things that might be said in time of peace are such a hindrance to its effort that . . . no Court could regard them as protected by any constitutional right." [156] In other words, the Constitution and the Bill of Rights mean one thing in peacetime and another thing in wartime.

Aside from this, the Supreme Court on more than one occasion has narrowed what may be said in peacetime. In fact, the justices have frequently employed the scale of values implicit in a revealing utterance of Mr. Chief Justice Vinson. In 1951 the Court upheld the conviction of eleven leaders of the Communist party of the United States for *advocating* certain ideas. According to the Chief Justice, "the societal value of speech must, on occasion, be subordinated to other values and considerations." [157] Nothing reveals more unmistakably than this statement the importance of the attitudes of the Justices in *interpreting* the Bill of Rights.

The historical evidence does not therefore vindicate Madison's faith in judges as almost Platonic guardians of the Bill of Rights. In fact, they have not resisted *every* encroachment upon rights expressly stipulated. Madison also did not fully appreciate the impact of socioeconomic inequalities, a fifth reason for the less-than-complete efficacy of the Bill of Rights. These inequalities strongly condition real access to the law and the effective exercise of constitutional rights. The wealthy, the well-educated, and the powerful have on paper precisely the same constitutional rights as the poor, the ill educated, and the powerless. Yet the latter tend in practice to have fewer effective rights than the former. For "there is [real] equality before the law only when the price of admission to its opportunities can be equally paid." [158] Since this price has not been and is not now equal, equality before the law is more of an aspiration than a fact.

These various factors constitute some of the reasons why the Bill of Rights has been of limited efficacy. To say this is not to imply, however, that it has been entirely inefficacious. Efficacy is, after all, a matter of degree. The real question is not *whether* the Bill of Rights has been efficacious, but *how* efficacious it has been. Unfortunately, a detailed response to this problem is the subject of a separate essay. Nonetheless, the record vindicates James Madison's calculation that the Bill of Rights would not be "altogether useless."

To begin with, courts have struck down numerous legislative encroachments on property rights. Of course, the language of the Bill of Rights offers only limited protection for these rights. The fifth amendment contains the most explicit guarantees, but it expressly prohibits only how property may be taken. No person shall be "deprived of life, liberty, or property, without due process of law; nor shall private property be taken for public use, without just compensation." Nonetheless, the due process clauses of the fifth and fourteenth Amendments have been interpreted to bar many state and federal regulations of property. Indeed, at times these clauses of the Constitution have been stretched to rule out the most beneficent social legislation.[159] To that extent, these guarantees *as interpreted by the courts* have at times been all too effective. At any rate, Madison and the other Founding Fathers believed that the right to own and acquire property is basic.

Aside from this, the courts have struck down *some* encroachments on other rights expressly stipulated. They include certain encroachments by the federal government, most notably since 1958. According to Jonathan Casper, from 1958 to 1974 the Court declared thirty-two provisions of federal law unconstitutional in twenty-eight cases. Twenty-seven of these decisions were based upon provisions of the Bill of Rights, primarily the first and fifth amendments.[160] Aside from this, prior to 1958 the Court struck down numerous state actions that violated basic rights. Even the critics of judicial review admit that the record of the Court in these kinds of cases is quite impressive.[161] Moreover, the frequency of either state or federal infringements of basic rights might have been even worse without the Bill of Rights.

CONCLUSION

In sum, James Madison persuasively explained the need for protection of basic rights. He also accurately estimated the limited efficacy of the Bill of Rights as a means to satisfy this need. To say this is not to imply that bills of rights are either a necessary or sufficient condition for protection of fundamental rights. The example of Great Britain suggests that these measures are not absolutely necessary for this purpose, though whether they are desirable is now a debated question in that country.[162] The American experience indicates that bills of rights are not sufficient to prevent severe deprivations of basic rights. It is possible, however, for a mechanism to be useful without being either necessary or sufficient for the achievement of a goal. The conclusion of this essay is that the Bill of Rights is just such a mechanism.

1. The title of "Father of the Constitution" was apparently first bestowed on Madison by John Quincy Adams. See Adair, "The Tenth Federalist Revisited," 8 *William and Mary Q.* 48, 51, n. 6 (1951).

2. Burns, *James Madison: Philosopher of the Constitution,* ix (1938).

3. See Dewey, "The Sage of Montpelier: James Madison's Constitutional and Political Thought, 1817-1836," (unpublished thesis at University of Chicago). Adair, " 'That Politics May Be Reduced to a Science'; David Hume, James Madison and The Tenth Federalist," 20 *Huntington Library Q.* 346 (1957); Adair, "The Tenth Federalist Revisited," 8 *William and Mary Q.* 48 (1951); Burns, *James Madison, Philosopher of the Constitution* (1938); Carey, "Majority Tyranny and the Extended Republic of James Madison," 20 *Modern Age* 40 (1976); Ingersoll, "Machiavelli and Madison: Perspectives on Political Change," 85 *Pol. Sci. Q.* 259 (1970); Koch, *Jefferson and Madison: The Great Collaboration* (1950); Koch, *Power, Morals, and the Founding Fathers: Essays in The Interpretation of the American Enlightenment* (1969); Koch, *Madison's "Advice to My Country"* (1966); Ketcham, "James Madison and the Nature of Man," 19 *J. History of Ideas* 62 (1958); Padover, "Madison as a Political Thinker," 20 *Social Research* 32 (1953); Riemer, "The Republicanism of James Madison," 79 *Pol. Sci. Q.* 45 (1954); and Riemer, "James Madison's Theory of the Self-Destructive Features of Republican Government," 65 *Ethics* 34 (1954). For studies of *The Federalist Papers* which include analyses of Madison's political ideas, see Mason, "The Federalist—A Split Personality," 57 *Am. Hist. Rev.* 625 (1951); Diamond, "Democracy and the Federalist: A Reconsideration of the Framer's Intent," 53 *Am. Pol. Sci. Rev.* 52 (1959); Dietze, *The Federalist: A Classic on Federalism and Free Government* (1960); Eidelberg, *The Philosophy of The American Constitution* (1968); Scanlon, "The Federalist and Human Nature," 21 *Rev. of Politics* 657

(1959); Smith, "Reason, Passion, and Political Freedom in the Federalist," 22 *J. of Politics* 525 (1960); and Wright, "The Federalist on the Nature of Man," 59 *Ethics* 1 (1949).

4. The best studies of the adoption of the Bill of Rights, which necessarily describe Madison's role and some of his ideas, are Rutland, *The Birth of the Bill of Rights, 1776-1791* (1962); Dumbauld, *The Bill of Rights and What It Means Today* (1957); and Schwartz, *The Great Rights of Mankind* (1977).

5. One such development is the adoption by the United Nations in 1948 of the Universal Declaration of Human Rights. See Korey, *The Key To Human Rights—Implementation* (1968). For useful comparative studies, see Duchacek, *Rights & Liberties in the World Today* (1973) and *Comparative Human Rights* (Claude ed., 1976).

6. Dahl, *A Preface to Democratic Theory,* 134 (1956).

7. *Id.* at 135.

8. See *id.* at 76, 82-83, 135-137.

9. See Locke, *Two Treatises of Government,* 308, 366, 395 (Laslett ed., 1965).

10. Madison, "Property," in 6, *The Writings of James Madison,* 101, 102 (Hunt ed., 1910) [hereinafter cited as *WJM*]. In *The Federalist Papers* Madison does not systematically analyze the ends of government. To the extent that he refers to them, he does not cite property as *the* end. Rather, he says that the happiness or the happiness and safety of the people are "the objects at which all political institutions aim and to which all such institutions must be sacrificed." Madison, Jay, and Hamilton, *The Federalist Papers,* 279 (Rossiter ed., 1961). Also see *id.* at 253, 380.

11. According to Dumas Malone, Jefferson cherished most "such rights as freedom of mind, conscience, and person. . . . These unquestionably were inalienable, and also desirable in themselves." Malone, *Jefferson The Virginian,* 227-228 (1948).

12. 6 *WJM* 101.

13. *Id.*

14. *Id.*

15. *Id.* at 102.

16. Hamilton, Madison, and Jay, *The Federalist Papers,* 322 (Rossiter ed., 1961).

17. Madison, "Government," in 6 *WJM* 91.

18. Letter from Thomas Jefferson to John B. Colvin, September 20, 1810, in 12, *The Writings of Thomas Jefferson,* 418 (1904) [hereinafter cited as *Writings*].

19. See Rutland, *supra* note 4. The absence of a bill of rights from the Constitution was probably the most powerful weapon of the Anti-

Federalists. For a convenient collection of their writings, see *The Antifederalists* (Kenyon ed., 1966).

20. 2, *The Records of the Federal Convention of 1787*, 588 (Farrand ed., 1911).
21. *Id.*
22. *Id.*, 3, at 143-144.
23. Hamilton, *supra*, note 16, at 515.
24. *Id.* at 513.
25. *Id.*
26. *Id.* at 514-515.
27. Letter from James Madison to Thomas Jefferson, October 17, 1788, in 5 *WJM* 271. Madison subsequently implied that he had favored a bill of rights *during the Constitutional Convention at Philadelphia.* "I am not of the number if there be any such, who think the Constitution lately adopted a faultless work. On the contrary there are amendments which I wished it to have received before it issued from the place in which it was formed. These amendments I still think ought to be made, according to the apparent sense of America and some of them at least, I presume will be made." Letter from James Madison to G. L. Turberville, November 2, 1788, 5 *WJM* 298. I have been unable to discover any evidence which supports this interpretation of Madison's thought in the summer of 1787.
28. Brant, *James Madison: The Virginia Revolutionist*, 234 (1941).
29. Letter from Thomas Jefferson to James Madison, March 15, 1789, in *The Life and Selected Writings of Thomas Jefferson*, 461 (Koch and Peden ed. 1944) [hereinafter cited as *Selected Writings*].
30. Letter from Thomas Jefferson to James Madison, December 20, 1787, *id.* at 437.
31. *Id.* at 438.
32. Letter from Thomas Jefferson to A. Donald, February 7, 1788, in *Selected Writings*, 442. Jefferson's views of what should be done about the absence of a bill of rights from the Constitution changed in the course of time. For a good analysis of the evolution of his thought on this question, see Malone, *Jefferson and the Rights of Man*, 171-179 (1951).
33. See Rutland, *supra* note 4, at 130-193.
34. See Letter from James Madison to Alexander Hamilton, June 27, 1788, 4, *Documentary History of the Constitution*, 803 (1905); 3, *The Debates in the Several State Conventions on the Adoption of the Federal Constitution*, 93 (Elliot ed., 1888); and Letter from James Madison to G. L. Tuberville, November 2, 1788, 5 *WJM* 298-300.
35. See Rutland, *supra* note 4, at 149-193.
36. *Id.* at 128-129. Rutland may well have overemphasized the extent to

which the omission of a bill of rights was the "main chant" of the Anti-Federalists. For a very different interpretation, see Kendall, "The Bill of Rights and American Freedom," in *Willmoore Kendall Contra Mundum*, 303 (N. D. Kendall ed.).

37. Letter of James Madison to Rufus King, June 22, 1788, in 1, *The Life and Correspondence of Rufus King*, 336-337. Madison had indicated some interest in *subsequent* amendments several months prior to this date. See letter from James Madison to Governor Randolph, April 10, 1788, in 4, *Documentary History of the Constitution*, 573 (1905).

38. Madison, *supra* note 27, at 271.

39. *Id.*

40. *Id.*

41. Elliot, *supra* note 34, at 620.

42. *Id.*

43. Madison, *supra* note 27, at 272.

44. *Id.*

45. *Id.* at 271.

46. *Id.* at 271-272.

47. Madison, *supra* note 16, 324.

48. 5 *WJM* 176.

49. Madison, *supra* note 16, at 324. This emphasis on the importance of social pluralism is one reason why Dahl's interpretation of Madison is unsatisfactory.

50. I, *The Debates and Proceedings in the Congress of the United States* 448-449 (Gales ed., 1834) [hereinafter cited as *Annals of Congress*].

51. *Id.* at 453.

52. *Id.* at 449-450.

53. *Id.* at 459.

54. *Id.* at 450.

55. *Id.* at 452.

56. *Id.* at 457.

57. *Id.*

58. Madison, *supra* note 27, at 273.

59. See Letter from James Madison to George Eve, January 2, 1789, 5 *WJM* 319-320. Madison began the letter in this manner: "Being informed that reports prevail not only that I am opposed to any amendments whatever to the new federal Constitution, but that I have ceased to be a friend to the rights of Conscience . . . I am led to trouble you with this communication. . . . But having been induced to offer my services to this district as its representative in the federal Legislature, considerations of a public nature make it proper that . . . my principles and views should be rightly understood." *Id.* at 320.

60. *Id.*
61. I, *Annals of Congress* 449.
62. It is difficult not to agree with Cecelia Kenyon that although "one may regard some of the fears expressed by the Anti-Federalists as somewhat fanciful and possibly exaggerated for propaganda purposes, there is no mistaking . . . the force and validity of their arguments in demand for [a bill of rights]. On this point the Federalists showed a puzzling obtuseness, and their attempt to defend the omission was as unconvincing then as it is now." Kenyon, *supra* note 19, at lxx.
63. Jefferson, *supra* note 29, at 463.
64. *Id.*
65. *Id.*
66. *Id.* at 462.
67. See Letter from Thomas Jefferson to Spencer Roane, September 6, 1819, in 15, *Writings,* 212, and Letter from Thomas Jefferson to William C. Jarvis, September 28, 1820, *id.* at 276.
68. For the amendments themselves, see I, *Annals of Congress,* 451-453. A good analysis of the various changes which these amendments underwent in the process of being approved by the Congress may be found in Dumbauld, *The Bill of Rights and What It Means Today,* 33-50 (1957).
69. I, *Annals of Congress,* 735.
70. *Id.* at 451.
71. *Id.*
72. *Id.*
73. See Levy, *Jefferson and Civil Liberties: The Darker Side* (1963). It is also true, however, that Jefferson expressed approval of Madison's initial amendments to the Constitution. Indeed, he went so far as to say that they did not go far enough. See letter from Thomas Jefferson to James Madison, August 28, 1789, in 5, *The Writings of Thomas Jefferson,* 107 (Ford ed., 1895).
74. I, *Annals of Congress,* 458.
75. *Id.* at 78. The margin by which the Senate defeated this measure is not known.
76. *Id.* at 784.
77. Madison, *supra* note 27, at 274.
78. *Id.*
79. *Id.*
80. Levy, *Freedom of Speech and Press in Early American History: Legacy of Suppression,* 221 (1965). Madison was well aware of the limitations of language as a guide to decisions. See Madison, *supra* note 16, at 229.
81. According to Martin Shapiro, "the Court has committed itself less

firmly to the First Amendment than to nearly any other of the individual rights specifically guaranteed by the Constitution." *Freedom of Speech: The Supreme Court and Judicial Review,* 172 (1966).

82. For studies of the different doctrines evolved by the Court, see Shapiro, *supra* note 81, and Emerson, *The System of Freedom of Expression* (1970).

83. For a recent study of the problem, see Abraham, *Freedom and the Court: Civil Rights and Liberties in the United States,* 3d ed. (1977).

84. 5 *WJM* 381.

85. Thus in his very important letter to George Eve, Madison wrote: "the Constitution ought to be revised, and . . . the first Congress meeting under it ought to prepare and recommend to the States for ratification, the most satisfactory provisions for all essential rights, particularly the rights of Conscience in the fullest latitude, the freedom of the press, trials by jury, security against general warrants etc." Letter from James Madison to George Eve, January 2, 1789, 5 *WJM* 320.

86. Madison, *A Memorial and Remonstrance on the Religious Rights of Man,* in *Cornerstones of Religious Freedom in America* 86 (Blau ed., 1949).

87. 1, Annals of Congress, 458. For discussion of the status of personal freedom in the various states prior to the ratification of the first ten amendments, see Rutland, *supra* note 4, pp. 84-110, and Schwartz, *supra* note 4.

88. For a useful study of the nature and evolution of the "preferred position" doctrine, see Abraham, *supra* note 83, at 9-32, 238-240.

89. 5 *WJM* 382.

90. For a useful analysis of whether the first amendment should be enforced against private organizations, see Emerson, *supra* note 82, at 675-696.

91. Madison, *supra* note 16, at 77.

92. *Id.* at 78.

93. *Id.* at 77.

94. Wood, *The Creation of the American Republic, 1776-1787,* 393 (1969).

95. *Id* at 414.

96. Madison, *supra* note 16, 79.

97. *Id.* at 78.

98. *Id* at 80. Martin Diamond, Ralph Ketcham, and Neal Riemer have persuasively argued for the genuine commitment of Madison to republicanism. See Diamond, *supra* note 3; Ketcham, *id.;* and Riemer, "The Republicanism of James Madison," 69 *Pol. Sci. Q.* 45, 49, 63 (1954).

99. Madison, *supra* note 27, at 272.

100. Letter from James Madison to Thomas Jefferson, October 24, 1787, in 5 *WJM* 17, 28-29.

101. *Id.* at 29.

102. See Robinson, *Slavery in the Structure of American Politics 1765-1820* (1971).

103. Letter from James Madison to Francis Cordin, November 26, 1820, in 9 *WJM* 40.

104. Letter from James Madison to Lafayette, 1821, *id.* at 85n.

105. Letter from Madison to Thomas R. Dew, February 23, 1833, *id.* at 500.

106. Letter from James Madison to Francis Wright, September 1, 1825, *id.* at 224-225.

107. Madison, Speech before Congress, June 17, 1788, in 5 *WJM* 210.

108. Madison, *supra* note 16, at 309.

109. Sam Adams, quoted by Bailyn, *The Ideological Origins of The American Revolution*, 60-61 (1967).

110. *Id.*

111. The words were spoken at the New Hampshire Convention of 1781, as quoted by Wood, *supra* note 94, at 447.

112. Madison, *supra* note 16, at 322.

113. *Id.* at 317. For useful studies of Madison's view of the relationship between reason and the passions, see the articles by Scanlon and Smith, *supra* note 3.

114. Hume, *A Treatise of Human Nature*, 415 (Selby-Bigge ed., 1888). According to Ralph Ketcham, "Of all the philosophers of the eighteenth century, the one who was in many respects closest to the edge of Madison's mind ... was David Hume." Ketcham, *supra* note 3, at 73. For a close analysis of the *causal impact* of Hume upon Madison and in particular *Federalist* 10, see Adair, " 'That Politics May Be Reduced to a Science'; David Hume, James Madison, and the Tenth Federalist," 20 *Huntington Library Quarterly* 346 (1957).

115. Madison, *supra* note 16, at 268.

116. *Id.* at 384.

117. *Id.* at 309.

118. *Id.* at 350.

119. Wood, *supra* note 94, at 409.

120. Madison, *supra* note 27, at 272.

121. Madison, *supra* note 16, at 310.

122. *Id.*

123. Madison, *supra* note 100, at 27.

124. Madison, *supra* note 16, at 309.

125. *Id.* at 322.
126. *Id.*
127. Madison, *supra* note 100, at 31.
128. Madison, *supra* note 16, at 245-246.
129. 5 *WJM* 385.
130. Letter from James Madison to Thomas Jefferson, June 27, 1823, in 3, *Letters and Other Writings of James Madison,* 327 (1884), and Letter, 1834, *id.,* 4, at 350.
131. Madison, "Report of the Resolutions," 6 *WJM* 351. For other examples of Madison's critical attitude toward judicial review, see Letter from James Madison to Thomas Jefferson, June 4, 1810, in 2, *Letters and Other Writings of James Madison,* 478 (1884) and Madison, Remarks on Mr. Jefferson's "Draught of a Constitution for Virginia," I, *id.* at 194.
132. Madison, "Report of the Resolutions," 6 *WJM* 351.
133. *Id.* at 352.
134. *Id.*
135. Letter from James Madison to N. P. Trist, December 1831, in 9 *WJM* 472.
136. Letter from James Madison to Trist, February 15, 1830, *id.* at 357n.
137. 6 *WJM* 402.
138. Madison, *supra* note 135, at 471.
139. Madison, *supra* note 137, at 398.
140. Madison, "Outline," 9 *WJM* 351, 353.
141. Madison, *supra* note 136, at 356.
142. For some famous illustrations of Marx's explanation of social conflict, see Marx and Engels, *Manifesto of the Communist Party,* in *Karl Marx and Frederick Engels, 1, Selected Works,* 32 (1951), and Marx, *Preface to a Contribution to the Critique of Political Economy, id.* at 327.
143. See Plato, *The Laws* (trans., Saunders, 1970). For Plato's constitutionalism, see Morrow, *Plato's Cretan City* (1960), and Morrow, "Plato and the Rule of Law," 50 *Philosophical Review* 105 (1941).
144. *Dred Scott* v. *Sandford,* 19 How. 393 (1857). For an important study of the judicial response to slavery, see Cover, *Justice Accused: Antislavery and the Judicial Process* (1975).
145. For a brilliant recent study of the entire problem, see Kluger, *Simple Justice: The History of Brown v. Board of Education and Black America's Struggle for Equality* (1976).
146. *Korematsu* v. *United States,* 323 U.S. 214 (1944). See Ten Broek *et al., Prejudice, War and the Constitution: Causes and Consequences of the Evacuation of the Japanese Americans in World War II* (1954); Dembritz, "Racial

Discrimination and Military Judgments," 45 *Col. L. Rev.* 175 (1945); Rostow, "The Japanese American Cases—A Disaster," 54 *Yale L.J.* 489 (1945); *Weglyn, Years of Infamy: The Untold Story of America's Concentration Camps* (1976); and Blum, *V Was for Victory: Politics and American Culture During World War II* (1976).

147. These and some other rights not included in the Bill of Rights are contained in the United Nations' Universal Declaration of Human Rights. See Korey, *supra* note 5.

148. See *Barron* v. *Baltimore*, 7 Pet. 243 (1833).

149. For a good recent account of this development, see Abraham, *Freedom and the Court: Civil Rights and Liberties in the United States*, 33-105, 3d ed. (1977).

150. John Morton Blum writes: "While the passing months of a grim and debilitating incarceration generated increasing tensions among the internees, few Americans protested against the barbarous and unconstitutional course of national policy . . . . most of [the] . . . protests were tempered by at least a rhetorical concession to military necessity." Blum, *supra* note 146, at 162.

151. See De Tocqueville, I *Democracy in America*, 265-280 (Bradley ed., 1954).

152. Rodell, *Nine Men: A Political History of the Supreme Court from 1790 to 1955*, 25-26 (1955).

153. *Id.* at 23.

154. Dahl, *Democracy in the United States: Promise and Performance*, 241, 3d. ed. (1976).

155. Two examples are obscene expression and "fighting words" in face-to-face conduct in public places. See *Miller* v. *California*, 413 U.S. 15 (1973), *Paris Adult Theater I* v. *Slaton*, 413 U.S. 49 (1973), and *Chaplinsky* v. *New Hampshire*, 315 U.S. 568 (1942).

156. *Schenck* v. *United States*, 249 U.S. 47, 52 (1919).

157. *Dennis* v. *United States*, 341 U.S. 494, 503 (1951). Also, see *Chaplinsky* v. *New Hampshire*, 315 U.S. 568, 572.

158. Laski, *The State in Theory and Practice*, 153 (1947).

159. For three classic examples, see *Lochner* v. *New York*, 198 U.S. 45 (1905); *Adkins* v. *Children's Hospital*, 261 U.S. 525 (1923); and *Morehead* v. *New York ex. rel. Tipaldo*, 298 U.S. 587 (1936). These decisions were overruled in *West Coast Hotel Co.* v. *Parrish*, 300 U.S. 379 (1937).

160. Casper, "The Supreme Court and National Policy Making," 70 *Am. Pol. Sci. Rev.* 50, 52-54 (1976). For a similar interpretation, see Dionisopoulos, "Judicial Review in the Textbooks," 11 *DEA News* 1 (1976).

161. See Commager, *Majority Rule and Minority Rights,* 65-66 (1943); Rodell, *supra* note 152, at 24-25; and Dahl, *Democracy in the United States: Promise and Performance,* 236, 3d ed. (1976).

162. See Zander, *A Bill of Rights?* (1976), and "Comment," *Public Law* 109 (Summer 1976). For defense of the idea that the United Kingdom does *not* need a bill of rights, see Lloyd of Hampstead, "Do We Need a Bill of Rights?" 39 *Modern L. Rev.* 121 (1976).

7

NIGERIAN CONSTITUTIONALISM

CHRISTOPHER C. MOJEKWU*

INTRODUCTION

Nigeria is the largest of all former British possessions on the African continent; its size is that of Texas and Oklahoma put together. The British crown took over the official administration of Nigeria on January 1, 1900, and did not give it up till October 1, 1960. Throughout this period, English law and British constitutional practices were gradually introduced into the country's

* Dr. Christopher C. Mojekwu was the Attorney General of the former Eastern Region of Nigeria, and later the Minister of Home Affairs and Local Government in the defunct Biafran regime. Educated in England and the United States, Dr. Mojekwu holds an LL.B. degree from London School of Economics, the University of London; LL.M. and S.J.D. from Northwestern University School of Law, USA. He is Barrister-at-Law of the Honourable Society of Gray's Inn, London, a member of the British and the Nigerian Bars, and an Associate member of the American Bar Association. Presently, he is an Associate Professor of Politics at Lake Forest

political administration. From 1900, English language became the medium of instruction in most primary and in all postprimary schools. Because the British dominated internal and external trade and politically administered the country for so long, English language is officially used for all government and commercial transactions today. In Northern Nigeria, however, the Hausa language is also used extensively for business and local administration.

Nigeria, since independence, has continued to retain and, in some cases, adapted for its use, the British parliamentary system, the legal and judicial processes, and the rule of law, which it inherited from the British colonial experience. Nigeria has over the years, slowly evolved what it may now call its own laws and its own constitutionalism.

The term "constitutionalism" is used here to mean "adherence to or government according to constitutional principles." By "constitution" we mean "an established law or custom" by which a state or society is organized, governed, and ordered. Constitutionalism, therefore, has to do with the system by which the basic principles and laws of a nation, state, or tribal group predetermine the limits of the powers and duties of various institutions and organs of government in a society.

As Professor Ben Nwabueze, a leading Nigerian constitutional scholar, has pointed out, the essence of constitutionalism is not "democracy" or the existence of a "written constitution. . . . The crucial test is whether the government is limited by predetermined rules." The problem with man and governments has always been how to limit the arbitrariness of political power which man can manipulate in a government. "It is this limiting of the arbitrariness of political power that is expressed in the concept of constitutionalism." [1]

We will judge various forms of government, not on the elegance

College, Lake Forest, Illinois, and a visiting faculty member of the School for New Learning, De Paul University, Chicago, Illinois.

The author is indebted to Dr. Charles A. Miller, Associate Professor and Chairman of the Department of Politics at Lake Forest College, for reading over the original drafts of this paper and for the invaluable advice he gave in the production of the article.

of their formal constitutional documents, but on how the systems impose limitations to the arbitrary nature of governments. A written constitution may proclaim lofty ideals as its objectives, but without the will or ability to limit the "use or abuse" of power by the power holders such a government is unable to enforce legal restraints on the officeholders and could turn into a dictatorship. Although we may not find written documents in the traditional African governments, the test is still the same: How does the system in the society limit the arbitrary powers of those who govern? As will be discussed later, the African traditional experiences have examples of limited governments within the monarchical, republican, and single-executive or presidential systems.[2]

BRITISH COLONIAL CONSTITUTIONALISM

It is quite often forgotten that Nigeria is not one people or one nation. It is composed of divers culturally different nations, city-states, and kindship societies.[3] Each has its own history, language, custom, religion, and culture. This diversity has been at the root of the major problems of Nigeria. British colonialism in Africa was not designed to socialize the Nigerian masses into western political culture. Colonialism in Africa meant subjugation and economic exploitation of the people. Indeed, socialization into Western political culture was what colonialism prohibited and avoided.

In 1900, the British claimed that, in order to protect the interest of the various African subnations in Nigeria, as well as their own commercial interest, they had no option but to superimpose English law and British colonial constitutionalism on the Nigerian traditional structures. By the time the British left the country, the Nigerian political elites utilized these British systems to develop what we have described as Nigerian law and constitutionalism.

Students of Nigerian constitutional history are aware of the problems of the country's constitutional development. From the policy of separate Northern and Southern Nigeria governments, the Lugard constitution of 1914, at least on paper, brought the two Nigerian governments under one central government.[4] In 1922, the "elective principle" was introduced into the Nigerian Constitution by the governor, Sir Hugh Clifford, though only two small portions of the country, Lagos and Calabar, were permitted to exercise the right to elect their representatives.

The next major constitutional advance was in 1946 under Governor Sir Arthur Richards (now Lord Milverton). The constitutional arrangements which still bear his name, the Richards constitution, are remembered for introducing regionalism in the Nigerian constitutionalism. Although the Richards Constitution was federal in nature, accommodating the major ethnic groups in the regional governments, it failed to reduce the fears of the many ethnic minorities about the domination of the apparatus of political power by the Hausa, Yoruba, and Igbo people, the three majority tribes on which the three regional governments were based. The Richards constitution was criticized by the nationalists as the sower of the seeds of regionalism, tribalism, separatism, and uneven development in Nigeria. Yet this concept of federalism has continued to guide constitutional development of the Nigerian state. Subsequent constitutional development, notably the Macpherson constitution of 1951, the Lyttelton constitution of 1954, and the Independence Constitution of 1960, were based on federalism.

Through each of these constitutional advances, Her Britannic Majesty introduced progressive measures that increased the Nigerian people's participation in the political decision-making of their country, and phased out British imperial involvement in the political administration of the country. All these culminated into the 1960 Constitution by which Britain granted political independence to Nigeria.

NIGERIAN INDEPENDENCE CONSTITUTIONALISM

Although Nigeria became free and independent in 1960, it was not without tears and hard political bargaining on the part of Nigerian political leaders with Her Britannic Majesty's imperial government. But as one Nigerian political leader, former President Nnamdi Azikiwe, described the whole process, "Nigeria got her independence on a platter of gold." Nigeria did not have to fight a war against Britain before independence, as was the case in French Indochina, or Portuguese Guinea Bissau, Mozambique, and Angola. The transfer of power was an extremely convivial occasion, bringing tears of joy from both the Nigerian and the British participants. Following the memorable midnight ceremony of September 30, 1960, Nigerian independence was ushered in during the early-morning hours of October 1, 1960.

The Independence Constitution of 1960 was a document produced as an order in council from Her Britannic Majesty, in London's Court of St. James. It named Nnamdi Azikiwe the queen's representative and the governor general of Nigeria. Accordingly, the queen of England continued, after independence, to be the queen and head of state of Nigeria. Sir Abubarkar Tafawa Balewa, as the leader of the Northern Peoples' Congress (NPC) that won the 1959 federal elections, became the first prime minister. In 1963, however, by an act passed by the Nigerian Parliament, the country became a Republic, though still remaining within the British Commonwealth of Nations.

The 1963 Constitutional Act changed nothing substantial, except to remove the queen as Nigeria's head of state and to designate the governor general president of the Republic—with mere ceremonial functions and few political powers. As became apparent during the Western Region crisis of 1963, and the election crisis of 1964, the president discovered that he had very little power under the Constitution to intervene in the political crisis. The prime minister, who apparently had all the powers, treated the Western Region crisis—in which there were two rival claimants to the position of the permier of that region—as an emergency situation. With the backing of the federal Parliament he controlled, he suspended that government and ruled the region through an administrator whom he had nominated. The weakness of presidential authority in an emergency was further demonstrated in the federal elections of 1964 at which grave allegations of rigging and electoral malpractices were made. To his chagrin, the president discovered that he had no power to nullify the results of such bizarre elections. He had no alternative but to comply with the formal Constitution and call on the person who appeared to command the majority of members on the floor of the federal Parliament to become the prime minister. Accordingly, Sir Abubarkar, leader of the NPC, continued to be Nigeria's prime minister in the 1965 government.

FAILURE OF THE FIRST REPUBLIC

The British had, in 1954, resolved to make Nigeria into a federation as a solution to the social and political problems that were apparent because of the heterogeneity of the Nigerian society. Although the Nigerian Federation was more likely to suffer the same fate as the East African Federation, the West Indies Federation, the Central African Federation or the Malayan Federation, the British persisted in launching it. Professor Kalu Ezera commented that it was the military coup of January 15, 1966, that, indeed, saved the country from disengagement into several nation-states as happened in the federations mentioned above.[5]

For a federation to be successful, no one unit of the constituent states can be so powerful as to overrule the rest or so manipulate the central government to be it own tool. The Northern Region of Nigeria was much larger than the other three regions put together, both in population and in area. The North, in consequence, was destined to dominate the central authorities indefinitely. This imbalance was a constant threat to the stability and unity of the Nigerian Federation.

The regions in Nigeria were created by the British to be coterminous with the three major tribes in Nigeria: The Hausa, the Yoruba, and the Igbo. The domineering attitude of these tribes in their respective regional governments, was equally a threat to the ethnic minorities in those regions. Because the large tribes were dominant in their respective regions, the regional governments operated on regional politics, which were dominated by tribal loyalties. Regionalism and tribalism thus became major evils in the first Nigerian Republic.

Because of regional politics, Nigeria had problems with national leadership. Nigeria failed to produce a dynamic objective and courageous leader at the center who had the vision and experience to face difficult political decisions with determination and resolution. Indeed, as Professor Kalu Ezera said, "leadership on the national scene was fickle and sick: it condoned compromise after compromise, even of crucial fundamental issues and specialized in the rare feat of walking on a tightrope." [6] Consequently, when the military took over in 1966, all Nigerians hailed them as the "saviors of the nation." [7]

The Republican Constitution of 1963 was notorious for being vague and ambiguous. As was stated earlier. the powers of the president were not clearly defined. The numerous provisions for fundamental human rights were surrounded with so many provisos and exceptions that it looked as if what was guaranteed with one hand was taken away with the other. For example, Section 19 (1) provided that "no person shall be subjected to torture or to unhuman or degrading punishment or other treatment." Subsection (2) immediately added that "nothing in this section shall invalidate any law by reason only that it authorises the infliction in any part of Nigeria of any punishment that was lawful and customary in that part on the first day of November, 1959." Such a provision obviously derogated from the essence of the rights already guaranteed and confirmed discriminatory practices and treatment of Nigerian citizens.

Worse than the formal constitutional weaknesses was the corruption of the body politic. Many people entered politics at very great expense to themselves by virtually buying each vote. Having secured a parliamentary seat in that manner, they had no intention of rendering honest and dedicated service to the people. Politics became an avenue of getting rich quickly by fair means or foul.

Soon after 1960, the clouds of the political storm had begun to gather. The first Republican government, flouting accepted British parliamentary practice, gave poor recognition to Chief Awolowo, the official opposition leader. His trial, conviction, and imprisonment under charges of "treasonable felony" in plotting to overthrow the federal government by force left the Western Region and twelve million Yoruba people without their popularly acclaimed political leader. The ensuing parliamentary crisis of that region in which there were two rival premiers, Adegbenro and Akintola, resulted in the breakdown of law and order in the West, creating a sense of frustration in the general population.

The census figures of 1963 were also in dispute. Although the NPC and the National Council of Nigerian Citizens (NCNC) were a coalition government in Lagos, the NCNC claimed that the North grossly inflated its census figures for political advantages. The

NCNC government in the Eastern Region took the federal prime minister to court to nullify the census figures, but without success. Also, a corrupt federal election in 1964 produced a crisis of confidence between the president and the prime minister.

Finally, there was the abortive military coup of some majors in January 1966. The federal prime minister, the federal finance minister, the premiers of Northern and Western Nigeria, and three senior military officers, one each from the North, the West, and the East were assassinated. With the president away from the country on an alleged health cruise, what was left of the federal cabinet panicked and handed over the government of the Federation to General Ironsi, head of the Nigerian army, which was still loyal to the government. General Ironsi was an Igbo, as were four of the six majors who precipitated the military coup. And because the North and the West lost senior civilian and military leaders, the Igbos as a group were blamed for the coup, and Ironsi's assumption of power was interpreted as an Igbo plot to rule Nigeria.

The assassination of the Northern premier, a direct descendant of Othman dan Fodio, the nineteenth-century religious leader that created ths Fulani Empire, was both a political and a religious tragedy. The Northern response to General Ironsi's assumption of power was the systematic killing of southerners, mainly Igbos, who were resident in the North. In July 1966, the killings included the assassination of General Ironsi himself and Colonel Fajuyi, the Yoruba governor of the West, who was hosting the general at the time. Yakubu Gowon, "another Northerner," took over the government, thus superseding the senior officers in the military hierarchy. This supersession created a crisis of confidence within the Nigerian military government. Ironsi's regime had been unable to deal as decisively and expeditiously as a government should with the original coup. Further, it attempted overcentralization of the Nigerian government. The succession regime of Gowon was unable to stop the killings that accompanied Ironsi's death and continued thereafter.

Tribal or subcultural nationalism, which had always lain dormant in the Nigerian political environment, was dramatically reactivated. It was such subcultural nationalistic loyalties which had induced the Northern peoples to present their own eight-point program at the 1954 Lyttelton Constitutional Conference in

London. There the North had stated that Nigeria was not one country and in effect asked for the right of the North to form a separate government and to secede from Nigeria. This same subcultural nationalism caused Chief Awolowo of the West to demand the insertion of a "secession clause" in the 1954 Lyttelton constitution. When his additional demand that Lagos become part of the Western Region was rejected, he threatened to pull Western Nigeria out of the Federation. The colonial secretary responded with a sharp warning that such an act would be treated as "secession by force" and would be met by equal force. In all these secession threats by the North in 1953 and the West in 1954, the Igbos and the Eastern government were the unflinching champion of a United Nigeria, which opposed dismemberment of the Federation.

constituted mainly of Igbos, completely disillusioned by the political incapacity of the then federal military government to protect their lives and property, pulled out of the Federation, and declared themselves the Republic of Biafra. The federal response was, like Lyttelton to Awolowo, to declare war on Biafra on July 6, 1967. The civil war continued for thirty months, until January 12, 1970, when Biafran resistance collapsed because of unmitigated and widespread hunger and starvation.

From the ashes of the thirty-month civil war, and from the economic stability based on the oil resources, a new Nigeria has arisen, resolved and determined to reconcile and reconstruct, to march together, recognizing the diversity and subcultural mosaic of the Nigerian society by the creation of nineteen states. In further demonstration of this resolve for a new Nigerian nation, the military regimes have assiduously pursued the task of drafting a new constitution.[9] A Constitutional Assembly of 223 members was duly elected in October 1977 and appointed to debate the draft constitution. A veteran politician and a Federal Supreme Court judge, Sir Udo Udoma, has been appointed chairman or speaker of the Nigerian Constitutional Assembly. These processes are prerequisites for Nigeria's return to civilian rule, envisaged by the military rulers for 1979.

NIGERIA'S HOMEGROWN CONSTITUTION

It is in the light of these factors that one must examine the marked departure of the Nigerian draft Constitution from parliamentary to presidential government and from capitalist economy to a more socialist-oriented political philosophy. The fifty-member Constitution Drafting Committee (CDC) were all Nigerian professional men,—politicians, academicians, and businessmen—except Professor J. B. Dudley, a black American who has been on the faculty of Nigeria's premier university at Ibadan for many years. Unfortunately, there were no women on the committee. Chief F.R.A. Williams, who was attorney general and minister of justice in the Western Region government under the 1954 Lyttelton constitution, was the chairman.

The CDC was set up by the federal military government in September 1975 and had its inaugural meeting in October. The committee held a two-day general debate on the basic cause of instability in Nigeria during the first Republic and the possible constitutional remedies which the draft must provide. It called for memorandums from the general public but rejected the idea of public hearings. In the next months it received a little over four hundred memorandums from persons in Nigeria and abroad. Concluding its work in August 1976, the committee was able to submit its report before the deadline of September 1976, one year after its establishment.

The CDC set up seven subcommittees to study various subjects, as follows:

1. Fundamental objectives and public accountability;
2. The executive and the legislature;
3. The judiciary;
4. The economy, finance, and division of power;
5. Citizenship, citizenship rights, fundamental rights, political parties, and electoral laws;
6. The public service, including the armed forces and the police

The seventh subcommittee had the responsibility of producing the first draft out of the various studies for the full committee's final consideration.

The final product, The Draft Constitution for Nigeria, contains 212 sections divided into 10 chapters or major headings. Seven schedules of details are attached to the Draft Constitution.

NIGERIAN CONSTITUTIONALISM: THE STRENGTHS AND WEAKNESSES OF THE DRAFT CONSTITUTION

We may now examine some of the strengths and weaknesses of the Draft Constitution in terms of its claim to constitutionalism. We would also examine the sources of these strengths and weaknesses from the background of traditional, colonial, and contemporary Nigerian experiences in constitutionalism. We would also examine the problems Nigeria had in drafting an American-type constitution with her British cultural background and constitutional experience.

GENERAL SOURCE OF STRENGTH

This is the first time that the Nigerians, by themselves, produced a draft constitution for the governance of their own people. In general terms, therefore, the strength of the Draft Constitution is that it is homegrown and the historic effort of a free people reacting to their recent and remote experiences to provide, in advance, well thought out rules by which the Nigerian people are to be governed. In the same document they have provided clear limits to the arbitrary political powers of future Nigerian democratic governments by predetermined rules.

In these attempts, the CDC wisely took a long look at what were regarded as the problems of the Nigerian society and the ills of the first Republican constitution and government. They took note of the history and behavior of the Nigerian politicians and public officeholders and inquired into the reasons for the lack of national unity. The CDC examined the causes that produced conflict and threats of disintegration of the Nigerian society. The drafters took note of the fact that "Commonwealth African Constitutions speak only in terms of power and rights, but never of duties." The latter, they said, are taken for granted.[10] The drafters considered that in a developing country like Nigeria, a constitution which is the fundamental law of the land should be categorical in stating the principle or ideology on which the state is organized. Such a document should spell out the ideals and objectives of the social order. The constitution should also "make it clear that powers are bestowed upon organs and institutions of government, not for the personal aggrandisement of those who wield them from time to time, but for the welfare and advancement of the society as a whole. It should, therefore impose on the state definite duties towards its subjects." [11]

The strength of the Draft Constitution is to be judged on its ability to provide solutions for the ills of the previous government and to lay a solid foundation for the future. In general terms, the Draft Constitution attacked this problem in four significant areas.

First, in order to secure "National Unity and Stability," the Draft, in Chapter 1, declares Nigeria once more a federation with nineteen states in place of four in the first Republic and twelve under the Gowon military regime. The Draft further stipulates in Chapter 2 that the federal government or any of its agencies must conduct their affairs "in such a manner as to recognize the federal character of Nigeria and the need to promote national unity and to command national loyalty." It stipulates that the predominance in the federal government or its agencies of persons from a few states or from a few ethnic or other sectional group is to be avoided.[12] Section 123 (2) of the Draft requires the president to conform with these provisions in selecting his ministers, so as to promote national unity and loyalty.

Second, it declares in Chapter 2 what it calls "Fundamental Objectives and Directives Principles of State Policy," consonant with the committee's views that, in developing countries, a constitution should no longer be just a catalogue of "powers and rights" but should contain what the duties of the government toward the subjects should be. Section 7 (1) of the Draft states quite clearly that all organs of government and all persons or authorities exercising executive, legislative, or judicial functions have "a duty and responsibility" to "conform, observe and apply the provisions" of these objectives and directives. Although these provisions are not justiciable in any court of law, they remain the guidelines on which the state and the officeholders are to be judged by the Nigerian people.

Third, in order to provide for and insure continuing effective leadership at the national level, the Draft in Chapter 4 creates a presidential form of government for Nigeria. Rejecting the Westminister parliamentary model and opting for a modified American presidential system, the CDC argued that the British system would hamper effective government in Nigeria because it depended on the legislature for its right to govern. Besides, the committee claimed that a plural executive by which the head of state and head of government are vested in two different persons would undermine responsibility. The CDC stated that a single chief executive could decide and act promptly, even if it meant imposing his will on his cabinet when they threatened to paralyze his government.[13]

Finally, because the CDC was aware of the danger inherent in a developing country of concentrating vast political power in one person's hands. it provided several checks and balances and guidelines for the public conduct of the president while he is in office. Accordingly, the Draft, in Section 128, creates twelve special bodies called "commissions" or "councils," which in fact share the executive functions of the president with him. The commissions, like the Civil Service Commission and the Electoral Commission, have direct executive functions to perform and are constitutionally independent and autonomous bodies. In the exercise of their executive functions, two of the commissions, the Civil Service and Police Service, are not subject to the direction or control of any other authority. In like manner, the National Population Commission is not subject to the direction or control of any other person or authority, which includes the person of the president.

Councils, such as the Council of State or the National Security Council, chaired by the president, advise the president in the constitutional exercise of his executive powers. It is envisaged that the president will act on a council's advice, or he must produce very convincing reasons to depart from it. In the alternative, the president will seek a compromise.

Although the Draft provides in Section 4 that no civil or criminal proceedings shall be instituted against the president. the vice-president, state governors, and deputy governors while they are in office, Section 117 makes very clear and elaborate provisions for the removal of the president or the vice-president by impeachment.

Althought the need for dynamic leadership at the center was the overriding purpose of establishing the executive president, the Draft has taken care to make adequate provisions to forestall the dangers of misrule or dictatorial tendencies in such a powerful individual. For example, the president must comply with certain rules in exercising power of appointment. For most appointments he must obtain the consent of the House of Representatives, the Senate, or the Council of State. The president is also enjoined to hold regular meetings with the vice-president and all ministers of the government of the Federation for determining the general direction of domestic and foreign policy of the federal government and for coordinating the discharge of his executive responsibilities. It may be recalled that the cabinet of the American president is not a constitutionally designated body, nor must the president call it into regular meeting.

The major weakness of the Nigerian presidential model may be found generally in the fact that the Draft overcircumscribed the president with constitutional limits in the attempt to prevent him from being a despot or a dictator. The Nigerian president may not, after all, have the same scope and freedom to use his initiative or have the flexibility the American president has. The various commissions and councils provide too many checks. Not only must the president consult his cabinet regularly, he must act on their advice, and in other matters act only on the advice of the various constitutional bodies. Further, by being required to select his ministers and make various national appointments reflecting diverse ethnic groups, the president is denied the real opportunity to select the best people for the government. The Constitution's emphasis on guarding against fragmentation lessens the likelihood of achieving national unity. For these reasons, the Nigerian Constitution may produce a president who must continually compromise, very much like the prime minister of the parliamentary system.

Because his ministers have a right to participate in the debates in the National Assembly, the president may be forced by circumstances to frequent the Assembly also, in order to explain some of his actions. It is very probable that the strong chief executive with effective leadership, which was the goal of the switch from parliamentary to presidential, may not, after all, be attainable in the Nigerian model.

Political parties have been banned in Nigeria since 1966, and no date has yet been set for the resuscitation of political activities. When parties are revived, moreover, they come under elaborate provisions for their control in the Draft Constitution. Yet this control of political activites by predetermined constitutional rules derogates very much from the essential elements of democratic principles and may reduce party activities to a one-party system, which would eventually lead to a one-party state. For example, Section 170 interprets the word "association" to include ethnic, social, and cultural bodies. Section 171 provides that no association other than a political party should canvass for votes for any candidate in any election or contribute to the funds for electing any candidate. Section 172, however, makes it obligatory that membership in any political party must be open to all Nigerian citizens irrespective of their place of origin, religion, ethnic group, or sex.

INFLUENCE OF THE NIGERIAN TRADITIONAL SYSTEM ON THE DRAFT

In precolonial Nigerian society, age was an important factor in holding traditional political office. Elders, who were the political decision-makers, were credited with wisdom because of their age and experience. They were to be persons of honor, integrity, and respect, serving their community selflessly and loyally and following traditional codes of behavior. Public officeholders were expected to be honorable in their public and private affairs and truthful, fair, and impartial in the discharge of their administrative and judicial functions. They were expected to promote unity and harmony in the community. The Draft Constitution seems to have drawn some strengths from this traditional, precolonial culture. The Draft prescribes minimum age of twenty-one years for members of the House of Representatives, thirty-five years for senators, forty years for the president, and fifty years for members of the Electoral Commissions.

Although the powerful executive chieftain did not exist in all Nigerian communities, particularly in the so-called chiefless or stateless societies, traditional African political organization has its parallel both in the single executive or in an executive president associated with, and limited by, a council. Thus the Draft's executive president, surrounded with statutory commissions and a kind of council of elders, the Council of State, is amply supported by tradition.[14]

The Council of State includes former presidents, former chief justices, and one chief representing each state of the nation. The functions of the council, among other things, are to "constitutionally advise" the president on matters connected with the thorny national population census in Nigeria, including the acceptance or rejection of the hitherto disputable and controversial census figures. The Council of State is to advise the president on matters concerning the exercise of his powers under prerogative of mercy, award of national honors, and the maintenance of public order within the Federation.[15] Another feature of the Draft that dates back to traditional Nigeria is the provision in Schedule 4 of a "Code of Conduct" for public officers. It is comparable to traditional codes of conduct prescribed for elders and titled officeholders.

A weakness in the Draft, however, may be seen in its lack of incorporation, in some way, of traditional Nigerian symbols such as language or motifs. For example, Ghana's Constitution incorporated by convention the traditional drumming by Asante royal drummers in announcing the arrival of the president into Ghana's National Assembly and other state functions. The pouring of a libation to the ancestral spirits of Ghana has also been elevated to a national ritual and symbol, a prelude to the saying of national prayer. Another example is the swearing-in ceremony of the president of Nigeria, which should be followed by the handing over to him of a "traditional staff of office" designated to represent the Federation of Nigeria. This staff should be the symbol of Nigeria's unity, which the president is expected to preserve and protect. The use of the *kakaki,* or special trumpet, to herald the arrival of the president at state occasions would incorporate Nigeria's traditional rituals, as is done in Ghana.

INFLUENCE OF THE COLONIAL SYSTEM

The Draft Constutution, in Chapter 4, draws some strength from the colonial constitution by enunciating more forcefully the fundamental human rights and freedoms without the colonial restrictions, provisos, and abridgments. Prominent among the fundamental rights and freedoms now established are the right to life; the dignity of the human person; personal liberty; fair hearing or due process; private and family life; freedom of thought, conscience, and religion; freedom of expression; peaceful assembly; freedom from discrimination; and freedom of property ownership. During an emergency, however, some of these fundamental rights and freedoms are subject to curtailment.

On the other hand, the Draft has evidently inherited the fears held by colonial governments against freedom of the press and freedom of expression. While Section 32 (1) of the Draft provides that "every person shall be entitled to freedom of expression, including freedom to hold opinion and to receive and impart ideas and information without interference" and subsection (2) provides that "every person shall be entitled to own, establish and operate any medium for the dissemination of information, ideas and opinions," the same Subsection (2) states that "no person other than the Government of the Federation or a state or any other person or body authorised by the President, shall own, establish or operate a television or wireless broadcasting station for any purpose whatsoever."

The real constitutional dangers to free expression lie not just in the government monopoly of radio and television, however. More important, the military government has bought interests in some of the leading newspapers in the country, and the government has thus been involved in the direct control of the major news media. Alhaji Babatunde Jose, doyen of Nigerian newspaper editors and a member of the Nigerian Constituent Assembly, speaking on the freedom of the press, has stated that Nigeria's past experience should have suggested the need for more specific protections for freedom of the press.[16]

INFLUENCE OF AFRICAN AND
CONTEMPORARY SYSTEMS

The Draft has drawn further strength from contemporary events in Nigeria and abroad. The CDC looked at the constitutions of several other countries in Africa in order to provide in advance against forces of instability. It also tried to provide for more effective leadership, which is necessary if Nigeria is to develop economically and socially. After examining the African scene, the CDC concluded that African executives, especially presidents under parliamentary government, were never satisfied with playing mere ceremonial roles: they wanted action and power. Accordingly, the dual executive of the parliamentary system has always yielded to that of a single chief executive. For the provision of social and economic rights the CDC looked at India, Pakistan, and the provisions of the United Nations Charter in similar needs. The "Directive Principles" was modeled after the Indian Constitution and the "Principles of State Policy" was drawn from the Pakistan Constitution. The example of incorporating a code of conduct into the written Constitution was drawn from Tanzanian and Zambian experiences. The two have codes of conduct, originally for party members, incorporated into their constitutions for all public office holders.[17] The most recent experience of the civil war gave the Nigerian Draft the urge to provide, as it were, "for a more perfect union" among the peoples of Nigeria. As had been said, Chapter 2 "directs" in very eloquent terms what would be necessary to keep all parts of the country involved in the administration of the Nigerian nation. With all its bold attempts the Draft has not solved all the ills of Nigeria and certainly has not met the desire of some minorities who want to have their own state.[18] The solution does not lie in making it impossible to create more states but in accommodating every ethnic group by making them feel that they belong to the Nigerian nations.

PROBLEMS OF DRAFTING AN AMERICAN-TYPE CONSTITUTION WITH BRITISH CONSTITUTIONAL HERITAGE

As should be expected, the attempt to write an American presidential-type consitution by and for people whose society had developed largely on British heritage—language, political economy, parliamentary system, the legal and judicial systems, and education—was beset by problems. The historical origins of the United States and Nigerian societies are so different that the motivating force of individual freedom and liberty which impelled the American founding fathers to declare themselves independent of the British monarchy in 1776 are totally lacking in Nigerian society.

A comparison of the preambles of the American Constitution and that of the Draft Nigerian Constitution show only one common objective—in the United States, the desire "to form a more perfect Union," and in Nigeria to consolidate "the unity of our people." Nigerian lawyers and members of the Drafting Committee were trained in British law and legal drafting techniques. The result is evident in the wordiness required to explain what the drafters meant in very clear terms. For example, the American Constitution has five chapters or articles, with twenty-one sections altogether, and twenty-three amendments, covering twenty pages of a given-size paper, but the Nigerian Draft contains 10 chapters, with 212 sections and seven schedules, covering 42 pages of the same-size paper.

The American presidential pattern involves rigid separation of the personnel of the executive and the legislature, as well as clear separation of powers between the three organs of government. Neither the U.S. president nor the members of U.S. executive branch are members of Congress nor may U.S. ministers participate in any debate in the Senate or the House of Representatives. But the British political ethos brings the head of state, like the queen, as a constituent part of the legislature. This tradition influenced the Nigerian Draft to establish a legislature composed of the president, the Senate, and the House of Representatives.[19] Although the intention is not to fuse the executive with the legislature, as is the case in the parliamentary system, the expression did not indicate clear separation of powers, as in the American system. Because the Nigerian elite are more socialized into the British parliamentary system, the Draft provided, as stated earlier, for the ministers in the president's cabinet to attend and participate in the proceedings in the Senate and the House.

The American model vested judicial powers in the one Supreme Court. Accordingly, judicial finality is vested in that Court also. The British, however, have allowed plurality in judicial finality—the House of Lords for domestic cases and the Judicial Committee of Her Majesty's Privy Council for colonial cases and Commonwealth countries. The Nigerian Draft seems to have introduced plurality in judicial finality also. Section 179 (1) provides that the judicial power of the Federation should be vested in the Supreme Court. Subsection (2) provides also for the judicial powers of the states to be vested in the Supreme Court, the Federal Court of Appeal, and the Federal Sharia Court of Appeal as applicable.

Anomalously, the Federal Sharia Court of Appeal appears to be elevated in terms of judicial finality so as to rank as co-equal with the Supreme Court. The Sharia courts are special courts that hear civil cases under the Muslim law. It has been argued that, although it was necessary to provide Sharia courts in the states, all appeals from state Sharia courts, like all other cases from the states, should be heard by the one Federal Court of Appeal. It has been suggested that the Federal Court of Appeal should have a division competent to hear appeals in which Muslim civil law is involved. The provision of two federal courts of appeal, the "Sharia Court" for Muslim cases and the "Federal Courts" for everyone else, including Muslims, is not only a duplication of efforts but discriminatory in favor of the Muslim members of the Federation.[20]

It looks as if the drafters clearly intended to have this duality in judicial finality, for Section 182 (1) gave the Supreme Court exclusive jurisdiction to hear and determine appeals only from the Federal Court of Appeal and the Code of Conduct Tribunal. Section 184 (1) also gave the Federal Sharia Court of Appeal exclusive jurisdiction to hear and determine appeals from state Sharia courts. Since no further mention was made in Section 182 (1) about the power of the Supreme Court to hear and determine appeals from the Federal Sharia Court of Appeal, it follows that it has been excluded from supervising the Federal Sharia Court of

Appeal. Such clear exclusion makes the Federal Sharia Court of Appeal the final court for all Muslim cases and a coequal of the Supreme Court in possessing judicial finality in some respects: the Muslim law. This duplication of judicial finality is characteristic of the British system which, no doubt, has influenced the Nigerian drafters.

CONCLUDING REMARKS

Two important questions immediately arise from this discussion of Nigerian constitutionalism. First, has the Draft Consitution so overcircumscribed the president with constitutional rules that he can no longer be the effective, dynamic leader that the drafters sought to create? Second, will the Nigerian masses be able to participate actively in politics as they traditionally did in the precolonial days?

With regard to the first question, it looks as if the Nigerian president is very much restricted by constitutionalism. It looks as if his job would be to see that the twelve councils and commissions act in accordance with the Constitution and that every government agent complies with the directive principles and the code of conduct. But this image is, indeed, misleading. Nigerian traditional chiefs and leaders have always been circumscribed by a code of conduct, a council of elders, titled societies, and secret societies. In the egalitarian societies, the leader's real role is to secure consensus and establish a compromise solution. The ability to do just this earns ths leader great support, followership, and effectiveness. An effective leader in the heterogeneous Nigerian society must reckon with a multitude of tribal and ethnic considerations. The various councils and commissions are created to do just that within their executive authority. The approval of various presidential nominees by the Senate, the Council of State, or the House of Representatives means that the chief executive must seek the strategy that the majority of ethnics would support. His role is not like that of the prime minister, whose authority to continue to rule is always tied with the support of the legislature. Indeed, the Nigerian president has the potential to rule much more justly than a prime minister. The president must satisfy the whole country, with all its diversity, rather than just the legislature.

With regard to the second question, traditional mass participation was highly successful only in small-scale societies. It is, therefore, doubtful how much the masses would really want to participate on a regular basis with Nigeria-wide issues, Except for the election of the chief executive, the masses would have little interest beyond events in their own villages.

In anticipation for this local interest and participation, the Draft provides in Schedule 3 very detailed duties and functions of the local government councils. The councils are to participate in what may be called "the politics of development," because they have the responsibility to make recommendations to the State Economic Planning Commission on the economic development of the state. In making their recommendations, the councils primarily are to take into consideration the needs of their own areas. The emphasis laid by the Constitution on local government indicates the importance of mass participation at the local level.

It is to be hoped that the Nigerian masses, themselves, are ready to cooperate with the government and all its agencies in accepting the discipline that is necessary in a democracy.

Constitutionalism is a man-made device to limit the arbitrariness of governments. Good government insures justice. Good government requires the vigilance of all the people to see that power-holders conform with the Constitution.

NOTES

1. B. Nwabueze, *Constitutionalism in the Emergent States* (Rutherford: Farleigh Dickinson University Press, 1973), pp.1-3. See also B. Nwabueze, *Presidentialism in Commonwealth Africa* (St. Martin's Press, 1974). The two works of Nwabueze are invaluable in this study. Professor Nwabueze was a member of the Constitution Drafting Committee and the Chairman of the Sub-Committee on Fundamental Objectives and Public Accountability.

2. For more insight into constitutionalism in traditional African government, see Nwabueze's two books, *op cit.*

3. There are well over 200 distinguishable groups of societies in Nigeria. The three most populous are the Hausa/Fulani in the North, about 35 million; the Yoruba in southwest Nigeria, 12 million; the Igbo in

south central Nigeria, 12 million. For a closer study of the subnational groups in Nigeria, consult F.A.O. Swartz *Nigeria* (M.I.T. Press, 1965); J.S. Coleman, *Nigeria* (Berkeley, 1958); M. Crowder, *Short History of Nigeria* (Faber, 1966).

4. For a more detailed study of the Lugard and colonial era, the following books should be consulted: A.H.M. Kirk-Greene, *Lugard and the Amalgamation of Nigeria* (Frank Cass, 1968); I. F. Nicolson, *The Administration of Nigeria, 1900-1960* (O.U.P., 1969); Kalu Ezera, *The Constitutional Development of Nigeria* (Cambridge, 1964).

5. See Kalu Ezera, "The Failure of Nigerian Federalism and Proposed Constitutional Changes," *African Forum* 1966), p. 17.

6. *Ibid.*, p. 20.

7. Between January 17 and 20, 1966, all the leading Nigerian newspapers, the Times, The *West African Pilot, the Morning Post,* all in Lagos, came out with strong editorials in support of the army for taking over from the civilian government. On May 26, 1966, when the military unified Nigerian administration, these same newspapers extolled them.

8. In his first speech to the nation after taking over power in August 1966, General Gowon described himself as Yakubu (the Muslim word for Jacob, his Christian name), and as "another northerner" who has come to head the government of Nigeria. These were interpreted as political moves to assuage the wounded feelings of the North in the loss of their political leadership, and to assure them that the government of Nigeria would always remain. in the hands of a northerner.

9. The CDC has published a two-volume report on its work. Volume I contains the report of the CDC and the Draft Constitution. Volume II contains reports of the work of the various committees before they were reconciled into one report as in vol. I.

10. Report of the Constitutional Drafting Committee, vol. I, p. v; vol. II, p. 35, hereinafter referred to as CDC Report.

11. *Ibid.*, vol. I, pp. v!vi; vol. II, pp. 35 and 36.

12. Section 8 (2).

13. CDC Report, vol. I, p. xxx.

14. For a more detailed reading on African forms of constitutionalism, see Professor Nwabueze's two books, *op. cit.*

15. Section 137.

16. *West Africa,* no. 3149 (November 14, 1977), p. 2290.

17. See CDC Report, vol II, pp. 39 and 40.

18. The debates in the Constituent Assembly give this impression. See

West Africa, no. 3151 (November 28, 1977). Although Mr. M. T. Mbu was reported not to have pressed the issue of creation of Ikom-Obubra state, it is clear that as a seasoned diplomat he had said enough for interested parties to know what he means.

19. Section 42.
20. See *West Africa*, no. 3151 (November 28, 1977, pp. 2395 and 2397.

PART III

8

CONSTITUTIONALISM: AN ANALYTIC FRAMEWORK

THOMAS C. GREY

Constitutionalism is one of those concepts, evocative and persuasive in its connotations yet cloudy in its analytic and descriptive content, which at once enrich and confuse political discourse. The long-standing confusion about the meaning of the term appears in the numerous mutually inconsistent simple definitions that have been confidently asserted in its name. Thus, Gierke wrote that "the principle of popular sovereignty never played any serious part in the theory of constitutionalism," [1] while Tom Paine insisted that the essence of a constitution was that it be "the act of a ... people constituting a government." [2] Paine also thought a true constitution had to be both written and supreme law;[3] Bentham thought constitutional law had to be written but should not be supreme; [4] while Professor McIlwain insisted only that constitutions must at least be law: "constitutionalism has one essential quality; it is a legal limitation on government." [5] What these three inconsistent definitions have in common is only their insistence that a constitution must be legal in character, and even that proposition most students of the British constitution would deny.[6]

More promising than these summary definitions of constitutionalism are the three familiar distinctions, each of which has been thought to divide constitutions into their two fundamental categories. The oldest and best known of these is the distinction between written and unwritten constitutions. Lord Bryce called that distinction "old-fashioned" and "superficial" and offered as a substitute the distinction between rigid and flexible constitutions.[7] Finally, Dicey suggested the distinction between the conventions and the law of the constitution as the key to understanding the varieties of constitutionalism.[8]

In truth, all three of these are useful distinctions when properly understood, but even when added together to provide a six-way division of the conceptual field occupied by the idea of constitutionalism, they do not provide an adequate analytic scheme for the study of the relevant phenomena. What follows has the modest aim of suggesting such an analytic scheme—a vocabulary for the classification and comparison of different kinds of constitutions and constitutional practices. It is a pure exercise in formalism, not purporting to deal with substantive and normative problems, offered only with the excuse that a little form may help clarify the substance.

The scheme of analysis is founded on two basic premises. The first is that the primary object of discourse in the study of constitutionalism should be constitutional *norms,* and not entire constitutions. A given constitution may not be classifiable as written or unwritten, rigid or flexible—to mention some of the traditional categories of analysis—because a single system, a single constitution, may contain written and unwritten, flexible and rigid norms. For example, the British constitution as commonly understood contains both customary "unwritten" principles and "written" statutes. Similarly, the body of American federal constitutional law contains both rigid principles (those not subject to change by legislation) and flexible ones (which can be altered by federal statute).[9]

The second premise is a negative one: there is no reason to suppose that an adequate conceptual analysis of constitutionalism must produce a *definition,* a set of necessary and sufficient conditions which justify either describing a norm as constitutional or describing a set of norms as a constitution. The focus on definition leads to largely verbal dispute, or to stipulative fiat masquerading as discovery or analysis. A debate about whether the British constitution is *really* a constitution insofar as it is not legally binding would involve effort misdirected from the more fruitful endeavor of analyzing and evaluating the actual differences between the British and American (or French) styles of constitutionalism. The group of ideas, institutions, and practices gathered under the terminological umbrella of the term "constitution" may bear "family resemblances" to each other without necessarily sharing any single quality or small group of qualities as their common essence.[10]

With these two premises as background, the framework of analysis can be introduced. Constitutional norms can be classified along three significant dimensions. First, they may have different normative force or hierarchical *status*. Some constitutional norms are purely *extralegal* in status: these are the "merely" customary, moral, or political norms. Others impose legal requirements, and of these, some have the status only of *ordinary law,* while others have the status of *fundamental law.* Second, constitutional norms (at least those conceived as legally binding) vary in their method of *enforcement.* Some are left entirely to *political* enforcement; others are subject to *special* ("nonpolitical") enforcement devices and institutions, including the various forms of judicial review. Third, constitutional norms differ in the source of their authority. Some derive their force from *enactment;* these are what have traditionally been called the "written" constitutional norms. Of the remaining ("unwritten") constitutional norms, some derive their authority from *acceptance* in the relevant community ("customary" or "traditional" constitutional norms), while others are founded on the claim that they express moral or political *truth* ("natural law" norms).

THE STATUS OF CONSTITUTIONAL NORMS

The first dimension along which constitutional norms may be arrayed is the dimension of force or hierarchical *status*. In order of increasing status, constitutional norms may be *extralegal,* they may have the force of *ordinary law,* or they may have the force of higher or *fundamental* law. The last of these is by far the most significant in the contemporary world, though the first two play a large role in the history of constitutionalism.

Extralegal Norms

The unwritten British constitution provides the best-known examples of norms limiting government that are generally considered at the same time constitutional in status and yet lacking in legal force. The British monarch, for example, has the legal power to prevent a bill that has passed both houses of Parliament from becoming law by withholding the royal assent. Similarly, the monarch may legally dismiss a ministry that still has a working majority in Parliament. Britons would describe such actions as "unconstitutional," indeed as gross violations of their constitution. But the principles the monarch would have violated in taking these actions are not considered to be legal restrictions, but rather only—in the term introduced by Dicey—"conventions of the constitution." [11] These unconstitutional royal actions would not be disturbed by British courts, but to say that these norms of the British constitution are extralegal is to say still more than that. There can be constitutional restrictions that, although not judicially enforceable, are thought of as legally binding, in the sense that official violation of them are naturally criticized as "illegal" or "contrary to law"—a point to be discussed in more detail in the next section. The British "conventions of the constitution" are not of legal character even in this relatively weak sense.

There may be some American analogies to these extralegal norms of the British constitution. First, some unwritten customs generally thought to be without legal force nevertheless are deep-seated features of our governmental system. Examples might be some aspects of our two-party system; the tradition that members of the electoral college will vote for the candidate for president and vice president in whose name they have been listed on the ballot; and perhaps some features of the separation between military office and civilian government—would not the objections to an active chairman of the Joint Chiefs of Staff serving as president be properly described as constitutional or at least "quasi-constitutional" in character? [12] In at least one case, constitutional tradition became constitutional law. After Franklin Roosevelt successfully defied the traditional requirement that presidents should not serve more than two terms, it was enacted as a formal constitutional restriction through the process of amendment.[13]

Second, besides these unwritten and extralegal but arguably "quasi-constitutional" traditions, one might consider those provisions of American state constitutions that appear rather to state general ideals of good government than to impose legal restrictions. For example, the Virginia Declaration of Rights provides (in language repeated in the subsequently enacted constitutions of many other states) that the people shall have the right both to pursue and to "obtain" happiness.[14] It further provides that the community has the right to "alter or abolish" its government when that government shall be found "inadequate."[15] These stirring provisions are surely constitutional norms, yet they seem better characterized as extralegal ideals than as legal requirements.

Ordinary Law

The British constitution does not consist entirely of the extralegal usages that Dicey called "conventions." Matters such as the respective powers of the Houses of Parliament and the selection of the House of Commons are regulated by law. The more important of these legal provisions are commonly thought of as parts of the constitution, though they differ from the norms of most other modern constitutions in having formal legal status no greater than that of ordinary legislation. In the history of constitutionalism, there have occasionally been constitutions which were entirely statutory, subject to amendment by the ordinary process of legislative enactment—the 1848 Italian Constitution and the present New Zealand Constitution are examples.[16] Jeremy Bentham's model constitution, which with its text and commentary fills an entire volume of his collected works, was proposed as an ordinary statute—a Benthamite "Code"—which would be subject to ordinary legislative amendment.[17]

Though constitutional norms with the status of ordinary law do not bulk large in practical significance today, the existence of this category suggests one of the ways in which the field of constitutionalism is marked off from other norms. British constitutional statutes, and the entirely statutory constitutions just mentioned, differ from the rest of the ordinary norms of the legal systems, not by virtue of their legal force or their origin, but by virtue of their subject matter. Constitutional norms in this sense are, roughly, the more important of those rules that define, distribute, and restrict the institutions and powers of government. But this characterization should not be thought of as stating necessary conditions for describing something as a constitutional norm. Other norms with the status of fundamental law, particularly those placed in a document labeled a constitution, are often quite properly characterized as constitutional in character. Examples of provisions in the United States Constitution which do not confine themselves to public law matters are the Thirteenth Amendment, which prohibits slavery or involuntary servitude, and the now repealed Eighteenth (Prohibition) Amendment.[18] No useful purpose would be served by describing these provisions as not *truly* constitutional norms.

Fundamental Law

Just as Dicey distinguished between the law and the conventions of the constitution, so Bryce distinguished between flexible and rigid constitutions. According to Bryce's distinction, if the constitution can be changed by the ordinary procedure of statutory enactment, it is flexible; if amendment requires an extraordinary and more difficult procedure, it is rigid. Since extralegal norms such as the British usages and customs making up the conventions of the constitutions cannot be changed at all by deliberate action—though they can evolve, and though they can be supplanted by legal norms—it is evident that Bryce's distinction applies only to constitutional norms with legal force.

The distinction presented here, between constitutional norms with the status of fundamental law and those with the status of ordinary law, is for practical purposes probably equivalent to the "rigid-flexible" distinction proposed by Bryce, though in this analysis the categories apply to norms rather than entire constitutions. Law is fundamental when it is accepted as controlling in cases of conflict with ordinary law. This description leaves to intuitive recognition what is to constitute "ordinary" law; statutes take precedence over municipal ordinances not because the statutes are fundamental but because the ordinances are "inferior law." The conceptual difference between the "flexible-rigid" and the "ordinary-fundamental" distinctions arises from the absence of any logical compulsion that law with fundamental status *must* be subject to a different enactment procedure than ordinary law—one can at least imagine a system in which a legislature could use precisely the same procedure to pass two classes of laws, ordinary and fundamental, and courts would be directed to give effect to earlier-adopted fundamental laws over even later adopted ordinary ones. It is more difficult to imagine why one should want to adopt such a system.

As further warning against the attempt to find defining characteristics of constitutional norms, it must be pointed out that hierarchical superiority over ordinary law is not a sufficient condition for describing a legal rule as a constitutional norm. In the United States (and indeed in all federal systems), valid central government legislation takes precedence over the ordinary statutes of the states or other constituent members of the federation. And even within a unitary legal system, statutes adopted by initiative and referendum may be superior to statutes adopted by the ordinary legislative process, and yet not be considered as constitutional norms—indeed they are themselves typically inferior to constitutional norms, which have normally been adopted by a more onerous procedure, perhaps a referendum requiring a supermajority.

THE ENFORCEMENT OF CONSTITUTIONAL NORMS

Who is to interpret and enforce legally binding constitutional norms? For Americans accustomed to the native tradition flowing from *Marbury* v. *Madison* [19] a single natural response is likely: the courts of law must have the last word in interpeting the Constitution and must enforce it through judgments disposing of lawsuits coming before the courts in the ordinary course of judicial business. The American tendency to link legal constitutionalism with judicial review is reinforced by one school of positivist jurisprudence, which insists that the linkage is a conceptually necessary one—that constitutional norms not enforced in courts of law are *by definition* only extralegal norms. But an adequate theory of constitutionalism must resist the American and positivist tendency to equate legal constitutionalism with judicial review if it is to avoid theoretical dogmatism and parochialism about the varieties of legal culture.

There are a number of mechanisms of constitutional enforcement, but for purposes of analysis they can usefully be divided into two rough classes—the "political" and the "special." Mature legal systems typically have institutions authorized to make law guided by what might be called the general or "all-things-considered" standard, the standard of "the common good" or "the public interest." These typically include legislative bodies and may also include the electorate acting through referendums and the executive acting through a veto power. Where institutions authorized to apply this "all-things-considered" standard to the making or invalidating or ordinary laws also have the final authority to interpret and enforce a constitutional norm that might come into conflict with those laws, the mechanism for the enforcement of that norm will be said to be "political." By contrast, where a constitutional norm is subject to authoritative interpretation by an institution that does not have authority to apply the "all-things considered" standard to the ordinary laws, the enforcement mechanism for that norm is "special."

Political Enforcement

Constitutional norms are subject to political enforcement if the decision of ordinary lawmaking and law-approving bodies is final on the question of the constitutionality of laws that arguably conflict with them. In some systems, there are no special institutions of constitutional enforcement, and hence all constitutional enforcement is political. In other systems, special enforcement (such as judicial review) exists in some instances, but in others enforcement is political only; this is the situation in the United States, where, though most constitutional norms are judicially enforceable, situations remain in which final constitutional decisions are left to political institutions.[20]

Are constitutional norms subject only to political enforcement properly considered legally binding norms? Is not a constitutional norm, nominally restraining a legislature, but subject to authoritative construction by that same legislature, really only a moral or extralegal limitation? The challenge raises an old and much-debated issue in jurisprudential theory, the question whether a norm can be characterized as legal only if it is backed by some form of institutional sanction or remedy. Most contemporary legal philosophers, even those of a positivistic bent, have tended to reject the Bentham-Austin-Kelsen position that as a matter of logic there can be no law without a sanction, no legal right without a remedy.[21] The analytic scheme proposed here follows that contemporary tendency, which in the context of constitutional norms preserves an important distinction.

The claim that constitutional norms not enforced by special institutions like judicial review are *extralegal* resembles the traditional "hard positivist" claim that international law is *not law*.[12] In each case, the claim has on its side the always useful insight that when legislatures, or nation-states, are left free to interpret the legal norms meant to restrain their own powers, they will naturally have a greater tendency to find justification than might a more independent body. Norms are more likely to be effective if externally enforced. But this is the kind of useful observation that can readily be kept in mind without resorting to radical definitional claims that exclude such norms from the field of law altogether. For instance, it is also true that positive laws are likely to be more efficacious when they are consistent with deeply rooted social mores and behavior patterns than when they are not. Yet it would be an odd and inappropriate way of expressing this observation to claim that regularly enacted and regularly enforced statutes, which run strongly counter to prevailing mores and for that reason are relatively likely to be frequently violated, are on that account *not law*.

This is in no way to denigrate the importance of a realistic sociology of law. The distinction between law in action and law on the books is worthy of constant attention, in the study of constitutionalism as in the study of other legal phenomena. But to attend realistically to the actual relationships between norms, attitudes, and behavior is by no means the same thing as automatically to classify constitutional norms as extralegal because they lack external enforcement mechanisms. Norms of constitutional law differ from extralegal norms in significant ways, quite apart from any enforcement mechanisms they may have. Many officials sincerely believe that they are under a particularly stringent sort of obligation to comply with the legal requirements surrounding their official role. Those who have no such belief, or who are generally not much moved by the tugs of conscience, know that other officials, and the public generally, believe in the specially binding force of legal obligation and may adjust their behavior accordingly. Personal and political enemies are given especially potent ammunition if they can plausibly argue that an official has flouted the law; partisan opponents of proposed legislation have their practical position noticeably strengthened when they can claim with some support that the contested bill is unconstitutional, quite apart from the likelihood that the courts will strike it down.

The character of the response that is called for by the charge that an official action or a proposed law is unconstitutional is quite different on the whole from the response summoned by the claim that it violates tradition, morality, or standards of good policy. In questions of constitutional law as in questions of international law, such a charge brings the paraphernalia of legal argument into play: precedents are cited, analogized and distinguished; law books are examined; learned commentators are consulted or asked to testify. If the constitutional (or, to continue the analogy, the international) standard is truly a legal one, it generally has sufficiently definite content to permit only a moderately restricted range of disagreement among the informed as to what it permits. Where the standard simply directs government to act as is right, just, or in the public interest, it is fair to say that the standard is not legal at all. However, it should be noted that standards phrased in sweeping terms of this sort are sometimes legal standards of a different sort—instructions to courts or other decision-makers to apply a set of genuinely legal and more determinate standards immanent in the shared case-by-case intuitions of the commmunity. The legal standard of reasonable care used in accident law is an example of this sort of norm, as are some vague constitutional provisions.[23]

The paraphernalia summoned forth by the challenge to the legality of a law or official action can be simply a charade, trotted out to camouflage a predetermined and unalterable decision reached on other grounds. And this is probably more often the case when the legal decision is made by the very institution the legal norm was designed to check. But the results of institutional decisions are very often *not* predetermined when the legal apparatus is injected into the process—whether for reasons of the decision-makers' own conscientious sense of fidelity to law, the political divisions among them, or their need to reconcile the public to the decision before it can be implemented. In these instances a distinction of real import is abandoned if one purports to apply Occam's razor to lop off the concept of a restraining norm that is legal in character though it lacks external institutional enforcement.

Consider some examples from American experience The Constitution requires that members of the House of Representatives meet certain qualifications: they must be at least twenty-five years old, citizens of the United States, and residents of the state they represent.[24] At the same time the Constitution makes the House the "judge" of the qualifications of its members, and this has generally been taken to preclude any judicial review of the House's determination that an elected member has failed to meet one of the enumerated qualifications.[25] In terms of constitutional law backed by sanctions or remedies, the House is thus "free" to exclude an unpopular member-elect on the grounds of age by finding that he is twenty-three although he is in fact thirty-six, or that he is not a resident of the state although he has never left it in his life. But it is difficult to believe that any such determination would be made, however strongly a majority of the House might prefer to have the member-elect excluded. The very existence of the standards of qualification as part of the Constitution, which is in its own terms the supreme law of the land, and which every member of Congress has taken an oath to support, realistically places an important check on the freedom of action of congressmen. The check may be that of conscience, of public opinion, or of pressure from other congressmen who take (or purport to take) the constitutional restriction seriously.

Similarly, in other instances in which the Constitution imposes restrictions on the political branches of government which for one reason or another may not be enforceable in court, the very fact that the constitutional check is seen as legal in character imposes a more than merely adminitory restraint. The president and other civil officers are to be impeached only for "high crimes and misdemeanors"; judges are to be free from removal "during good behavior." [26] In each case, the House as the charging body and the Senate as the trier of the charge are thought jointly to have the last word on whether these standards are met.[27] The character of the impeachment process as one controlled by legal standards whose final interpretation is left to the two houses is very different from what it would be if the process were unguided by constitutional standards. The absence of judicial review does not make an impeachable offense "whatever a majority of the House of Representatives considers it to be." [28] The general acceptance that the issue is partly a legal one gives a very different tone to an impeachment proceeding than, say, to a vote of no confidence in the British Parliament. Charges are preferred; only evidence arguably relevant to the charges is openly considered; the meaning of the impeachment standard is debated in lawyers' terms, with attention to the language and background of the impeachment clauses, and the precedent developed under it.

None of this absolutely excludes the possibility that all the legal trappings are only a charade. The fact that Congress proclaims itself to be bound by the Constitution, that it debates an issue in terms of constitutional law, *might* have absolutely no effect on the actual process of decision. But to assume that this *must* be the case, in the face of the common human experience that the forms, ideals, and rhetoric which surround a decision process often substantively affect the outcome of that process, is surely to succumb to the contemporary penchant for crackpot realism.

Special Enforcement

Constitutional norms are subject to special enforcement when, in addition to their consideration by political lawmaking and law-approving institutions, they are enforced by institutions that do not have general authority to prevent the enactment of laws they judge to be on the whole undesirable. Judicial review is by far the most common and familiar form of special enforcement; it can be carried out by ordinary courts, as in the United States, or by a specialized constitutional court, as in a number of other countries.[29] Another form of special enforcement is exemplified by the Conseil Constitutionnel of the French Fifth Republic. Proposed laws and treaties may be referred to the Conseil by the president, the prime minister, and certain other designated officials, and the conseil must then rule on the constitutionality of the proposal. If the law or treaty is found unconstitutional, it cannot become law without amendment to the Constitution.[30] Finally, if the executive veto were limited to cases in which the executive judged the law in question to be unconstitutional, the veto would be yet another form of special enforcement of constitutional norms.[31]

The distinction between political and special enforcement of constitutional norms suggested here is based on the thought that the assignment of the enforcement of constitutional norms to an institution without general lawmaking (or law-vetoing) power is likely to elevate the significance and efficacy of those norms by a quantum leap. Constitutional norms are more specific than that general standard of "wise policy" (or good politics) that a legislature applies in making laws and an executive with a general veto applies in approving or rejecting them. The general "all-things-considered" standard subsumes within itself constitutional standards, along with considerations of morality, policy, and politics. In such a decision process the constitutional standards are likely to receive less than fully focused attention—though as was argued in the preceding subsection, a decision process subject to the general "all-things-considered" standard *plus* the constitutional restraints still seems sufficiently likely to respond to those restraints to justify ascribing to them legally binding character.

By contrast to a decision-maker operating under the "all-things-considered" standard, an institution whose authority is confined to enforcement of a limited set of more definite standards is likely to focus more clearly on those standards. Of course the focus required to justify the decision in terms of the limited and definite standards cannot *guarantee* that the outcome of the decision will be actually guided by those standards. But here, as in the case of the political decision-maker, the presumption is that officials are substantially enough influenced in what they do by the prevailing standards governing what they are supposed to do to make the study of those standards a worthwhile enterprise.

THE SOURCES OF CONSTITUTIONAL NORMS

Where are constitutional norms to be found, and how is it to be determined what they prohibit, require, or allow? It is with respect to this inquiry that the traditional distinction between written and unwritten constitutions is made. Bryce argued that this "old-fashioned" and "superficial" distinction should be replaced by the "more essential" one between flexible and rigid constitutions which he proposed.[32] But in truth the two distinctions are not in competition. Bryce's distinction concerns the hierarchical status of constitutional norms, whereas the "written-unwritten" distinction expresses differences in the sources of norms, whatever their hierarchical status may be.

What have been called written constitutions (or written constitutional norms) are those that derive their status from the fact of their *enactment* by some authorized body, according to some established procedure. The content of an enacted constitutional norm is derived by interpretation of the enactment itself—the text of the enacted document, as well as what can be learned from other evidence of the meaning intended by those who enacted it. Unwritten constitutional norms have other sources of authority than enactment, and their contents must be elucidated by techniques other than interpretation. It is possible to distinguish two sources of unwritten constitutional norms, each of which has its corresponding method of elucidation. First are those norms whose authority is based upon their general acceptance; the content of these norms is determined by investigation, impressionistic or scientific, of the usages generally accepted as binding by the community in question. Second are those norms whose authority rests on their status as moral and political truths; the content of these norms must be ascertained by some method of arriving at true moral and political value judgments, whether it be direct intuition, inference from a determinate human nature, deduction from self-evident moral axioms, or identification of normatively significant laws of historical development.

Reason and Truth

American constitutionalism was born in a climate of opinion which accepted the rational ascertainability of normative principles of ethics and politics. It was "self-evident" that human beings had "certain inalienable rights": what is more, the principles enforcing these rights were legally binding fundamental law, superior in status to enacted ordinary law. James Otis's summary expression of these ideas in the *Writs of Assistance* case is well known: "As to Acts of Parliament, an Act against the Constitution is void: an Act against natural Equity is void. . . [33] The relation between legality, natural law, and the Constitution in the eighteeth century Whig mind is perhaps best reflected in the statement of a great English lawyer, Lord Camden, who in 1766 denounced taxation without representation as "illegal, absolutely illegal, contrary to the fundamental laws of nature, contrary to the fundamental laws of this constitution . . . a constitution grounded on the eternal and immutable laws of nature." [34] For Otis and Lord Camden, the unwritten British constitution incorporated and gave fundamental-law status to principles of natural law.

This idea has shown a remarkable persistence in American constitutionalism despite the decline of the intellectual prestige of natural-law ideas since the eighteenth century. Even after the enactment of written constitutions, American courts through much of the nineteen century invalidated statutes they considered in violation of "general principles of republican government," [35] and "limitations on power which grow out of the essential nature of all free governments." [36] In this century, the due process clauses of the federal Constitution have been held to protect those rights that could be said to be "of the very essence of a scheme of ordered liberty." [37] The United States Supreme Court continues today to discern and enforce as constitutional norms values such as the integrity of the family and the right of adults to order their own sexual relationship that have no conceivable basis in the "written" Constitution, the Constitution regarded as an enactment or legislative act.[38]

The place of natural-law ideas in constitutionalism of course extends far back in history beyond the eighteenth century, and in modern times is not confined to the Anglo-American world.[39] The impressive recent growth of affirmations of support for "human rights" and the increasing interest in providing institutional mechanisms for the definition and protection of such rights on the international scene [40] suggest that the influence on constitutional development of the age-old conception that human beings can, by reason, ascertain universal moral and political truths has by no means come to an end.

Usage and Acceptance

An unwritten constitution or constitutional norm need not be conceived as embodying universal and immutable moral or political truth. Deeply rooted in history and in political and legal theory is the Burkean conception that each human society is founded upon historically unique set of organically integrated and evolving values and institutions. The idea that these deeply rooted customary and traditional norms are incorporated into the constitution of the community has been a central and persistent idea in Anglo-American thought. Just as influential as the concept of natural law on early American constitutionalism was the idea that Americans inherited specifically English constitutional rights whose authority was derived from their immemorial antiquity.[41]

Like the ideas of natural law and natural rights, the notion of constitutional norms discerned from the shared and strongly felt values and beliefs of the community continues to play an important part in contemporary American constitutional law. The courts have spoken of the constitutional protection of due process of law as including "the notions of justice of English-speaking peoples" [42] and "moral principles so deeply imbedded in the traditions and feelings of our people as to be deemed fundamental."[43] In implementing the constitutional prohibition against cruel and unusual punishment, the Supreme Court has said that it is to be seen as embodying those "evolving standards of decency which mark the progress of a maturing society." [44]

The content of these socially based standards is developed by the courts through the traditional process of case-by-case common-law adjudication. In one respect, this method is well suited to keeping law in tune with contemporary values; an important aspect of the common-law tradition is its stress upon close attention to the facts of the particular case, and its presupposition that the concrete facts will themselves dictate the result in the case—the idea of "decide first, explain later." On the other hand, law extracted by this method is not likely to be a pure representation of unreflective general sentiment, such as accurate opinion research might discern. First, the values underlying judicial decision will be those of an educated elite. Second, the requirement that reasoned explanation accompany the intuitive case-by-case decision will press the law in the direction of society's proclaimed ideals and away from it more covertly held (but often strongly felt) prejudices. Law developed in this way is thus likely to be a blend of usage and "natural law," prejudice and reason, and indeed that seems an apt characterization of the unenacted norms of American constitutions.

Enactment

Virtually every modern state has an enacted constitution, which contains norms structuring and limiting the powers of government. The authority of enacted constitutions is today invariably ascribed to their status as the most solemn expression of the will of the sovereign people. Typically, constitutional norms are enacted and can be repealed or amended only by some procedure closely linked to popular participation—in twentieth-century constitutions, normally a referendum. In this sense, enacted constitutions are a legal expression of the political theory of popular sovereignty, and they embody Tom Paine's axiom that a constitution must be "the act of a . . . people constituting a government." [45] Nevertheless, written or enacted constitutions have not always drawn their authority from popular roots. Professor Kenyon's paper in this volume reminds us of the classical tradition that the constitution of a state must be the product of a single wise lawgiver.

The tradition of distinguishing between written and unwritten constitutions can suggest the misleading conclusion that the two forms of constitution are alternatives, so that where there is an enacted constitution—as there is in virtually every modern state—there can be no unwritten constitution. The focus upon constitutional *norms* rather than constitutions as units of analysis permits the correction of this error. A supreme enacted constitution may coexist with unenacted constitutional norms that have the full status of judicially enforceable fundamental law. The clearest examples of this phenomenon were the "general principles of republican government" that American courts enforced against legislation throughout much of the nineteenth century quite independently of any reference to written or enacted constitutional norms.[46] Today, though this sort of judicial review is no longer found, courts continue to enforce with full constitutional status customary and ethical principles whose content they do not even purport to derive from the enacted constitution. These unenacted principles, however, are today attributed to constitutional enactments—typically broad constitutional clauses, such as the due process and equal protection clauses of the United States Constitution—in another way. These broad constitutional provisions are often said to have established a "living constitution," which delegates to contemporary judges and other decision-makers the power to apply, with constitutional force, contemporary concrete norms that the framers of the relevant constitutional text did not intend, and in some cases would clearly have rejected. These concrete norms—for example, those that prohibit school segregation, gender discrimination, and laws against the sale of contraceptives—are themselves unenacted constitutional norms in the full sense.

The existence of an enacted constitution—or, better, of enacted constitutional *norms*—does not, then, preclude the existence within the same system of unenacted norms derived by moral reasoning, sociological investigation, or case-by-case decision. However, what does invariably seem to be the case, at least in modern constitutional schemes, is that an enacted constitutional norm takes hierarchical precedence over an unenacted norm where the two conflict. It is assumed as a matter of course that the constitutional amendment or enactment process is available to override restrictions laid down in the name of unenacted constitutional norms by courts or other authorized enforcement institutions. The claim that a procedurally valid constitutional enactment cannot take effect because it violates unwritten constitutional law—fundamental tradition or natural justice—is not generally available as an accepted argument in contemporary constitutional systems. To allow the enforcement of unenacted constitutional norms over enacted ones would be to insulate altogether the decisions of constitutional enforcement agencies like the courts from correction by more popularly based political institutions. There would of course be nothing logically inconsistent or incoherent in such an arrangement. Its unacceptability is a matter of substantive political theory and practical necessity. On the theoretical level, it expresses the ultimate dominance of popular sovereignty as the source of political legitimacy in the contemporary state. And as a practical matter, the pervasive effect of change—change in technology, in social structures, in values—requires that some means for the conscious legislative alteration of the fundamental law governing a modern society should always be available.

NOTES

1. Otto von Gierke, *Natural Law and the Theory of Society,* p. 152, trans., Barker (1934).
2. Thomas Paine, "The Rights of Man," in *The Essential Thomas Paine,* p. 246 (1969).
3. *Id.* at pp. 203, 248.
4. Jeremy Bentham, "Constitutional Code" in vol. 9, *Works of Jeremy Bentham,* pp. 119-124, Bowring ed. (1838-1843).
5. Charles McIlwain, *Constitutionalism: Ancient and Modern,* p. 21 (1947).
6. See, e.g., Albert V. Dicey, *The Law of the Constitution,* pp. 417-474, 10th ed. (1959).
7. James Bryce, "Flexible and Rigid Constitutions" in vol. 1, *Studies in History and Jurisprudence,* pp. 124, 126-27 (1901).
8. See *supra* note 6.
9. The whole body of constitutional doctrine which governs the extent to which the states may regulate interstate commerce is of this latter sort; see *Prudential Insurance Co.* v. *Benjamin,* 328 U.S. 408 (1946).
10. This follows Wittgenstein's celebrated assault upon the obsessive search for definitions of general concepts, Ludwig Wittgenstein, *Philosophical Investigations,* pp. 31-33 (1963).
11. See *supra* note 6. Compare the *Wensleydale Peerage* case, 5 H.L.C. 957, 969 (1856): "things may be legal and yet unconstitutional."
12. On extralegal constitutional norms in the United States, see Christopher Tiedeman, *The Unwritten Constitution of the United States* (1890), ch. 3 ("The Electoral College"), and ch. 4 ("The Re-eligibility of the President").
13. U.S. Const., Amend. 22.
14. For the Virginia Declaration of Rights, see vol. 7, Thorpe, *The Federal and State Constitutions, Colonial Charters and Other Organic Laws,* p. 3813 (1909). Compare Article 1, Section 1, of the California constitution: "All men . . . have certain inalienable rights, among which are those of . . . pursuing and *obtaining* safety and happiness." (Emphasis added.)
15. Thorpe, note 14 *supra,* at 3814.
16. On the Italian Constitution of 1848, see James Bryce, note 7 *supra,* at p. 176; on the New Zealand Constitution, see Kenneth Wheare, *Modern Constitutions,* pp. 5-6 (1966).
17. Jeremy Bentham, note 4 *supra.*

18. According to Professor Wheare, the Swiss Constitution was amended in 1893 to prohibit the sticking of animals for butchers' meat unless they had previously been stunned. Kenneth Wheare, note 16 *supra,* at p. 32.

19. 1 Cranch 137 (1803).

20. The "political question" doctrine has attracted a voluminous literature; a good brief discussion is Lawrence Tribe, *American Constitutional Law,* pp. 71-79 (1978).

21. See, e.g., H. L. A. Hart, *The Concept of Law,* pp. 27-41, and ch. 10 (1961); Joseph Raz, *The Concept of a Legal System,* pp. 147-156 (1970).

22. See, e.g., John Austin, *The Province of Jurisprudence Determined,* pp. 141-42 (1954); compare the "soft positivism" of Professor Hart, note 21 *supra,* ch. 10.

23. On the conception of enacted constitutional provisions incorporating by reference a set of more definite socially determined norms, see note 47 *infra* and accompanying text.

24. U.S. Const., Art. I, Sec. 2.

25. U.S. Const., Art. I, Sec. 5. It has been held that the provision making each house the judge of its members' qualifications does not insulate from judicial review the exclusion of a member-elect on grounds other than his failure to meet the constitutionally enumerated qualifications. *Powell* v. *McCormack,* 395 U.S. 486 (1969).

26. U.S. Const., Art. II, Sec. 4; U.S. Const., Art. III, Sec. 1.

27. See, e.g., Lawrence Tribe, note 20 *supra,* at pp. 215-216, n. 2.

28. The words are those of then Representative Gerald Ford in connection with the proposed impeachment of Supreme Court Justice William O. Douglas in 1970, quoted in Raoul Berger, *Impeachment: The Constitutional Problems,* p. 53 (1973).

29. The distinction between centralized judicial review by a constitutional court and decentralized review by the ordinary courts is made by Mauro Cappelletti, *Judicial Review in the Contemporary World,* ch. 3 (1971). Professor Cappelletti makes a broader distinction between "political" and "judicial" constitutional enforcement which differs from the one suggested here between "political" and "special"; for Professor Cappelletti, all enforcement that is not carried out by courts of law is "political."

30. *Id.* at pp. 2-6.

31. Professor Cappelletti suggests that the veto power possessed by the president of Italy, and perhaps also that of the president of West Germany, is of this nature. *Id.* at pp. 6-7.

32. See note 7 *supra.*

33. Quincy's *Reports* (Mass.) 473.

34. 16 *Parliamentary History,* 178 (1813).

35. *Fletcher* v. *Peck,* 6 Cranch 87, 139 (1810).
36. *Loan Association* v. *Topeka,* 87 U.S. 655, 663 (1974).
37. *Palko* v. *Connecticut,* 302 U.S. 319, 325 (1937).
38. See, e.g., *Eisenstadt* v. *Baird,* 405 U.S. 438 (1972); *Moore* v. *City of East Cleveland,* 97 S. Ct. 1932 (1977).
39. Edward Corwin, *The "Higher Law" Background of American Constitutional Law* (1955); on the influence of natural law ideas on twentieth-century continental constitutional theory, see Dietze, "Judical Review in Europe," 55 *Mich. L. Rev.* 539 (1957).
40. See generally Louis Sohn and Thomas Buergenthal, *International Protection of Human Rights* (1973).
41. See generally H. Trevor Colburn, *The Lamp of Experience* (1965).
42. *Malinski* v. *New York,* 324 U.S. 401, 417 (1945).
43. *Solesbee* v. *Balkcom,* 339 U.S. 9, 16 (1950) (Frankfurter, J., concurring).
44. *Trop* v. *Dulles,* 356 U.S. 86, 101 (1958).
45. See *supra* note 2.
46. See *supra* notes 35 and 36.
47. On this point, see Thomas Grey, "Do We Have an Unwritten Constitution?" 27 *Stan. L. Rev.* 703, 708-710 (1975).

9

A COMMENT ON CECELIA KENYON'S "CONSTITUTIONALISM IN REVOLUTIONARY AMERICA"

WILLIAM J. BENNETT

Professor Kenyon speaks of the success of the American Revolution as due in part to a "pervasive spirit of, and commitment to, constitutionalism." [1] It was a revolution that never abandoned law and equity; the tread of marching feet was bordered on the one side by the contract arguments of the Declaration of Independence and on the other by arguments from the common law and "higher law" for and in the Constitution. It was, as Irving Kristol has written, a revolution infused to a remarkable degree by mind. And to the men of the Revolution speaking in state constitutions and in defense of the federal version, this constitutionalism meant more than a rule of law. Professor Kenyon writes that at that time it was

a commonplace of conventional political theory that virtue is both the necessary and peculiar characteristic of republics. The virtue ordinarily meant was the willingness of individual citizens and groups to subordinate their private selfish interests to the public interest or the general welfare. [2]

The point on which I want to focus is Professor Kenyon's conclusion about the Framers' estimate of the importance of virtue to the health of this constitutional republic:

> [This] classical meaning of virtue was not abandoned at the time of the Revolution, but I think its meaning and sig- nificance were *eroded* by the emergence of other ideas and assumptions which left its status ambiguous. . . . One of these assumptions was the belief that men were by nature creatures motivated by self-interest.[3]

Because of this, she suggests parenthetically that the dictum about virtue "may have been relegated to a liturgical status." [4]

I shall concentrate my brief remarks on this requirement of virtue in constitutional republics and urge three points:

1. A recognition of the degree and extent to which men are motivated by self-interest does not erode the significance of virtue but highlights it.

2. The authors of *The Federalist* "still" believed in the necessity and primacy of virtue correctly defined by Professor Kenyon. To them it had more than liturgical status.

3. As teachers, when we address the topics of constitutionalism or constitutional law or the constitutional heritage, we should empha- size in addition to law the importance of the morality out of which constitutions emerge and the virtue on which they depend. Atten- tion to the right nurture of constitutions requires attention to the character of the citizenry.

First, virtue's significance is not eroded when it is recognized the degree to which it is no simple or natural outgrowth of history or men's lives. Indeed, it is only with a sound recognition of the obstacles to virtue that it can be appropriately considered an achievement of good societies and men. Without self-interest there is no virtue; there is only behavior. An exhortation to virtue is not a call to asceticism, nor does belief in it imply a belief that civil society is a happy empire of perfect wisdom and perfect virtue. Men are not angels nor do angels govern them, and dependence on virtue does not require this. Precisely, the belief in virtue is not a belief that all or most men are good, but a belief that the temporizing of self-interest does occur on some occasions by some men, and sometimes many men, for the sake of values of the polity that transcend self-interest narrowly conceived. This is not to ask of men what they cannot give: it does not defy human nature. There is nothing insensible about believing in a sometimes virtuous citizenry while maintaining an ardent, healthy skepticism about the capacity of virtue usually to override self-interest in the springs of conduct. It is neither contradictory nor foolish to believe, as the Puritans believed, that a community of sinners can make a good church.

Second, in *The Federalist* Publius worries that the observer who indulges in no idle speculation about human perfection and thus recognizes the extent of self-interest may as a consequence be blind to the existence of better motives in men. On the basis of the facts of politics and history, Publius instructs us to assume neither a universal venality nor a universal rectitude in man,[5] and we are reminded that "as there is a degree of depravity in mankind which requires a degree of circumspection and distrust, so there *are* other qualities in human nature that justify esteem and confidence," [6] Although it is true, as Professor Kenyon writes, that constitutions were designed to compensate for our defects of virtue, these structural compensations, the contrivances for which *The Federalist* is famous—a republic rather than a democracy; the system of representation; the separation of powers; these buffers, devices, "ropes and chains" as Patrick Henry called them—are all described as *auxiliary* precautions to the major, principal precaution which is the wisdom and virtue of the people themselves.[7] How do we decide that Publius does not mean what he says when he says this, or decide that Madison did not mean his statement in the Virginia Convention of 1788, that no government can secure liberty or happiness without virtue in the people? [8] It is correct to argue that a rule of law with well-conceived state and federal constitutional law at the summit can compensate for much defect of citizen virtue, but not for all. Because we do not always or even often act up to snuff, it does not follow that goverment must therefore be founded exclusively on a notion of what we fail to be rather than on what we can be. With an awareness of man's self-interest, both Publius and John Adams nevertheless refuse to limit themselves to a cynical, Hobbesian account of the state's legitimacy and purposes. They propose a good society, a system of ordered liberty where virtue provides part of the order. In the view of the people who founded this government, the purpose of civil society is not merely to preserve life but to provide an occasion and condition for living a good life.

Third, I would like to make a point relating education, constitutionalism, and virtue. This is not intended as a direct comment on Professor Kenyon's paper but it is a point of importance that is suggested by issues she raises.

I believe we misallocate our resources and energies if in teaching about constitutionalism we neglect to talk about the "ordinary" values citizens—our students—must have in daily commerce with each other. We often neglect this for the sake of talking about constitutionalism and great dissents; we talk about nifty ways to put together arguments extending the Fourteenth Amendment into new areas when the students with whom we are working are at a point where they believe some or all of the following spectacularly unrepublican notions: that all values are subjective; that all questions of right reduce to questions of power; that the Constitution is not primarily an order or structure for fair dealing and for providing justice "for friends as well as enemies" but is a bludgeon to be used to beat the unregenerate, the big, and the powerful into submission. It seems to me that the spirit of constitutionalism requires, perhaps primarily, a commitment to the possibility of citizens' reaching sound conclusions about right and wrong through the deliverances of judgment and sound principle, and the commitment to responsible action on that basis. A skeptical, cynical citizenry that likes to say "it's all subjective" or "you'd do it too if you could" is a diminished citizenry insufficient to the task of the maintenance of civility and to the constitutional heritage written in its most venerable codes. Professor Freund, a great constitutionalist, has written that regeneration comes from within. In our fever for post-Watergate celebrations of the Constitution, we ought to be mindful of this. With a recognition of what lawyers, journalists, and critics can do, we ought to see as well that we teachers may have much to do with the maintenance of the spirit of constitutionalism when we engage our students in serious discussions about their responsibilities as citizens and moral agents.

Professor Kenyon ends with a tribute to John Adams's tribute to the laws. It is a wonderful and important passage. It would be fine to have complete confidence in a government of laws and not of men if the laws by themselves were good and capable of flexibility, change, application, and extension, but this is not the case. The laws are not self-executing.

It has been well said that no system of law and no constitution can hold a people to ideals it is determined to betray. I therefore offer my dissent to the notion that the framers thought, or should have thought, that virtue's significance had eroded and could be compensated for by a rule of law and a constitution not fundamentally dependent on virtue and the probity of citizens.[9]

NOTES

1. This volume, p. 84-85.
2, 3, 4. These comments on Cecelia Kenyon's paper were written on the basis of a version of that paper delivered at the meetings of the Society. The statements here quoted were omitted from her revised version; accordingly, they should be considered as applying to the views expressed in the original paper, whether or not they represent her present judgment. (The Editors)
5. *The Federalist* 76.
6. *The Federalist* 55.
7. *The Federalist* 51.
8. Irving Brant, *The Complete Madison* (New York: Harper & Brothers, 1953), p. 339.
9. I have written a paper, "The Constitution and the Moral Order," which offers a fuller discussion of constitutional law and "virtue" in the American policy. It appeared as the lead article in a symposium in *The Hastings Constitutional Law Quarterly*, Vol. III, No. 4, Winter 1976.

10

REMARKS ON THE PROCEDURES OF CONSTITUTIONAL DEMOCRACY

GEORGE KATEB

In the discussion that followed her presentation, Professor Kenyon raised the subject of political and legal procedures. She said,
and Professor Bennett concurred, that procedures were "neutral,"
and to be valued for their neutrality. Her remarks were brief, but I
thought she had expressed a common view, and one that I found in
need of consideration. I objected, saying that the great political and
legal procedures of constitutional democracy—to leave aside the
characteristic procedures of other polities—were not neutral, but
rather intrinsically valuable. They contained values—qualities that
made them worthy of praise or, at least, amenable to moral
judgment. My remarks were also brief. The entire discussion was
thus really incidental to the occasion. Yet I thought then, and still
think, that the subject of the intrinsic moral worth of procedures is
an important one. The origin of this paper is in that exchange.

I would like to explore tentatively the view that certain political
and legal procedures, those of constitutional democracy, have
intrinsic moral value.[1] This contention is hardly novel; [2] it is also
full of difficulties. I would be satisfied if I could make a few

215

distinctions and perhaps add a bit to the labors of the contributors to the *Nomos, XVIII Due Process.*[3]

1. Undoubtedly, it is extremely tempting to think of procedures as neutral. On many occasions in the life of any institution, as well as in talk about public matters, one hears that disagreement over ends or values, over policy and choices, is endless and would be fatal in the absence of a procedure to work things out. The assumption is that the essence of any procedure is regularity; that regularity is both the antithesis to strife and the guarantor of its absence; that regularity is a matter of efficient functioning; that inefficiencies are corrected by technical improvements; and that though the results of a procedure, the decisions or "outcomes" are ends or values, the procedure itself has worked neutrally to attain them.

Why is it tempting to think of procedures in this way? (I do not here pretend to give an account of the reasons of Professors Kenyon and Bennett.) One main reason is to seek relief from moral perplexity. A procedure in its seeming automatism may appear to be an impersonal agent; some great machine which, once activated, accomplishes its task without the intervention of personality and all its deviations, all its deviance.[4] It seems to be a way of choosing in which no one chooses, like throwing dice or picking the short straw. Human agents are involved, but not as real agents—only as the vehicles of something not human, something outside themselves. Those unhappy with the decision may be told that they have no reason to complain: they had their chance, and no one can be blamed. The procedure was neutral and its decision must be accepted. To refuse to accept it is to try to replace neutrality by partisan or willful imposition, to reintroduce the moral confusion which the procedure was meant to dissipate.

This way of thinking need not be malign. Yet insofar as it is in the service of exonerating an established arrangement it can operate to discredit a proper sense of grievance, to silence complaint by a counterclaim of helplessness. But whatever the conservative uses of the view of procedures as neutral, the view itself is inadequate, as I hope to indicate. If we seek relief from moral perplexity in procedures, we seek it in the wrong place. If failure to agree on ends is felt as intolerable, we would inevitably have the same feeling when we looked again at the nature of procedures. Procedures are not "value-free" devices of deliverance but morally charged and therefore morally problematic modes of activity.

Alternatively, one may believe that procedures are merely means to a clearly specifiable end, a serviceable technique that has been discovered under the stimulus of a commonly experienced lack. A job has to be done; everybody knows that a job has to be done. The people need a government, or there has to be a system in which a man will be tried for a crime he has been accused of committing. If, in the first account, all ends but peace appear as hopelessly contestable on any given occasion, here, in the second account, ends appear as obvious: they pertain to the most basic and general human needs. Circumstances will dictate which government or which legal system (or which particular procedures) will be the best. The ends are fixed and not affected by the means used to attain them; the means have no separate moral identity and may be picked up and dropped without moral compunction. Nothing is morally at stake in the choice of procedures.

From this practical-minded or pragmatic outlook, political and legal procedures appear, then, as neutral, without intrinsic moral meaning. In response, one must acknowledge that procedures are means, are methods of getting a job done; that they would not exist without some initial need, some end in view; and that unless they are seen to get the job done, they will be impaired and perhaps discarded. Such acknowledgment, however, is compatible with further assertions which this practical outlook ignores. The great political and legal procedures of constitutional democracy are means, but not merely means; and they partly redefine the ends they serve, as they are changed by their own consequences and the emergence of new ends for them to attain. Called into being by some necessity, they convert that necessity into a positive moral opportunity, while altering the very understanding of necessity. Procedures may transcend their own root nature and become the real ends (though not statically), the real raison d'être, of the society in which they exist. Certain procedures are the soul of constitutional democracy, precisely because of their intrinsic value. I hope to indicate how the pragmatic view, like the morally skeptical view, is seriously deficient.

Other reasons for finding the idea of procedures as neutral

tempting may be given. And of any given procedure one can rightly say that it shows neutrality in the sense, for example, of impartial maintenance or enforcement of the rules of a procedure. I do not mean to say that this idea as a whole is either implausible or without the power to instruct. I want, rather, to resist it, certain that it is immune to annihilation: the temptations to espouse it are strong.

2. We usually say that restriction or limitation on the power of the government is the soul of constitutional democracy and that the political and legal procedures are modes of restriction (or limitation). Specifically, the political procedure—the filling of offices through contested elections held at suitably frequent intervals, decided by the majority, on the basis of universal adult suffrage; and the legal procedure, due process of law—are modes of restriction. These two procedures would seem to be the most important procedures of constitutional democracy. We go on to say that one other mode of restriction is characteristic of constitutional democracy: absolute prohibition of governmental intervention in certain areas of life, such as religion, speech, press, and assembly. Taken together, all these restrictions are initially justified in the name of avoiding oppression. Submission to the electorate is meant to keep officeholders on their best behavior; acceptance by the government of rules guiding it in its dealing with suspected or actual violaters of the law is meant to prevent arbitrary action; total abstention by the government in regard to the most sensitive areas of life is meant to leave them strong and spontaneous. Putting aside the absolute prohibitions of the First Amendment, we may say that, at its simplest level, the defense of the procedures of constitutional democracy is oriented toward an outcome or result, even if "negative" in nature—the avoidance of oppression. The pragmatic outlook on procedures in general (to which I have referred above) is thus brought to bear on the political and legal procedures of constitutional democracy. The end is defined in a fairly clear way: the avoidance of oppression; and the appropriate means, if not forever, then in the modern age, is some version or other of the electoral system and some version or other of due process of law. The means have enormous importance, but only as instruments; they are not considered to possess intrinsic value.

At the same time, the morally skeptical outlook may furnish

another initial justification of the procedures of constitutional democracy. They may be seen as peculiarly likely to elicit popular acceptance because of the overall indulgence the people receive by means of them. Elected government gives the people what they want; due process of law makes it comparatively easy on them in their waywardness. With such complaisance, with this congruence of what the people want and what officeholders do, the question of values subsides. Consequently, complaint should be severely limited: it should not touch the procedures themselves, while complaint about any outcome is tolerated but seen only as a subjective expression. The political or legal procedure has spoken: the vote or verdict must be accepted. To say it again, those unhappy with the result had their chance; no one can be blamed. Hence, the procedures, if understood by society in this way, attain the valuable outcome of stability but have no intrinsic value.

3. But the procedures of constitutional democracy deserve a richer defense. This is not to disparage either the avoidance of oppression or the stability of popular acceptance. It is only to say that valuable outcomes are not the only matter of value attached to the political and legal procedures of constitutional democracy. These procedures are not neutral or value-free in themselves. They attain values but are also themselves valuable. Even when we take the broadest possible view of the valuable outcomes (besides the avoidance of oppression and the stability of popular acceptance) which the procedures attain,[5] we have not reached the essential matter. Even when we say—on the assumption that our reality permits us to—that the electoral procedure conduces to the attainment of wise and just social policy, and the due process procedure conduces to the attainment of criminal justice, and each procedure is more likely to attain these things than other procedures, we have still not reached the essential matter. We still have not given constitutional democracy the defense it deserves—or that it would deserve if social conditions were different and better.

We may say that the procedures of constitutional democracy not only *attain* valuable outcomes (attain values); they also *accommodate, embody,* and *express* values. The meaning of saying that these procedures have *intrinsic value* or that they *contain values* is that they accommodate, embody, and express (or sponsor) values. (We cannot discuss here the question of the intrinsic value, if any, of other political and legal procedures, or of other kinds of procedure. The unelaborated intuition is that the political and legal procedures of constitutional democracy are the most intrinsically valuable of all political and legal procedures.)

Let us take up the three terms and suggest briefly what they mean and how they are illustrated.

The electoral system [6] accommodates values by giving citizens—both episodic citizens, and "the political stratum" (including officeseekers) [7]—the opportunity to have morally valuable experience; but not only experience that is morally valuable, but also aesthetically, spiritually, or existentially valuable. The experience is enriching, even transforming. Within the basic ground rules covering elections, such forms as the campaign, party caucuses, public opinion groups, pressure groups, protest groups, and other politically connected voluntary associations provide the occasions for regulated contest, "serious play," the democratic agon. The electoral system (and all that supports and sustains it) withdraws quantities of possible experience from the rigidities or quirks of such nonelectoral strategies as inheritance of office, personal favortism, meritocratic promotion, or the lottery. By these withdrawals, the electoral system elicits, shapes, restrains, intensifies, civilizes, makes intelligible, and beautifies energy, courage, alertness, conflict, and aspiration; and it does so noninjuriously. Or, if it does so not entirely noninjuriously, then at least the right-minded will see that the injuries are mostly to the vanity: injuries that must hurt but should not count.

The electoral system embodies values by establishing formal relationships (first) between the government and all citizens, and (second) among all citizens. These relationships reach directly to many aspects of personal identity. The first relationship is a crystallization of the idea that superiors (officials who make and enforce the law and policies) are inferior to those whom they govern, because their authority is merely temporary and revocable, and they must ask for it and win it, and yet not think of themselves as deserving or meriting it. Authority is dependent on the sufferance, the suffrage, of those who are to obey it. And the obedience is not to natural persons, inspired understandings, or naked wills, but to officeholders using their authority by means of rules and manifesting it in rules. The electoral system is not really consonant

with the idea of sovereignty. The second relationship is a crystallization of the idea that though I am only a voter, and only then when I
choose to be, I may nevertheless find in that status—as all the rest
may find in it—a series of attributions to me as a citizen affirmed
and acknowledged by my fellows, as theirs are by me. These
attributions include: I count; I count only as one; I am owed an
account; I take part guiltlessly; I help to determine; I press myself
forward without feeling shame; I can talk back; I have a right to be
talked to; I am part of the ultimate constitution of the body politic;
I take sides without wickedness; I should have access; I judge and
accept judgment without the odium of presumptuousness; I win
even when I lose. (In passing, I would say that certain values some
theorists have found embodied in the electoral system, such as
individual self-determination or autonomy, and *individual* consent
[as opposed to the consent of the people], seem to me not present, or
present in an extremely attenuated, not to say spectral, form. Thus,
the present theory of the intrinsic value of the procedures of
constitutional democracy itself needs revision, when the matter at
issue is the values embodied in the two relationships I have just
taken up. The work of enlarging our sense of the worth of our
procedures must also incorporate some important deflation.)

The electoral system expresses values by teaching valuable
lessons—again, lessons that are not only morally valuable, but also
aesthetically, spiritually, or existentially valuable. Those who are
willing to contemplate the electoral system as a whole may find in
its opportunity for experience and in its relationships, models for all
sorts of institutions and for all sorts of informal, even intimate
relationships as well; and, besides, a sense of self, of identity
characteristically democratic. The values accommodated and embodied in the political procedure may be transferred out of public
life and put into social and domestic and personal life. The electoral
system may be reproduced, say, in some organization; or those in an
organization or institution may demand not only representation but
actual direct, democratic participation; or daily life, family life,
relations between men and women may all be democratized or
politicized, changed into something more citizenly or egalitarian.
The spectacle of the electoral system may radiate a large number of
influences; it may indeed help to form or maintain a culture that
thus reflects it, though sometimes distortedly or only superficially;

and, of course, for good and bad. Good and bad: in reference to the
health of the electoral system itself, and the health of all the
electorally influenced nonpublic institutions and relations, too.
What is involved is the capacity of the electoral system to work on
the imagination of the beholders and lead them to see in that system
illustrations of truths that spill over all confines. It operates as a
continuously potent force of suggestiveness. The electoral system
exemplifies (or may be thought to exemplify, or may only appear to
exemplify) permanently valuable qualities; or to "instantiate"
them. All of these may exist first in nonpublic life. But they are
vivified and strengthened in nonpublic life when seen in the public
realm. And as the public realm may alter them in absorbing them
into itself, so it may alter them, by expressing them, outside itself.
The spectacle is brought home.

The continuities between public and nonpublic life are complex,
sometimes hidden, sometimes only incipient. Then, too, there are
perhaps ineffaceable discontinuities and peculiarities; and they are
probably desirable, from the point of view of both public and
nonpublic life. Where, however, significant continuities appear,
there we may speak of at least a partly integrated culture. To put it
briefly: the electoral system helps to promote a culture of energy
and dignity. Energy names the main value accommodated; dignity
names the compound value embodied. Because of the public way in
which the electoral system accommodates and embodies its values,
it may be said to express values that are the colloquial translations
(so to speak) of those accommodated and embodied; and thereby to
invite their extension, in variously "translated" or adapted forms
throughout society.

Of the three aspects of intrinsic value, which is the most
important? I cannot answer with any confidence, except to speak
quantitatively. The quantity of voters and observers is much larger
than that of the more active citizens, even though almost anyone
can become active. That would lead to supposing that the
embodied and expressed values are more important than the
accommodated values. Furthermore, embodied and expressed values seem to me to be seamless: the mere voter, influenced if only
half-consciously by his status as voter, may be the very person who
demands greater democracy in his immediate surroundings. What is
more important: public status or private and social relations? To

assess their relative importance is artificial. What prevents this effort from being totally unprofitable is that leftist criticism of the authenticity of the embodied values may be true, and the electoral system still manage to express values transferrable to nonpublic life. Inauthentically democratic as a political procedure, it may still work to democratize the rest of life. The greatest kind of intrinsic value in the electoral system would then turn out to be the expressive value. The power to teach valuable lessons, however, would end if most people thought that the leftist critique was correct, that the embodied values were only deceptively present.

Let us turn now to the other great procedure of constitutional democracy: due process of law.

I realize that in speaking of due process of law one is using a term that is restricted to English-speaking jurisdictions (and other jurisdictions that have come under their influence). That means, quite baldly, that it will turn out that the English-speaking constitutional democracies contain a legal procedure—one of the two most important procedures in any constitutional democracy— that is intrinsically more valuable than the corresponding legal procedure (usually that of the civil-law tradition) in non-English-speaking constitutional democracies. Due process of law is intrinscially more valuable than the civil-law tradition of dispensing criminal justice.

I also realize that the term "due process" has a long history. It has been given competing interpretations. In American jurisprudence, as we know, these questions have been raised: What does the phrase mean? What is the relation between due process and the rights and entitlements specified in amendments four to eight in the Bill of Rights? If it is assumed that most or all the specified rights and entitlements are part of the meaning of due process, how should each of them be interpreted? Are the states of the union bound by the prevailing federal interpretation of due process?

When I speak of the intrinsic superiority of due process to the civil-law tradition, I mean due process in the conceptualization made of it by Herbert L. Packer in *The Limits of the Criminal Sanction* under the name of the "Due Process Model." [8] I suppose another name for it could be "enlarged due process." Packer's contrasting term is the "Crime Control Model," which names that tendency in American jurisprudence and legal practice to narrow due process as much as possible, while still retaining a process recognizably Anglo-American. This latter tendency either excludes most or all of the specified rights and entitlements from the meaning of due process, and thus frees the states from them (where the state constitution permits); or includes them in a narrowly interpreted form, asking even less procedurally of the states than of the federal government. (Needless to say, when exponents of this tendency are faced with the clear necessity of holding the federal government to amendments four to eight, they provide narrow interpretations.)

For our purposes it does not especially matter whether or not due process includes amendments four to eight as part of its very meaning, as long as it is understood that, in this context, I do use due process to mean just that, to mean enlarged due process. It stands not only for the minimal requirements of nonarbitrary rule of law (as formulated by Lon Fuller in *The Morality of Law* [9]) but also for the adversarial system and the rights and entitlements specified in amendments four to eight, generously interpreted and read to include the exclusionary rule. (I would however, like to think that the reasons given for having due process in the narrowest sense are sufficient to necessitate enlarged due process.) Let us put these complications to one side and consider our notion of due process.

The citizen—voter, episodic citizen, or officeseeker—is the basic unit in the electoral system, the agent who finds in it an opportunity for experience, and who is implicated by it in significant and influential relationships. The experiencer of the intrinsic value of the political procedure is the citizen (as he is also the presumed beneficiary of its valuable outcomes). What do we say about due process? The government is the agent. It creates and administers a system of criminal justice. Within this continuous activity of seeking to attain the valuable outcome of legal justice, due process asserts itself by forcing abstentions and inhibitions on the government. From the perspective of intrinsic value, the government is the principal agent or actor in due process, and its intrinsically valuable actions are abstentions and inhibitions. It is restrained from doing (it restrains itself, ideally, from doing) what it would like to do, what it may think it must or should do, what other governments do as it were without thinking. (More properly, officer holders connected with the administration of criminal justice are so restrained, or restrain themselves. They are as a group the principal actor.)

But to say that is not to say that the principal agent is the principal experiencer of intrinsic value. He who is, so to speak, the target of the abstentions and inhibitions, he whose due process rights are recognized, is the principal experiencer of the embodied values. On the other hand, the people at large, if they are receptive, stand to learn the great lessons taught by due process, to be the principal experiencers of the expressed values.

I would now take up the aspects of intrinsic value, in order.

Due process accommodates values by giving various individuals the opportunity for certain kinds of valuable experience. It gives the relevant officeholders the experience of restraint; judges, the experience of impartiality; juries, the experience of deliberation; and lawyers, the experience of serious play. But, above all, it gives suspects, defendants, and prisoners the experience of having their dignity respected when they seem, in the eyes of others and often in their own, to have lost their dignity because they failed to respect that of others. In that sense, they are the principal experiencers of the intrinsic value of due process.

But I do not think that the values accommodated by due process are nearly as important as the values it embodies and expresses. Where I find it dubious and difficult to estimate the comparative moral importance of the various aspects of the intrinsic value of the electoral system, I think we should do so when considering due process. I will only mention here this asymmetry between the political procedure and the legal procedure.

Due process embodies values by establishing formal relationships between the government and certain persons, those caught in the toils of the criminal law. In defending the extension of the particular privilege against self-incrimination to pretrial interrogation, the late Chief Justice Warren succinctly stated the values which, in effect, due process as a whole embodies. In a key sentence, he wrote:

> To maintain a "fair state-individual balance," to require the government "to shoulder the entire load," . . . to respect the inviolability of the human personality, our accusatory system

of criminal justice demands that the government seeking to
punish an individual produce the evidence against him by its
own independent labors, rather than by the cruel, simple
expedient of compelling it from his own mouth.[10]

By recognizing the great rights in amendments four to eight, the
government creates relationships which have moral meanings of
immeasurable worth. To expand Warren's passage: no matter what
you do, you can never be thought of or treated as having forfeited
certain rights; vice and error have their rights; your status as person
before the law is not diminished by the evil you may have done; the
government may not use any means, even if efficacious, but only
some means, even if seemingly inefficacious, to attain indisputably
valuable outcomes; the benefit of every doubt is given to the person
who is now at the mercy of the government; government will
strengthen its adversary so that the contest be a good one; unequals
are to be treated equally; the government cannot profit from its
wrongdoing; the government takes no pleasure in punishing; there
is no majesty in condemning and punishing; leniency is part of strict
morality; appealing a verdict is normal; it is indecent to force a
person to cooperate in his own hurt; strife is justice; and so on.
Customarily, the words "fairness" and "justice" are used to name
the totality of due process restraints and inhibitions. We may
therefore say that due process embodies the values of fairness and
justice, provided we see that both are embodied in a fully developed
way. Due process seeks to do legal justice within the constraints of
fairness and justice. Crudely: justice is done justly. There is a unity
of means and ends, not only some vague consonance. Due process is
no mere luxury or trifle.

Due process expresses values by teaching valuable lessons. The
way the government restrains itself and yet seems to get the job
done composes a pattern which the prepared beholder may revolve
in his mind and from which he may derive attitudes and motivations for his whole life. What is at stake is more than fairness in the
narrow though perfectly estimable sense: the right to notice and a
hearing, and the right to know what is expected of one. What is at
stake is also more than rationality, estimable as that, too, is: to let
everyone have a say, to consult, to lay down clear rules and stick by

them, and so on. Due process is somewhat reduced when it is equated with fairness and rationality in these senses. It is good, but not the greatest good, when the government's employment of due process in criminal law, thus reduced and adapted, serves as a model for the internal workings of all types of organizations and institutions, or at least encourages preexistent tendencies. It is, in truth, a great good to have "fundamental fairness" and decent sense spread throughout the culture.

Beyond these expressed values lie those which any individual may internalize as he goes about his life. He may imitate the government in its dealings with those caught in the toils of the law by practicing the everyday equivalents of the restraints and inhibitions of due process. Whereas the electoral system promotes energy (though disciplined by the rules of contest), due process promotes restraint (though not paralysis). It teaches the transcendent importance of scruples; while, to be sure, tending to inculcate some readiness to forbear altogether from some actions and to expect to feel remorse after many actions. Herbert Packer speaks of the self-doubt and self-correction that are inherent in due process.[11] We see these qualities as the essence of the values expressed, the values radiated through the society, by due process.

It may be that as a moral phenomenon constitutional democracy is most interesting when the tensions and resemblances between the electoral system and due process are studied.[12] The two major procedures absolutely belong together. But it would be wrong to say that a fine harmony prevails between them. Nor are they constantly at odds. In the values they attain as well as those they accommodate, embody, and express, they have in common a devotion to the idea that the individual is the moral center of society. Both are committed to the principle of dignity or "respect for persons." But they give different emphases to that principle.

The electoral system, like due process, respects the person in his capacity to suffer. They both try to reduce suffering. But in regard to the two other capacities which fill out the notion of that which in any person deserves respect—the capacity to be a free agent, and the capacity to be a moral agent—the two procedures diverge. As we have said, the electoral system is actually and symbolically a procedure of energy. Its workings demand energy; its relationships create energy by creating self-respect. For that reason it pays enormous homage to the person as free agent and as moral agent; more, by far, than any modern alternative. It liberates.

What of due process? It begins and ends by trying to reduce suffering, to reduce the suffering of those who may have caused others to suffer. The kinds of energy it liberates in judges, juries, lawyers, and even in shrewd and alert suspects and defendants, are commendable for the most part, but not large. They are anyway found in many sectors of the culture and do not need their presence in due process to survive and flourish outside it. In fact, they are all found—even judiciousness—in the electoral system. The frame which due process provides for the free agency of these participants cannot finally count hugely. What does count hugely is that due process (in the values it embodies and expresses) tends toward the absolutist end of the moral scale. Not that in its treatment of suspects and defendants (to leave aside prisoners) it exemplifies the morality of altruism; or of resist not evil, or never inflict pain; or always be merciful or charitable or loving or caring. Nor does it show forth only leniency (though, in some secondary respects, it does). Rather, it redefines the concept of justice to embrace such qualities as generosity, detachment, and honor—the honor that consists of being willing to win only on certain terms and to lose because of a little lapse of form. If we take due process seriously, we say that we owe each other, all through life, generous, detached, and honorable conduct. The values embodied and expressed in due process comprise one of the ultimate refinements of secular morality—of *morality*, not supererogation. And due process does all this negatively, as it were: by its abstentions and inhibitions.

4. I would say, without elaboration, that some of the arrangements or structures (as distinguished loosely from procedures) of constitutional democracy can be analyzed for their intrinsic value. In American constitutional democracy, the separation of powers, checks and balances, judicial review, the federal division of powers, and a written fundamental law all may be prized for more than the valuable outcomes they were established to attain or do, in fact, attain.

5. In discussions of the intrinsic value of procedures, the question always arises, and rightly, as to how to compare the relative

importance of the values contained (the intrinsic value) and the values attained. It is helpful, but not sufficient, to acknowledge that procedures are valuable apart from the valuable ends they attain. One must go on to reconnect procedures with their ends. The question is unmanageably big and amorphous. All I can do is to offer a few suggestions.

Obviously one can propose that the values accommodated, embodied, and expressed (all somehow added up) are less valuable, equally valuable, or more valuable than the values which the given procedure more or less regularly attains. Or one can simply say the procedures not only attain values, they also contain values, and then stop. Without being able to explain adequately my position, I believe that this way of talking is not the best way, even though it is useful and probably necessary. It is not only that the difficulties of comparing the relative importance of values is, in most cases, tricky, inconclusive, and maybe even misguided. In addition, talking in this way tends to create a disjunction between means and ends, procedures and outcomes, even as it tries to effect a connection between them. Of course, common sense is right to hold that means and ends can be judged independently of each other. What have I been doing so far in this paper, if not examining procedures independently of their outcomes? How could it be in any way objectionable to do as simple a thing as to judge a method for its own sake, while reserving to oneself the right to look also at its results, and then enter a judgment on them, too?

The paradoxical and therefore tentative answer is that though the need to attain some end is (conceptually) at the origin of a means (method, procedure), a means, once established, may come to be seen as the only morally right and permissible means; and that the valuable ends thought to be attained by some other means are not really the ends they are supposed to be but rather a shadowy or parodied form of those ends. To consider the value of procedures apart from outcomes is only a first step and is made necessary by the prestige of the view that the procedures of constitutional democracy are neutral instruments. The real aim is to show that outcomes cannot be valued apart from the procedures which have attained them. The intrinsic value of the electoral system and due process is not merely great, or greater than any particular outcome or pattern of outcomes; it is unique and incommensurable. Camus's remark that the means justifies the ends is not a cheap reversal but another way of making our point.[13]

Rejected, on this line of argument, are two views: first, there are many means for attaining the end of, say, humane governance or dispensing legal justice; and second, the view that the best means may truly turn out to be those of constitutional democracy (the electoral system and due process), but they could as easily have turned out to be other ones. What I propose is not a new view but one that may still be thought extreme or muddled. That is that without the electoral system as the modern basis of governance, governance lacks legitimacy; and it is therefore governance only in a manner of speaking. Without due process as the basis of criminal justice, legal justice cannot be done. Without the electoral system all sorts of ends may be attained; but respect for persons (in the full sense) has been denied; the ends attained cannot, for that reason, be considered as ends that serve human persons, but only, at best, human creatures. Without due process, legal justice has been attained at the expense of certain individual rights, and hence of justice, and is, for that reason, a contaminated legal justice. (Some want to say that the only guilt is legal guilt and that the only way of ascertaining legal guilt is through due process.) To put it analogically, when you change the form, you change the content.[14]

The electoral system is a *frame* for action: almost any particular result attained within it is acceptable, just as the characteristic types of ends it attains, like welfare and social innovation, are valuable. Due process is a *sieve*: almost any particular verdict that survives its abstentions and inhibitions is acceptable, just as its characteristic end, legal justice, is valuable. Both procedures, like games, create the activity they confine. The inexact metaphors of frame and sieve are intended to suggest the difference between a procedure that is used joyously and one that is used reluctantly. Indeed, though both procedures convert, as we have said, a necessity into a moral opportunity, we would not, in good conscience, lament the evaporation of the necessity for due process. We would rather have a world without crime, provided it remained a world of persons and not of sheep. On the other hand, insofar, but only insofar, as government makes electoral politics possible and necessary, we could not imagine a world of persons without government. And the only legitimate (modern) government is that formed by the electoral system.

In sum, when we consider political and legal procedures, we may insist that these are the only permissible means, and that they alone really attain the ends we posit. The fundamental reason for this unyielding position is that the values contained in these two procedures are necessary to establish the principle of respect for persons in society as a whole, in all its relations and institutions. The values these procedures accommodate, embody, and express are necessary to the existence and growth of persons. (Also necessary are other guarantees and conditions: most especially, an "absolutist" First Amendment.) The means are the only means and they are more than means.

Ends certainly matter when we consider the interests of a society as a whole. In smaller groups, it may very well be that almost all that mattered was, say, the quality of participation or the quality of personal relations. In forsaking ends small groups may convert life into art. A society of tens of millions cannot be theorized in this way. Our subject is procedures in such a society. But I want to be able to say that we are allowed to look at the ends only after we have looked at the means. The ends are not secondary: rather, they are not the ends we think they are unless they are attained by intrinsically valuable procedures of the sorts we have been discussing.

6. The foregoing position is shaky, I am sure. One cannot just turn away from the serious charges that have been made against both the electoral system and due process on the grounds: first, that they fail to attain what they are supposed to attain; and second, that they accommodate, embody, or express vice or irrationality. The principle of the indissolubility of procedures and outcomes which I have put forward can be accepted, and the charges still made.

It could be said that it takes no great wit to see that the outcomes of the electoral system and due process are open to *systemic* criticism. It is not that on occasion both procedures lapse. It is that their outcomes compose a pattern that cannot withstand moral scrutiny. If that is so, then it is likely that the procedures accommodate, embody, and express vice and irrationality. Granted that the connection between procedures and outcomes is essential and not slight or accidental: that is precisely the trouble. We are familiar with the leftist critique of the electoral system: roughly, the procedure of energy is a procedure that accommodates deception, manipulation, corruption, and irrationality; that embodies relationships of unchanging inequality between the government and all citizens and among all citizens; and that expresses values no better and really not different from those it accommodates and embodies. The electoral system is rigged in behalf of various kinds of privilege, but especially wealth. When it does not serve as an empty ritual which distracts attention from those unelected people who wield the basic power in society, it works with an irreversible bias toward the preservation of inequality. Its contests, struggles, differences, choices, debates all take place within a preposterously narrow range—especially preposterous because falsely thought indefinitely wide. The electoral system in a capitalist society is an instrument of elite dominance.

We are also familiar with the rightist critique of due process, a critique summarized in Herbert Packer's "Crime Control Model," [15] Enlarged due process (what I have been calling due process) accommodates the distortions and withholdings of lawyer and client; the general sophistry and trickery of counsel; and the irrational pedantry of old, complex, and inconsistent rules; it embodies relationships of irresponsibility, evasion, and egocentrism; and it expresses the general idea that it is all right in everyday life to go easy on yourself, to get away with anything you can, to use any method to gain an advantage, to misrepresent yourself, and to avoid merited penalties. The upshot, inevitably, is that guilty people go free or are punished much less severely than they deserve; while individual victims go unrequited, and the whole of society suffers from a legal procedure that encourages crime itself, not just noncriminal selfishness.

(A rightist critique of the electoral system and a leftist critique of due process have also been made; but, at the present time, they are less intimidating than the two I have just mentioned, and I can do no more here than refer to them.)

Another line of criticism challenges the indissolubility of procedures and outcomes, and the hesitations I have indicated concerning my view partly derive of course from awareness of this line. At issue is the constant possibility that a procedure—understood rightly as a mode of human activity—must fail on not infrequent occasions to attain ends that are worthy of that procedure. This is not systemic criticism. All it asks is that we remember that human agency is imperfect. The defense of an enhanced view of procedure should not, in its turn, repeat the inadequate idea that procedures work with an impersonal agency. Once we recall that, we are enabled to retain the right to examine the outcomes and judge them independently of the procedure which attained them. That is, we should be allowed to say that some outcomes are so gravely wrong (evil done or not prevented or rectified) that the intrinsic value of the procedure cannot outweigh them. Impossible as it is, the effort to compare the relative importance of the values attained with the values contained must be undertaken. Ordinarily, we go along: we accept the outcome just because it is the outcome of an intrinsically valuable procedure that is preponderantly nonatrocious in its outcomes—and is nonatrocious precisely because of the nature of the procedure and the values it contains. But there are supervening occasions of individual or constitutional conscience when rejection is the rightful response, especially in regard to the political procedure.

The last line of criticism I would point to is reducible to the insistence that some outcomes, actually end results or steady conditions, are attainable variously. They do not gain their identity from the procedures which bring and keep them in being. Some examples are the preservation of life; the reduction of violence; the avoidance of war; the successful conduct of diplomacy and war; the provision of the means of subsistence; the toleration of many religious, intellectual, cultural, and technological endeavors; and many other policies. Specifically, governments not constituted by the electoral system may attain all these end results. In addition, the "Crime Control Model" or, indeed, some other legal procedure, may, despite all sophistry to the contrary, be able to ascertain guilt and innocence. A murderer is a murderer.

Answers to these several lines of criticism are beyond me—certainly within the limitations of this paper. To the last one, I can only concede the point. Some ends are variously attainable. But then I would insist that the status and activity of citizenship remake the world in which they exist. Life is life, peace is peace; but there is no truth in modern constitutional and democratic theory if we would be right to settle for order and security on any terms. We are not supposed to want any benefit if it is imposed, when we can have that benefit as well as an entirely transformed conception of benefit in general without nondemocratic imposition. Constitutional democracy is a way of life. Its distinctive features constitute its claim to moral superiortiy; and these features are accommodated, embodied, and expressed in its political and legal procedures. On due process, specifically, no other legal procedure does justice justly. That is its specific claim to moral superiority. A murderer is a murderer, and due process will find him out without having the government itself perpetrate wrong by refusing to recognize the murderer's rights. A government loses its status as government when it does unnecessary wrong in pursuit of good; good ceases being good when unneccesary wrong has produced it.

The first two main lines of criticism are more vexatious. What they have in common is the demand that any defender of an enhanced notion of procedure pay attention to the context, to the social reality in which the procedures work. If in some respects political and legal procedures are like games in that they seem to constitute a whole world, gathering all our interest into the play, we would be mistaken if we were to lose sight of the elementary fact that a political or legal procedure is not a game. The social world is not constituted anew every day. It is there day after day in its overwhelming presence and it will intrude on the playing of a game (or the performance of any self-contained activity). Indeed, "intrude" is too remote a word, too connotative of aestheticism. Procedures absorb or "process" what is external to themselves, problems and issues; and do so because they exist to do so. Procedures have a reciprocating influence on the society that influences them. Games do not, or at least not nearly to the same degree. History and nature and culture do their mysterious work to create interests, attitudes, commitments, prejudices, traditions, passions, and reasons. People become what they are. And they, after all, are the agents and experiencers of the procedures, and the ones who are influenced by them inwardly and who benefit or fail to benefit from the results of their working. It cannot but be the case that the same procedures will, in different circumstances, yield different results. But to say that is not only to readmit the rightness of judging the procedures and the outcomes independently; it is also to say that social reality substantially affects every aspect of a political or legal procedure. I think this consideration applies with special force to the political procedure.

In America, the political procedure coexists with, preserves, elicits, and rewards so much inequality of various kinds that its own integrity is impaired. To revert to our analogy, the content spoils the form because the context is not wholly appropriate to the form.

Yet this point marks the limits of the concessions I would make to the view that procedures and outcomes may be judged independently. The (conceptual) right to judge in this way is a sign of the serious imperfection of social reality. With lesser imperfection we would be entitled—or more entitled—to insist on the indissolubility of means and ends, procedures and outcomes. This is not to say that the means morally outweigh the ends, but that the ends are really the ends because the only morally permissible means have attained them.

I would hold on, then, to the belief that, ideally, the social reality of constitutional democracy could be such as to permit its great procedures to be perfectly themselves, untrivialized or undistorted by excessive inequalities and other deficiencies. That society does not exist in America, except approximately, or in some sectors, or in recurrent phases, or for some groups. However, only that society is genuinely a constitutional democracy, the developed civilization of constitutional democracy. Far from being neutral, the great procedures must be at the heart of thought about the moral nature of that civilization.

NOTES

1. I want to thank Professors L. A. Babb, E. Bruss, J. Dizard, T. Kearns, B. O'Connell, and A. Sarat, my colleagues in the Kenan Colloquium at Amherst, for all that I have learned from them on the general subject of constitutional democracy, as a political form and as a civilization. I would also like to acknowledge the stimulation given to thought about procedures by John Rawls in *A Theory of Justice* (Cambridge, Mass.: Harvard University Press, 1971). This paper is a revision and continuation of an earlier article, "Imperfect Legit-

imacy," presented in 1972, and printed in Dante Germino and Klaus von Beyme, eds., *The Open Society in Theory and Practice* (The Hague: Martinus Nijhoff, 1974), pp. 164-87.

2. For the intrinsic moral value of the political procedures of constitutional democracies, see, among other works, Henry B. Mayo, *An Introduction to Democratic Theory* (New York: Oxford University Press, 1960; Henry S. Kariel, *The Decline of American Pluralism* (Stanford: Stanford University Press, 1961); and Carl Cohen, *Democracy* (Athens, Georgia: University of Georgia Press, 1971). For the intrinsic value of the legal procedures, see Sanford H. Kadish, "Methodology and Criteria in Due Process Adjudication—A Survey and Criticism," *Yale Law Journal,* 66 (January 1957), 319-363; Charles Fried, *An Anatomy of Values* (Cambridge, Mass.: Harvard University Press, 1970), esp. ch. 8; and Robert S. Summers, "Evaluating and Improving Legal Processes—A Plea for 'Process Values,' " *Cornell Law Review,* 60 (November 1974), 1-52.

3. The whole volume is rich. My position is closest to that of David Resnick, "Due Process and Procedural Justice," in J. Roland Pennock and John W. Chapman, eds., *Due Process, Nomos XVIII* (New York: New York University Press, 1977), pp. 206-228.

4. See Duncan Kennedy, "Legal Formality," *Journal of Legal Studies,* vol. 2 (1973), pp. 351-98, at p. 357.

5. See, for example, Mayo, *An Introduction to Democratic Theory,* ch. 9; and Cohen, *Democracy,* ch. 14.

6. I speak throughout of the electoral system. My attention is on the procedure of filling offices through contested elections held at suitably frequent intervals, decided by the majority, on the basis of universal adult suffrage. The obvious assumption is that this way of filling offices is, in its nature, a way of determining the broad outlines of public policy. The filling of offices is thus instrumental to the continuous making of policy in the largest sense. In turn, the making of policy involves other procedures, formal and informal, which may be intrinsically valuable, but which I do not specifically discuss in this paper. All this, in addition to the value of the experience of holding office, though, of course, democratically filled offices are hardly the only ones that afford this opportunity. And, most important, there are the varieties of valuable experience in regular or episodic involvements in helping to make policy, without holding formal office. Democratic political life as a whole is full of accommodation for valuable experience. But my stress in this paper is on the electoral system which is the basic frame and hence the decisive procedure.

7. For the concept of the political stratum, see Robert A. Dahl, *Who*

Governs? (New Haven: Yale University Press, 1961), pp. 90-94, and throughout. Dahl also throws light on the notion of episodic citizenship, though the book was published before the New Left gave its version of such participation.

8. See Herbert L. Packer, *The Limits of the Criminal Sanction* (Stanford: Stanford University Press, 1968), chs. 8-12, and throughout.
9. See Lon L. Fuller, *The Morality of Law,* rev. ed. (New Haven: Yale University Press, 1969), ch. 2.
10. *Miranda v. Arizona,* 384 U.S. 436 (1966) at p. 460.
11. See Packer, *The Limits,* pp. 167-177.
12. See, for example, Edmond Cahn, *The Predicament of Democratic Man* (New York: Macmillan, 1961); and Herbert J. Spiro, "Privacy in Comparative Perspective," in J. Roland Pennock and John W. Chapman, eds., *Privacy, Nomos XIII* (New York: Atherton, 1971), pp. 121-148.
13. See Albert Camus, *The Rebel* (1951), trans. Anthony Bower (New York: Vintage, n.d.), p. 292.
14. See Packer, *The Limits,* p. 166.
15. A general defense of this model is found in Macklin Fleming, *The Price of Perfect Justice* (New York: Basic Books, 1974); and in recent various opinions by Chief Justice Burger and Justices White, Rehnquist, and Powell. Of course, elements of this tendency are found in countless other court opinions on various levels through the years, and in many announcements by lawyers and officials.

11

RAWLS ON CONSTITUTION-MAKING [1]

RONALD MOORE

INTRODUCTION

Although it scarcely seems possible, at least one portion of John Rawls's monumental study, *A Theory of Justice,*[2] has still attracted relatively little critical attention. It is that development that Rawls designates stage 2 (in the four-stage sequence described generally throughout Part II of *TJ*), the point at which the "veil of ignorance" is partially lifted, and the just-minded but still somewhat benighted parties to the social contract of the "original position" reassemble "to design a system for the constitutional powers of government and the basic rights of citizens" (pp. 196-97). I suspect that this portion of Rawls's vast and complicated conceptual program has struck many of his commentators as intermediate and hence of less consequence than the conspicuously important themes of contractarian choice and fully applied political policy between which it appears. Constitution-making is, however, a crucial moment in the development of *TJ*'s overall thesis, and one which therefore warrants close scrutiny. In what follows, I do not pretend to scrutinize all of the features of Rawls's account of constitution-making that deserve critical attention. Instead, I concern myself exclusively with a narrow range of central elements and assumptions upon which that account vitally depends.

My aim is to expose some of the inherent difficulties of applying Rawls's theory of justice to the enterprise of constitution-making. It is not to show that a successful application is in principle impossible. For the purposes of the present discussion, I do not quarrel with the celebrated justice principles Rawls takes his rational, self-interested contractors to have adopted in stage 1.[3] I assume that Rawls's two principles (stated most fully on p. 302) do identify the concept of justice for social institutions and that these principles have been chosen in the "original position" and carried forward into stage 2. I hope to show, however, that the use to which these principles are put by the delegates to the constitutional convention to some degree undermines the point of the deliberations. Stage 2 is designed to furnish a stable and just foundation for legislation and legal application at subsequent stages. It is crucially important, therefore, that its proceedings be both recognizably just (i.e., fully faithful to the previously adopted justice principles) and "a reasonable approximation to and extension of our considered judgments" (p. 195) (i.e., fully demonstrative of the varied virtues we commonly expect of democratic constitutional processes). In his effort to make stage 2 serve both of these ends, Rawls is forced into a difficult balancing act. On the one hand, he wants the justice principles to exercise a dominant *control* over the proceedings, and through them, to what lies beyond. On the other hand, he wants to leave room in the convention for open debate, meaningful dissent, and genuine compromise.

Undeniably, Rawls is a master equilibrator. In *TJ*, he manages to traverse a lofty, treacherous, and remarkably complicated network of theoretic highwires while juggling a dazzling variety of conceptual devices; and throughout the performance he maintains the impression in his audience that he is moving on solid ground. From a distance, every step looks as natural and inevitable as that of the average citizen strolling down a familiar street in his hometown. The traditional accolade is apt: he makes it all look so easy! But, of course, we know it isn't easy. When we look more closely, the concentrated effort and the strain are evident. The balancing act of stage 2 is, perhaps, the toughest act in *TJ*. If the control of the justice principles over the proceedings is too strong, the open-forum features we associate with constitution-making will be lost; but if it is too weak nothing will prevent the centrifugal effects of heterodoxy from wrecking the rest of the show. I shall argue that in the end the delicate equilibrium proves too difficult to be sustained. First, by hanging some "safety nets," in the form of simplifying background assumptions, Rawls injects a false air of facility into the performance and invites an overbold use of the justice principles. This overboldness is later accentuated as Rawls tries to skirt some of the potential hazards of dissenting opinion. And, ultimately, the balance is lost when Rawls gives the justice principles an effective monopoly over competing forces of political values.

THE AIM OF STAGE 2

Without a doubt, Rawls's penetrating account of the role of justice in modern constitutionalism is, or will soon become, the benchmark against which future discussions of the subject must be measured. And justifiably so. Rawls's analysis, developed in Part II of *TJ*, applies to such inherently problematic issues as liberty of conscience, equality of political rights, the limits of toleration, and the like, a level of rigor, a clarity of vision, and a respect for the irreducibles and intractables of social theory that are, in their felicitous combination, to be found nowhere else in the literature—except, it must be said, in Sidgwick. The main thread of this analysis, and the characteristic that makes it so distinctive, is a special form of contractarianism whose key elements, both methodological and substantive, it carries over from the celebrated derivation of justice principles in Part I. Rawls would have his readers arrive at a concept of the just constitution by imagining what choices rational, self-interested delegates to a hypothetical constitutional convention, operating with limited information, and constrained by certain assumptions regarding their bases of choice, might make.

It is important to remember that Rawls's account of constitutionalism and its forms is not meant to describe *real* constitutions, constitutional conventions, political choice, and so on. Rawls's interest is confined to *just* constitutions, and specifically to those that reflect a moral commitment to the principles argued for in *TJ*, Part I. Thus, although the "four-stage sequence," the key organizing feature of constitution-making and later developments of the political process, was suggested by history,[4] it is not in any way historical:

> The idea of the four-stage sequence is part of a moral theory, and does not belong to an account of the working of actual constitutions, except insofar as political agents are influenced by the conceptions of justice in question. In the contract doctrine, the principles of justice have already been agreed to, and our problem is to formulate a schema that will assist us in applying them. The aim is to characterize a just constitution and not to ascertain which sort of constitution would be adopted, or acquiesced in, under more or less realistic (though simplified) assumptions about political life, much less on individualistic assumptions of the kind characteristic of economic theory. (p. 197n.)

All of this does not quite amount to saying that choices at stage 2 are *determined* by choices at stage 1. To be "influenced" by prior moral choices and to "apply" principles conscientiously, one need not think of oneself as a sorting and subsuming mechanism. And to insist that what comes out of a lengthy process be judged just is not to say that the position of justice in the end result would be immediately apparent to (or perhaps even assented to) by those first entering upon the process. The issues of influence, application, and outcome must, one might suppose, be understood in the light of conditions and operations that are held to obtain in the constitution-making enterprise itself. If these conditions and operations did not differ substantially from those of stage 1, stage 2 would plainly be redundant. In that case, the parties to the original position might as well have made their constitution as soon as they had chosen their basic political principles. Or, better still, they might as well have made those principles their constitution. Stage 2 does, however, differ from its predecessor in respect to information at hand, kinds of choice required, and conduct of choosing. Of these, the first difference is clearly controlling. Stage 1 contractors are taken to choose as they do because, in the informational situation they face, the choices they make seem to them to be peculiarly reasonable. Presumably, stage 2 constitution-makers will wish to make a second estimate of what seems reasonable, based on the information they now have.

One item of this information will of course be their previous contractual decision. Other items are provided by a partial lifting of the "veil of ignorance," the set of restrictions on knowledge which had been imposed at stage 1 (p. 197). The process of veil-lifting continues through each of the succeeding stages until, at the final stage, "everyone has complete access to all the facts" (p. 199). In the second stage, the delegates to the constitutional convention are not vouchsafed information about particular individuals (including themselves), about their own social position, about their place in the distribution of natural attributes, and about their conception of the good. They are, however, now permitted to know "the relevant general facts about their society, that is, its natural circumstances and resources, its level of economic advance and political culture, and so on" (p. 197). They are also permitted to know "the beliefs and interests that men in the system are liable to have and . . . the political tactics that they will find it rational to use given their circumstances" (p. 198). Now, such formulas as these do not provide us with an accurate means of deciding whether in specific cases, particular items of information are or are not available to the delegates. However, we are assured that "[t]he flow of information is determined at each stage by what is required in order to apply these principles intelligently to the kind of question of justice at hand, while at the same time any knowledge that is likely to give rise to bias and distortion and to set men against one another is ruled out" (p. 200). In its simplest terms, the project (the "question of justice at hand") is this: delegates are to use their prior theory and new-found facts to select from among a variety of feasible alternatives the best just constitution. Presumably, then, the only details of information revealed to stage 2 delegates by the partial lifting of the veil will be those needed beyond what was previously known to enable delegates to make the choices required to fulfill this aim. It follows that the key questions for assessing stage 2 decision-making are: What choices must be made in order to frame a just constitution, given the constraints otherwise imposed by Rawls's constructive theoretic project? And, what information will be relevant to the choosing process?

Answers to these questions do not come easily. The blunt counsels of common sense, often undeniably useful in similar contexts, will take us only a short distance. A major reason for this is that Rawls has hemmed in the delegates' deliberative situation with a set of "simplifying assumptions," background conditions stipulated in posing the initial contractual problem, attaching themselves to the solution to that problem, and sustaining themselves through the later stages. These background assumptions simplify the business of finding applications for the previously selected justice principles in the constitution-making forum; but at the same time, and to a corresponding degree, they complicate the business of determining what the choices within that forum shall be. By ruling out certain potential counterexamples to proposed applications of the justice principles, they also rule out consideration of ways in which delegates under more familiar conditions might reasonably wish to deal with the principles. Chief among these background assumptions are the postulates Rawls calls: (1) the "well-ordered society"; (2) the "basic structure"; and (3) the "primary goods." [5] We shall briefly examine each of them in order.

BACKGROUND ASSUMPTIONS

Rawls's treatment of justice does not concern itself with the tangled features of real, that is, ongoing, society. Rather, Rawls takes as the arena in which various proposed concepts of justice are to be examined the "well-ordered society," one in which certain key problems of self-governing polity are presumed to have been solved. A well-ordered society is one that is "designed to advance the good of its members" and is "effectively regulated by a public conception of justice" (p. 5). By the latter condition, Rawls means that it is a society in which "(1) everyone accepts and knows that the others accept the same principles of justice, and (2) the basic social institutions generally satisfy and are generally known to satisfy these principles" (p. 5). Rawls has spelled out (or compiled from various locations in *TJ*) further features of this well-ordered society in more recent publications.[6] In the hypothetical well-ordered society, Rawls says there are conditions of moderate scarcity, reasonable beliefs (on which to ground the public conception of justice), generally accepted methods of inquiry, fundamental and divergent individual aims and interests supporting claims on the design of social institutions, various opposing and incompatible basic beliefs, and so on. *All* of the features defining a well-ordered society, Rawls tells us, are incorporated into the description of the original position.[7] He also tells us that "the only principles which authorize claims on institutions are those that would be chosen in the original position" (p. 218). So the conditions of a well-ordered society are more than a base on which stage 2 delegates may build; they set the bounds within which whatever is built must stand, and the standards by which it is to be approved.

Rawls thinks that the conditions of the well-ordered society are recognizably reasonable, since they are arrived at by the process of asking ourselves what form of society we might wish to live in.[8] At the same time, he admits that "existing societies are of course seldom well-ordered in this sense" (p. 5). Manifestly, however, the entire set of conditions is *never* satisfied by existing societies.[9] And, although these conditions may seem reasonable to us (in the flush of our present social knowledge), they may not seem transparently reasonable to the constitution-makers of stage 2. The chief reason they may not is that Rawls's account of the institutions of a well-ordered society assumes as made and well made what to the stage 2 delegates will appear to be something in the making. To them, it is bound to seem that they inherit the very conclusions they are supposed to be striving to secure. The postulate of the well-ordered society determines that institutions these delegates choose *will* legitimate the claims citizens make on each other based on their fundamental aims and interests, conduce to a supporting sense of justice, provide a more or less sufficient and productive scheme of social cooperation for mutual good (where productivity means a better-than-zero-sum game), and so on. The fact that these ends are fixed before the business of the convention is begun makes stage 2 decision-making *safe* by ruling out many of the familiar hazards of social choice, but it cannot help but make it seem correspondingly *unnatural*. The unnaturalness is most clearly manifested in the fact that stage 2's parasitic relation to stage 1 inhibits application to it of our intuitively clear concepts of debate and voting.

The point I am urging here is simply the converse side of Norman Bowie's objection to Rawls's blurring of the boundaries between the stages. As Bowie pointed out, "the constitutional convention and the constitution which results partially determine the meaning of the first principle by providing an explication of the phrase 'most extensive total system of equal basic liberties compatible with a similar system of liberty for all.' " [10] Just as Rawls's first justice principle is ultimately dependent for its meaning on the constitution, so it appears the constitution is ultimately dependent for its meaning on conditions assented to in order to facilitate agreement on the first principle at stage 1.

The impact of this objection becomes more obvious when we consider what Rawls says regarding the "basic structure," a notion tightly interlocked with the postulate of the well-ordered society. One of the defining features of the well-ordered society is that its members take the basic social institutions and their arrangement into one scheme as the "primary subject of justice" to which the justice principles apply.[11] These institutions in their arrangement constitute the basic structure.

> For us the primary subject of justice is the basic structure of society, or more exactly, the way in which the major social institutions distribute fundamental rights and duties and determine the division of advantages from social cooperation. By major institutions I understand the political constitution and the principal economic and social arrangements. (p. 7)

Now, it would seem from this definition that the question of what basic structure a society shall have will be left primarily to the constitution-makers. Surely society's chief interest in having a constitution is to secure by formal rules a favored distribution of rights, duties, cooperative advantages, and so on. But it can hardly be said that stage 2 decision-makers determine such rules by debating and voting their rational preferences (as informed by current evidence of distributional options) if the basic structure itself was already available for stage 1 decision-makers to use in formulating justice principles for a well-ordered society. Rather than simply voting allocational policies and the like into effect, stage 2 decision-makers must consider whether what they now make fits with the stage 1 prevision of those policies, and so on. And that prevision has veto power over their decisions. For, we may be reminded, claims on institutions are authorized *only* by principles which would be adopted at stage 1. The constitutional delegates seem, on this view of things, to be caught up in an elaborate shuttle between the stages, baptizing rules of the basic structure, rather than fathering them.

Another set of problems arises from the way in which Rawls seeks to use the basic structure postulate to confine the scope of *TJ* to a system of social relations considerably narrower than that of society in general. The basic structure simplifies political theory chiefly by excluding consideration of justice as it relates to international and interstate relations, on the one side, and the practices of private associations, on the other. For these extremes, Rawls tells us, we may need "different principles [of justice] arrived at in a somewhat different way" (p. 8). The basic structure, it is argued, allows us to solve problems for a "special case," with the expectation that the solutions we find will make problems in other cases more tractable. "For the time being," then, Rawls explains, we may consider the basic structure of society "as a closed system isolated from other societies." [12]

In his most recent writings, Rawls has amplified somewhat the notion of basic structure and has argued at some length for the importance of taking it as the primary subject for a theory of social justice.[13] These writings have not, however, mitigated Rawls's earlier remark that "the concept of the basic structure is somewhat vague. It is not always clear which institutions or features thereof should be included" (p. 9). In *TJ*, Rawls is satisfied to proceed on an "intuitive understanding" of the basic structure, passing off the admitted vagueness with the declaration that "it would be premature to worry about this matter here" (p. 9). But intuition scarcely seems capable of settling what needs settling in this case. By assuming that people are barred from emigrating from the societies into which they have been assigned at birth by fate, Rawls magnifies the importance of each of the assumptions he makes about that society, assumptions such as that it contains significant social and economic inequalities, children, and a scheme of family organization in which the parents' control over their children's early years is great and greatly influenced by the parents' economic position, and so on. If we believe that familial, economic, and social relations acquire their full meaning only in a supersocietal (e.g., international) context, or if we believe that they are reducible to functions of private transactions, we shall object to some features of

Rawls's basic structure. If we believe all social relations are dominated by, and explicable only in terms of, some deep-seated psychological determinants such as fear or agapistic love, we might quarrel with the (apparent) exclusions of these features from the basic structure. It is hard to say how much weight should be assigned to such objections as these. Perhaps the subject matter boundary of the basic structure can be adjusted to accommodate such apparently divergent claims. As things stand, however, there is no way of knowing whether this can be accomplished; for Rawls has left his "intuitive" notion of basic structure so vague that it is impossible to identify features it does include and exclude. What is beyond doubt is that Rawls's employment of the notion narrows in some significant ways the scope of decision-making at each of the stages of the four-stage sequence. If it were to lack this effect, it is plain that the basic structure could not be discriminated from the wider social background it is meant to simplify.

A third simplifying assumption in Rawls's program is his stipulation that social decision-making throughout the stages is restricted to a consideration of the distribution of what he calls "primary goods." Broadly speaking, these are rights and liberties, opportunities and powers, income, wealth, and (considered somewhat separately from the rest) a sense of personal worth (p. 92). Rawls has been forcefully critized for refusing to allow any "looking behind" these primary goods in the process of constructing a just social system, both because this refusal seems to rule out the provision of extra benefits for those with special needs,[14] and because his assumptions about the goods he denominated "primary" seem to bias the decision-making process in favor of individualism and against communitarian values.[15] In responding to his critics, Rawls has fleshed out somewhat the barebones notion of primary good he employed in *TJ*, amplifying the problematic component "good-notions" of wealth and income, and clarifying the easily misinterpreted motivational assumption of mutual disinterest that attends them.[16] More importantly, perhaps, he has sought to clarify the way in which the doctrine of primary goods makes sense as part of sound sociological and psychological strategy. The suppositions involved in this strategic interpretation are: (1) (sociological)—"that, given a just distribution of primary goods, individuals and associations protect themselves against the remain-

248 RONALD MOORE

ing institutional forms of injustice"; and (2) (psychological)—"that
strong or inordinate desires for more primary goods on the part of
individuals and groups, particularly a desire for greater income and
wealth and prerogatives of position, spring from insecurity and
anxiety." [17] Undeniably, these are weighty suppositions whose
projected consequences, if correct, bolster considerably the plausibility of the doctrine of primary goods laid down without
particular attention to strategic consequences in *TJ*. But, they will
obviously not go far toward carrying the convictions of anyone
whose general sociological and psychological views are greatly at
odds with these assumptions, or, for that matter, of anyone who
views all assessments of the place of (primary) goods in social theory
as immune to considerations of sociological and psychological
strategy.

The fleshed-out notion of primary goods may seem elastic enough
to embrace almost anything which could be construed as goods,
simpliciter. What could a person possibly want that could not be
construed as, in some extended sense, a power, an opportunity, or
wealth? But, the notion of primary goods is, after all, supposed to be
another simplifying assumption; and we may take it from this alone
that Rawls intends it to reduce the complexity of decision-making
in the various stages by eliminating consideration of some social
factors some people might wish to regard as goods. His idea seems to
be this: just as the demonstration that desirable effects follow from
applying the justice principles to the basic structure of a well-
ordered society will give momentum to the suggestion that these
same principles will be useful in wider arenas, so the demonstration
that reasonable justice calculations can be made against a limited
list of primary goods will give momentum to the suggestion that
they can work on a longer list. To be of use, the primary-goods list
must restrict decisions throughout the four stages to what can be
weighed in terms entered on it. The list is quite short; if it were very
long the point of discriminating primary goods from others would
be lost and Rawls's arduous defense of the primacy of the primary
goods chosen would be wasted. But, because the list is short, there
are bound to be some potential decision-makers who can legit-
imately complain that considerations they believe to be relevant to
constitution-making, and so on, have been assigned no weight.
Disregarding some putative goods *ab initio* (as weightless) differs

sharply from determining that they are outweighed by other consideration in the open process of choosing details of social design. Plainly, then, Rawls's vision of constitution-making will diverge to some extent from the common view that everyone's sense of goods, primary, secondary, or *n*-ary, is to be given *some* weight. And, to that extent, the simplifying assumption of primary goods is an obstacle rather than an aid in our efforts to determine whether Rawls's hypothetical choosers choose as we would. In the following section, we shall pursue this last question more directly, by examining what Rawls has to say about the stage 2 process of just constitution-making itself.

THE PROBLEM OF DISSENT

When Rawls's stage 2 delegates arrive at the door of their imaginary convention hall to draft a constitution, they have accepted the twin principles of justice articulated in stage 1, and they have accepted them against the backdrop of various simplifying assumptions. They enter the hall, and the veil of ignorance is raised somewhat, revealing -the information requisite to their enterprise. What comes next? We can answer this question only with guesswork. Rawls has left the scene very dim. My guess, based mainly on the evidence that Rawls hasn't troubled to spell out anything to the contrary, is that he assumes the convention will proceed more or less in the manner in which constitutional conventions typically proceed. As an example, the federal Convention of 1787 may well come to mind. Thanks to Madison, we have a pretty clear idea of how delegates to that "great debate" behaved. We know that they were mutually suspicious, parochial, contentious, earnest, high-minded aristocrats; that they prided themselves in assuming a perspective *sub specie aeternitatis* through reason and natural law; and that they created the basic text of American government mainly by wrangling, wheedling, compromise, and wearing each other out. More importantly, however, we know that these delegates subscribed unanimously to what Rawls calls the "basic ideas" of modern constitutionalism, the ideas of "the sovereign people who have final authority and the institutionalizing of this authority by means of elections and parliaments, and other constitutional forms" (p. 385).

To what extent should we assume that Rawls's stage 2 convention will conform to the paradigm we inherit from the great Convention of 1787? For one thing, we know that Rawls's delegates vote. They adopt (on another simplifying assumption) "a variant of majority rule suitably circumstanced" as "a practical necessity" (p. 354). And we know that they institutionalize governmental authority through the usual majority-constraining mechanisms of constitutionalism (e.g., a bill of rights) (p. 228). Unless, therefore, there is more than meets the eye in Rawls's somewhat mysterious qualification "suitably circumstanced," it seems likely that the patterns will first begin to diverge over what the different delegates think of "the final authority of the people." It is manifestly apparent that Rawls's delegates are somewhat less willing than the founding fathers to regard this principle as a warrant for unrestraint in the forum.

In the open-forum convention (of which the 1787 Convention is an approximate, though admittedly imperfect instance), nobody's ideas regarding the design of government are ruled out of court. Rules that everyone has grounds for thinking later generations might find unpalatable may still be enacted, on the theory that these rules can be changed when the people choose to exercise "final authority" through their amending power. Rawls appears willing to have his delegates move part way but not all the way toward this ideal. He does, as I have mentioned, make *some* room for dissidence. In constitution-making, he says, "the principle of loyal opposition is recognized, the clash of political beliefs, and of the interests and attitudes that are likely to influence them, are accepted as a normal condition of human life" (p. 223). How far is this "principle of loyal opposition" allowed to go? At times, Rawls suggests that constitutional controversy reaches only "the circumstances of justice": "A lack of unanimity is part of the circumstances of justice, since disagreement is bound to exist even among honest men who desire to follow much the same political principles" (p. 223). And at other times, he seems to suggest that it may extend to justice itself:

[A]lthough at the stage of the constitutional convention the parties are now committed to the principles of justice, they must make some concession to one another to operate a constitutional regime. Even with the best of intentions, their opinions of justice are bound to clash. In choosing a constitu-

> tion, then, and in adopting some form of majority rule, the parties accept the risks of suffering the defects of one another's knowledge and sense of justice in order to gain the advantages of an effective legislative procedure. There is no other way to manage a democratic regime. (pp. 354-55)

This formulation, framed in terms of controversy over "opinions" and "senses" of justice, rather than concepts or conceptions of justice, opens the questions of how far and in what ways the principles of stage 1 may be eroded and amended at stage 2. What sort of "concessions" does Rawls have in mind? There is little in *TJ* to help answer this question. The very admission that differences of opinion aired at the constitutional convention may extend to justice itself, however, raises fundamental problems for Rawls's account. The principles of justice were adopted *unanimously* at stage 1; and as the rational contractors move to stage 2, they acquire the *same* increment of information about their society. Whence the diversity, then? It is easy to see how men as we know them, neither fully rational nor equally informed, might make differing judgments about the rules appropriate to ambiguous circumstances. However, Rawls's contractors are, *ex hypothesi*, fully rational; so it is hard to see how equal lack of information could skew or alter their judgments about justice itself. Moreover, the mere lack of information should make no difference, if, as Rawls maintains, justice turns on rationality, not on information.[18]

It is with the arrival of the maverick—the delegate who accepts the justice principles, but who insists at the same time that they must be limited by other considerations in certain circumstances— that the ill-fated balancing act begins. The conditions of equality, Rawls says, require that delegates should have "a fair chance to add alternative proposals to the agenda for political discussion" (p. 225). Yet, "the test of constitutional arrangements is always the over-all balance of justice" (p. 231), construed according to the initially agreed-upon justice principles. What sort of maverick is welcome, then, and to what extent are his views to be given a fair hearing? Rawls maintains that the constitution which the delegates are charged to draft is an instrument for the protection of liberties and that these liberties ("when the constitution itself is secure," p. 219) should be extended to the intolerant. This position is argued on the analogy with religious toleration. In the arena of religion diversity of opinion is welcome: "Each person must insist upon an equal right to decide what his religious obligations are," and "a person is always free to change his faith" (p. 217). By pursuing the analogy of religious and political toleration further than Rawls would like, however, Victor Gourevitch seems to have come upon one sort of dissenter not likely to be well received at Rawls's convention.[19] This is the old-fashioned religious zealot who would not have constitutional protection of liberties extend to the equal freedom of conscience for everyone. He believes that he has the truth and that everyone should believe as he does. To him it appears that securing protection of liberties by a constitution which allows equal freedom of conscience to all will entail sacrificing his former belief that liberty of conscience requires everyone to believe as he does. And such a sacrifice would be the epitome of unreason. Gourevitch argues that, inasmuch as reasonable men have differed on perfectionist grounds regarding the balance of such benefits, Rawls's exclusion of this hypothetical maverick view is, itself, a gesture of dogmatic intolerance. He says:

> Rawls, who certainly inclines to the view that the benefits brought about by the great change in political opinion that has occurred during the past two or three centuries far outweighs [sic] the losses, if he thinks that it has involved any losses, and who bends all of his considerable powers to consolidate this change, strives, throughout his work, to establish that a society which forces all men, as far as society can, to be rational, equal, and free, is both a juster and a better society for it. He does not think it even worth discussing whether such a society is just or good for those who might not have willingly chosen to be free, or rational, or equal, but might, for religious or spiritual reasons, or because they recognize their limitations, have preferred a more restricted political or spiritual freedom.[20]

Now, it is far from clear whether Gourevitch's religious zealot should be counted a true maverick, under the description given above. It is not apparent from Gourevitch's account that his zealot accepts the first justice principle. Rawls might well reply to this form of dissent that justice, freedom, rationality, equality, rightly understood, entail each other, as the original position hypothesis shows. Thus, the proposed opposition between some of them is false. And, in *TJ,* section 35, Rawls argues at some length that under a just and secure constitution toleration ought to be extended to the intolerant up to the point where they threaten the constitution by suppressing the views of those who disagree with them. In the latter case, Rawls says, intolerance has no legitimate complaint against counterintolerance (p. 220). On the other hand, Gourevitch might point to the fact that Rawls extends a privileged status to the right of self-preservation (p. 218) and that one might consequently reason that, because what touches the soul must intimately touch the self, one who puts religious principles in jeopardy puts himself in jeopardy. Other lines of counterrebuttal appear open as well. Two suggested by what Gourevitch says are that Rawls's position on the entire matter is clouded by a suspect psychological assumption (occurring at p. 219) and that the original position hypothesis covertly and illegitimately embraces religious skepticism.

Even if Gourevitch's zealot should not qualify, another, more clearly eligible maverick is not hard to find. Delegate Jones has all his credentials in order. He has been to the original position and loved it. He arrives at the stage 2 convention bubbling with enthusiasm for both justice principles. Jones is, however, neither brave nor bright. In fact, stupidity and timidity (which I take to be compatible with self-interested rationality) are as much ingrained in him as religious zeal was in Gourevitch's delegate candidate.[21] As soon as the relevant general facts of society are revealed behind the lifting veil, Jones rises trembling to declare that, in light of the apparent perils of the times (which he probably overestimates), the right of equality of respect (which appears to be a sacred, immutable right to Rawls) should be subordinated to the right of general safety in certain areas. He does not argue that the twin principles of justice should be abandoned; nor does he argue that equality of respect should be foresworn as a general rule. Jones merely insists that a "side constraint"[22] should be placed on the original principles in light of current conditions: when the situation gets sufficiently threatening (by some criterion he may or may not be able to spell out), some justice-correlated rights should be suspended. And he is happy to have his rider principle applied to himself as much as to others. If he is reminded of the manner in which constitutional guarantees derive from the original contract, he will respond indignantly that the original contract was conceived in ignorance and that new information requires an adjustment in the rules. Is it beyond belief that such a dissenting view might gather support among the delegates? What if Smith, who is timid but not stupid, agrees with him? Could the support build toward majority? If so, how are the orthodox Rawlsian delegates to respond?

Rawls has, I believe, left open two—perhaps three—lines of response for them. First, they might invoke a procedural principle Rawls lays down for the conduct of the convention:

> The parties in the constitutional convention . . . must choose a constitution that guarantees an equal liberty of conscience regulated solely by forms of argument generally accepted, and limited only when such argument establishes a reasonably certain interference with the essentials of public order. (p. 215)

Following this rule, the body of delegates might regard repression of the maverick's dissenting opinion as justifiable in the name of safeguarding the essentials of public order. And, indeed, given certain general facts about society, a fearful dissident's willingness to suspend some of the rights otherwise guaranteed by the justice principles *would* be dangerous to public order. Recent history has provided all-too-ample illustrations of the hazards that follow from official paranoia when phantom perils are invoked to legitimate the curbing of rights. On the other hand, the loose criterion, "reasonably certain interference with the essentials of public order" may strike us as rather uncomfortably like the notorious "national-security" touchstone, also of recent memory. Whether or not the "public-order" criterion worries us by reminding us of such things (and whether or not, moreover, we are worried when so reminded), we are likely to be bothered by its glaring vagueness. Rawls leaves the phrases "reasonably certain" and "interference with the essentials of public order" wholly uninterpreted. Consequently, they provide no legible guidelines for the reasonable control of dissent.

On the face of it, the Rawlsian delegates' second line of response seems more plausible. It is to invoke the notions of "original

position" and "reflective equilibrium" as a means of neutralizing
the controversy between themselves and the dissident maverick.
Rawls provides that "at any time we can enter the original position,
so to speak, by following a certain procedure, namely, simply by
arguing for principles of justice in accordance with [certain named]
restrictions" (p. 19). (It may be recalled that such a "shuttle"
strategy—a checking back and forth between positions—seemed to
be implied by the basic structure assumption.) Once the delegates
have projected themselves back into the original position's situation
of choice, they may "go back and forth" in their construction of
justice and its consequential principles, letting conditions and
particular cases lead to the revision of judgments (pp. 20-21). Thus,
it may be argued, stability can be restored to the convention by the
very process of equilibration that led initially to stability (indeed,
unanimity) in the original position, the process Rawls speaks of as
"working from both ends" (p. 20). But, when the disequilibrium
occurs in the second stage, rather than the first, a serious question
arises as to what the *ends* are from which one is supposed to work. If
reentry into the original position for the purpose of reflective
equilibration means putting aside the incremental information
acquired at stage 2 and checking back on the basis of moral
judgment earlier accepted, the effort seems a pure redundancy.
Reenacting the prior deliberations, undertaken with the veil fully
down, cannot settle problems which arise out of conditions which
appear only when it is partially lifted. This would be hollow
"memento ritual," incapable of settling anything because it reminds
the decision-makers of what they are *assumed* to remember. But, if
the reentry procedure allows importation into the subject matter of
reflective equilibrium the stage 2 increment, it is hard to see how
the procedure can be spoken of as a reentry into the original
position. For, the concept of "original position" is defined in terms
of its own restrictions on information. If the conditions that obtain
in stage 2 are allowed to have a corrective effect on decisions made
at stage 1, a real question arises as to why the stringent restrictions
on knowledge characterizing stage 1 were imposed in the first place.
If, that is to say, "going back and forth" means reopening all stage 1
questions in light of events occurring in the stage 2 convention,
there would appear to be no purpose served by Rawls's contractors

deciding anything prior to stage 2. Since everything is known there that was known at stage 1, and more, that, it would seem to follow, is where the work should begin.[23]

The first two lines of response to dissent by the orthodox Rawlsian delegates seem, for these reasons, to be less than persuasive. A third line, bolder than these, but perhaps more ominous in its implications, may be thought to remain open. It is to say that Jones, our genuine but unintelligent maverick, expresses views that cannot be credited simply because they are false, and that Smith, the maverick whose agreement with Jones is based on a realistic, informed appraisal of the general facts of society, is an impossibility. According to this view, both hypothetical mavericks (and Gourevitch's as well) are impostors. If they really know the facts and principles proposed as the basis of stage 2 choice, they will agree with the rest of the delegates; if they don't know them, they have lost their credentials as delegates. After all, isn't it Rawls's pervasive, underlying theme that, in the basic structure of a well-ordered society, interests *do* fall in line with the pattern according to which primary goods are distributed by the justice principles? And isn't the whole point of "checking back and forth," of the assumptions of rationality, stability, finality, and the rest, simply to confirm that the reasonable man's intuitions will, as a matter of course, lead to the conclusions he describes? According to one way of reading Rawls, at any rate, it is clear why mavericks pose no problem on the stage 2 convention floor. They simply don't show up.[24]

Such an argument, I firmly believe, makes a mockery of what Rawls says about the clash of opinions, the contrast between notions of justice, and the need for compromise in stage 2. To make sense of Rawls's remarks in these directions we must, I think, assume that some delegates who are as dedicated or as informed as the rest may believe that their interests (or the interests of society in general) do not coincide with what justice requires for its own sake. Barry has argued that "the essence of Rawls's political thinking is that laws must be made by people who desire to do what justice requires for its own sake, and not because it happens to coincide with their own interests." [25] But Rawls has, in fact, left this vital issue entirely unclear. He says, on the one hand, that "[t]he principle of participation compels those in authority to be responsive to the felt interests of the electorate" (p. 227). And he says, on the other hand:

first (regarding the constitutional stage itself) that "Where issues of justice are involved, the intensity of desires should not be taken into account (p. 231); and second, that the legislative discussion, which is subject to the constraints of the constitutional stage, "must be conceived not as a contest between interests, but as an attempt to find the best policy as defined by the principles of justice" (p. 357). In the face of such apparently conflicting remarks, I am at a loss to say with confidence what role "interest" has in Rawls's theory. I am, however, prepared to say that if the view that in certain circumstances "the intensity of desires should not be taken into account" means that disagreement and controversy (even if founded on misapprehension) will have no role in constitutional design, then Barry is entirely right in saying that such an admission imparts to the overall program a conspicuously "sinister" aspect.

JUST AND JUSTIMIFIC

While Rawls has drawn both agreement and disagreement into the picture he gives us of stage 2, the overall impression we have of his hypothetical convention is not likely to be a stalemate between them. There is room for dissent on the floor, to be sure; but, on the whole, the accumulation of tempering background assumptions, the presence of a spirit of compromise, and the mutual commitment to the fundamental principles of justice will appear to have a settling and solidifying effect on the proceedings. It is hard to escape the impression that Rawls conceives the convention as a by-and-large harmonious, cooperative working out of governmental design, a process whose smooth efficiency is guaranteed by the fact that its main business consists of educing specific constitutional provisions from premises all parties accept. Such a view of the proceedings may strike us as unrealistic if we think of constitutional conventions as inherently wild and woolly battles of values and interests. And it may strike us as vaguely disquieting in the way that an all-too-mechanical dream is disquieting.

But the apparent general stability of the convention floor (which I may have overestimated) is not the root reason why we should find Rawls's vision of constitution-making unrealistic. It is the purported stability of what the delegates enact, rather than their way of enacting it, that should bother us most. The constitution these delegates draft is supposed to be prospectively stable. The provisions it contains are not only just; they are such as will lead to a continuing predominance of justice in social arrangements in the future. Having gotten us to agree that it will be good for the convention to be run in accord with the principles of justice, Rawls would have us tacitly consent to the permanent supervenience of these principles over other social values through the institutional forms enacted at the convention.

To be sure, plenty of features in the four-stage sequence threaten to undermine the prospective stability of the just constitution. Under majority rule, Rawls admits, mistakes (owing both to lack of knowledge and judgment and to partial and self-interested views) are inevitable (p. 354). To gain the benefits of effective legislative procedure at stage 3, the delegates of stage 2 are forced to submit to the consequences of each other's defective knowledge and mistaken senses of justice (p. 355). More importantly, the information at the delegates' disposal for making sound predictions is itself far from perfect. The delegates know the relevant general facts about their society, but "the tendencies of the general social facts will often be ambiguous and difficult to assess" (p. 357). And, in assessing these tendencies, the delegates are supposed to estimate the net balance of primary social goods; but the theory of primary goods "depends on psychological premises and these may prove incorrect" (p. 260).

Working against these potential destabilizing factors, however, and winning out, is Rawls's supposition that a just system musters its own support through generating among its members "an effective desire to act in accordance with its rules for reasons of justice" (p. 261). Thus, the stability of the system of government that the constitution sets into motion is secured through justice itself. Stability, as Rawls conceives it, is a matter of justice checking injustice: "[S]tability means that when tendencies to injustice arise other forces will be called into play that work to preserve the justice of the whole arrangement" (p. 219). (In this sense, even civil disobedience and conscientious refusal may be regarded as institutional stabilizing devices, although extralegal ones (p. 384.) But the efforts of the constitution-makers to maximize constitutional stability are not limited to counteracting social tendencies toward injustice. They go beyond this, to counteract the tendencies of other positive virtues that might compete with justice in the ordering of social policy.

The constitution Rawls wants his delegates to make is more than just; it is *justimific.*[26] Rawls tells us repeatedly that the only constitution authorized is one calculated to maximize justice at the later stages. "The fundamental criterion," he says, "for judging any procedure is the justice of its likely results" (p. 230). Applied to the task of constitution-making, this criterion requires that delegates select from the inventory of feasible constitutions the one "best calculated to lead to just and effective legislation" (p. 197). Or, stating the objective in the language of stage 4 rather than stage 3, they are to select the one that "will most probably result in effective and just social arrangements" (p. 198). This justimificity principle has the effect of discounting values and desires which might otherwise be weighed in with justice in shaping the future social order. Rawls takes what is, in fact, quite a hard line on the exclusion of alternative values. Speaking of the principles that would be chosen in the original position as "the kernel of political morality" (p. 221), he makes it abundantly clear that the justimific constitution is supposed to be the hard shell around this kernel: "When persons with different convictions make conflicting demands on the basic structure as a matter of political principle, they are to judge these claims by the principles of justice" (p. 221). And, again: "[T]he test of constitutional arrangements is always the overall balance of justice. Where issues of justice are involved, the intensity of desires should not be taken into account" (p. 231).

Surely the "overall balance of justice" is *one* worthwhile test of the merit of a constitution; but it is far from obvious that it should be *the* test. Justice may be conceded to be a necessary condition for a constitution's being desirable (i.e., the best alternative) without its following that justimificity is the sufficient condition. Rawls reminds us in "Constitutional Liberty and the Concept of Justice" that "justice is but one of many virtues of political and social institutions, for an institution may be antiquated, inefficient, degrading, or any number of other things without being unjust." [27] Suppose that, bearing this thought in mind, the stage 2 delegates decide that they will do all that they can to make a constitution that is perfectly undegrading, say, without being perfectly justimific. Does this, in and of itself, mean that the constitution they select

from among the plausible options cannot be "the best"? It would
seem not. If in their system for all the virtues, the principle of
nondegradation weighed heavily, the delegates' failure to adopt
principles giving strong effect to this principle in contest with other
virtues would simply be irrational. There seem to be no compelling
reasons, even on Rawls's terms, not to allow that such a course
might be preferred by such delegates as he has described.

Or suppose that the gods hate the word "maximin" and propose
a bargain with the constitution-makers: "If you make it a constitutional precept that no one speak that word, we will guarantee that
no one will contract cancer for one hundred years." Should the
delegates say, "No soap! We can restrict liberty through our laws
only for liberty's sake, and not for health's sake"? (That the
principle of restricting liberty only for the sake of liberty is part of
the moral geometry of justice is argued for in *TJ*, section 32.) Surely,
it is not unthinkable that the constitution-makers may wish to
change one rule, the rule of free speech, perhaps even on a
temporary basis (until the hundred years run out, say), fully
realizing that doing so will not maximize liberty, and hence not be
justimific.

It may be responded to this line of objection that it runs afoul of
the condition of finality that Rawls attaches to the justice principles. Rawls does stipulate that "the original agreement is final and
made in perpetuity, there is no second chance" (p. 176). And he insists repeatedly that the contractors' choice must prevail at all later
stages because it is an "agreement in perpetuity," a "once and for
all choice," and so on. But, it is important to remember in reading
such remarks that when the notion of finality is first introduced, it is
held that "the final court of appeal" for practical reasoning is a
"fully general theory which has principles for all the virtues" (p.
135). It is not manifestly apparent that, in a *system* of final
principles, considerations of justice will invariably override other
considerations based on other virtues.

There is, we should note, an ambiguity in Rawls's position
regarding justimificity calculations that gives rise to an objection
parallel to the stage-blurring objections raised earlier (see Section II,
above). The justimificity rule appears to require of stage 2 delegates
calculations that are strictly prospective estimates of probability.
Rawls charges the delegates with the responsibility of framing that

constitution that is *"more likely than any other* to result in a just and effective system of legislation," and, he adds, "the justice of the constitution is to be assessed . . . in the light of what circumstances permit, these assessments being made *from the standpoint of the constitutional convention"* (p. 221; emphasis added). Elsewhere, however, Rawls says, "[b]y moving back and forth between the stages of the constitutional convention and the legislature, the best constitution is found" (p. 198). Here, admittedly, he is speaking about the issue of just legislation; but that fact does not make the statement any less revealing. If we can, as this suggests, "move back and forth" between stages 2 and 3 at will, the incremental information barrier set up by the veil-of-ignorance mechanism would seem to be a sham. Why, if it is possible to shuttle between stages in this way, should assessment of justimificity be confined to the constitutional standpoint? And why should the delegates settle for probability estimates when, by direct comparison, they can be certain of their constitution's effects on legislation? [28]

It seems to me that Rawls largely assumes, and does not argue for, the doctrine of justimificity. The basis for his assumption, however, seems to be that justice, like liberty, is one of those political concepts that we cherish so dearly that we are willing to insist that nothing can circumscribe their scope except themselves. So, for example, he is willing to declare that "arguments for restricting liberty proceed from the principle of liberty itself" (p. 242); and likewise, we may presume, for arguments restricting justice. H. L. A. Hart has argued persuasively that Rawls's argument regarding the restriction of liberty is incoherent, except perhaps in the simplest cases of weighing claims. He points out that in more complicated, genuinely problematic, constitution-making problems "conflicts between basic liberties will be such that different resolutions of the conflict will correspond to the interests of different people who will diverge over the relative value they set on the conflicting liberties." [29] And he adds: "Rawls fails to recognize sufficiently that a weighing of advantage and disadvantage must always be required to determine whether the general distribution of any specific liberty is in a man's interest, since the exercise of that liberty by others may outweigh the advantage to him of his own exercise of it." [30] I should think that Hart's line of attack on Rawls's liberty doctrine may be easily adapted for an assault on the doctrine that justice is to be limited only for the sake of justice. Rawls, in fact, leaves the door open for this form of response when he remarks, at the outset of *TJ,* that "even though justice has a certain priority, being the most important virtue of institutions, it is still true that, other things equal, one conception of justice is preferable to another when its broader consequences are more desirable" (p. 6). Surely what Hart has said about the role of interests in the resolution of conflicts between basic liberties in constitution-making applies equally to the connection of interests and "broader consequences" in constitution-making. That is to say, the weighing of "broader consequences" will also turn on the divergent appraisals delegates make of the relative values of differing blends of basic social virtues; and the various resolutions struck will reflect the interests, (i.e., the primary estimates of desirability) of these parties. That the delegates do not know at stage 2 much about what their interests are does not, I think, militate against their seeking to keep open the grounds of decisions respecting those interests when they are known. We should, in this context, remember that Rawls's decision-makers are presumed to know at every stage that, at the final stage, they will, at last, have all the facts before them.

Near the end of *TJ,* Rawls, almost despite himself, adds fuel to this attack on the doctrine of justimificity by allowing that the justice principles themselves are not as eternal and immutable as he first makes them out to be. Several hundreds of pages after all the talk of the rational contractors' "once-and-for-all choice," "agreement in perpetuity," and so on, he comes around to saying: "We have to concede that as established beliefs change, it is possible that the principles of justice which it seems rational to choose may likewise change" (p. 548). If this is so, it would seem reasonable for constitution-makers to incorporate into the institutional forms some rules based on virtues that are less pervious than is justice to the corrosive effect of changing beliefs. Even if none of the other virtues of the "total system" turn out to be more immune to change than justice, they may still wish to institutionalize certain virtues that may be expected to harmonize with justice, and thus conduce to a stable total political system. Here again, the choice turns ultimately on the delegates' estimate of the desirability of "broader consequences." And, clearly, nothing that we know about the constitution-makers tells us that their reasoning as to this question will be dominated by considerations of justice alone.

To be fair to Rawls, we should admit that the context in which the statement cited above about the change in justice principles occurs makes it appear that only one kind of alteration in belief, and, correspondingly, only one alteration in the justice principles, are under consideration. The change in belief comes when a society has attained a sufficient degree of economic development to make the value of liberty more attractive than that of other basic goods. And the change in principles is only a departure, legitimated by this historical development, from the "general" form of the justice principles to the "special form" (i.e., the form in which a "priority rule" orders them serially, prohibiting the trading off of basic liberties for economic or social gains). Under the most favorable interpretation, Rawls can be construed as saying that shifting from the general to the special conception of justice does not violate the principle of finality. As he sees it, the parties to the original contract are not barred by the veil of ignorance from perceiving that the crucial change in the material conditions of their society is in the works. So they can adopt the special conception of justice *conditionally;* that is, they can accept it as effective just when the appropriate stage of social well-being has been attained. Rawls suggests, in fact, that to do otherwise would be irrational:

> As the conditions of civilization improve, the marginal significance for our good of further economic and social advantages diminishes relative to the interests of liberty, which become stronger as the conditions for the exercise of the equal freedoms are more fully realized. Beyond some point it becomes and then remains irrational from the standpoint of the original position to acknowledge a lesser liberty for the sake of greater material means and amenities of office. (p. 542)

But surely, if the point can be allowed for liberty, it should be allowed for justice itself. There might, for all the contractors know, come a point beyond which it becomes and remains irrational to prefer a perfectly just but, say, degrading rule over a nondegrading one which is somewhat less just. When does that point come? How

can we recognize such a point, if it comes? Such questions as these
are not answerable within the ideal framework of Rawls's theory.
Neither, however, are the corresponding questions directed to the
general-special breaking point. We cannot answer such questions
because, in the end, we do not know enough about the delegates,
confined within their network of simplifying assumptions, and
barred from certain forms of information, to know what they might
prefer. We simply do not know what "broader consequences" they
will, on balance, find "more desirable." Manifestly, however, we
should not conclude from the fact that we do know that they find
justice desirable that they find desirable the exclusion of other
values in the name of justice.

AFTER THE CONVENTION

At some point, of course, the job of the constitution-makers will
be finished. The convention will adjourn, and the discussion of
policy will move on to later stages. At this point, it is to be expected
that some of the "final authority of the people" will be put into the
hands of a Supreme Court, whose justices will have the task of
informing the people and their legislatures what the constitution
says they may and may not do. How are these justices to proceed?
According to one view, they should decide the constitutionality of
statutes and acts by recurring directly to the principles of justice
pervading and ordering the constitution as a whole. According to an
alternate view, they should decide such issues by referring to the
particular express rules of the constitution, thinking of each rule as
embodying a policy directed by a (possibly unique) blend of
primary social values. Readers who warm to the ideal majesty of
Rawls's stage 2 convention may prefer the former. Readers unable
to shed their fondness for the 1787 convention's wide-open free-for-
all atmosphere, may be pleased to hear what Justice Black had to
say in *International Shoe Co.* v. *Washington:*

> There is a strong emotional appeal in the words "fair play,"
> "justice," and "reasonableness." But they were not chosen by
> those who wrote the original Constitution or the Fourteenth
> Amendment as a measuring rod for this Court to use in
> invalidating State or Federal laws passed by elected legislative

representatives. No one, not even those who most feared a democratic government, ever formally proposed that courts should be given power to invalidate legislation under any such elastic standards. Express prohibitions against certain types of legislation are found in the Constitution, and under the long settled practice, courts invalidate laws found to conflict with them.[31]

NOTES

1. I have profited greatly from conversations with Professor Rawls concerning some themes touched on in this paper. I should also like to acknowledge my indebtedness to Professors Peter Radcliff, J. R. Pennock, J. Chapman, and to Nancyanne Moore for their very useful comments on earlier versions of this paper. All errors of interpretation, analysis, and so on, are, of course, my own.
2. John Rawls, *A Theory of Justice* (Cambridge: Harvard University Press, 1971). Hereafter referred to as *TJ*. Page references to this work are indicated parenthetically in the text.
3. My quarrel with these principles is taken up in "What Hath Rawls Got?" *Journal of Chinese Philosophy,* 2 (1977), 143-160.
4. Specifically, by the history of the United States Constitution *(TJ,* 196n.).
5. The list is far from exhaustive. We might add the "principle of lexical priority," the "principle of pure procedural justice," the empirical bar to the "great disparities" objection, and so on. The three chief assumptions named, however, appear to be the most sweeping in their consequences for decision-making in the four-stage sequence, and it is therefore appropriate to focus the discussion on them.
6. An annotated list of twelve characteristics defining the "well-ordered society" is provided in John Rawls, "Reply to Alexander and Musgrave," *Quarterly Journal of Economics,* 88 (November 1974), 634-636. The first seven items in this inventory are also discussed in John Rawls, "Fairness to Goodness," *Philosophical Review,* 84 (October 1975), 547-551.
7. Rawls, "Fairness to Goodness," p. 548.
8. John Rawls, "A Kantian Conception of Society," *Cambridge Review* (February 1975), p. 94.
9. Indeed, it is certain that no society has ever satisfied even the *first* of Rawls's conditions: that "Everyone accepts, and knows that others accept, the same principles (the same conception) of justice" ("Reply to Alexander and Musgrave," p. 634).

10. Norman Bowie, "Some Comments on Rawls' Theory of Justice," *Social Theory and Practice,* 3 (Spring 1974), 71.

11. Rawls, "Reply to Alexander and Musgrave," pp. 635-636.

12. *TJ,* 8. It is hard to say what Rawls means by saying that the basic structure should be conceived as a closed system "for the time being." This formulation suggests that, at some future point, the basic structure itself may be viewed as something more than a "closed system." But when, later in *TJ,* Rawls does get around to discussing the relations of justice to the law of nations (e.g., '58), and so on, it appears that he is speaking of something *beyond* the basic structure, and not an ampler form of that structure. Since the *point* of the basic structure as a methodological device was simplification to the special case, it is altogether unclear what an open-system basic structure would be if it is to remain something separate from the concept of society in general.

13. See "A Kantian Conception of Equality," p. 95, and especially, "The Basic Structure as Subject," a paper read by Rawls at the Fifty-first Annual Meeting of the American Philosophical Association, Pacific Division, March 25-27, 1977.

14. See Brian Barry, *The Liberal Theory of Justice* (Oxford: Oxford University Press, 1973), pp. 55 ff.

15. See, generally, Adina Schwartz, "Moral Neutrality and Primary Goods," *Ethics,* 83 (1973), 294-307, and Michael Teitelman, "The Limits of Individualism," *Journal of Philosophy,* 69 (1972), 545-556. My summary formulation of the core of Schwartz's and Teitelman's attack is that provided by Rawls in "Fairness to Goodness," p. 540.

16. Rawls, "Fairness to Goodness," pp. 540-545.

17. *Ibid.,* p. 546.

18. I may have overestimated the degree to which "concession" and disagreements over "opinions" and "senses" of justice at issue here are matters concerning conduct of the convention proper, rather than prospective considerations, identifying problems delegates should anticipate as likely to occur in the later operation of the constitutional regime. A conversation with Rawls has helped me to see more of the latter motive in the passage in question (pp. 354-355). I think, however, that the language of the text as it stands does lay itself open to the objections I raise.

19. Victor Gourevitch, "Rawls on Justice," *Review of Metaphysics,* 28 (March 1975), 498.

20. *Ibid.,* pp. 498-499.

21. At this point it may be objected that anyone qualified as rational under Rawls's criterion of rationality is ipso facto intelligent (or, at any rate, not outright stupid) and perhaps also reasonably brave (or,

at least not vulnerable to irrational fears). It must be said, however, that the concept of rationality Rawls invokes does not make the necessity of these relations at all apparent. Rawls tells us that, with the important exception of an envy-exclusion proviso, the concept of rationality at work in *TJ* is "the standard one familiar in social theory" (p. 143). In a general way, one may suppose, this should be taken to mean that the deliberations rational agents make are to be viewed in abstraction from many features peculiar to individuals in their specific settings of choice. One might, for example, wish to eliminate consideration of a wide range of egocentric psychological characteristics as having no bearing on rational deliberation. Rawls's model is apparently abstract in much the way that microeconomic theory is abstract. Still, Rawls does feel compelled to provide a special exclusion category for envy. Shouldn't the reader infer that his failure to provide similar special exclusions for fear and stupidity leaves these features open as possibilities for rational agents? Certainly the references to philosophical discussions of rationality made at p. 143n. throw little light on the issue. One can, for example, imagine stupid and timid superbees who are rational, taking everything else that Bennett says about them as correct.

22. The notion of side constraints is developed by Robert Nozick in *Anarchy, State, and Utopia* (New York: Basic Books, 1974), pp. 28-35.

23. Rawls does, of course, occasionally talk about justification being a matter of "everything fitting together into one coherent view" (p. 579). But it seems to me that a general equilibrium notion and the four-stage strategy are plainly incompatible. The point of the differences between stages is lost if we can conveniently check their overall coherence at any point in the game.

24. This way of disposing of the problem may be thought reminiscent of Rawls's attempt to finesse the problem of great disparities as it relates to the difference principle. To the objection that it would seem unreasonable for the justice of increasing the wealth of the more well off by a billion dollars to hinge on the prospect of the loss or gain of a penny by the least well off, Rawls's blunt reply is, "The difference principle is not intended to apply to such abstract possibilities. . . . The possibility which the objection envisages cannot arise in real cases; the feasible set is so restricted that they are excluded" *(TJ,* 147-158). This apparently empirical rejoinder seems altogether out of keeping with the *avowedly* abstract "ideal theoretic" approach maintained in the rest of the text. If, granting the background assumption, the knowledge restrictions, and acceptance of the justice principles, it is "empirically" possible for the maverick to dissent, it is not persuasive to respond that his objection "cannot arise in real cases." If,

in this case, the "feasible set" of decision-options is so restricted that this objection is excluded, then it is proper to conclude the set is overrestricted.

25. Barry, *The Liberal Theory of Justice*, p. 144.
26. It is necessary at this point to coin a term for the propensity to maximize justice. Admittedly, "justimific" is clumsy, but it recommends itself as the natural Rawlsian correlate to "optimific" as used in utilitarian theory.
27. John Rawls, "Constitutional Liberty and the Concept of Justice," *Justice, Nomos VII*, eds. C. J. Friedrich and John Chapman (New York: Atherton Press, 1963), p. 98.
28. It might also give us pause that Rawls speaks here of "finding" the best constitution through the shuttle technique. Making something—a car, a dinner, a constitution—is a matter of assembling, adjusting, and perhaps replacing parts; finding something is coming upon what was (in some sense) there all along. In this passing suggestion that the best constitution might be *found*, Rawls gives us a tantalizing clue that there may be more Platonism in his program than is at first apparent.
29. H. L. A. Hart, "Liberty and Its Priority," *University of Chicago Law Review*, 40 (1973), 545.
30. *Ibid.*, pp. 550-551.
31. 326 U.S. 310, 66 S. Ct. 154, 90 L. Ed. 95.

12

THE JURISPRUDENTIAL USES OF JOHN RAWLS*

RICHARD B. PARKER

I

In December 1973, the Association of American Law Schools met in New Orleans. At the convention's major luncheon, with the Chief Justice of the United States in attendance, the announcement was made that a book by a Harvard philosophy professor [1] had won the Coif Award as the best book written in law in the three preceding years. The strangeness of the occasion can be more easily appreciated against a list of earlier winners of the Coif Award. They were:

1964: *Selected Essays on the Conflict of Laws* by Brainerd Currie
1967: *Security Interests in Personal Property* by Grant Gilmore
1970: *The Oracles of the Law* by John P. Dawson and *The Limits of the Criminal Sanction* by Herbert O. Packer [2]

One explanation for the award which I heard expressed at the convention was that the selection committee was unduly influenced

* A draft of this essay was read to the Tuesday Evening Club at New York University Law School on December 6, 1977. I am indebted to the members of the club for several helpful suggestions and criticisms. I am

by several members with abnormally strong philosophical interests.[3] Why otherwise should a book of social philosophy, however meritorious, be given an award ordinarily going to a book about law? Were important books in sociology or economics given consideration?

Events since 1973, however, seem to support the selection committee's view of the unusual interest for lawyers of this particular work of social philosophy. Citations to the book in law reviews have become increasingly numerous. The book is required reading for a larger and larger percentage of law students. Law professors with no special interests in philosophy increasingly feel some professional obligation to become acquainted with the main ideas of the book. My own impression is that *A Theory of Justice* has been more enthusiastically received by lawyers than by philosophers and political theorists. Part of the explanation for the enthusiasm may be the unprecedented publicity which the book has received.[4] But the main purpose of this essay is to show that lawyers have uses of their own for *A Theory of Justice* and have discovered virtues in it that many philosophers have failed to appreciate fully.

A law professor friend, educated in Europe, once remarked to me that Rawls's book reads as though the nineteenth century had not happened. He then noted that the United States is still governed by an eighteenth-century constitution. One reason for the inclusion of Rawls in a legal education is that *A Theory of Justice* articulates some fundamental values protected by the United States Constitution. To put it more strongly, it is arguable that *A Theory of Justice* formulates as well as any book to date the principles of justice expressed by the Constitution. This thesis, if true, would be sufficient to establish the importance of the book for lawyers regardless of the truth of Rawls's theory or the cogency of his reasoning.

The initial plausibility of the idea that any constitution expresses a single conception of justice rests on the picture presented by Rawls's own four-stage sequence.[5] Recall that Rawls sets out his four-stage sequence as a framework to simplify the application of the two principles of justice.[6,7] The first stage is the original position

indebted also to David A. J. Richards, Kenneth I. Winston, and the editors of *Nomos* for their very useful correspondence on that earlier draft.

behind the veil of ignorance in which Rawls's two principles of justice are chosen. The final statement of Rawls's two principles with some accompanying priority rules which Rawls offers to aid interpretation of those principles is as follows.

First Principle:

Each person is to have an equal right to the most extensive total system of equal basic liberties compatible with a similar system of liberty for all.

Second Principle:

Social and economic inequalities are to be arranged so that they are both:

(a) to the greatest benefit of the least advantaged consistent with the just savings principle,[8] and

(b) attached to offices and positions open to all under conditions of fair equality of opportunity.

First Priority Rule (The Priority of Liberty):

The principles of justice are to be ranked in lexical order [9] and therefore liberty can be restricted only for the sake of liberty. There are two cases:

(a) a less extensive liberty must strengthen the total system of liberty shared by all;

(b) a less than equal liberty must be acceptable to those with the lesser liberty.

Second Priority Rule (The Priority of Justice over Efficiency and Welfare):

The second principle of justice is lexically prior to the principle of efficiency and to that of maximizing the sum of advantages; and fair opportunity [clause (b) of the Second Principle] is prior to the difference principle [clause (a) of the Second Principle]. There are two cases:

(a) an inequality of opportunity must enhance the opportunities of those with the lesser opportunity;

(b) an excessive rate of saving must on balance mitigate the burden of those bearing this hardship.[10]

After the choice of this conception in the original position, the contractors move to the second stage, a constitutional convention, where, subject to the constraints of the principles of justice already chosen, they are to design a system for the constitutional powers of government and the basic rights of citizens.[11] At this second stage, the veil of ignorance is thinned a bit so that the contractors now know "the relevant general facts about their society, i.e., its natural circumstances and resources, its level of economic advance and political culture, and so on." [12] The third stage is the legislative stage where the veil of ignorance is totally lifted except that contractor-legislators do not know particular facts about themselves.[13] The fourth stage is the following of rules of law by judges, administrators, and citizens.[14] Everyone has access to all the facts. At each of the first three stages, the veil of ignorance keeps out that information that is not relevant from the point of view of justice to the decisions to be made at that stage.[15] At each stage, the conclusions of the prior stages are binding upon the participants: the constitution is chosen to implement the principles of justice, the legislators are bound by the constitution, and the citizens are bound by the law.[16]

The veil of ignorance and the four-stage sequence are only expository devices.[17] The story of contractors in the original position behind the full veil of ignorance is a graphic way of summarizing a whole set of normative and empirical premises, few of which are argued for in the book.[18] I discuss this point in more detail in the next section of this essay.

The thesis the truth of which would justify and explain lawyers' interest in *A Theory of Justice* is that the United States Constitution as it presently exists with all of its amendments might have been chosen by contractors who had already chosen Rawls's two principles and were now charged with drawing up a constitution, given knowledge of the relevant general facts of present-day American society, including the fact that we now have the Constitution we do have. Another way of stating the thesis is that Rawlsian contractors already committed to Rawls's two principles of justice would not significantly alter the United States Constitution. In this sense, the Constitution is an expression—an expression relative to American economic, political, and social history—of Rawls's two principles of justice.

The thesis that the contractors would choose not to change the present-day United States Constitution does not entail that Rawls's conception of justice has been realized in present-day America. Having a constitution does not guarantee that everyone's constitutional rights are respected. The United States Constitution sets standards that are often not met. The thesis holds only that those constitutional standards are an attempt to apply Rawls's two principles to the particular circumstances of American economic, political, and social history.

It is important to realize that the truth of the thesis does not require that the United States Constitution be a unique solution to the application of Rawls's principles of justice to present-day America. The principles are very general, and many constitutions might fill the bill.[19] The federal system, for example, is not explicitly required by the two principles. Yet given that the facts of present-day American society include a federal system to which everyone is accustomed, it seems reasonable to suppose that the contractors would presently choose a constitution which provides for a federal system.[20]

Analogously, the truth of the thesis does not require that difficult cases of constitutional interpretation be solvable by direct application of Rawls's two principles of justice. That would be to expect too much of theory and to give too little credit to the importance of the lawyers' craft.[21] Both Rawls's principles of justice and many of the most interesting provisions of the United States Constitution are too abstract to be mechanically applied. Their application requires practical wisdom, and skill in the arts of casuistry in which lawyers are trained.

A counter-example to the thesis would be a provision in the Constitution clearly incompatible with Rawls's two principles. Examples are the provisions for the institution of slavery in the United States Constitution of 1789.[22] Fortunately for the thesis, these provisions were removed by the Civil War amendments.[23]

It appears that the major arguments against the thesis are not positive provisions in the Constitution which directly contradict Rawls's two principles, but the absence of provisions that seem to be dictated by the two principles. For example, if the proposed Equal Rights Amendment [24] is necessary to insure equal citizenship to women, that is, if the equal protection clause of the Fourteenth Amendment [25] is in fact not sufficient, then the present absence from the Constitution of the Equal Rights Amendment would weigh against the thesis that the Constitution expresses Rawls's two principles.

The most telling arguments against the thesis arise with Rawls's Second Principle. The Constitution of the United States seems designed neither to insure that all offices and positions shall be open to all under conditions of fair equality of opportunity nor, especially, that all social and economic inequalities are to be arranged so that they are to the greatest benefit of the least advantaged (the "Difference Principle").[26] Part of the solution to these difficulties may be to view the Constitution as designed to further only the First Principle of justice insuring that each person have an equal right to the most extensive total system of equal basic liberties compatible with a similar system of liberty for all. Rawls himself assigns the labor of insuring expression of the Second Principle to the legislative stage.[27] But a defense of the thesis should not rest on a strict distinction between the constitutional convention and the legislative stage. Rawls also says that the best constitution is found by moving back and forth between the stages of the constitutional convention and the legislature.[28] And, in the United States, all serious matters of the justice of the basic structure of society [29] that become political issues become issues of constitutional law as well. The compliance of the basic structure of society with the Second Principle may have to be governed to some degree by constitutional rights to a minimum income and to the material means for equal opportunity.[30] That the United States Constitution does not seem to require equal opportunity, and clearly does not require the Difference Principle, is a problem for the thesis.

Most Americans, including lawyers, would, contrary to Rawls,[31] defend some notion of moral desert based on effort as basic to social justice. While they believe that such desert should not condition one's basic liberties, the majority of Americans do not believe that sheer citizenship is sufficient to support the constitutional right to the benefits of the Difference Principle. On the other hand, Rawls's First Principle, as well as, to some degree, the requirement of equal opportunity in the Second Principle, and the priorities established between the two principles, seem to most American lawyers to give expression to basic constitutional values. To the degree that the Difference Principle can be defended as a necessary consequence of the theory unifying so much else of what American lawyers believe about the Constitution, it may in time be accepted that the Constitution requires realization of the Difference Principle. Rawls's theory may simply be the spelling out of the implications of taking human equality seriously. If such equality is also basic to our Constitution, then perhaps the Constitution requires the Difference Principle.

It may be said in derogation of the thesis considered here that the views on social justice of the Founding Fathers or of the authors of the Civil War amendments were closer to Robert Nozick's [32] than to John Rawls's. Two responses can be made to this charge. Both are partially true, and each provides part of the answer.

First, the charge can be denied. It can be asserted that differences between what the founding fathers or the authors of the Civil War amendments believed the Constitution requires and what we believe it requires are only differences over means to achieve Rawlsian ends. The Founding Fathers may have thought—and it may have been true in 1789—that certain property rights were necessary to protect a system of basic equal liberties. But times and the social and economic organization of society have changed so drastically that preservation of equal liberty may now require much more governmental control over private property. Similarly, experience has taught us what the authors of the Civil War amendments could not have known: that doctrines of separate but equal are not adequate means, in the American context, to achieve equal protection of the laws for blacks. Insight into what means are necessary to achieve the vision of society inherent in the Constitution has affected our conception of what the Constitution requires in particular contemporary situations, but the basic principles expressed by the Constitution, and the meaning of the provisions of the Constitution, remain the same.

Second, to the extent that the charge is true, the views of the Founding Fathers or of the authors of the Civil War amendments are not dispositive. They must be considered, as we shall expect future generations to consider our views; but the Constitution is the constitution of those living under it. Accordingly, it must be interpreted to give expression to our own best vision, all things considered, of what is just. Rawls's book is useful as the best available formulation of that vision and, accordingly, the best

available description of the principles underlying the best judicial
decisions of the last twenty-five years.

Another indication that the Constitution expresses Rawls's two
principles of justice, or something very close to them, is what many
lawyers and law students experience upon reading *A Theory of
Justice*.[33] They find that a reading of the book strengthens their
commitment to the Constitution by clarifying for them what they
themselves believe about social justice. Read as an expression of
belief, lawyers experience the book as an exciting reaffirmation of
constitutional and personal values. They are moved by Rawl's
vision in Part III of his book of a New Englandish society composed
of a hierarchy of town meetings. *A Theory of Justice* seems to function
among lawyers as a handbook for the faithful. For those out of
sympathy with the Constitution, and few lawyers are out of
sympathy, Rawls is unsatisfying because so much that is basic is
simply asserted without argument. But as I shall argue below, *A
Theory of Justice* is not designed to persuade the heathen.

II

It is important to keep in mind in reading Rawls that both the
original position with its veil of ignorance and the four-stage
sequence are only expository devices used to set out in summary
form the many normative and empirical premises which Rawls
accepts without argument and from which he argues to his two
principles of justice. In his interesting reconstruction and critique of
Rawls, Robert Paul Wolff argues that when Rawls began to develop
his theory in the 1950s, he hoped to show that his two principles
were binding on any rationally self-interested agent willing to
commit himself to a moral point of view.[34] Wolff argues that Rawls
came over time to see that he had set himself an impossible task and
that he came to regard his theory more and more as a rational
reconstruction of his and his reader's views on social justice.[35] On
this view of what Rawls is doing, the normative and empirical
premises which are built into the notion of the original position and
the veil of ignorance are acceptable if they are in fact our premises.
No further argument is necessary if Rawls is simply reconstructing
and ordering our own views for us. It seems clear that this is what

Rawls is doing,[36] which makes him less interesting to philosophers but much more interesting to lawyers.

Philosophers often criticize Rawls either (1) for not providing argument for debatable premises, or (2) for not being specific enough regarding the practical application of his conception of justice.[37] Rawls would and must plead guilty to both charges.

Rawls does knowingly assert virtually without argument that: (1) justice is the first virtue of social institutions; (2) a "well-ordered society," that is, a society composed of free and equal moral persons adhering to a single conception of justice, is both possible and desirable; and (3) the conception of justice most suitable for a "well-ordered society" is the one which would be unanimously agreed to in a hypothetical situation that is fair. None of these three propositions is argued for in *A Theory of Justice* except that Rawls hopes that the coherence and scope of the entire picture painted by the book may convince the uncertain reader.[38] What is argued for in the book is that given these three assumptions plus several others, the particular conception that will be chosen in the fair hypothetical situation will be Rawls's two principles. Societies based on aesthetic values, or on warrior virtues, are not seriously considered. The moral equality of persons is taken for granted. Caste systems are beyond the pale. Rawls also knowingly assumes the same mildly pessimistic view of human nature that is presupposed by the United States Constitution. He does offer in Part III some arguments from developmental psychology to counter a deeper pessimism that would regard the vision of a human society organized around Rawls's two principles as a dangerous pipe dream.[39] He does not consider more optimistic views of mankind that would allow the possibility of human societies not organized by the jealous virtue of justice. Given that Rawls takes all this as given, it is no wonder that some social philosophers and political theorists complain that he has begged all the interesting questions. But lawyers, self-selected into American law schools, and educated in the American constitutional tradition, already believe what Rawls assumes about equality and human nature. They are willing to grant Rawls all of his basic premises, for they are interested in his actual enterprise of showing how a single determinate conception of justice follows from his, and their, premises. To the degree that Rawls's conception of justice is an articulation of what they already believe, his principles of justice provide lawyers with a common starting point and an enriched vocabulary for discussion of how to apply the only slightly less abstract provisions of the United States Constitution to contemporary problems.

At one point Robert Paul Wolff says of Rawls's theory:

> So long as we remain in the realm of rational reconstruction [of the readers' beliefs about social justice] the logical status of the project is clear, and not terribly satisfactory. The ground for asserting the principles arrived at by the analysis is merely the general agreement of the audience with the original moral convictions of the author. In short, the entire procedure can be no more than aimed for a sophisticated rendering of the *consensus gentium.*[40]

I think that rational reconstruction is all that Rawls is doing, or claims to be doing. Wolff is expressing a philosopher's disappointment that Rawls did not do more. But what is disappointing to philosophers is exciting to those who agree with the *consensus gentium,* which includes most American lawyers. Even statements as abstract as Rawls's two principles of justice eliminate many possible justifications for decisions made by American legislatures and courts.[41]

As for the second charge that Rawls is not specific enough, if Part II of *A Theory of Justice* is viewed as a serious attempt to address the problems of designing a particular constitution, or of weighing liberties against one another in concrete cases, or of designing particular economic systems, then it is obviously inadequate. But the fact that Rawls does not spell out in much detail how his principles are to be applied does not usually bother lawyers. They do not expect it from a philosopher. They view Part II of *A Theory of Justice* as Rawls intended it, as a clarification of the conception set out in Part I, not as an attempt to apply that conception to the hard problems of designing in a particular social context, particular social and political institutions.[42] They understand that actual application of Rawls's two principles requires the intervention of at least two more levels of specialists: first, philosophically trained lawyers to translate Rawls's conception of justice into principles of constitutional law; and second, sophisticated practicing lawyers and judges willing to apply those principles of constitutional law in complex factual settings.

A growing literature by philosophically trained lawyers takes Rawls's two principles as starting points and attempts to apply them to particular public policy issues.[43] This literature, and Rawls' book, can be seen as the two middle stages of a developing five-stage unification of theory and practice.

At the first stage there is traditional social philosophy and political theory, the classical authors such as Locke, Rousseau, and Kant, and the secondary literature and commentary comprising "the familiar theory of the social contract"[44] which underlies not only Rawls's theory but also the United States Constitution.[45]

The second stage is Rawls's theory which picks up where much traditional political theory leaves off and argues to a formulation attractive to, and applicable in, our own society (attractiveness being one of the conditions for applicability).[46]

The third stage is the work of philosophically inclined lawyers who begin where Rawls leaves off and discuss the application of his conception of social justice to particular problems of constitutional law.[47]

The fourth stage is the work of the practicing lawyer, bureaucrat, or judge who applies the analysis of the third stage to particular cases.

The fifth stage is that of the citizen who, under the Constitution, is often called upon to make an independent evaluation of the work of lawyers, judges, and legislators, and decide whether to dissent or disobey.[48]

A major virtue of this five-stage sequence of theory and practice is that, in addition to being more detailed and complete than anything that has gone before, its further development does not depend on the existence of the extraordinary man who combines in himself both theoretical and practical wisdom. People can be trained to do good work at one of the stages, and also trained to appreciate and work with specialists at adjacent stages. Rawls is accessible to academic lawyers as Kant and Rousseau are not. Practicing lawyers will apply the work of academic lawyers who speak directly to a problem on which the working judge or attorney must write a brief or opinion. The work of the capable judge, attorney, or administrator becomes philosophically informed, more reflective, and more internally consistent—in short, better and more worthy of the respect of the citizen. The results at the fourth and fifth stages will in turn stimulate theoreticians in the first three stages to cooperate consciously in developing a more detailed articulation of the prospectives and values inherent in the American constitutional tradition.

The prospect of a unified theory of the United States Constitution spanning the distance from the best philosophical arguments for the basic moral premises inherent in the Constitution to justifications for decision in actual cases is an exciting one. The lasting effect of Rawls may be that, by working so effectively on an uncharted part of the distance between theory and practice, he has demonstrated both how great that distance is and also how it might be traveled.

III

There is another reason for the success with lawyers of Rawls's book apart from its contribution to the articulation of an ethical tradition already accepted by most lawyers. When the book is viewed as the second stage of a full working out of the "American constitutional tradition" from first premises to specific cases, it becomes clear that that tradition has only one serious competitor within the American legal and political system. That competitor is utilitarianism.[49] Often the unarticulated basis for public policy decisions hidden in some "neutral" consideration such as "efficiency," utilitarianism is rapidly developing its own five-stage sequence. In the first stage are the classical utilitarians such as Bentham and Mill and the large body of sophisticated philosophical literature which makes up utilitarian theory. The analogue to Rawls are those scholars, primarily economists, who begin from utilitarian premises and argue to general principles attractive to and applicable to American society. The third stage is illustrated by Richard Posner's and Guido Calabresi's analysis and criticism of legal doctrines.[50] The fourth stage is the work of the lawyers, judges, and administrators who see their proper role as the fostering of economic efficiency. The beliefs of citizens who justify obedience or disobedience to law in utilitarian terms constitute the fifth stage.

A case could be made that at the present time the utilitarian five-stage sequence is more theoretically developed and more influential in American law and public policymaking than what I have called the American constitutional tradition.[51] In some areas of law, such as antitrust law, where considerations of economic efficiency provide the express reason for the law's existence, the utilitarian sequence easily holds the central place. In areas of law touching immediately on important personal rights such as the case law on provisions of the Bill of Rights and the Civil War amendments, economic efficiency seems to lawyers a much less important, if not bizarre, consideration.[52] In still other areas of law, lawyers increasingly realize that many of the major issues in their fields can be instructively viewed as presenting a choice between a theory that maximizes some conception of the good, whether it be efficiency of some sort, pleasure, productivity, or happiness, and a theory that takes rights seriously enough to honor them even though the sum total of the common good suffers thereby.[53] A major reason for the interest of lawyers in Rawls is that he provides a common point of reference for those presenting the rights side of these debates.

The conscious unification of theory and practice in the five-stage sequences described above, whether the utilitarian sequence or the rights-oriented sequence, represents a new sort of jurisprudence that might be termed "ethical jurisprudence." The double meaning is appropriate. "Ethical jurisprudence" is an apt description of the activity in that ethical premises are appealed to as grounds for justifying, explaining, and criticizing legal doctrine. And the people who engage in the activity regard justifying and criticizing from ethical premises as the ethically required way to handle legal doctrine.

(Some writers at the third stage of the utilitarian sequence attempt an ethically neutral stance.[54] In part, this rhetorical neutrality is a remnant of the view that economics can be, in some important way, value neutral. The original attraction of economic analysis to many lawyers was that it seemed to give value neutral yet nonarbitrary anwers to questions of what the law should be.[55] As economic analysis of law is increasingly seen to be an application of a kind of utilitarian ethics, the rhetorical neutrality will be dropped in favor of substantive argument that the law should above all be economically efficient because, in a world where resources are limited and people are in need, it is wrong above all to be wasteful.)

The primary problem that many readers who are not philoso-phers will have with ethical jurisprudence is: whose ethics are to determine decisions when different ethical premises dictate different results in a difficult case or policy decision? Part of the answer is that most of those decisions should involve explicit argument for and against various ethical premises. Ethical jurisprudence builds on the work of philosphers over the last twenty-five years, which shows the possibility of rational discussion of ethical questions.[56] Ethical positions are not simply subjective matters of taste insuscep-tible to justification or refutation.

Another part of the answer is that many questions open to the moral philosopher are closed to a lawyer arguing from points of authority—statutes, cases, legal principles, and constitutions. His decisions are controlled by the ethical premises contained in those points of authority. The Constitution of the United States, for example, is not some ethically neutral set of procedures for regulating conflict between subjective differences of opinion. Ac-cepting the Constitution as authoritative commits us to a definite and controversial set of ethical premises which forecloses many possible ways of deciding cases or deciding what legislation to pass. Lawyers, all of whom have sworn an oath to uphold and defend the Constitution of the United States or one of the state constitutions, have committed themselves to uphold and defend a definite set of ethical premises. The hard part is to discover just what those premises are and what they require of us. If *A Theory of Justice* comes even close to being an articulation of the ethical premises contained in the United States Constitution, it is no wonder that the book won the Coif Award.

The jurisprudence of one generation of lawyers is often the accepted practice of the next generation. When Oliver Wendell Holmes, Jr, refers to jurisprudence in his 1897 essay, "The Path of the Law," [57] he means the activity of abstracting basic principles of law from the cases. Examples are his own groundbreaking treatise, *The Common Law*,[58] published in 1881, and the later *Restatements of the Law* published by the American Law Institute beginning in the 1920s. In the 1930s and 1940s, the use of sociology and psychology to explain legal decisions was urged and illustrated in jurisprudence courses. Now such explanations are incorporated routinely into many courses in the law school curriculum. In twenty years, the techniques of ethical criticism of legal decisions will, I think, be part and parcel of legal education. Now those techniques are the stuff of jurisprudence courses around the country (I include courses in economic analysis of the law where the ethical basis of the analysis is explicitly recognized), but are scarcely used in other courses. The hope of a value-neutral "science of law" dies hard. Rather than reject principled justification of legal results in favor of causal explanation and prediction as the legal realists did, ethical jurisprudence rejects only the hope of ethically neutral principles as a sufficient basis for legal decision and affirms the possibility of a principled ethical justification of legal doctrines.[59] Just as the legal realists made clear that law could be improved by using the social sciences, ethical jurisprudence attempts to show that the law will improve when legal doctrines are explicitly justified in ethical terms.

Although Rawls's book is the expression of an eighteenth-century moral and political tradition which happens to be our own, *A Theory of Justice* is in one respect a twentieth-century book. Rawls does not view himself as putting forward *the* theory of justice. He concedes that some might not find compelling the ethical and empirical premises that he builds into his description of the original position. Nor does he appeal to any authority beyond the reader's own well-considered beliefs. The question can always be raised: why should the reader not change his beliefs, or the country change its traditions? Rawls is important to lawyers as a description of what we believe and as an aid to making decisions consistent with the Constitution which we have sworn to uphold and defend. Whether we might hold other, better beliefs, and have different, better traditions is an important question, but one which does not seem to lawyers as urgent as the question of what is required of us by our present traditions and beliefs.

NOTES

1. John Rawls, *A Theory of Justice* (Cambridge, Mass.: Harvard University Press, 1971) [hereafter cited as *TJ*].
2. Information supplied by Ms. Jessie Petcoff, Administrative Assistant to Professor Frank Strong, National Secretary-Treasurer of the Order of the Coif.

The winner of the 1976 Coif Award was Lawrence M. Friedman, *A History of American Law* (New York: Simon & Schuster, 1973).

3. The Selection Committee for the 1973 award was: Dean Francis A. Allen, Chairman, University of Michigan Law School; William T. Coleman, Jr., Esq., Dilworth, Paxon, Kalish, Levy & Coleman; Professor Ronald M. Dworkin, Yale Law School; Professor Marian G. Gallagher, University of Washington School of Law; Hon. Frank R. Kenison, Chief Justice, Supreme Court of New Hampshire; Dean James A. Rahl, Northwestern University School of Law; Professor Yosal Rogat, Stanford University Law School; Professor Franklin E. Zimring, University of Chicago Law School.

4. See the Introduction to *Reading Rawls: Critical Studies of A Theory of Justice,* ed. Norman Daniels (New York: Basic Books, 1974), p. xi, for an account of the publicity received by *A Theory of Justice.*

5. *TJ,* 195-201.

6. *TJ,* 195.

7. It is essential to keep in mind that the four-stage sequence is a device for applying the principles of justice. This scheme is part of the theory of justice as fairness and not an account of how constitutional conventions and legislatures actually proceed. It sets out a series of points of view from which the different problems of justice are to be settled, each point of view inheriting the constraints adopted at the preceding stages. Thus a just constitution is one that rational delegates subject to the restrictions of the second stage would adopt for their society. And similarly just laws and policies are those that would be enacted at the legislative stage. Of course, this test is often indeterminate: it is not always clear which of several constitutions, or economic and social arrangements, would be chosen. But when this is so, justice is to that extent likewise indeterminate. Institutions within the permitted range are equally just, meaning that they could be chosen; they are compatible with all the constraints of the theory. Thus on many questions of social and economic policy we must fall back upon a notion of quasi-pure procedural justice: laws and policies are just provided that they lie within the allowed range, and the legislature, in ways authorized by a just constitution, has in fact enacted them. This indeterminacy in the theory of justice is not in itself a defect. It is what we should expect. Justice as fairness will prove a worthwhile theory if it defines the range of justice more in accordance with our considered judgments than do existing theories, and if it singles out with greater sharpness the graver wrongs a society should avoid. (*TJ,* 200-201)

8. The just savings principle is a limitation on consumption in any one generation, in order to provide for future generations. See *TJ,* 284-293.

9. Lexical order requires complete satisfaction of the First Principle before moving to the Second Principle. Thus, the First Principle cannot be weighed against the Second because the First Principle has an absolute weight with respect to the Second Principle. First Principle considerations cannot be sacrificed to Second Principle considerations. See *TJ,* 40-45.

10. *TJ,* 302-303.

11. *TJ,* 196-197.

12. *TJ,* 197.

13. *TJ,* 198-200.

14. *TJ,* 199-200.

15. It may be that some remnant of the veil of ignorance is also necessary at the fourth stage, that is, that some ignorance of some facts is necessary to an impartial application of any law. Those facts not necessary to the application of a law, yet liable to influence or distract the person applying the law, should ideally be kept from the person applying the law. This is, in fact, the major purpose of the legal rules which govern the admissibility of evidence at trials.

16. *TJ,* 200.

17. *TJ,* 21, 200-201. See the quotation *supra* note 7.

18. Robert Paul Wolff, in *Understanding Rawls: A Reconstruction and Critique of "A Theory of Justice"* (Princeton, N.J.: Princeton University Press, 1977) [hereafter cited as Wolff], pp. 119-132, questions the possibility of knowledge of "general facts about human society" or knowledge of general facts about present American society. Wolff draws a sharp distinction between our knowledge of natural reality and our knowledge of social reality. The former can be atemporal, but social knowledge is always "historical, self-reflective, and constitutive as well as descriptive" (Wolff, p. 126). Therefore, according to Wolff, the knowledge conditions of the ahistorical original position, and, presumably, of the constitutional convention and of the legislative stage as well, are defective.

Wolff explicitly denies that he is making the naive objection that there could never in fact be beings such as Rawls's contractors. He appreciates that the veil of ignorance is a literary device "designed to bring to life a logical claim" (Wolff, p. 121). He appreciates that, for example, it does not matter whether there could be persons without envy (Wolff, p. 121). I think Wolff would agree that Rawls's exclusion of envy from the original position is simply another way of stating the normative premise that envy of a certain sort is not to be taken into account in determining what is just. Similarly, Rawls's exclusion of facts about individuals is a vivid way of stating what is a controversial moral premise of his argument for his two principles, namely that facts about individuals are irrelevant to the choice of principles of social justice. It is that premise which marks Rawls as Kantian. Indeed, Rawls excludes so much from the original position and describes the contractors in such a way that there can be no real bargaining. All contractors reason exactly the same way because none has any reason to reason differently from the others. There might as well be only one "person" in the original position. This aspect of the story of the original position is simply a vivid way of saying that Rawls's two principles follow logically from the premises he builds into the original position. *(TJ,* 121). The problem is, as Rawls acknowledges, that he cannot produce the deduction, so he gives us the story of the original position instead *(TJ,* 121). It is a story that, like the stories of traveling through time in science fiction, may be incoherent when examined closely. But Rawls's deduction of his two principles from his assumed premises does not turn on the coherence of the story that Rawls uses in place of a full working out of the logical deduction.

I think Wolff would respond that his objection goes to the premises of Rawls's deduction, without regard to the coherence of the story of the original position. But Wolff or the reader make general statements all the time about human societies or about present day American society. Judicial opinions are filled with such statements, as are the preambles to all sorts of legislation. Are these statements, since they are statements about social reality, always defective because social reality cannot be known in the same way that natural reality can? I think Wolff would say that they are (Wolff, p. 210). But his objection is a point against not only Rawls's theory but against "the entire tradition of political philosophy of which *A Theory of Justice* is perhaps the most distinguished product" (Wolff, p. 210). The arguments pro and con are beyond the scope of this essay or, for that matter, beyond the scope of Rawls's book. Rawls limits his enterprise to developing "the familiar theory of the social contract" *(TJ,* 11). See Roberto Mangabeira Unger, *Knowledge and Politics* (New York: Free Press, 1975) and *Law in Modern Society: Toward a Criticism of Social Theory* (New York: Free Press, 1976) for an extended argument by a Harvard law professor against the tradition of political philosophy which includes Rawls's book and American constitutional law.

19. See the quotation *supra* note 7.

20. A federal system might also be more conducive to the high degree of decentralization which is implied by much of Rawls's argument in Part III of *A Theory of Justice* that a society well ordered by his conception of justice is psychologically possible and would contribute to the individual good of its members. In his discussion of envy, Rawls relies on a plurality of associations, each with its own secure internal life, to reduce the visibility, or at least the painful visibility, of variations in men's prospects (*TJ*, 536).

On the other hand, the federal system makes more difficult protection by the federal judiciary of individual rights as required by Rawls's two principles. Yet state courts may in the long run provide better protection for those rights. See Justice William J. Brennan, Jr., "State Constitutions and the Protection of Individual Rights," *Harvard Law Review*, 90 (January 1977), 489.

21. See the discussion in the text at pages 270-272 on the manner in which Rawls's conception of justice, or any abstract conception of justice, might be applied in the legal process.

22. "The Migration or Importation of Such Persons as any of the States now existing shall think proper to admit, shall not be prohibited by the Congress prior to the Year one thousand eight hundred and eight, but a Tax or duty may be imposed on such Importation not exceeding ten dollars for each Person" (U.S. Const., Art. I, Sec. 9, cl. 1).

"Representatives and direct Taxes shall be apportioned among the several States which may be included within this Union, according to their respective Numbers, which shall be determined by adding to the Whole Number of free Persons, including those bound to Service for a Term of Years, and excluding Indians not taxed, three fifths of all other Persons . . ." (U.S. Const., Art. I, Sec. 2, cl. 3).

"No person held to service or labor in one State, under the laws thereof, escaping into another, shall, in consequence of any law or regulation therein, be discharged from such service or labor, but shall be delivered up on claim of the party to whom such service or labor may be due" (U.S. Const., Art. IV, Sec. 2, cl. 3).

23.   AMENDMENT XIII [1865]

Section 1. Neither slavery nor involuntary servitude, as a punishment for crime whereof the party shall have been duly convicted, shall exist within the United States, or any place subject to their jurisdiction.

Section 2. Congress shall have power to enforce this article by appropriate legislation.

AMENDMENT XIV [1868]

Section 1. All persons born or naturalized in the United States, and subject to the jurisdiction thereof, are citizens of the United States and of the State wherein they reside. No State shall make or enforce any law which shall abridge the privileges or immunities of citizens of the United States; nor shall any State deprive any person of life, liberty, or property, without due process of law; nor deny to any person within its jurisdiction the equal protection of the laws.

Section 2. Representatives shall be apportioned among the several States according to their respective numbers, counting the whole number of person in each State, excluding Indians not taxed. But when the right to vote at any election for the choice of electors for President and Vice President of the United States, Representatives in Congress, the Executive and Judicial officers of a State, or the members of the Legislature thereof, is denied to any of the male inhabitants of such State, being twenty-one years of age, and citizens of the United States, or in any way abridged, except for participation in rebellion, or other crime, the basis of representation therein shall be reduced in the proportion which the number of such male citizens shall bear to the whole number of male citizens twenty-one years of age in such State. . . .

Section 5. The Congress shall have power to enforce, by appropriate legislation, the provisions of this article.

AMENDMENT XV [1870]

Section 1. The right of citizens of the United States to vote shall not be denied or abridged by the United States or by any State on account of race, color, or previous condition of servitude.

Section 2. The Congress shall have power to enforce this article by appropriate legislation.

24.   Section 1. Equality of rights under the law shall not be denied or abridged by the United States or by any State on account of sex.

Section 2. The Congress shall have the power to enforce, by appropriate legislation, the provisions of this article.

Section 3. This amendment shall take effect two years after the date of ratification.

25. See note 23 above for the text of the Fourteenth Amendment.
26. See text, page 271 above for the full statement of the Second Principle.

27. *TJ*, 199.
28. *TJ*, 198.
29. Rawls limits himself in *A Theory of Justice* to the justice of "the basic structure of society," which he defines as the major social institutions that distribute fundamental rights and duties and determine the division of advantages from social cooperation. Examples of such institutions are the legal protection of freedom of thought and freedom of conscience, competitive markets, and the monogamous family (*TJ*, 7-11).
30. Just what combination of constitutional rights, legislative programs, and social institutions would produce realization of the Second Principle in the United States is beyond the present ability of the social sciences to determine. The advantage of viewing the Constitution as requiring realization of a relatively determinant conception of social justice is that if we have some very general sense of the society we wish to achieve, it gives some point to empirical investigations of how to change things. See also *TJ*, 221-234.
31. *TJ*, 312.
32. Robert Nozick, *Anarchy, State and Utopia* (New York: Basic Books, 1974).
33. The remarks in this paragraph are based primarily upon reactions of my law students, to whom I have been teaching the book since before it won the Coif Award.
34. Wolff, p. 17 and pp. 180-181.
35. For a summary of the problems which forced this change, see Wolff, pp. 180-186.
36. *TJ*, 46-53. See also Rawls, "Reply to Alexander and Musgrave," *Quarterly Journal of Economics*, 88 (November 1974), 633-655 where he says, "The aim of a theory of justice is to clarify and to organize our considered judgments about the justice and injustice of social forms" (p. 633). See note 38 below.

    Unlike Wolff, I am using the term "rational reconstruction" so that it includes the results of being in "reflective equilibrium" and includes all of our best judgments evaluating the stability and applicability in practice of our conception of justice. See note 46 below. All of these factors affect what our actual conception of justice is; and it is our actual conception of justice that Rawls reconstructs for us.
37. An example of (1) is Milton Fisk, *History and Reason in Rawls' Moral Theory*. An example of (2) is H.L.A. Hart, "Rawls on Liberty and its Priority." Both of these essays are printed in *Reading Rawls: Critical Studies of "A Theory of Justice"*, ed. Norman Daniels (New York: Basic Books, 1974). Hart's essay also appeared in *University of Chicago Law*

Review, 40 (Spring 1973), 534. Most of the points made by Wolff fall within either (1) or (2).

38. That Rawls does not intend to provide argument for these three assumptions is, I think, clear in *A Theory of Justice.* It is made clearer by Rawls in "Reply to Alexander and Musgrave," *Quarterly Journal of Economics,* 88 (November 1974), pp. 633-655, in which Rawls summarizes his theory of justice from a different point of view. Instead of starting with the story of rational self-interested persons in an original position behind a veil of ignorance, he begins with the notion of a well-ordered society. A well-ordered socity is one made up of members who are and who view themselves as free and equal moral persons. A well-ordered society is also effectively regulated by a public conception of justice and is a society in which the basic social institutions generate an effective supporting sense of justice. To this definition, Rawls adds the assumptions of moderate scarcity, a divergence of fundamental interests and ends, and the assumption that social organization is not a zero-sum game. It can benefit all. Given all of these assumptions, the role of the principles of justice is to assign rights and duties in the basic structure of society and to specify the manner in which it is appropriate for institutions to influence the overall distribution of benefits and burdens. Rawls then asks, "[W]hich conception of justice is most appropriate for a well-ordered society, that is, which conception best accords with the above conditions" (p. 637). His answer for which he gives little argument is, "[T]he conception that is most appropriate for a society is the one that persons characteristic of that society would adopt when fairly situated with respect to one another. This hypothetical situation is the original position" (p. 637). Then follows the discussion of which principles would be chosen in the original position. That discussion forms the main argument of the article and of *A Theory of Justice.* Although Rawls makes clear in both the book and the article the value premises contained in the notion of a well-ordered society, argument for these premises is not the main purpose of the book or the article.

> Clearly the value of the notion of a well-ordered society, and the force of the reasoning based upon it, depends on the assumption that those who appear to hold incompatible conceptions of justice will nevertheless find conditions (1) to (7) congenial to their moral convictions, or at least would do so after consideration. [(1)-(7) specify the notion of a well ordered society.] Otherwise, there would be no point in appealing to these conditions in deciding between different principles of justice. But

we should recognize that they are not morally neutral (whatever that would be) and certainly they are not trivial. Those who feel no affinity for the notion of a well-ordered society, and who wish to specify the underlying conception in a different form, will be unmoved by justice as fairness (even granting the validity of its argument), except of course as it may prove a better way to systematize their judgments of justice. (pp. 636-637)

In the book, where he starts from the notion of the original position rather than from the notion of a well-ordered society, the assumptions characterizing the well-ordered society and the circumstances that make crucial the choice of a conception of justice are assumptions built into the definition of the original position.

See also Rawls, "Fairness to Goodness," *Philosophical Review*, 84 (October 1975),pp. 536, 539-540, and 547-551.

Rawls does provide some argument for his premises in Part III of *A Theory of Justice* by arguing for the possibility and desirability of a society well ordered by his two principles. See, for example, the arguments for the conclusion that "the collective activity of justice is the preeminent form of human flourishing" (*TJ*, 529). These arguments depend on interesting and controversial assumptions of developmental psychology set out in *TJ*, 453-512.

39. See esp. *TJ*, 453-512.
40. Wolff, p. 182.
41. See the literature cited in note 43 below.

42. In the three chapters of Part Two my aim is to illustrate the content of the principles of justice. I shall do this by describing a basic structure that satisfies these principles and by examining the duties and obligations to which they give rise. The main institutions of this structure are those of a constitutional democracy. I do not argue that these arrangements are the only ones that are just. Rather my intention is to show that the principles of justice, which so far have been discussed in abstraction from institutional forms, define a workable political conception, and are a reasonable approximation to and extension of our considered judgments. (*TJ*, 195)

43. The best example is David A. J. Richards, *The Moral Criticism of Law* (Encino, Calif.: Dickenson, 1977). See also some of the later chapters on particular policy issues in Ronald Dworkin, *Taking Rights Seriously* (Cambridge: Harvard University Press, 1977); ch. 4 of Bruce A.

Ackerman, *Private Property and the Constitution* (New Haven: Yale University Press, 1977); Charles Fried, *Medical Experimentation: Personal Integrity and Social Policy* (Amsterdam: North Holland Publishing Co., 1974); and much of Frank Michelman's work, for example, "In Pursuit of Constitutional Welfare Rights: One View of Rawls' Theory of Justice," *University of Pennsylvania Law Review*, 121 (May 1973), 962.

44. *TJ*, 11, although the "contract" in Rawls is a metaphor. See note 18 above.

45. See Bernard Bailyn, *The Ideological Origins of the American Revolution* (Cambridge: Harvard University Press, 1967).

46. Wolff is puzzled as to why Rawls makes one of the considerations for selecting the principles in the original position the ability of the set of principles to produce stability and harmony. If Rawls intends simply to describe what we believe about social justice, why, asks Wolff, should the fact that a society governed by such principles is unstable and disharmonious be a reason for altering our principles. (Wolff, p. 189). The answer is that if society would be unstable and disharmonious under a given set of principles, that is evidence that those principles do not express what we believe about social justice and are not the principles expressed by the Constitution.

47. See the work cited in *supra* note 43.

48. For development of a theory of civil disobedience, see *TJ*, 363-391, and Dworkin, *Taking Rights Seriously,* ch. 8.

49. Philosophers and political theorists have made the point that Rawls's justification for his two principles may be a sort of utilitarianism in which the rule is to maximize the minimum. If so, the conflict between the two five-stage sequences is an intramural struggle within utilitarian theory. But however described, the real conflicts noted in the text at note 53 and the work cited in note 53 between rights and other sorts of efficiencies remain.

50. Richard A. Posner, *Economic Analysis of Law*, 2d ed. (Boston: Little, Brown, 1977); Guido Calabresi, *The Costs of Accidents* (New Haven: Yale University Press, 1970). See also Guido Calabresi and A. Douglas Melamed, "Property Rules, Liability Rules, and Inalienability: One View of the Cathedral," *Harvard L. Rev.*, 85 (1972), 1089, reprinted in *Economic Foundations of Property Law*, ed. Bruce A. Ackerman (Boston: Little, Brown, 1975); and Calabresi, "Concerning Cause and the Law of Torts: An Essay for Harry Kalven, Jr.," *U. Chi. L. Rev.*, 43 (1975), 69.

51. Bruce A. Ackerman, in his interesting book, *Private Property and the Constitution* (New Haven: Yale University Press, 1977) agrees that Utilitarianism is a powerful force in contemporary American law. We

disagree on the nature of the major competitor to Utilitarianism. Ackerman sets out in his book (p.17) the following table of "forms of legal thought":

		Objective of Legal Analysis		
		Policymaker	v.	Observer
Nature of Legal Language	Scientific v. Ordinary	Scientific Policymaker		Scientific Observer
		Ordinary Policymaker		Ordinary Observer

According to Ackerman, the ordinary view of legal language views legal language as having its roots in ordinary English. "While legal specialists, naturally enough, will sometimes be called upon to make refinements generally ignored in ordinary language, recourse to everyday, nonlegal ways of speaking can be expected to reveal the basic structure and animating concerns of legal analysis" (p. 10). The scientific view of legal language "conceives the distinctive constituents of legal discourse to be a set of technical concepts whose meanings are set in relation to one another by clear definitions without continuing reliance upon the way similar-sounding concepts are deployed in nonlegal talk" (pp. 10-11). Ackerman gives Wesley Hohfelds's system of terms as an example.

With respect to the objective of legal analysis, for the Observer, "[t]he test of a sound legal rule is the extent to which it vindicates the practices and expectations embedded in, and generated by, social institutions" (p. 12). The Policymaker, on the other hand, aspires "to view seemingly disparate legal issues within a common framework provided by a relatively small number of abstract and general principles that are assumed to permit the consistent evaluation of all the disputes the legal system is called upon to resolve" (pp. 11-12). Such a framework is called by Ackerman a "Comprehensive View." Benthams' "Utility" or Posner's "Efficiency" are given as examples of "Comprehensive Views."

Ackerman views the struggle between Utilitarianism and what he calls Kantianism as an intramural struggle between Scientific Policymakers with different Comprehensive Views. He regards the major battle for the possession of the modern American legal mind as being between Scientific Policymakers and Ordinary Observers. He sees

294   RICHARD B. PARKER

Rawls's book as an important reformulation of Kantian concerns, enabling those concerns to be more easily applied to contemporary social issues by Kantian Scientific Policymakers.

Ackerman's characterization of the Scientific Policymaker may fit the Utilitarian analyst. It does not fit the sort of "Kantianism" which Rawls advances and Richards and Dworkin (see note 43 *supra*) apply to legal issues. This "Kantianism," which I have called the American constitutional tradition, bases its authority primarily on the fact that it is a reconstruction of our personal beliefs and of American constitutional values. It tries to systematize those beliefs and values but does not claim to provide a unique solution to every case. It has a strong and clear sense of the limits of abstract theory and leaves room for the important casuistical work of the application to hard cases which is the special skill of lawyers. And that casuistry is to be carried on in ordinary language. Richards and Dworkin use virtually no technical terms. If the American constitutional tradition had to be placed somewhere on Ackerman's chart, it would seem to me to be a sophisticated form of ordinary observing. The conflict between it and ordinary constitutional lawyering is a struggle between more and less sophisticated ordinary observing. The conflict between the American constitutional tradition and Utilitarianism is indeed the major battle for possession of the modern American legal mind.

Harry H. Wellington says in "Common Law Rules and Constitutional Double Standards: Some Notes on Adjudication," *Yale Law Journal,* 83 (December 1973), 221, 285, "The Fourteenth Amendment, as Holmes has said, does 'not enact Mr. Herbert Spencer's *Social Statics.*' Nor does it enact Mr. John Rawls's *A Theory of Justice.*" Wellington does not consider whether Rawls might be a reconstruction of "ordinary morality" on which Wellington relies heavily in his theory of constitutional adjudication. Wellington might, on reflection, deny what Rawls asserts, that "everyone has in himself the whole form of a moral conception" (*TJ,* 50). But if not, might not Rawls's conception of justice be "ordinary morality"?

52. See, for example, Richard Posner's discussion of school segregation in which the point is made that one justification for the decision in *Brown v. Board of Education,* 347 U.S. 483 (1954) is that any minority bears a proportionally greater share of the economic burden of discrimination because opportunities for economic exchange between a minority and the majority are economically more valuable to the minority. Posner, *Economic Analysis,* note 50, pp. 528-529. This is no doubt a reason for outlawing discrimination, but a relatively unimportant one. Posner notes in the same discussion that the Court could have exploited the

value which whites attached to school segregation by requiring that communities which desired to segregate contribute X dollars to black education in exchange for being allowed to segregate. If X were a high enough number, blacks would gain from segregation. The discussion serves to illustrate the minor role of economic gain or benefit when fundamental rights are at issue.

53. For example, see George Fletcher, "Fairness and Utility in Tort Theory," *Harv. L. Rev.,* 81 (1972), 537, and Frank I. Michelman, "Property, Utility, and Fairness: Comments on the Ethical Foundations of Just Compensation Law," *Harv. L. Rev.,* 80 (1968), 1165.

All of the material cited in note 43, much of which deals with specific legal issues, takes this distinction to be basic. For a good discussion of the distinction itself without reference to legal issues, see *TJ,* 22-27.

54. For example, Posner, *Economic Analysis,* note 50, pp. 10-12 and 17-23.

55. For a criticism of this hope, see C. Edwin Baker, "The Ideology of the Economic Analysis of Law," *Philosophy and Public Affairs,* 5 (Fall 1975), 3.

56. See, for example, Rawls's early article, "Outline of a Decision Procedure in Ethics," *Philosophical Review,* 60 (1951), 177. See also *TJ,* 46-53, and the work of Kurt Baier, Philippa Foot, David Gauthier, and G. R. Grice, much of which is cited by Rawls in *TJ.*

57. *Harv. L. Rev.,* 10 (1897), 61.

58. Oliver Wendell Holmes, Jr., *The Common Law* (Boston: Little, Brown, 1881).

59. See David A. J. Richards, "Rules, Policies, and Neutral Principles: The Search for Legitimacy in Common Law and Constitutional Adjudication," *Georgia Law Review,* 11 (September 1977), 1069.

PART IV

13

THE SEPARATION OF POWERS: A CRITIQUE OF SOME UTILITARIAN JUSTIFICATIONS

GEORGE P. FLETCHER

One of the assumptions of modern constitutional government is that the functions and powers of government should be allocated to discrete branches, typically called the executive, legislative, and judicial branches of government. This process of allocation has come to be called the doctrine of separation of powers. It presupposes a coherent standard for determining whether a particular exercise of governmental authority appropriately belongs in the province of one branch or another. The classic standard for allocating governmental powers to these three branches turns on the relationship of each branch to the process of making and executing laws. As it is usually put, the legislature makes or passes the laws; the judiciary interprets them; and the executive enforces them. Implicit in the doctrine of separation of powers, then, is the assumption that governments act only by means of laws. It follows that governmental powers are necessarily limited, for that which is not done in the execution of a law is not authorized within the system. As a result, constitutional government presupposes that some decisions are reserved to the citizenry. The overall process of allocating functions, then, requires attention to four sources of power within the system: the executive, the legislature, the judicial, and the private citizen. This scheme is complicated in a federal government, like that of the United States, by the allocation of power between the states and the federal government. There is an ambiguity, for example, in the American Constitution whether the authority of the federal government derives from a grant made by the states or from a grant of authority coming ultimately from the people.[1]

This description has a naive ring to it today. The reason is that very few people, particularly few lawyers, put much stock in the standards once used to assign powers to the branches of government. If lawyers once knew the difference between making, interpreting, and enforcing the law, they now regard those distinctions as folklore of the past. If there were once limits to the powers of the federal government relative to the states, those limits have been distended to their ultimate demise. Virtually any law can be interpreted as one that is necessary and proper to the regulation of interstate commerce. Further, the Supreme Court now treats federal and state law as interchangeable in assessing the constitutionality of provisions that might offend the Bill of Rights. The limits of federal power are no longer to be found in the body of the Constitution. These boundaries, like the boundaries of legislative power in the states, are to be found in the theory of natural rights that percolates through the first ten amendments to the Constitution. These claims of natural right are camouflaged in the legal idiom of free speech, due process, and cruel and unusual punishment. Yet they unmistakably find their warrant in judicial conceptions of human dignity and decency. The decisions of the Supreme Court in the fields of abortion[2] and capital punishment[3] are only the most dramatic examples of the survival of natural law as the limit on legislative power. All of this is replete with irony. For in a positivistic jurisprudence that scorns the law as "brooding omnipresence in the sky," the judges bank almost entirely on transcendental claims in order to salvage the notion of a government limited by a written charter.

The paradoxical survival of natural rights in positivistic America is the symptom of a deeper jurisprudential crisis of modern constitutional government. Even if we do not believe in natural rights, we can manufacture that belief as a way of justifying the allocation of power as between the government and the people. But there is no analogous virtue that we might assume in allocating powers among the branches of government. If the judiciary intrudes upon the customary powers of the legislature, what arguments can we muster to reprove the well-meaning judges? If the police, as the agents of the executive, intrude upon the powers of the judiciary, what can we say about their disturbing the customary balance of power? These are the day-to-day agonies of the legal system. Judges and legislatures joust for authority, for example, in reforming the rule of contributory negligence by the more discriminating standard of comparative negligence. On another front, the judges and police clash daily in claiming authority to decide whether a suspect should be arrested or a home searched. These jurisdictional conflicts could once be resolved by talking about the differences between making, interpreting, and enforcing the law; they can no longer be solved so simply.

One major school of modern legal thought, sometimes called the school of legal process, seeks to solve these jurisdictional tensions in modern government by assessing institutional competencies and assigning tasks to the institutions best suited to handle them. Thus, courts are thought better suited than legislatures to protect minorities, and therefore judicial intervention to protect the rights of the poor and the disenfranchised is thought desirable. Conversely, legislatures were once thought better at resolving delicate political issues, and therefore the courts arguably should abstain from resolving questions like the reapportionment of political districts. The State Department is thought to be in the best position to make judgments affecting our foreign relations, and therefore courts should abstain from decisions that might undermine the executive's conduct of foreign affairs. This way of thinking has gained considerable currency in the law schools. Its central tenet is that allocations of power among the branches should be made on a case-by-case basis, with the over all effectiveness of government as the ultimate goal.

This way of thinking is rife with ambiguities. It never is quite clear whether the devotees of legal process describe or prescribe; whether, if they do prescribe, their standards are utilitarian; and whether, if their standards are utilitarian, the theory is one of act or rule-utilitarianism. The whole school of thought is still wanting in adequate exposition. Yet the general drift of law teaching today is that some kind of standard of prospective effectiveness should be invoked to resolve jurisdictional conflicts among the branches of government.

The appeal of the utilitarian reasoning is strongest when the relevant standard of the law is itself premised on the balancing of competing interests. Two examples are the standards of reasonableness in assessing the legality of searches and seizures and the standard of lesser evils in providing a justification of nominally criminal conduct. Both of these are substantive standards that turn on the assessment of competing interests. And both arise at the intersection of competing claims of authority to decide whether the standard applies. The conflict in the context of search and seizure, as we shall see, is between the judiciary and the police; in the litigation of lesser evils, between the legislature and the private citizen. Further, in both contexts, it turns out to be tempting and superficially plausible to work the resolution of these jurisdictional conflicts into the matrix of utility governing the substantive standard of reasonableness or lesser evils. This is a highly condensed version of two arguments whose steps remain to be sorted out. The exposition of these arguments and their critique is the task that we have before us.

One preliminary word about philosophical usage. The term "utilitarian" is used loosely in this paper to refer to any argument for the right decision that turns on assessing competing interests and determining which of two competing interests is of superior value. The term "interest" is used to refer to considerations that are prospective relative to the time of decision and that lend themselves to variable assessment and comparison. The term is used in distinction to the concept of rights, though there is no effort in this paper to formulate a rigorous distinction between interests and rights. The phrase "cost-benefit" analysis is used interchangeably with the notion of a "utilitarian" standard.

SEARCH AND SEIZURE

The law of search and seizure provides us with a well-plowed field of decisions allocating power between the judiciary and the executive—specifically, between magistrates and the police. The power in question is the authority to decide when the police should arrest a suspect, search his person or his home, and seize evidence that might be used against him at trial. The basic rule of the Fourth Amendment, as interpreted by the Supreme Court, is that the power to make these decisions is reserved to the judiciary. The general rule is that there shall be no search or seizure (1) except by warrant and (2) "no warrant shall issue, but upon probable cause supported by oath or affirmation, and particularly describing the place to be searched, and the persons or things to be seized." [4] The principle that only a warrant can legitimate an arrest, search, or seizure is an affirmation of judicial supremacy in making decisions intruding upon individual privacy. The police should not be able to decide for themselves when there is probable cause to legitimate a search or seizure. In the Court's words, the decision must be made by a "neutral and detached magistrate instead of . . . the officer engaged in the often competitive business of ferreting out crime." [5]

Admittedly, the principle of judicial supremacy over the conduct of the police is not explicitly prescribed in the Fourth Amendment. The amendment ambiguously prescribes the formal requirements for warrants when they are issued; but it does not specify that warrants provide the only means for legitimating police searches and seizures. Nonetheless, the dominant line of Supreme Court authority reasons that the amendment would not provide detailed rules about when a warrant should be issued unless the framers intended implicitly to adopt the warrant requirement as the basic rule of search and seizure.

Offsetting the principled supremacy of the warrant requirement is an array of judicially recognized exceptions permitting the police to arrest and search without prior judicial approval. The most notable of these exceptions are the well-established rules: (1) permitting the police to arrest a suspect whenever there is probable cause to believe he has committed a crime; (2) permitting the search of a person validly arrested; and (3) permitting the search of an automobile whenever the police have probable cause to believe that the automobile contains contraband, instrumentalities, or evidence of crime. There are other exceptions, such as those pertaining to border searches [6] and some cases of routine building inspection. [7] And there are some narrowly defined exceptions in cases in which: (1) evidence is in the process of being destroyed; [8] (2) the police seek to take a blood sample of an unconscious person suspected of drunk driving and they must act without a warrant or not at all; (3) the police search the home of a suspect within hours after assassination of a United States senator.[9] Although we will work with these examples in our effort to understand the Fourth Amendment, we should keep in mind that there is no *numerus clausus* of exceptions and that the courts have demonstrated their willingness to recognize new exceptions when the occasion demands.

If we leave aside the few cases that seem to turn on a theory of implied consent (some administrative searches, perhaps border searches), a common thread appears to unite the bulk of the exceptions. In most of these cases there is a strong element of necessity that makes it imperative to search or arrest without a warrant or forgo the search or arrest altogether. In the case of persons suspected of committing a felony, the exception is tolerated for fear of the suspects fleeing during the time necessary for the issuance of a warrant. The same is true of the exception recognized for mobile vehicles. Either they are searched when the officer has them under observation or they are likely never to be searched at all. The same rationale obviously applies to the exceptions for evidence being destroyed. With regard to searches incident to arrest, the traditional rationale is that these searches are imperative in order to protect the safety of the officer and to prevent the destruction of evidence. In the dominant line of its opinions, the Supreme Court describes these and analogous situations as "exceptional circumstances," when the "impracticability" of acquiring a warrant justifies the police taking the decision on their own.[10]

The Argument of Reasonableness

If this is the dominant view, there is a strong and persistent line of thought that seeks to undercut the primacy of the warrant requirement and to treat the issue of the warrant as but one factor bearing on the overall reasonableness of the search. This is a mode of thinking about the Fourth Amendment that we shall call the argument of reasonableness. It consists of the following claims. First, that it is a mistake to treat the warrant clause as the dominant and defining that clause of the Fourth Amendment. The first and more general clause of the amendment merely prohibits "unreasonable searches and seizures." Therefore, reasonableness is the ultimate issue, and the question of the warrant is but one issue bearing on the reasonableness and constitutionality of the search. Further, the argument goes, the Court's own analysis of the exceptions to the warrant clause conform to the calculus of reasonableness. By its own admission, the Court assays the constitutionality of searches without a warrant by "balancing the need for effective law enforcement against the [individual citizen's] right of privacy." [11] Balancing these two interests is but one aspect of the calculus of utility underlying the Fourth Amendment. Therefore, the question whether the warrant clause should govern is part of the encompassing inquiry whether the search is reasonable on utilitarian grounds. What emerges from this argument is a unidimensional theory of the Fourth Amendment based upon the overriding question of weighing the social benefit of searching against the social costs of intruding upon individual privacy.

The argument of reasonableness reached its zenith twenty-five years ago in *United States* v. *Rabinowitz* when Justice Minton wrote for the Court: "The relevant test is not whether it is reasonable to procure a warrant, but whether the search was reasonable." [12] Though the logic of the argument need not generate a more tolerant view toward searches without a warrant, the effect of the argument in practice has been precisely that. The argument of *Rabinowitz* has been dethroned by subsequent cases tightening the warrant requirement.[13] Yet the argument of reasonableness still lives in exile with ever more followers on the Court. It warrants our attention, not only because it may soon be returned to its former glory, but because it raises an interesting array of problems in the theory of utilitarianism. In particular, the argument assumes that if standards like "impracticability" and "necessity" turn on the balancing of competing interests, it follows that they are standards reducible to a straightforward cost-benefit analysis. Eventually, I shall attempt to show that this assumption is a tempting but basic error, with implications going beyond the law of search and seizure. First, it would be useful to work our way through the legal materials and show the way in which the argument of reasonableness is inconsistent with the premises that now govern the law of search and seizure.

The Legal Materials

The argument of reasonableness asserts that the warrant is but one factor among many in deciding whether a search is reasonable. Other factors would include a state's interest in searching, as indicated by the gravity of the crime being investigated [14] and the probability of finding incriminating evidence in the place to be searched. These interests yield a net value to the government, which is offset by the costs in individual privacy. These costs are measured presumably by the temporal and spatial features of the search as well as by the degree of intrusiveness into intimate matters of the person being searched. These benefits are measured against the costs to determine whether the search is justified.

The question that we are concerned about is whether the issue of the warrant can be integrated into the calculus of competing interests that we have just outlined. In other words, we are concerned with the question whether the allocation of power to decide Fourth Amendment questions is to be resolved by the same kind of criteria that apply in deciding whether searches are reasonable. These criteria, as I have suggested, are essentially utilitarian. They require a prospective balancing of the social interest in suppressing crime against the individual's interest in maintaining privacy. Before we address ourselves to the integration of the warrant requirement into this calculus, we should note that there are other issues that might not be readily assimilable to a cost-benefit analysis of reasonableness. One unresolved issue in the analysis of the Fourth Amendment is whether it should matter whether the person whose privacy is affected is the one suspected of criminal activity. There is some authority for the view that it does matter. In *Stanford Daily* v. *Zurcher*,[15] the police searched the offices of the newspaper for snapshots that would identify suspects at a riot. The *Daily* was not implicated, but their privacy was compromised. Although the police had a warrant, the federal district court ruled that the search of an innocent party's offices required something more than a warrant based upon probable cause of finding the photographs. Unless there was good reason to believe that the photographs would be destroyed, the police had to proceed by way of subpoena—that is, by way of a judicial order directing the *Daily* to surrender the photographs to the court. The intriguing question is why it should matter whether the person searched is suspected of wrongdoing; and if it does matter, how did this factor enter into the balancing process leading to a judgment of reasonableness?

There appears to be no simple way of resolving the issue. One rationale for considering whether the suspect is the party to be searched would be that the rationale for the loss of privacy was personal responsibility for generating signs of probable or apparent guilt. This would be an adaptation of one theory of retributivism to the justification of search and seizure: the suspect brings the search on himself as the criminal brings his punishment on himself. The only difference is that the threshhold of evidence is lower to justify search than it is to legitimate punishment. Injecting a factor of desert is problematic, for if it prescribed a necessary condition for a legitimate search, it would be impossible to justify the search of the *Daily*'s offices. Of course, the *Daily* might be responsible for the appearance of their having the photographs on their premises, but they are not responsible for the appearance of criminality justifying the police desire to procure those photographs. Obviously, there are important distinctions to be worked out in the formulation of this argument. At the level of principle, it is not so clear why it should be objectionable to search totally innocent parties.

Alternatively, one might seek to subsume responsibility for suspicious signs under the general role of avoiding the destruction of evidence. The claim might be that criminal suspects are likely to destroy evidence, but not innocent third parties like the *Stanford Daily*. Yet transforming the issue in this way also proves too much. It implies that whenever there is a minimal risk of destruction, whether the party searched is the suspect or not, then the police must proceed by way of subpoena rather than by way of the search warrant. Alas, that is a reading of the law that finds little support.

This discussion illustrates the general difficulty of integrating the factors bearing on the legitimacy of searches into a single calculus of utility. Admittedly, the warrant requirement might be easier to work into the crucible of competing interests. The argument would be that the suspect had an interest in having a "neutral and detached" magistrate decide whether there is probable cause to support a search. If a magistrate rather than a police officer decides the issue, the suspect is more likely to secure a decision in his favor.

Therefore, in those cases in which it is impracticable for the magistrate to decide, such as in the case of automobile searches, there should be greater attention paid to the other interests of the suspect. To maintain the same threshhold of reasonableness there should be some adjustment in the demands made on other factors in the balancing process. Yet what are the factors that could be adjusted in favor of the suspect? As we have noted, the list is short: (1) the gravity of the offense; (2) the likelihood of finding incriminating evidence; and (3) the intrusiveness of the search. Of these variables, the first and last are fixed for any particular search that the police wish to undertake. If the police wish to search a particular house in the course of a murder investigation, both the gravity of the offense and the intrusiveness of the search are prescribed by the circumstances. The only free variable is the likelihood of finding the contraband or evidence being sought. To offset the increased cost of a warrantless search, there should be a greater benefit to the state. The only way to generate a greater benefit is to demand a higher probability of success in conducting the search. In brief, if there is no warrant, the threshold of evidence justifying a search should be higher.

Yet there is little evidence in the case law that the standards justifying a search are higher in cases where the warrant requirement is waived.[16] Typically, all one finds is a more favorable rule on the burden of persuasion in cases where there is no warrant. If a magistrate has already passed on the issue of probable cause, then the burden is on the criminal defendant to attack the warrant and to prove there was insufficient evidence to support the search. If the search was conducted without a warrant, the burden is then on the government to establish both that an exception to the warrant requirement obtains and that there was probable cause to justify the search. Thus, one can interpret the Supreme Court's reasoning that "in a doubtful or marginal case a search under a warrant may be substainable where one without it would fall." [17] A ruling as to who wins borderline cases is in effect to allocate the burden of persuasion or, as it is sometimes called, the risk of nonpersuasion.

The Argument of Principle

We may safely conclude that as the law now stands, the affirmation of the warrant requirement does not adhere to a single calculus of interest governing the Fourth Amendment. This is the implication of there being no mode of adjusting the standard of decision in cases where the search is legitimate absent a warrant. What one finds is not a single decision but rather a two-staged process of analysis. The first stage poses the question: Who decides whether the search is reasonable? The second stage is the substantive question whether the search is indeed reasonable. This is not a surprising conclusion. It merely affirms that the allocation of governmental functions is a question that is independent and preliminary to the application of substantive standards.

Yet this is not all there is to the refutation of the argument of reasonableness. The argument still exercises a powerful pull on the legal mind—for reasons that are now ripe for analysis. Those who advocate the all-encompassing nature of reasonableness scoff at the rigid separation of the issues of competence to decide and the standard to be applied. Their point is that deciding who decides—the magistrate or the officer on the beat—requires the same kind of balancing of interests that recurs at the second stage of assessing the reasonableness of the search. It is always a matter of balancing the needs of law enforcement against the citizen's interest in privacy. If the same process of balancing occurs at the two distinct stages of the process, what is the point of holding them distinct? They should be collapsed into one integrated matrix of competing interests. If the law does not acknowledge interdependence of the warrant requirement with the threshold of evidence required to justify a search, then the law should be changed.

There are at least two responses to this challenge. One is that even if the same process of balancing occurs at two different stages, there is some point to recognizing the conceptional distinction between competence to decide and that which is to be decided. This is a weak reply, for we can recognize the distinction in principle even though we collapse the two stages of analysis into one calculus of utility. A stronger response is that even though the question of competence requires attention to the needs of law enforcement as well as the interests of the suspect, the process of balancing is structually different from the attempt to decide whether one interest outweighs another. It is important to recall that the Court itself treats the exceptions to the warrant requirement as cases where the process of obtaining the warrant is "impracticable." What I shall attempt to show is that the concept of "practicability" belongs to a special class of balancing processes with important distinguishing features.

A close analogue to the concept of impracticability is the concept of involuntary conduct in the substantive criminal law. The core case of involuntary, excusable conduct is strict physical involuntariness. If someone acts as a result of a brain tumor, psychosis, or hypnosis, his conduct is readily classified as involuntary. The more problematic cases are those typified by a witness' committing perjury in order to avoid a threatened reprisal, or a group of shipwrecked sailors killing and devouring one of their number in a desperate attempt to avoid starvation. In these cases, the criminal conduct in not strictly involuntary, yet in many legal systems the actor is excused on the ground that his conduct is coerced or necessitated.[18] These are cases that Aristotle described as "mixed" for the conduct is voluntary in one respect and involuntary in another.

How does one go about deciding whether conduct is sufficiently coerced to be treated as involuntary and to be excused? It seems that initially one should seek to determine whether the situation of the witness committing perjury under dire threats is sufficiently akin to the core case of physical involuntariness to warrant the same treatment. Yet that inquiry is not so easily resolved, for various cases are more or less like the core situation and there is no guideline for determining when a case of coercion is sufficiently like psychosis to be treated in the same way. As one begins to compare cases, it becomes obvious that the conflicting interests in the situation influence our judgment of involuntariness. For example, it makes a difference how grave an injury the person causes under threats of reprisal. It matters whether he testifies for the defendant and thereby prevents a conviction or whether he commits perjury against an innocent defendant in a capital case, thereby risking the death of an innocent person. Similarly, it matters whether in order to avoid personal injury, he commits larceny, rape, or murder. On the other side of the balance, we need to consider how much harm is threatened against the person who allegedly acts involuntarily. An imminent risk of death is more likely to excuse than an impending assault or deprivation of property.

Now the balancing between these two conflicting interests is not a simple matter of choosing the superior interest. In cases of duress it is well recognized that the coerced actor may commit greater harm to others than he prevents from occurring to himself.[19] The balancing is askew; the question is always whether the disproportion between the harm done and the harm avoided is so great as to preclude the defense. It would obviously be too great if the actor committed rape in order to avoid the loss of property; but perhaps not too great if he killed two innocent persons in order to avoid the threatened homicide of his child. Thus, we see that there are two different aspects to the analysis of involuntariness. One aspect is the attempt to decide whether a case of coercion is sufficiently like physical involuntariness to be treated in the same way. And the other aspect is the implicit balancing that underlies the attempt to classify conduct as involuntary. The important point to note is that the balancing in the case of duress and necessity does not represent the pursuit of the greater interest. It is rather an aid in deciding whether, as a matter of justice to the accused, the conduct is to be treated as involuntary.

The concept of impracticability bears many of the features that we note in the structure of involuntariness. The core cases where it is impracticable to procure a warrant are those in which it would be pointless to search if a warrant were required. A good example is the problem of taking a blood sample from an unconscious person suspected of drunk driving. In the time necessary to procure a warrant, the suspect would assimilate the alcohol in his bloodstream and there would be no point to taking the reading. A similar case is the exception permitted where the police know that evidence is in the throes of being destroyed. Of course, in these core cases the police could forgo the search altogether. Yet if the search is not to be precluded, it is patently impracticable to require a warrant. Clustering about these core cases are a variety of less obvious exceptions, such as those permitting the warrantless search of mobile vehicles and the warrantless arrest of ambulatory suspects. Either the police act when they have a chance or they may never make the search or the arrest. Yet these situations invite the balancing of competing interests in order to justify their assimilation to the core cases. What precisely is the risk that the car or the suspect would not be seen again? How long would it take to procure a warrant? These are questions that must be resolved in deciding how much efficiency law enforcement should sacrifice in the interest of maintaining judicial supremacy over the Fourth Amendment. An even more problematic situation is the *Sirhan* case, where the problem of waiving the warrant requirement required sensitivity to the sense of imminent danger triggered by the assassination of Robert Kennedy.[20] Waiving the warrant requirement in this type of case would seem to suggest that any time there is imminent danger, the police may enter a private dwelling and search it without a warrant. Yet the Supreme Court has not been willing to go that far.[21] The case law adheres to the requirement that the search be "pointless" if the police took time to procure a warrant. This means that there are some situations in which the police must sacrifice the acquisition of evidence or the making of an arrest. That sacrifice would be difficult to justify if the process of decision were based on the pursuit of the greater interest. For in no particular case does the suspect's interest in having a magistrate decide the question appear to be as important as the tangible promise of seizing contraband or evidence of crime.

This analysis does not account for all the exceptions to the warrant requirement. There are some that seem to be based upon a theory of implied consent. Others, such as border searches, are justified, if at all, only by persistent historical practice. Yet the point that we have tried to make is that the process of analyzing competence to decide questions of search and seizure is different in priciple from assessing the utility of the search. As we have seen, balancing competing interests is an important aid to the assessment of impracticability, as it is indispensable in assaying the concept of involuntariness. Yet the intellectual process is sufficiently distinguishable from assessing the reasonableness of the search that we may adhere to the sharp differentiation between the question of competence and the question of substance. Whether the magistrate should decide is one issue; whether the search is reasonable is another.

The most we have been able to conclude is that assessing the competence of magistrates should not be integrated into the substantive issue that either the police officer or the magistrate is called upon to decide. We have not given an affirmative account of the rule that magistrates ought to decide the legality of arrests, searches, and seizures unless it is impracticable to do so. It is hard to give a utilitarian account for judicial supervision of police searches, for, as we have noted, in the particular case it would be hard to justify a loss in the effectiveness of law enforcement by the countervailing benefit to the suspect of having a magistrate decide rather than a police officer. In the individual case the benefit of having one person decide rather than another—even if one wears a black robe and the other a badge—would appear uncertain and unquantifiable; yet the loss in time and the possible loss of evidence would be tangible and substantial. It would be hard indeed to see the magistrate's deciding as the superior interest.

One could shift to a version of rule-utilitarianism and argue that there is some virtue in a clear, transmittable rule allocating competence to a neutral and detached decision-maker. Yet the contours of the rule permitting exceptions where the warrant are impracticable is hardly stable and teachable. The benefits of searching without a warrant seem still to prevail in individual cases.

Another tack would be to argue that the warrant requirement, together with its exceptions, formed a received practice of our legal system. This practice, taken as a whole, might be justifiable on the basis of long-range utility. It would seem to be better than two competing alternatives: (1) a practice in which the magistrate always decided; and (2) a practice in which the police always decided. Yet shifting to this vantage point would hardly explain why we draw the line within the practice where we do: Why is it that there is a deep-seated preference for magistrates? It is hardly persuasive to refer to the conventions of the practice. Nor is it enough to appeal to the authority of the Constitution. It is both the conventions of the practice and the constitutional pattern that we are seeking to justify.

It may be that we can say nothing more profound about the preference for magistrates except that where basic rights and interests are at stake we should institute the fairest proceeding at our disposal. Of course, the proceeding before the magistrate is not particularly fair. The suspect is not represented, even by a "devil's"

advocate.[22] Yet the proceeding is taken to be significantly more
objective than one in which the police officer is the decision-maker.
Pending a more general analysis of fair procedures, we may have to
settle for this admittedly partial account of our constitutional
practice.

THE INDIVIDUAL AND THE LEGISLATURE

Having labored the tension between the judiciary and the police,
I should like to turn to a totally different context in which there are
ongoing problems of allocating decision-making competence. The
issue that I turn to now is the interface between legislative
competence, on the one hand, and individual decision-making
under the law, on the other. This is a problematic area that has not
received due attention, largely because individual decisions about
the law are much less visible than the quantitatively dominant
activities of legislatures. Indeed, as I shall point out, it is even
problematical whether a positivistic jurisprudence can accommodate the notion of individuals making decisions about the law.

The context in which I shall explore the issue is the defense of
necessity to charges of criminal conduct. Consider a case in which
an individual is faced with the conflict between violating the law
and helping a person in distress. In order to get a sick person to the
hospital, he might have to violate rules of the road, take someone
else's car without permission, and even commit an assault against
the owner trying to prevent him from taking the car. The question
is whether any or all of these violations is justified by the defense of
lesser evils. Though the common law has never explicitly recognized
the defense, the Model Penal Code and most commentators now
commend its adoption, and it is gradually becoming a general
principle of American law. Most continental European systems
have long had the defense, either as a matter of judicial adoption or
legislated rule.[23]

The defense typically contains two requirements. First, it provides
that violations of the law may be justified if they favor the greater
interest under the circumstances. Getting a sick person to the
hospital would readily justify many unavoidable legal violations,
including speeding, larceny, and even assault. It all depends on how
important we take the competing interests to be. There are some

problems at the fringes of this justification, such as whether the defense applies in cases of homicide. And there are differences among statutes as to whether the interest furthered by the violation need be "substantially" greater than that protected by the law or whether it is sufficient for one merely to overbalance the other. Though interesting and important, these problems need not detain us here.

Of greater relevance is the limitation typically prescribed in the formulation of the defense. To appreciate that limitation we have to note the anomaly of holding that all violations of the law might be justified by appealing ot the greater interest. If this principle applied across the board, a socially sensitive judge might feel constrained to approve stealing from the rich in order to give to the poor. Or an ecologically minded judge would have to applaud an expedition of do-gooders going to Alaska to blow up the pipeline now under construction. It is not an adequate response to say that the judges must make their cost-benefit assessment by appealing to the dominant moral sentiment of the society. Redistribution of wealth and protection of the environment are important social values in the United States today. Even if the judge decided that "middle America" would approve of the actor's choice of values, there would be something awry in ruling that stealing from the rich or blowing up the pipeline was justified and therefore legal behavior.

What would be awry is that in our system of government the legislature strikes the balance between the competing interests in these cases. It is the legislature that decides the extent to which wealth should be redistributed by progressive income taxation. It is the legislature that decides whether the mercantile advantages of the pipeline outweigh the risk to the environment. To allow individuals, supported by sympathetic judges, to second-guess the legislature would be to undermine the system of legislative authority in making the basic political decisions of a democratic society. Accordingly, there must be some provision in the defense of lesser evils to distinguish between taking a sick person to the hopsital on the one hand, and blowing up the pipeline on the other. The effort to formulate that distinction underlies the typical limitation on the defense of lesser evils that the conduct in question be undertaken to avoid an "imminent" or "immediate risk of

316 GEORGE P. FLETCHER

harm." Though this is a standard requirement of the defense as it is formulated in Germany and the Soviet Union,[24] the Model Penal Code curiously overlooks the requirement and focuses instead on legislative intent as a guideline for limiting the range of decisions that individuals may make.[25] The soundness of this approach came before a federal court of appeals in a case in which the defendants broke into a Selective Service office and were apprehended in the act of stealing draft cards.[26] One of their defenses was that their conduct was justified by their goal of foreshortening the war in Vietnam and saving lives. Without assaying the question whether the end of saving lives justified these means, the judges ruled that this was not the kind of case in which the defense of lesser evils could come into play. They intuited the limitation explicit in European formulations of the defense: the defense could only apply in cases of action take to avoid a "direct and immediate peril." [27]

A Rationale for the Rule of "Direct and Immediate Peril"

One way to interpret this limitation on the defense is that the imminence of the risk serves to circumscribe the range of persons affected by necessary intrusions. If an accident victim lies bleeding on the sidewalk, and it is necessary to take someone's car to get him to the hospital, the range of available car owners is limited. The circumstances of the emergency preempt the good samaritan's authority to decide who should bear the burden of the rescue. This is not the case where the risk is muted and pervasive and the party intervening picks the time and place of his utility-maximizing conduct. The pipeline, for example, might endanger the Alaskan wilderness, but the activist who blows it up picks the time and place of his intervention for the common good.

This limitation imposed by the doctrine of imminent risk highlights a major difference between legislative decisions and individual decisions about social costs and benefits. The legislature is authorized to make general judgments about how the benefits and burdens of social organization are to be distributed. In a word, they are entitled to identify the victims of progress—be they the group that would suffer sonic booms or those who might lose their jobs as a result of closing a military base. The requirement of imminent risk, as a limitation on the defense of necessity, precludes the actor from identifying the victims of his nominally unlawful conduct. Of course, within a narrow range, he has some leeway in picking the car he will take in order to get an accident victim to the hospital. But the dominant tone in a case of justified necessity is that the circumstances dictate whose interests must be sacrificed for the sake of helping someone in distress. What the individual is allowed to do in the context of necessity is to make the judgment that the law should be violated. He is not entitled to channel the burdens of his violation with the same range of authority as that commanded by a legislature.

Thus we see that the standard of imminence functions much like the concept of "impracticability" in setting the limits to the supremacy of magistrates in ruling on the legality of searches and seizures. The standard of impracticability serves to delineate the spheres of judicial and police competence. Similarly, the requirement that the justifying peril be imminent serves to protect legislative authority against individual claims of superior wisdom in making utility-maximizing decisions. In analyzing the law of search and seizure, we considered a variety of efforts to integrate the issue of judicial authority into the calculus of reasonableness governing the Fourth Amendment. In the context of lesser evils, the analogous effort is to insist that the problem of delineating legislative authority in a democracy can somehow be worked into the matrix of conflicting interests that confronts the individual when he decides to violate the law for the sake of the greater good.

A Utilitarian Challenge

In the discussion that follows we shall consider an appealing argument that would merge the issue of proper legislative authority with the standard to be applied in deciding whether conduct was justified by the greater good. If this argument proves to be persuasive, it would enable us to dispense with the test of "imminence" in deciding which risks are covered by the defense of lesser evils. The argument, which we shall call the argument of democratic discipline, holds that the issue of legislative authority can be translated into one of the costs to be considered along with the other costs of an allegedly justified violation of the law. The danger of individuals departing from the prohibitions of the criminal law, such as those prohibiting speeding, unpermitted use of another's car or escape from prison, is that the example of one person's deciding that a violation of the law was justified might encourage others to make similar judgments in the future. The risk is that those encouraged might not weigh the interests as carefully as was done in the example they are following. The net result would be a diminution in social order. Of course, it is not ineluctable that those encouraged to violate the law for the greater good would make decisions contrary to the general welfare. Those who follow suit in the future might consist of a class of people acting for the common good who could not have acted, but for the example set by another. Yet if we suppose that the legislature acts rationally and with due regard for society's interests, those who interpose their own judgment might well turn out to be acting on the basis of a scheme of values that is askew with the dominant standard of the society. The argument in favor avoiding this cost is called the argument of democratic discipline, for it is expected of citizens in a democracy that they defer to legislative judgments about the common good. The defense of necessity triggers a process that can lead to the weakening of that disciplined deference to legislative judgment.

An instance where this kind of analysis has influenced the courts is in the context of justifying prison escapes necessary to avoid personal harm. The typical case is that of the convict threatened with homosexual rape. He or she has no practical alternative but to go over the wall. The courts have been uniformly reluctant to justify these escapes.[28] One of the arguments invoked is that a justified prison break tends to undermine prison discipline. Therefore this cost must be considered in deciding whether the convict should bear the risk of rape rather than escape. Once this factor is added to the scales, it invariably tips the balance against the justification of the escape. In the minds of the judges, the greater good turns out to be the preservation of discipline, even if the price of that discipline is the suffering of homosexual rapes.

The value of preserving prison discipline bears strong resemblance to the value of maintaining the democratic discipline of deference to legislative judgments. Both are social costs that derive from prior decisions to violate the nominal prohibitions of the law. And both are costs that are attributable to the undesirable behavior of other persons that might be encouraged by a prior decision to put other values ahead of the letter of the law. At first blush this appears to be a plausible technique for recasting the issue of legislative competence as a quantifiable cost to be included with the other costs and benefits in a situation of conflict. This effort appears to be more convincing than the move to subsume the warrant requirement within the calculus of reasonableness governing the Fourth Amendment. While the issue of competence could not there plausibly be integrated with the standard to be applied, there appears to be some hope here that all the relevant factors, including that of legislative authority, are reducible to a common calculus of utility. Yet as we shall see, this effort too is bound to fail, and for even more powerful reasons. The argument of democratic discipline is flawed by a contradiction that affects a wide range of utilitarian arguments. In order to explicate that contradiction, we need to formalize the problem more rigorously than we have until now.

A Critique of the Argument

Let T_1 represent the time that the actor must make a decision about the lesser evil. This is the time that an individual at the scene of an accident must decide whether to take emergency steps to help an injured party or the time in which the convict must decide whether he should escape from prison to avoid homosexual rape. Let T_2 represent the moment at which the judge or jury at a trial must decide whether the individual's conduct at T_1 is justified under the defense of lesser evils. Let T_3 represent the prolonged period during which society would suffer a breakdown of institutional discipline triggered by an initial decision to violate the law. As noted above, the social costs at T_3 might be a rash of cases in which individuals, encouraged by the event at T_1, would make rash decisions about the permissibility of transgressing the nominal prohibitions of the law. My assumption in this analysis is that the costs at T_3 occur after the judicial decision at T_2. This is a realistic assumption so far as the criminal trial follows hard on the violation occurring at T_1. To complete the formalization of the problem, let B represent the benefit of violating the law (e.g., getting the sick person to the hospital on time) and C the cost of doing so (e.g., impermissibly taking someone's car). Further, take D to stand for the costs attributable to a breakdown in democratic discipline (a

rash of car borrowings). For the sake of clarity, let C and D be
exclusive, so that the costs resulting from the future behavior of
other people are not included within the concept of direct costs
represented by C.

Now we are in a position to state the contradiction resulting from
the effort to translate the issue of legislative authority into an
interest to be weighed at T_1. The contradiction results from the
decisions at T_1 and T_2 having conflicting effects on the social cost D.
The decision to depart from the legal norm might produce D at T_3.
But the decision to punish the violator at T_2 would presumably
counteract the example set at T_1 and thus prevent the cost D from
accruing. To see the implication of this assumption let us further
formalize the problem by supposing that in a particular case, the
benefit B of taking someone's car without permission is 50, the cost C
in deprivation of the car is 40 and the potential cost D at T_3 is 20.
Now note the following chain of reasoning:

1. Initially B outweighs C 50 to 40; therefore the defendant should
   be acquitted.
2. If the defendant is acquitted, cost D would accrue, which means
   that the total cost at T_1 is 60. Therefore, the defendant should be
   convicted.
3. If the defendant is convicted, cost D would not accrue and
   therefore the total cost would only be 40. B outweighs C and
   therefore the defendant should be acquitted.
4. If the defendant is acquitted, cost D would accrue, etc.

There seems to be no way of breaking out of this bounded circle.
The analysis keeps looping back on itself. The reason is that the cost
D is hypothetical and contingent on *not* reaching the result that its
presence would favor. That is the antinomy of the argument of
democratic discipline, and there seems to be no way of avoiding it.
The problem posed by this argument is a general feature of all
utilitarian arguments in which a cost, like the cost D, is affected
differentially by (1) the act (T_1) to be judged by utilitarian criteria,
and (2) the act (T_2) of passing judgment under a utilitarian
standard. The kind of case where this is likely to occur is where one
of the costs to be considered is the cost attributable to the conduct

of others, who are likely to follow the example of the conduct whose justification is in question. We are led to conclude that if one proceeds by appealing to a utilitarian standard, one cannot consider costs of this sort. It follows that the cost D cannot be considered in assaying whether conduct is justifiable under the defense of lesser evils. And if cost D must be considered as irrelevant, then the argument of democratic discipline fails and we are left without a utilitarian substitute for the inquiry about the directness and the immediacy of the risk.

In the case of magistrates and police we found that we needed a two-stage process of decision. The same need obtains in working out proper spheres of individual and legislative judgment under the law. One stage in both contexts is the comparison of competing interests. A distinct step in the analysis is the question of the decision-maker's competence. That question is probed in the context of search and seizure by asking whether obtaining a warrant is practicable under the circumstances. In fashioning the defense of lesser evils, the analogous question is whether the peril to be avoided is direct and immediate. It is only when the risk is so imminent that the actor does not exercise discretion in selecting the victims of his act that it is appropriate for him to override the legislative judgment prohibiting the conduct in question.

It should be noted that the rationale we have provided for the defense of lesser evils and the requirement of imminent peril is only one version of the defense. It is a view that is based implicitly on a nonpositivist conception of law, namely a theory of Law or Right that encompasses both legislative and individual judgments about what the law is. That theory of law is incompatible with the positivist claim that all law derives from commands of the sovereign. If the entire body of law derives from legislative acts and perhaps as well from judicial decisions, then it hardly makes sense to speak of an individual's perceiving the law directly and overriding a legislative judgment about the permissibility of speeding of impermissibly using another's car. Thus, the positivist is led to the view that the conflict in cases of lesser evils is not between the legislature and the individual at all. Rather, it is between the legislature and the courts. The correct description of cases of necessity, the positivist would claim, is that the courts fill out the gaps left in the legislative plan. The legislature cannot be expected to foresee all cases that might arise. In totally unexpected cases, the courts are free to work out the appropriate rules of optimal conduct.

Thus, one is led to an alternative view of the requirement that the risk be imminent. The quality of the risk serves as a signpost of those cases in which the legislature is not likely to have anticipated the case before the court. But surely, there is no necessary connection between imminence of the risk and legislative foresight. Therefore, if one fashioned the defense of lesser evils in a positivist crucible, it makes more sense to discard references to the quality of the risk and add instead the ingredient of legislative intent. This is precisely the compound of elements reached by the positivist Model Penal Code, which, to the disappointment of American courts, banks entirely on legislative intent to the exclusion of the more typical requirement of an imminent peril.

SUMMARY AND CONCLUSION

In this essay we have attempted to assay two arguments for integrating issues of governmental competence into the standards to be applied in resolving disputes. If the analysis is persuasive, we must conclude that neither argument is convincing and that issues of competence must be kept extinct from utilitarian tests used in legal analysis. Yet we must stop short of giving an adequate theory of the separation of powers, and particularly the problems of resolving jurisdictional conflicts on a case-by-case basis. It is unfortunate that this paper does not address itself to the thorniest of all jurisdictional conflicts, that between the legislature and the judiciary; but that is a topic that requires deeper conceptual work than is needed to counteract the gravitational attraction of utilitarian standards in the law.

NOTES

1. Note U.S. Const., Amend. X, which ambiguously provides that "powers not delegated to the United States ... are reserved to the States ... or to the people."
2. *Roe* v. *Wade,* 410 U.S. 113 (1973).
3. *Furman* v. *Georgia,* 408 U.S. 238 (1972).

4. U.S. Const., Amend. IV.
5. *Johnson* v. *United States,* 333 U.S. 10, 14 (1948).
6. The permissibility of warrantless border searches has never been squarely presented to the Supreme Court. The exception is assumed in dictum in *Carroll* v. *United States,* 267 U.S. 132 (1925). Recently, in *Almeida-Sanchez* v. *United States,* 413 U.S. 266 (1973), five members of the Court concurred that border searches were to be treated as a special category. Yet implications of this view are yet to be worked out. There are some judges who would approve of searches in the border area on the basis of less evidence than probable cause. Others would reach the same result if the search were supported by a warrant.
7. *United States* v. *Biswell,* 406 U.S. 311 (1972).
8. This exception is supported by dictum in *McDonald* v. *United States,* 335 U.S. 411, 455 (1948); *Vale* v. *Louisiana,* 339 U.S. 30, 35 (1969).
9. *People* v. *Sirhan,* 7 Cal. 3d 710, 102 Cal. Rptr. 385 (1972).
10. E.g., *Vale* v. *Louisiana,* 399 U.S. 30 (1969); *Chimel* v. *California,* 395 U.S. 752 (1969).
11. *Johnson* v. *United States,* 333 U.S. 10, 14-15 (1948).
12. *United States* v. *Rabinowitz,* 339 U.S. 56, 66 (1950).
13. *Chimel* v. *California,* 395 U.S. 752 (1969).
14. In principle, the gravity of the crime should matter; but the author knows of no explicit judicial recognition of this factor in assessing reasonableness.
15. 353 F. Supp. 124 (N.D. Calif. 1972).
16. There is some recent authority for the view that when the state relies upon consent of the suspect or of a third party, it must establish the fact of voluntary consent by "clear and positive evidence." This standard is higher than the ordinary burden of proving facts by a preponderance of the evidence. See *People* v. *Reynolds,* 127 Cal. Rptr. 561 (C.A. 2d 1976).
17. *United States* v. *Ventresca,* 360 U.S. 102, 106 (1965).
18. For details and further elaboration, see Fletcher, *Individualization of Excusing Conditions,* 47 So. Calif. L. Review, 1269 (1974).
19. Model Penal Code, sec. 2.09 (Proposed Official Draft, 1962). Fletcher, note 18 *supra,* at 1289.
20. See *supra* note 9.
21. *Vale* v. *Louisiana,* 399 U.S. 30 (1969).
22. Representation by counsel and the opportunity to be heard are the primary advantages of proceeding by subpoena. See *Stanford Daily* v. *Zurcher,* note 15 *supra.*
23. See Fletcher, note 18 *supra,* at 1280-1288.
24. German Criminal Code of 1975, sec. 34; Criminal Code of the

RSFSR, sec. 14. See Judgment of July 12, 1951, 1951 *Neue Juristische Wochenschrift,* 769 (Bundesgerichtshof, Germany).
25. Model Penal Code, sec. 3.02 (1) (c) (Proposed Official Draft, 1962).
26. *United States* v. *Kroncke,* 459 F. 2d 697 (8th Cir. 1972).
27. *Id.* at 700-701.
28. *State* v. *Green,* 470 S.W. 2d 565 (Mo. 1971), cert. denied, 405 U.S. 1073 (1972); *People* v. *Richards,* 269 Cal. App. 768, 75 Cal. Rptr. 597 (1969). In contrast, there is a nascent case law recognizing the excusability of escapes under these circumstances, *People* v. *Lovercamp,* 43 Cal. App. 3d 823, 118 Cal. Rptr. 110 (1974).

14

COMMENTS ON
GEORGE P. FLETCHER'S
"THE SEPARATION OF POWERS:
A CRITIQUE OF SOME
UTILITARIAN JUSTIFICATIONS"

STEPHANIE R. LEWIS

Professor Fletcher distrusts utilitarian reasoning in the law. In his paper in this volume he is out to take one corner of the law away from the utilitarians: he argues that there is one species of legal decision that cannot be made on grounds of utility alone, and that is the jurisdictional decision to allocate power to one branch of government rather than another to apply a legally defined standard that is itself utilitarian in origin. He also defends the thesis that the legislature, not the court, is the proper branch of government to set standards of behavior. I am on Fletcher's side; I too believe that there is ample reason to distrust the kind of legal reasoning that answers every question in the law, solves every problem, by the single procedure of balancing burdens against benefits.

But I do not think that this campaign against the utilitarian foe succeeds. Fletcher's tactics—pursue the utilitarians point by point, case by case, and take on one utilitarian rationale at a time and show that it won't do—are not enough to defeat the utilitarian. In the last section of this paper I will suggest tactics that might do more lasting damage to the utilitarian foe.

Fletcher exhibits two utilitarian standards, each the result of weighing up the competing interests that are touched by one of the law's functions, and setting that standard so that the balance comes out right and utility seems to be served best when that standard is applied. Neither of the two standards is now a part of our law, but both of them are so attractive to the legal profession—in particular to the judges who are in a position to make them into law—that they are worth close attention. Further, they are typical utilitarian standards; their fate at the hands of Fletcher's attack tells us how the class as a whole does. One of these two standards is the standard of reasonableness as a test of lawfulness in the Fourth Amendment jurisprudence of search and seizure, and the other is the standard of necessity as a test to justify conduct that would otherwise be criminal.

Fletcher attacks these utilitarian standards by arguing that the jurisdiction to apply them cannot be successfully awarded on utilitarian grounds alone. He does this by setting out rival, utilitarian arguments that it can, and then demolishing those rival arguments.

The Reasonableness Test. Fletcher defends the existing standard, the warrant requirement, by refuting an argument that reasonableness of the search or seizure, as determined by the court, is the proper standard for justifying search and seizure. The utilitarian argument that he refutes goes like this: a search or seizure is permitted by the Fourth Amendment if and only if it is reasonable, and it is reasonable if and only if the court can see that the good it does outweighs the harm. This is then the one and only standard there need be of the lawfulness of search or seizure; on the reasonableness theory, any other tests, such as the warrant requirement, have merit only insofar as they can be derived from a utilitarian calculation and subsumed under the reasonableness test. The utilitarian standard decided the substantive question of legality and the jurisdictional question of who shall decide on the substantive question, at a stroke. It decides the jurisdictional question by yielding, on grounds of utility, the warrant requirement and its attendant swarm of exceptions.

But, Fletcher argues, the reasonableness test *cannot* account for the warrant requirement as the law has it, so it does not answer the jurisdictional question after all, because the calculus of utility comes out wrong. If you weigh up the good that a particular search would do against the harm, the searches undertaken without a warrant that pass the reasonableness test are not the same ones that meet the impracticability test that characterizes most of the exceptions to the warrant requirement. And, worse yet, the warrant requirement that normally obtains does not turn out to balance the competing interests so as to maximize utility. So the reasonableness test does not accord with the law.

One who would defend the reasonableness view against Fletcher's attack has a couple of tactics open to him. First, the defender might say that if some other award of jurisdiction to determine the legality of search and seizure produced better results than the warrant requirement, then so much the worse for the warrant requirement. The strategy here is to argue that a law that fails to maximize utility has for that very reason something the matter with it. This is a bold line of counterattack, not much suited to criticizing the received view in the law from a minority position, for it cannot be expected to cut any ice with people who are not already convinced that in general the best answer to questions about what the law should do is the utilitarian one. It rests on utilitarian principles that Fletcher does not admit.

But the defender of the reasonableness view has another tactic. He can offer a new version of the reasonableness theory, also grounded on utility. The user of this tactic first has to clear off the rubble of the old theory by arguing that the new one, not the old one, really maximizes utility. He might, for instance, want to discredit the version of his theory that Fletcher considers by arguing that this version does not use all of the machinery that is available for comparing the merits of various answers to the jurisdictional question, and say that the new version of the theory offers utilitarian calculations that lead to different conclusions.

Now I do not want to venture a theory of search and seizure of my own, but only to show how a defender of the reasonableness theory can get his theory back on its feet again. So all I will do is suggest some lines of argument that the defender might want to follow. I do not claim that these lines lead to conclusive arguments, but only that they have to be taken into account by the reasonableness theory's opponents.

The defender of the reasonableness view can answer the jurisdictional question, and he can have the warrant requirement, or something close to it, for his answer, by arguing like this: if the constitutional protection that we enjoy against unjustified search and seizure is to have any substance at all, the decision about whether or not some search is proper cannot be left to the policeman to make all by himself and at the same time as he makes the search. Now you do not have to take a particularly dark view of police behavior to think this. If it is only the policeman's-eye view at the time of the search that bears on its reasonableness, and if the searching policeman testifies about it only afterward, at a trial, then a search that turned out to bear fruit looks, after the fact, very reasonable indeed. And this is apt to color the policeman's report of his view of things at the time of the search. If you do take a dark view of police behavior, then you can add to this that the incentive to lie about the reasonableness of the search is great: after all, the policeman wants to have the evidence turned up by his search introduced at the trial, to help him get a conviction. And if his word is the only test of reasonability that there is, there is no way to stop him from lying, and no very reliable way to prove that he has lied. Under a police-administered test of the legality of search and seizure, we can suppose that suspicious behavior—the kind that makes it reasonable to search—will greatly increase, and reliable though unidentifiable informers will multiply. To keep the policeman from seeing reason to search by hindsight, he has to be made to put his reasons for searching on the record before he performs the search, and to keep him from manufacturing reasons somebody else has to make the decision as to when it is reasonable to search.

From here it is only a step or two to the requirement that a warrant, issued before the search it legitimates and issued by a judicial officer, is the measure of reasonability nearly all of the time.

So Fletcher's attack on the reasonableness view does not have any lasting success. That view can be rehabilitated by utilitarian reasoning. We could let the defender go on like this, deriving more and more of the law of search and seizure on grounds of utility, and all of it proof against the attack that felled the first version. Presumably this new version is no more to Fletcher's liking than was the old one, but if he wants to be rid of it he will have to start all over again and make a new attack.

The Necessity Defense. Nor do I think that Fletcher succeeds in his other attack, against the theory that uses only reasons of utility to award jurisdiction to decide where the burdens and benefits of living among one another shall fall. His attack is in the same style as his attack on the reasonableness view—demolish the utility of the utilitarian competition—and he fares no differently here. The reply to his attack is, again, to give a new utilitarian theory that is proof against his attack.

Fletcher attacks the necessity defense twice. He argues, against a particular version of the necessity defense, that it gives too much power to individuals to decide when their conduct is reasonable, because the necessity defense fails to account for the principle, absolutely critical to our democratic way of life, that these decisions are reserved to the legislature. It is a matter of law that an individual, or the court, can make his own decision that an unlawful act is nevertheless defensible only when that act is taken to avoid "direct and immediate peril." But, says Fletcher, the utilitarian theory cannot account for this result.

His second attack is a generalized version of this one. This second attack argues that the sort of utilitarian reasoning that underlies the necessity defense leads to contradictory results. We will look at the generalized attack in the next section.

A slightly different version of the necessity defense can resist the attack on the version that Fletcher gives and can get the jurisdictional question about defenses to nominally criminal conduct to come out the way Fletcher wants it to. I no more want to offer a justification of the necessity defense than I want to give a theory of search and seizure, so again I only suggest lines of argument. A new version of the necessity defense might go like this: if we are to flourish we need to be protected from each other, and furthermore we have to *expect* to be protected from each other. For it is not much use to you to *be* secure if you do not *feel* secure; security against harm is in this respect just like privacy. The only way to make us feel secure is to take utility-allocating decisions *out* of the hands of individuals and out of the hands of courts and give them to the legislature. For by and large people are not very good maximizers, and letting individuals decide which of their own possible actions will best serve utility, and where the burdens and benefits of their actions are to fall, will turn out to be much more costly than beneficial. We are all better off if the legislature decides which kinds of acts maximize utility, and decides how that utility is to be distributed, than if those decisions are left in individual hands. This means that some utility will be lost, for in some cases the lawful thing to do is not the maximific thing to do: statutes have to be broad and general, and they cannot be expected to get the outcome right for each and every circumstance under which they apply. We can get some of this lost utility back again by allowing behavior that would normally be criminal, like stealing a car, to be justified in special circumstances, like the urgent need to get somebody to the hospital. Thus, another necessity defense is derivable. But the standard of necessity is higher, to protect against bad decisions from individuals. This standard is higher than the one Fletcher considers, high enough to stay out of his loop. And it is high enough to let us rely on law-abiding behavior from other people in all but extraordinary circumstances, and so high enough to prevent a breakdown in democratic discipline.

Fletcher's Paradox. Fletcher generalizes his argument against the necessity defense into an argument that the legislature, not the court or the individual concerned, is always the proper agency to make decisions about the law based on utilitarian considerations. He argues that doing it the other way, using utility as a standard for justifying nominally criminal conduct and thus also as grounds for acquittal, always leads to contradiction. The contradiction arises in situations like this: first, at T_1, somebody is faced with a situation in which he has to decide whether he is justified in breaking the law to avoid some harm rather than standing aside and allowing that harm to come about.If he stands aside he does nothing to alter the course of events, so the net effect of his contribution to the situation is zero. If he acts to break the law and avert the harm and if he succeeds in averting the harm, he reaps benefit B, but at immediate cost C.

If the actor breaks the law at T_1 he is tried for his offense at T_2. The court knows what happened at T_1, it knows the utility of the various acts open to the actor at T_1 and has to decide if his unlawful act was justified. If the act turns out to be justifiable, then the actor is acquitted; if not, he is convicted. If he is convicted, then he suffers a bit, say J, but there is no net change in other people's behavior. (Fletcher does not count the disutility J of conviction, but he might just as well have done; taking account of J makes no difference to his argument, or to this reply to it.) If, on the other hand, the actor is acquitted because the court finds that his act at T_1 was justified, he suffers nothing. But other people hear about the acquittal and the reason for it and later on, during the interval T_3, there is "a rash of cases in which individuals, encouraged by the events at T_1 [and T_2], make rash decisions" (See Fletcher, p. 319) and break the law, with some benefits but greater burdens, so the net cost of the rash is D.

The standard for justifiability from which Fletcher derives the contradiction is that the actor must, for his unlawful act to be justified, reap an *immediate* benefit. That is, the court looks only at what happened at T_1 and acquits if $B > C$. This standard is backward-looking; there is no place in it for the court, or the actor, to take into account the utility of events after the trial. It asks the court to look only at the short-run consequences of an act: events after the trial, and in particular the possibility of a breakdown in democratic discipline at cost D, never enter into the court's calculation at all.

A standard for justifiability which takes the longer view, which looks forward as well as back and counts in long-run consequences as well as immediate ones, can avoid the contradiction. Consider whether an act, otherwise unlawful, can be justified on grounds of utility if long-run consequences as well as immediate ones go into the calculation: let us say that such an act is justifiable just in case the short-run good that it does is enough to outweigh *any possible* long-run harm. That is, an unlawful act is justifiable just in case $B > C + D$.

This requirement sets standards for justifiability of searches and seizures, unlawful acts taken to avert harm, and so on, much higher than the ones that Fletcher considers and rejects. These new, higher, standards can pretty easily be defended as replacements for the rejected ones: because the long-run costs of the violations of law that they allow are paid for by the harms prevented in the short run, the argument that any such standard maximizes utility is straightforward. So Fletcher's arguments have gained him no ground in his war against the utilitarians: he has battled one round of enemy arguments, but he has to stand in the same place and fight the new ones that have appeared.

The Hydra Utilitarianism. Here we have a method for keeping

Fletcher busy with utilitarian arguments for points he wants to win: every time he demolishes one argument for something, we can find another utilitarian argument for the same thing. If these new utilitarian arguments should happen to fall, others still will fill their places, perhaps calling on other values to put into the utilitarian calculation or on other predictions as to what the consequences will turn out to be of this or that legal decision. These new arguments are not necessarily very good ones, but Fletcher will have to deal with them in their turn. Utilitarian arguments are hydra-headed; destroy one, and another one (or two) grows up in its place. Fletcher's tactics may succeed in every battle, but they cannot win the war. A different line of attack altogether is needed to put the defender of utilitarian decision procedures in the law out of business once and for all, and that is to object to him, not case by case, but on methodological grounds. To get anywhere against a utilitarian you have to argue that his *method,* weighing and balancing the consequences of the various possible actions, has something the matter with it.

15

JUDICIAL ACTIVISM AND AMERICAN CONSTITUTIONALISM: SOME NOTES AND REFLECTIONS *

ARTHUR S. MILLER

INTRODUCTION

A generation ago Alexander M. Pekelis maintained that the time had come to develop a "jurisprudence of welfare." Recognizing that judges have much more freedom than the myth allows them—freedom, that is, to make law and to fashion remedies for purported grievances—he asked "freedom for what?" His was a "call for the growth of systematic participation of the judiciary . . . in the travail of society." Welfare, admittedly, is an ambiguous concept, but to Pekelis it assumed "as its end the ethical and political doctrine professed by our society and attempts to find in the arsenals of judicial doctrine and social science the means for their realization." Welfare jurisprudence is the rejection of "an issueless life and an issueless jurisprudence." [1]

* This manuscript was completed in December 1975; except for some citations, it has not been updated. I am therefore not taking into consideration such works as Berger, *Government by Judiciary* (1977) or Glazer, "Should Judges Administer Social Services?" *Public Interest,* no. 50, (Winter 1978), p. 64. Analysis of those and other offerings about the question of "judicial activism" must await another time and another forum.

There is no way of knowing how many lawyers and judges read or were otherwise influenced by Pekelis's views. Even so, it is now obvious that he presciently forecast what in fact has taken place since then: judges, most of all Justices of the Supreme Court of the United States but also on other federal and state courts, have indeed become deeply immersed in the travail of society; they are "activist" as never before in American history. Consider these examples:

Item: In December 1975 federal district Judge W. Arthur Garrity placed a Boston high school in "receivership" because of noncompliance with integration orders, appointed a receiver, and took over administration of the school.[2]

Item: In January 1976 Judge Frank M. Johnson, Jr., declared that Alabama's prison system amounted to cruel and unusual punishment contrary to the Eighth and Fourteenth Amendments to the Constitution and directed that forty-four guidelines designed to rectify prison conditions be followed. He also created a citizens' review board to monitor compliance and report to the court. Finally, Judge Johnson warned state officials that they could be held personally liable for monetary damages if they failed to comply.[3]

Item: In 1973 the Supreme Court, speaking through Justice Harry Blackmun—a Nixon "strict constructionist"—wrote the most sweeping Supreme Court opinion in recent memory in knocking down state abortion laws and establishing a trimester system when a state may regulate the woman's choice to have an abortion.[4]

Item: Beginning in 1962, with the decision in *Baker* v. *Carr,* federal courts have consistently either invalidated legislative reapportionments or, of more importance, told the state legislatures to reapportion under pain of having the judges do it for them.[5]

Item: In 1966 the Supreme Court, in *Miranda* v. *Arizona,* promulgated a little code of criminal procedure concerning what police officers must do while interrogating criminal suspects.[6]

Item: In *Perez* v. *United States,* the Court in 1971 held that purely local loansharking was reachable by Congress through the interstate commerce clause because loansharking was a national problem.[7]

Other examples could be given, but heeding William of Occam, one need not needlessly multiply them to make the point: the judiciary has indeed become an active participant in social affairs.

An "affirmative jurisprudence" is being created, complementary to the programs of the Positive State.[8] Not all judges so act, to be sure, but enough of them do in areas of social turmoil to make them the target of heavy attack—some of which comes from venal politicians or other know-nothings but some of which issues from a group of academics widely called "neoconservatives."[9] The fulminations of the know-nothings and opportunistic politicians can be dismissed as transient excrescences on the body politic; but the neoconservatives are worth serious attention. My purpose here is to analyze the new judicial activism in the light of the criticisms of neoconservatives, using Professor Nathan Glazer's provocative article in the Fall 1975 issue of *The Public Interest* as a point of departure.[10]

Glazer maintains *inter alia* that the Supreme Court "is engaged in a damaging and unconstitutional revolution"; that "the courts truly have changed their role in American life"; they "now reach into the lives of the people, against the will of the people, deeper than they ever have in American history"; the courts are "authoritarian" and "a free people feels itself increasingly under the arbitrary rule of unreachable authorities"; this, Glazer, asserts, "cannot be good for the future of the state."

Were such statements accurate, that would be a sweeping and damning indictment. Glazer raises important questions about the nature of an activist judiciary in the American constitutional order, but his assertions should be taken as just that—a statement of the questions rather than answers to complex problems. There is another dimension to the general question of judicial activism that was slighted in Glazer's exposition. In this essay, the contours of that differing perspective are suggested.

What follows develops the following themes: (1) The judiciary, speaking generally, has always been activist; this is particularly true of the Supreme Court. (2) There are, however, new twists on judicial activism in recent decades, in ways that in some respect go even further than Professor Glazer's criticisms. (3) Contrary to Glazer, an activist judiciary may well be the final, even desperate hope of a crumbling system of American constitutionalism to save itself from its own inconsistencies and inequities; in other words, those who are triggering the courts, for after all judges are not self-starters, are, as the slogan of several years ago goes, "working within the system." Like Ralph Nader and his efforts to create a competitive enterprise system, the litigants believe the rhetoric of American "democracy" and act accordingly. (4) Even so, despite superficial evidence to the contrary, the judges cannot and will not prevail in the ultimate resolution of the human disputes that characterize and at times disrupt American society.

Constitutionalism, Professor Daniel Bell (another neoconservative) tells us, may be defined as "the common respect for the framework of law, and the acceptance of outcomes under due process." [11] One need only consult Charles Howard McIlwain's text on constitutionalism to learn that other definitions exist; [12] but Bell's definition is accepted for purposes of the present essay. Major attention will be accorded the Supreme Court, but federal judges in general will also be scrutinized.

SOME BACKGROUND OBSERVATIONS

A beginning may be made with a sociological truism. The functioning of a state and its legal system are closely intertwined; a legal system, including the judiciary, does not operate in a political vacuum. Although truistic, these facts tend to become obscured, submerged in a bog of mythology about the nature of law and lawyers and legal systems. The prevailing ideology of American lawyers is "legalism"—the notion that law is a discrete entity in some way separate from the society which it helps to regulate and control. This means that the orthodox model of judicial decision-making is that of Blackstone. Judges find but do not make the law; they are limited by the nature of the adversary system to facts brought forth by opposing counsel plus "strict" judicial notice; they are impartial; and they are competent to deal with complex issues. [13]

The orthodoxy has long been under attack, and is not accepted by the cognoscenti. Nevertheless, a curious ambivalence in legal thought makes knowledgeable observers uneasy about publishing the shortcomings of the Blackstone model. Hence the pretense, as revealed in the standard texts used in law school classes in constitutional law, still is that constitutional decisions are babies brought by judicial storks. [14] Some go even further and argue that of course the orthodoxy is faulty but those shortcomings should be kept from the laity, else the symbolic position of the Supreme Court will be badly shaken and its place in the constitutional order jeopardized.[15] One consequence of this mindset, a part of the legal profession's ideology, is that thousands of law students sally forth each year armed with J.D. degrees and some facility with legal jargon, but with little understanding of law as an instrument of social control or of its relationships to the sciences, social and behavioral and natural.

The judiciary, furthermore, is not a "democratic" institution. Not only do federal judges have lifetime appointments, removable under the Constitution only by the extraordinary means of impeachment, but Supreme Court Justices are accountable to no one—only to the Constitution and their consciences, as Chief Justice Earl Warren said in his valedictory speech—for their decisions.[16] An essentially oligarchic institution, the Supreme Court operates with the authority and often with the opacity of a modern Delphic oracle. Moreover, it works in an atmosphere of strict secrecy; its public face is limited to largely ceremonial but at times helpful oral arguments and to periodic announcement of decisions. What takes place behind the red velour curtain of the Marble Palace is a tightly held secret, as are the internal operations of all courts.[17]

Lack of accountability plus secrecy plus what most observers assert is a considerable power add up to an untidy sum. It is a form of elitism, even despotism, often benevolent no doubt,[18] that fits uneasily into a constitutional order usually (unthinkingly) called democratic. (I believe that it is more confusing than useful to employ the word "democracy" as if it meant something commonly accepted. That it does not should be obvious, there being by one count at least two hundred definitions of the term.[19]) Hence the arguments since *Marbury* v. *Madison* about the role of the Supreme Court and the self-asserted power of the judiciary "to say what the law is." [20]

Judges, moreover, are part of the political process and in fact would be meaningless and functionless outside of politics. Excessive preoccupation, by lawyers and scholars alike, with law as legalism has by and large beclouded this indisputable fact. And if politics involve, as Harold Lasswell has said, answering the question of who gets what, where, when, and how?, then it is important to analyze the Court—the judiciary generally—as one does other political institutions. Who wins lawsuits becomes the basic, indispensable criterion—not, as some would have it, the reasoning of judges or the

way in which judicial opinions are written. The reasoning and
opinions are important only to lawyers; "result-orientation" is an
unavoidable aspect of the adversary system, as reflected in the
judicial process.[21] That means that judicial activism is to be
evaluated in terms of "democratic" theory—in terms, that is, of
furtherance of the values of due process and of equality. By
definition, the adversary system, as reflected in the American
judiciary and its operation, means due process; it is constitutionalism as Daniel Bell defined the term.

But the fact that the Supreme Court engages, as Professor Martin
Shapiro has said, "in the very stuff of routine politics," [22] should not
be taken to mean that it is equatable in all respects with the
avowedly political branches of government. It has functions different from those of Congress, in the main a charismatic role that
fulfills, as the Grand Inquisitor put it, some of the desires of
humans—for miracle, mystery, and authority. The Court, any court,
is clothed with mystery and speaks with authority; small wonder,
then, that people at times look to the judges for miracles, for ways to
save them—the people—from their own follies. That judges cannot
do that is obvious, but in a secular society imbued with religiosity
but not real religion there is no substitute. Shapiro has argued that
"the real problem" about the Court is how to enable it to make
policy—that is, act politically—while professing to be apolitical; as
Shapiro puts it, "without violating those popular and professional
expectations of 'neutrality' which are an important factor in our
legal tradition and a principal source of the Supreme Court's
prestige." [23]

He wants the impossible. A jurisprudence of nondisclosure about
the judiciary surely cannot—more, should not—be rebuilt. It is too
late in the day for "the distinction between what the Court tells the
public about its activities and what scholars tell each other" any
longer to have the semblance of validity. "It would be fantastic,"
Shapiro continues, "if the Supreme Court ... were to disavow
publicly the myth upon which its power rests." [24] Fantastic,
perhaps, but that is precisely what has happened since those words
were written. Justice Byron White, among others, has openly
acknowledged that the Court's task in constitutional interpretation
is one of creativity, of making law.[25] (That bespeaks a jurisprudence
of process, rather than one of logical principles internally consistent

one with another.) And the heavens have not fallen; the Supreme Court and the judiciary generally is still high in esteem among governmental institutions (President Richard Nixon knew that he could not defy the Court's unanimous decision in 1974 on the White House tape recordings); and federal judges, such as Garrity and Johnson, become obviously and deeply immersed in "political" matters. The public, as Professor Leonard Levy has acknowledged, cares about results: [26] it does not read judicial opinions. Contrary to those who, like Professor Shapiro, advocate "squid jurisprudence"— covering the operations of the judiciary in a dense cloud of black ink—the prestige and ultimately the power of the courts depends on something rather more substantial than adherence to a long-exploded myth.[27]

JUDICIAL ACTIVISM IN PERSPECTIVE

Led by a gaggle of professors, many of whom are votaries in the cult of Frankfurter worship, it has become fashionable in recent years to characterize, and usually to castigate, the Supreme Court (and other courts) as being too activist. The term is only loosely employed; it is never adequately defined. A high-level abstraction, it seems to mean that the Justices since Earl Warren became Chief Justice have been too ready openly to create new law and to break new constitutional ground. The advocates of judicial passivity appear to disagree with Justice William O. Douglas's assertion in 1962 that constitutional questions are "always open." [28] Refusing to concede that a refusal to decide is itself a decision, a decision at least to maintain the status quo, and failing to follow the logic of the open secret that judges are philosophically not fungible,[29] the passivists desire a somnolent judiciary which is not an active participant in the travail of society. Their views are, of course, fully entitled to First Amendment protection, although it should always be remembered that the amendment merely protects speech and that it does not require it to be "true" or accurate.

Activism, to be sure, does characterize much of the judiciary today, as Professor Glazer tells us. In at least three ways, that activism has characteristics not mentioned by Glazer. First, the judges—particularly the Justices of the Supreme Court—have since at least *Cooper* v. *Aaron* [30] at times issued general, as distinguished from specific, norms; second, they have begun to issue "back-door" advisory opinions *sua sponte;* and third, with the change in nature of the state from a negative, night-watchman posture to one of affirmative orientation, the judges have begun to operate to say "you must" at times as well as what they said historically: "you cannot." That Glazer is correct about the increased activity of courts does not mean that he is accurate when he says that judges are to enunciate "the will of the people"; nor is it at all clear that the state, if by that word is meant something different from the people, is harmed by judicial activism.[31] Each aspect requires explanation; but before doing so, it is desirable to discuss the general question of judicial activism.

Speaking generally, federal judges have always been activist. Since 1803 the Supreme Court has maintained that "it is emphatically the province and duty of the judicial department to say what the law is."[32] Since the beginnings of the republic the question is: What direction should judicial activism take? Brief reference to history will help to validate that statement. Since 1789, much of American constitutional law has revolved around the development of finance capitalism. Early on, the Supreme Court, as is well known, was a nationalizing influence. Under the domination of Chief Justice John Marshall, its decisions in *Marbury, Martin, McCulloch, Cohens, and Gibbons*[33] constitutionally permitted a vast increase in the powers of the federal government. *Marbury,* to be sure, was naysaying; but in a way that established the Court as the ultimate arbiter of constitutionality. At the same time, astute use of the obligation of contracts clause in such cases as *Fletcher* v. *Peck* and *Dartmouth College* v. *Woodward*[34] both cut away state-government regulation designed to curb the businessman and paved the way for the economic exploitation of the continent. The "basic doctrine of American constitutional law" was, as Professor Edward S. Corwin said, "vested rights."[35]

The Marshall Court's activism promoted government intervention into economic life in ways to aid the growing number of business corporations. As Professor Wallace Mendelson has put it: "Conservative tradition insists that by putting the sanctity of 'contracts' above other considerations of ethics and public welfare, Marshall and his associates promoted economic stability. Would it not be more accurate to suggest rather that they encouraged the flagrant corruption of state politics and reckless waste of natural resources that marked the nineteenth century? Surely judicial protection of fraud in the Yazoo land scandal paved the way for the Robber Barons and their Great Barbecue at the expense of the American people." [36] The point, for present purposes, is that the Supreme Court early on was quite activist—as much so as in recent years. Only the issues differ. Then it was finance capitalism; now it is civil rights and civil liberties. Moreover, Chief Justice Marshall in *Fletcher* v. *Peck* established the practice, since followed, of finding new rights and principles buried in the vague contours of the Constitution. Influenced by what Hamilton called "the first principles of natural justice and social policy," [37] he invalidated Georgia's attempt to prevent an enormous fraud (perpetrated, it is meet to note, by two United States senators; two congressmen; and three prominent judges, including an Associate Justice of the Supreme Court). The state of Georgia, Marshall went on to say, "was restrained" from passing a rescission of the fraudulent land sale "either by general principles which are common to our free institutions, or by particular provisions of the Constitution of the United States." [38] There should be little wonder, then, that judges today articulate political theories of what is socially proper when called upon to interpret the Constitution—particularly when one recalls what Justice William Johnson said while concurring in *Fletcher:* "I do not hesitate to declare that a state does not possess the power of revoking its own grants. But I do it, on a general principle, on the reason and nature of things; a principle which will impose laws even on the Deity." [39] The Warren Court at its most extravagant extension of doctrine—as, say, in *Miranda* v. *Arizona* [40]—or the Nixon Court, at times equally extravagant—as, say, in the abortion cases [41]—never went as far as did Johnson (to try to bind the deity).

Judicial activism after the Civil War took two directions. First was the continued protection of business enterprise, at the expense of the workingman, who was asked to bear many of the burdens of an industrializing nation; second, since 1937 the equality principle has been expanded to enhance civil rights and liberties. The half century between the time that the Justices casually agreed, without argument, that the corporation was a person under the Fourteenth Amendment,[42] and thus protected by the due process clause, and the time when hydraulic pressures of social protest peaked in the mid-1930s to create the "constitutional revolution" of 1937 was characterized by judges, in both private and public law, being in effect an arm of the business community and their minions in the political branches of government.[43] Activism, again, so much so that John R. Commons could in 1924 call the Supreme Court "the first authoritative faculty of political economy in the world's history." [44] Conservatives then, contrary to today, looked upon the Constitution and the Court as bulwarks against a rising tide of majoritarian democracy. Conservatives, in other words, welcomed judicial activism; their ox was not being gored at that time.

Judicial activism since 1937 is too recent and too well known for more than brief mention. The Justices first constitutionalized Keynesian economics and the American version of the welfare state; and then, having stripped themselves of their historical role of protecting finance capitalism, they cast around and found in the rising tide of equalitarianism ways to continue its position as "equal in origin and equal in title" [45] to the other branches of government. But in so doing the Court added new twists to its propensity for innovation.

The redefinition, first, took the posture of propounding norms of general applicability—something new under the constitutional sun. The landmark opinion is *Cooper* v. *Aaron*, the Little Rock school desegregation case. There a unanimous Court, in an opinion unique because it was individually signed by each Justice (rather than the usual practice of one member writing an opinion or of issuing decisions *per curiam*), maintained that "the federal judiciary is supreme in the exposition of the law of the Constitution." The Court went on to assert that "*every* state legislator and executive, and judicial officer is solemnly committed by oath taken pursuant to Article VI, cl. 3, to support the Constitution." The *Marbury* activism took an exponential jump; the writ of the Court ran generally, not merely to the parties before the bench. That type of activism has since been repeated in other contexts. In 1966, for example, a divided Court in *Miranda* v. *Arizona* [46] not only overruled past precedent but promulgated a little code of criminal procedure as to when lawyers must be present during police interrogations of suspected criminals.

Such a "back-door" advisory opinion is the second facet of the new judicial activism. The Justices at times go far beyond the facts of a given case and attempt to settle a number of problems at once. When in 1973 the Nixon Court, led by "strict constructionists" Harry Blackmun, Lewis Powell, and Warren Burger, not only validated voluntary abortion by consenting females but went much further to establish a trimester system when a state might regulate abortions,[47] it so staggered one law professor that he asserted, quite seriously, that the decisions were "not constitutional law," [48] a piece of intelligence that should interest the attorneys general of Texas and Georgia (where the suits were brought) as well as the Supreme Court itself. What the president and the Congress cannot do— obtain an advisory opinion from the Supreme Court—the Court at times does *sua sponte.* These opinions, furthermore, are general norms, far wider than even class actions. (It is wryly amusing to note that the same group of Justices who made class actions more difficult [49] at times make law wholesale by issuing opinions that they say bind everyone, not merely individuals or members of a class.)

Finally, modern judicial activism sometimes has an affirmative thrust. Rather than being a series of "thou shalt nots," from time to time it takes the form of judges saying what other governmental officials *must* do. Put another way, there has been a noticeable tendency in recent years for courts to impose affirmative duties upon government rather than leaving officials to determine their options after invalidating one of those options. Discretion over policy thus was taken from, say, school officials or state legislatures and vested (again, at times) in the judiciary. *Green v. School Board* provides an illustration. Said Justice William Brennan for the Court: "school boards operating [dual] school systems were *required* by *Brown II* 'to effectuate a transition to a racially nondiscriminatory school system.' " Brennan went on to say that under the second *Brown* decision school boards "then operating state-compelled dual systems were nevertheless clearly charged with the affirmative duty to take whatever steps might be necessary to convert to a unitary system in which racial discrimination would be eliminated root and branch." His conclusion merits close attention: "The Board must be required to formulate a new plan and, in light of other courses which appear open to the Board, such as zoning, fashion steps which promise realistically to convert promptly to a system without a 'white' school

and a Negro school, but just schools." [50] Other decisions of the same
genre are in the books, not only in racial matters, but also in
legislative reapportionment and criminal procedure.[51]

The net result, in school cases at least, is that the federal judiciary
has indeed become a "national school board." [52] The logical
extension of the Court enunciating affirmative duties was seen,
moreover, in December 1975 when District Judge W. Arthur
Garrity summarily removed a Boston school board and placed it in
"receivership," with himself in charge.[53] Receivership is a term in
the law of bankruptcy, and while in a loose sense the Boston school
might be bankrupt in that it had not complied with judicial orders
to integrate the system, surely it was not in the financial sense. All of
that presumably flowed logically from the Supreme Court's unanimous opinion, authored by Chief Justice Burger, in the *Charlotte-
Mecklenburg* busing case and the *Keyes* case.[54] It indicates once again
how a principle once enunciated often tends to be carried to its
logical extreme—a phenomenon that Glazer attributes to the
training of lawyers to see and value continuity.

The new activist posture, then, relates not only to the issues being
decided. True enough, the power of the federal government is
steadily being further constitutionalized, just as it was in John
Marshall's time. *Maryland* v. *Wirtz* and *Perez* v. *United States* provide
examples of that.[55] In the former, the application of the federal
wage and hour act of 1938 to state employees was upheld as a valid
exercise of the power of Congress to regulate commerce; while in
Perez an admittedly local criminal action (loansharking) was held to
be within the purview of federal law because, as Justice Douglas
said for the Court, "loan sharking in its national setting is one way
organized crime holds its guns to the heads of the poor and the rich
alike and syphons funds from numerous localities to finance its
national operations." In other words, organized crime (including
loansharking) is a national problem requiring a national solution.
Douglas did not mention *Kansas* v. *Colorado,* a 1907 decision holding
that because a social problem transcended state lines did not ipso
facto give Congress power to act.[56]

Activism by the courts today is principally in areas of individual
rights and liberties. And it is there that the Court has made a
mutational leap—an exponential jump into new forms of innova-

tion. Why such a foray into what had theretofore largely been judicial *terra incognita* should pose serious questions of the legitimacy of those exercises of power is completely mysterious. But that is precisely what is being argued, at times in words bordering on strident incredulity.[57] Like Edmund Burke after the French Revolution,[58] the neoconservatives see Jacobins at the gates of the city, led—astoundingly—by those men (and a few women) in black robes whose predecessors had manned the barricades against the onslaught of the mob. A strange twist to history, one might conclude, unless it be true, as I think it is, that the judges are the true conservatives. Like Franklin D. Roosevelt in the 1930s, they are trying to save the "system."

Professor Glazer sees "harm to the state" emanating from judicial activism—a cryptic remark proffered without explanation of the nature of the harm or of the nature of the state itself. Apparently Glazer equates the state with something different from the arithmetical sum of the interests of the people who live in the United States—perhaps an anthropomorphic superperson in the Gierkian sense.[59] It will do little good, in fact it will do much harm, to make such unsupported statements. One supposes that Glazer has not thought through the question.

THE WILL OF THE "LAW"—OR OF THE "PEOPLE"?

What, precisely, is the function of the Court in constitutional interpretations? Even now, two centuries after the formation of the republic, there is no settled conception of what Cardozo called "the nature of the judicial process." The ideal may be simply stated: the Court is to give effect "to the will of the law." As Chief Justice John Marshall said in 1824, possibly with tongue in cheek (could he actually have believed these words?):

Courts are mere instruments of the law, and can will nothing. When they are said to exercise a discretion, it is a mere legal discretion, a discretion to be exercised in discerning the course prescribed by law; and when that is discerned, it is the duty of the court to follow it. Judicial power is never exercised for the purpose of giving effect to the will of the judge; always for the purpose of giving effect to the will of the legislature; or, in other words, to the will of the law.[60]

Marshall in effect echoed Blackstone and Bacon. Said the former: a judge is "sworn to determine, not according to his own private judgment, but according to the known laws and customs of the land; not delegated to pronounce a new law, but to maintain and expound the old one." Said Bacon: "Judges ought to remember, that their office is *jus dicere,* and not *jus dare;* to interpret law, and not to make law, or give law. Else it will like the authority, claimed by the Church of Rome, which under pretext of exposition of Scripture, doth not stick to add or alter; and to pronounce that which they do not find; and but show of antiquity to introduce novelty." [61]

The problem is to understand the nature of judicial decision-making. Dean Edward Levi once called it "reasoning by analogy," pointing out that the pretense of the declaratory theory of law (as espoused by Marshall, Blackstone, and Bacon) has long been rejected. This may be close to the mark, but is not really helpful, for Levi does not explain the criteria by which one analogy is chosen over another.

On the other hand, Professor Glazer—amazingly—suggests that it is the duty of judges to give effect to "the will of the people," drawing on Lord Bryce for support.

"To construe the law," Bryce wrote of the Supreme Court, "that is, to elucidate the will of the people as supreme lawgiver, is the beginning and end of their duty." Bryce then adds in a footnote:

"Suppose, however," someone may say, "that the court should go beyond its duty and import its own views of what ought to be the law into its decision of what is the law. This would be an exercise of judicial will." Doubtless, it would, but it would be a breach of duty, would expose the court to the distrust of the people, and might, if repeated or persisted in a serious matter, provoke resistance to the law as laid down by the court.[62]

What, however, can "the will of the people" mean? At the very least, perhaps, it may suggest that in the ultimate resolution of social matters, nothing official—from whatever source—will prevail unless it is accepted by the people. But what will the people accept? And how are judges to know?

On the other hand, if the will of the people means that the judges are to intuit some sort of public consensus on specific issues, other problems obtrude. What is the "public"? And how is that consensus to be determined? Is a Gallup poll to be the test of constitutionality or of judicial propriety? Those questions answer themselves, and suggest that Professor Glazer either is not serious in his talk about the will of the people or that he has not thought through the implications of such a position. Furthermore, and this is of greater significance, the logical end of Glazer's position is one of majoritarianism—precisely what the neoconservatives in general appear to abhor. If constitutionalism has any core meaning in the United States, one aspect of it is that the majority does not always prevail, that the individual qua individual or qua member of decentralized group at times can win out over what majorities want.

It will simply not do, accordingly, to argue as does Professor Shapiro that "if the Court is to be successful as a political actor, it must have the authority and public acceptance that the principled, reasoned *opinion* brings." [63] Shapiro's focus is on the wrong part of the Court's work—the justification or rationalization rather than the *decision.* It is who won or who lost that counts, not how the game was played. Even most lawyers, Chief Justice Roger Traynor of the California Supreme Court once said, do not understand how appellate judges make up their minds.[64] How, then, can the opinions, as distinguished from the results, matter?

Rather closer to the mark was Professor Alexander Bickel, who in 1962 opined that "the Court should declare as law only such principles as will—in time, but in a rather foreseeable future—gain general assent. ... The Court is a leader of opinion, not a mere register of it, but it must lead opinion, not merely impose its own;

and—the short of it is—it labors under the obligation to succeed." [65]
Indeed it does; but what Bickel did not answer is how the Justices
can determine which principles can "gain general assent." Here, as
with Glazer and Bryce, one is reminded of the pungent remarks of
Judge Jerome Frank: In *Repouille* v. *United States,* a citizenship case
involving the question of whether Repouille was a person of "good
moral character," as the statute required, Judge Frank said:

> The precedents in this circuit constrain us to be guided by
> contemporary public opinion [in determining good moral
> character] about which, cloistered as judges are, we have but
> vague notions. (One recalls Gibbon's remark that usually a
> person who talks of "the opinion of the world at large" is really
> referring to "the few people with whom I happened to
> converse.")
>   Seeking to apply a standard of this type, courts usually do
> not rely on evidence but utilize what is often called the
> doctrine of "judicial notice," which, in matters of this sort,
> properly permits informal inquiries by the judges. However, for
> such a purpose . . . the courts are inadequately staffed so that
> sometimes "judicial notice" actually means judicial ignor-
> ance.[66]

If judicial notice at times becomes, as Judge Frank said later, mere
"cocktail hour knowledge," [67] then serious questions about the
nature of the adversary system of settling litigation—and in
constitutional questions, large questions of public policy—are raised.
There is simply no way under the way the system now operates for
judges to ascertain "the will of the people" or to determine which
principles will in time "gain general assent." Furthermore, "the will
of the law" cannot be determined if by that phrase it is meant that
the judge locates in what Jhering called "a heaven of legal
concepts" the *one* principle or rule to guide the decision. For it is
manifest that in any case that reaches the Supreme Court and gets
attention "on the merits"—and perhaps in all appellate litigation—
the principles of doctrinal polarity operates. There are always
inconsistent lines of doctrine—of the law—and it is the task of the
judge to choose from between them. In so doing, he must—as Justice
White has told us—create law.

We are left, then, in a parlous situation indeed if the goal is to have something other than "the will of the judge" in operation in constitutional and other decision-making. For when all is said and done, it is indeed the will of the judge that is articulated. There are no external standards of judgment that bind the Justices; they can pick and choose within the broad parameters of the adversary system and to the extent that they think their decisions will be accepted.[68] That evaluation must, of course, be intuitive; one has only to point to Frankfurter's cloudy crystal ball in *Baker* v. *Carr* to know that his fear of judicial intrusion into the briar patch of legislative reapportionment did not eventuate.

The basic question from the standpoint of American constitutionalism is to determine how much discretionary power the people are willing to consign to the judges in the making of what Frankfurter once called sociologically wise decisions. That problem, even today, has not yet been answered (almost two centuries after the Supreme Court began to operate as an informal council of revision of the acts of other governmental agencies). It is a problem that surely is not going to be answered by reference to Blackstonian theories or by citation of people long dead, including Lord Bryce. The vague contours of a possible way to approach it are suggested here.

A beginning may be made with the reminder that the courts are part and parcel of the political process. No one denies that they make law. But so do other, nominally democratic (in that they are elected) organs of government: the Congress and the president. And so does the appointed bureaucracy (as well as the private bureaucracies of the nation).[69] Judicial discretion thus should be seen in the context of the entire spectrum of governmental activities. In one of his last opinions, Justice William O. Douglas iterated one of his familiar themes: ". . . the entire federal bureaucracy is vested with a discretionary power, against the abuse of which the public needs protection. 'Administrators must strive to do as much as they reasonably can to develop and make known the needed confinements of discretionary power through standards, principles and rules.' " [70] Americans have become accustomed to and accept legislative discretion, even though the sanction of the ballot box is more apparent than real; and not only accept but appear to demand presidential discretion, including that of the bureaucracy (over which the president nominally rules). Only an occasional maverick, such as Justice Douglas, or a law professor, such as Kenneth Culp Davis, are perturbed by the well-nigh uncontrolled discretion vested in much of the bureaucracy, high and low.[71] Rather than being bothered by it, some observers applaud it as a necessary feature of government in the modern era.

That being so, why is there perturbation about the discretion of federal judges? Theirs is a power of decision that is usually final, whether it be district judges (the bulk of whose rulings are never appealed), or appeals judges who in the circuit courts operate as "mini-supreme courts" because most of their decisions are never reviewed on the merits, or the Supreme Court itself. Judges are like administrators in that their decisions are both discretionary and final, and both are not elected (and thus responsible to the electorate). Both groups of public officials are not "accountable" in the constitutional sense of having to answer in another place for their actions. The reference here is to the great bulk of decisions, judicial and administrative, not to the occasional one that does get reviewed in another place. The sporadic and happenstance should not be taken for the usual: judicial review of administrative action is a sometime thing (in which the bureaucrat is usually sustained), and the few appeals from lower court decisions usually do not prevail.

Life in the "administrative state" that is the United States of America has its drolleries. For a lawyer, who must get his amusement where he can find it, obsessive concentration upon a few hundred federal judges accompanied by little attention being accorded three million public and the several million private bureaucrats seems to be an odd misdirection of priorities. Furthermore, it is important to realize that only a relatively small segment of judicial discretion is under fire. Plea bargaining, for example, is seldom criticized, whether it is on the level of crimes in the streets or crimes in the (executive) suites. In both, and in between, a rough form of barter economics replaces the "rule of law." Prosecutors routinely engage in this practice, one in which judges equally routinely participate and which has the weighty authority of the Supreme Court to validate it. Sentencing practices of judges are notorious for being uneven, but that has not exercised many commentators (e.g., Glazer does not mention this aspect of what he calls an "imperial judiciary"). Moreover, thousands of decisions tumble each year from the judicial spigots without public or private reaction (or even knowledge).

WHY THE OPPOSITION?

In final analysis, there is no escape from the proposition that judges are entrusted with immense discretion. Even if in the vast majority of decisions there are no social ripples of dissent, at times the exercise of discretion does—as is obvious—draw fire. Consequently, it is necessary to determine *which* decisions of the federal courts today pose the question of *excès de pouvoir*. Four decisional areas may be noted: administration of the criminal law, separation of church and state, racial relations, and abortion. There may be others, but these are noteworthy for having been vociferously criticized by professional commentators and segments of the public alike—the basic criterion of choice. Legislative reapportionment is not placed in that listing, for the controversy appears to have died down; the legal doctrine is settled in large part, even if the politics remain. Is there a common thread running through the four categories that enables one to analyze the problem of judicial power? I believe that there is—and that it deals only partly with the new activism discussed above. General norms judicially promulgated are well on the way to acceptance.[72] Back-door advisory opinions raise hackles only if they deal with certain issues.[73]

The third leg of the new activism is somewhat different—where courts attempt to tell people what they *must* do, as distinguished from what they *cannot* do. Obviously there are semantic problems in perceiving judicially imposed "duties" as compared with "limitations," [74] but nonetheless it is here that some of the public and some of the professions unite, not in unanimous disagreement with examples of judicial fiat, but with enough anger or dismay that it is easy to perceive that something basic is at work. What, then, is their common denominator? It is fairly simple and equally obvious: Each of the decisional areas directly affects the personal life-styles of many Americans or deals with personally held, deeply felt, irrational beliefs. The attack, to be sure, has seldom been so bluntly put. For the professional critic, disagreement is couched in high-level abstractions: the reasoning of the Justices is subjected to scathing analysis; seldom is there a stated disapproval of the result reached. For the public it is different. The laity cares nothing for reasoning; it wants to know who won and who lost and, of supreme importance, what does it mean to me?

The question this poses is crucial—and unanswerable: Are the professional critics of the Court's decisions hiding their objections to the results reached behind a cloud of legalistic verbiage? And are those among the professoriate who are not concerned with reasons and structured opinions tacitly indicating their approval of the results? One would have to know the motivations of each commentator to state an adequate answer to that. However impossible it may be to answer, however, the problem should be faced. No one—lawyer or judge or layman or political scientist—is a dispassionate observer of the human comedy. We all tote our preferences and predilections around with us; these may be known but hidden or unknown and still hidden. That much, I think, is clear; there is a myth of neutrality in legal research and writing.[75] Gunnar Myrdal, who comes as close to being a modern (social science) Renaissance man as anyone in this century, has noted this in several books. He calls, as a consequence, for a person to "face his valuations" and to state them for all to see when reading some discourse.[76] In my judgment, he is correct: with deference to those who belabor the Supreme Court for alleged faults of omission and commission, it is of vital importance that we know where they stand on the substantive issues, as well as on the methodology of judges.[77]

Judicial lawmaking means that choices must be made between conflicting principles leading to opposing ends. These choices are not logical derivations from agreed premises.[78] The principle of doctrinal polarity being in operation, the law, by definition, is unclear; it is made by the decision of the Court, created anew in each case in some degree. If the choices that judges must make are, as Judge Braxton Craven maintains, always "result oriented," [79] then something of critical importance is at issue: *the problem of ends or of goals.* Yves Simon has asserted that in a democratic state "deliberation is about means and presupposes that the problem of ends has been settled." [80] But that is precisely what is lacking in the four decisional areas listed above.

Compare two types of cases. First, *Shapiro* v. *Thompson,* in which residency requirements for welfare were cut down; *Goldberg* v. *Kelly* making a hearing necessary before welfare payment can be terminated; *Baker* v. *Carr* and its progeny, which established "one person-one vote" as a constitutional principle; *Perez* v. *United States,* making local crime a federal problem; *Boddie* v. *Connecticut,* setting up a due process requirement of indigents' access to civil courts; and *Reid* v. *Covert,*[81] invalidating courts-martial of civilian dependents of military personnel serving abroad. In each the Court was activist; in each its reasoning was typical; in each it made new law. Second, *Miranda* v. *Arizona,* on the right to counsel for criminal suspects; *Engel* v. *Vitale,* outlawing prayers in public schools; *Swann* v. *Charlotte-Mecklenburg Board of Education,* permitting racial integration of public schools by busing students; and *Roe* v. *Wade* and *Doe* v. *Bolton,*[82] the cases establishing when abortion could be regulated by the state. Again, each was an activist decision; in each its reasoning was in the usual mold; and each made new law.

The second group, of course, is so controversial that constitutional amendments to overturn them have been seriously proposed in all save the *Miranda* situation—and there Congress, in the general area of criminal procedure, has dealt with some of the Warren Court decisions and the Nixon Court has chipped away slowly but steadily at the underpinnings of *Miranda* itself.[83] The problem is to understand why these decisional types have been so stoutly resisted, while passive acquiescence has characterized the first group. Professor Glazer attributes it to "the apathy of cynical and baffled people," in talking about why efforts of resistance to judicial decrees have failed thus far. (That probably means those people with whom he talks.) He ends his sharp critique of the Court by saying:

> In 1954 the Court abandoned prudence and for 15 years firmly and unanimously insisted that the segregation and degradation of the Negro must end. It succeeded, and eventually the legislative and executive branches came to its side and the heritage of unequal treatment was eliminated. That was indeed a heroic period in the history of the court. But even heroes may overreach themselves. It is now time for the Court to act with the prudence that must in a free society be the more regular accompaniment of its actions.[84]

But why would it have been prudential to refuse to rule in the designated (and similar) areas, and thus leave the final decision to the political branches? The answer is not self-evident. What values of constitutionalism are furthered by judicial passivity? Again, by no means is the answer obvious—or even ascertainable. It is idle, even mischievous, of Glazer to talk of "the will of the people" as if it could be ascertained or as if "the people" were an identifiable entity or, of more importance, as if "the will of the people" determined the decisions of legislatures or executives. The Supreme Court, to be sure, is an oligarchic institution, but so, too, are Congress and the state legislatures, as well as the ostensibly representative bodies of local government; and so, too, are executives at any level of government. To call the courts "authoritarian," as Glazer does, is to confuse the mythology of American governance with the reality. Judges are no more authoritarian than executive officials and bureaucrats—and surely are less so than those who control the giant corporations, financial institutions, and labor unions. Each of these groups probably exercises more power in fact, if not in constitutional theory, than do the judges. Judges, after all, are bound by the invisible chains of the adversary system and by institutional imperatives leading to conformity.

The Justices in each of the areas had three choices: to refuse to rule, to go along with the political branches, or to state their own understanding of the Constitution. Whatever the choice, they, consciously or not, had to make an evaluation of the probable harm of alternative decisions—to the people at large or to identifiable individuals. Both a refusal to rule and approval of the politicians' choices would mean that at least a few would be harmed, if not physically then psychically. If so, the Court would be approving majoritarianism; the rights of the individual would be swallowed up in a societal whole. The values of consensus would replace those of constitutionalism. Everyone of course has a full First Amendment right to such an opinion—that the majority—"the will of the people"—should always prevail, but that is hardly what constitutionalism is all about. That, be it noted, is precisely what is at issue in the efforts, seriously begun in 1974 and 1975, to have a written bill of rights promulgated in Great Britain. The fear is of legislative majorities, dominated by the unions.[85] There can be no doubt that the goals of white and black Americans do not coincide; nor do those who favor abortion against those who do not; nor those who fear an established religion and those who want subsidies for religious organizations from government; nor those caught in the toils of criminal-law administration and "society" at large. It is relatively easy to reconcile those goals politically. That is done routinely in legislatures and the public administration. But the problem is that the political system leaves many people dissatisfied and unhappy.

The critical issue, however, is whether a lone individual or a minority group should have to bow down against his conscience and at times against human decency to that principle of majoritarianism. The dilemma is clear: if the individual or group prevails, as in the four decisional areas, then others (in larger numbers) have to suffer losses. Who should bear the burden of conformity? And to what?

The best that can be hoped for is what we now have, something at times denigrated as the "guardian ethic," [86] but something for which in the American system there is no replacement. If Justices of the Supreme Court (and other judges) do not act at times to catch the conscience of the people, and to draw them up short and make them rethink their premises, there is no one else. Not Congress, not the president, not the leaders of private life; not one is up to the mark. In the American constitutional order, only the judges can—if they will, which by no means is certain—as Judge Learned Hand suggested in a famous passage.[87]

What, then, of the legitimacy of the Supreme Court's (and that of the other courts) activism in recent decades? The short answer is the same as that for the legitimacy of its *Marbury* role: it has been established. One decision alone proves the point: *United States* v. *Nixon*, in which the Court said that the now-disgraced president had to give up the famous tapes to the special prosecutor of the Watergate conspiracy. When Nixon capitulated, after hints by his counsel that he might not, for the first time in American history the writ of the Court ran against the president qua chief executive. As with his predecessor, President Truman,[88] Nixon clearly saw that defiance of the Court would have been disaster. An activist judiciary prevailed. The American people cheered. In general, it is not *excès de pouvoir* that is at the core of discontent; rather, it is the direction of the exercise of power—whose ox is being gored.[89] A "democratic" nation will continue to tolerate an activist judiciary; and if sheer numbers of people are concerned, they may demand it—as Glazer implies.[90] For he inveighs against the public interest lawyers, those who in recent years have helped to bring a flood of new types of litigation—and of litigants—into the courts. This means that more people are expecting relief for perceived troubles and also that they are using the established institutions of American constitutionalism to try to effect social change. When the avowedly political branches of government are unresponsive, what other peaceful avenue do they have? Close off the judiciary, as Glazer wishes, and the bottled-up furies of discontent may well explode. To oppose the use of the system by public interest lawyers is to oppose what Bickel called "the morality of process"—to him "the highest morality." [91] Furthermore, a judiciary adhering to the "passive virtues" means, in final analysis, a passive populace, one in which "the masses" know their place and keep it. But, again, is that what constitutionalism means? Hardly.

YES, BUT . . .

A court may pronounce but it cannot administer. It must, in the usual case, trust the *bona fides* of others—officials in other branches of the federal government and of the state and local governments—to translate its decree into operational reality. Judge Garrity's appointment of a receiver for the Boston High School is so unusual that it surely will not be quickly emulated.[92] In some of the reapportionment cases judges have, of course, told the legislatures to redraw the voting districts or the court would do it for them. Again, the legislatures capitulated. But a federal judge is not likely to drive a school bus or to monitor schoolrooms to learn whether prayers are being said. Nor is a judge likely to listen to the conversations of doctors and their female patients who want abortions. And those who administer the criminal law will do so without the presence of a man in a black robe or his designate. In net, there are and there will continue to be administrative checks on judicial power, just as there are lower court checks on Supreme Court power, as well as Supreme Court checks on lower court power. As Bishop Hoadly said in 1717 in his sermon to the King: "Whoever hath an absolute authority to interpret any written or spoken laws, it is he who is truly the lawgiver, to all intents and purposes, and not the person who first spoke or wrote them."

Whether an activist judiciary is also a powerful organ of

governance, in the sense of being able to promulgate binding, permanent norms on the people, is an unanswered question. Professor Glazer believes that the courts are "authoritarian" and are increasingly subjecting a "free people" to the "arbitrary rule of unreachable authorities." (But how can they be authoritarian when the adversary system is used? Is that not an example of "the morality of process"?) This, he says, has led to a loss of respect and trust of the courts by the people. Strong statements, those— particularly if they are accurate perceptions. But are they? I suggest not—that the judiciary is far from "imperial," and that in the long and perhaps even the short run the judges will not prevail. Americans are not close to having a government by judiciary, even with the new activism and the explosion of litigation. Societal decisions, insofar as they are made by public government, are in final analysis articulated by legislatures and, of much more importance, administrators. Adolf Berle said a few years ago that: "Ultimate legislative power in the United States has come to rest in the Supreme Court of the United States." [93] Professor Philip Kurland is nearer the mark when he recently said, "ultimate legislative power . . . resides not in the judicial branch but in the executive branch of the National Government." [94] Kurland echoed Professor Clinton Rossiter, who in 1960 called the president the "Chief Legislator," and Amaury de Riencourt, the European social critic, whose 1957 volume, *The Coming Caesars,* merits close attention as a description of American government.[95]

The basic question being one of power, how then can one assess that of the courts, particularly that very special court, the Supreme Court of the United States? Analysis should begin with the following kept in mind: (1) having neither purse nor sword, as Alexander Hamilton said, the judiciary still remains "the least dangerous" of the departments of government "to the political rights of the Constitution"; (2) the modern state is the administrative state; if with the fall of Richard Nixon, the presidency no longer can be called imperial, then surely the bureaucracy can; [96] (3) two factors characterize the social context in which American governmental institutions must operate: first, the growing realization of the finite nature of man, his resources and his power, and second, as Senators Frank Church and Charles Mathias said in July 1974, "emergency government has become the norm"; [97] and (4) the capacity of the law, however enunciated and promulgated, to change behavior patterns and thoughts of the American people is at best an open question; data do not exist to substantiate firm conclusions on the problem.

Lawyers and political scientists and Court watchers generally assume that the Supreme Court has enormous power. Any assessment should place it on a continuum with other governmental institutions, public and private.[98] The Court can then be viewed comparatively. If such a power continuum of the American polity were to be constructed, it would look something like this: at one end is the lone individual, who is relatively meaningless in the industrialized and urbanized nation-state that is the United States of America. Politically speaking—that is, in terms of power—an individual is significant only as a member of a group or groups.[99] The isolated individual does not exist as such. The group, the Constitution to the contrary notwithstanding, is the basic societal unit. Only groups have political or economic power. Robert Merriam put it well in 1944: "The lone individual does not figure either in family relations, in neighborhood relations, in state relations, or in the higher values of religion. Nowhere is he left without guiding social groups, personalities, and principles." [100]

At the other end of the continuum are the massive organizations of the bureaucratic state: Big Government, Big Business, Big Labor, Big Foundations, Big Farmers' Organizations, Big Veterans' Legions, Big Churches, Big Universities. These bureaucracies tend to interlock; they cooperate as much as they conflict; they make up the administrative apparatus for "the corporate state, American style." [101] No American is untouched by one and usually more of these organizational monstrosities. We all are beholden to them in one form or another. There the power lies in American government—and there it will remain. There is little or no likelihood that they will be broken up; the contrary will probably be true: they will continue and they will grow and they will envelop not only the nation but the world.[102]

Somewhere between those extremes lie the two embattled departments of government—Congress and the courts. Speaking generally, and with full recognition of recent attempts to regain lost power or attain new power, Congress is still the sapless branch of government. It is like a great beached whale, still alive, but mindlessly flipping its tail to and fro; now and then a flip of the tail can be lethal, as Richard Nixon and his merry men learned. But that is the exception and should not be taken as evidence of much more than that Congress still has *some* energy, but not much; it cannot govern— and what is more: it does not want to govern.[103] At most, Congress has an occasional but seldom used power of veto.

Without filling in the details of the range of power exercise in the American polity, where do the courts fit? Certainly not with the locus of public power in the bureaucracy; and not even with Congress. Somewhere toward the individual but of course relatively far from him. Judges, including those on the Supreme Court, can enunciate norms, but require a reservoir of public acceptance to make them stick. Little exploration beyond the superficial level of poll-taking has been made into the factors which work for or against such acceptance or confidence. Moreover, far too few empirical studies have been made about compliance with judicial decisions— "impact analysis," as it is sometimes called—to reach firm conclusions. What little is known with certainty is that at times there is compliance and at times there is not. Furthermore, the record, such as in church and state questions, varies from state to state throughout the country. The Justices shoot their thunderbolts from the Marble Palace on Mount Olympus, but whether they are merely hortatory pleas rather than acceptable commands depends upon some as yet little explored factors.

Two of those factors are worth special mention: first, if decisions, as suggested above, cut too close to the bone of primordial and no doubt irrational beliefs and preferences, then noncompliance may result; and second, if it is granted, as is obvious, that the courts are part of the political process in the American constitutional order, then as with any other part of public government they must receive the approval, tacit or overt, of the leaders of the elite groups in the nation.

As for the first, one example should suffice to illustrate the point: busing to achieve desegregation in the public schools. The fundamental issue about busing is not about the power of the judiciary; rather, it is the position of the black in American society. And of that this much can be said now: the white American, generally speaking, is not ready to accept the black as his equal and to accord him the same social status as whites receive. The National Advisory

Commission on Civil Disorders asserted in 1968 that the United States was moving toward the formation of two nations, one white and one black.[104] So we are, something presciently noted by Lerone Bennett in 1965: "The basic facts of the Negro situation is shattered community. Negro and white Americans do not belong to the same social body. They do not share that body of consensus or common feeling that usually binds together people sharing a common bond. ... Black man is incomprehensible to white man in America and vice versa: this is the root cause of the rebellion—broken community and the failure of Americans to create a single social organization." [105] Despite Supreme Court pronouncements by the score and such congressional statutes as the Civil Rights Act of 1964 and the Voting Rights Act of 1965, in the generation since the landmark decision in *Shelley* v. *Kraemer* [106] only surface changes have taken place. The black ghettoes still remain; the blacks are still at the low end of the pole of economic betterment; their unemployment rate is markedly higher than that for whites. In employment and elsewhere, "tokenism" has replaced separate but equal. Most blacks are still separate and still unequal, and as the United States celebrated its Bicentennial serious efforts were being made in several pillars of the Establishment to "prove" scientifically that they are genetically inferior.[107]

Two inferences may be drawn from that basic indecency to a long subjugated 11 percent of the populace. One is that the mass of whites want it that way and are quite content to keep the blacks in a condition of second- or third-class citizenship. The other is that the power structure of the American polity also is quite content to rock along with cosmetic changes for the blacks but with nothing fundamental being done. One would have to probe deeply into the psyche of the white American to learn why and how his fears and dislike of blacks are motivated.[108] That has not been done and perhaps cannot be done, but one thing is clear—the white intellectual leaders of the Civil Rights movement of the 1950s and 1960s, who told the people in the South what they ought to do, are strangely silent when it comes to such places as Detroit, Michigan, or Boston, Massachusetts. Ivy League professors and media pundits who during the 1960s became missionaries to the "benighted" southerners and spoke confidently about what should be done do not march to integrate the South Boston High School or pontificate about their backyard. Suddenly the ox has turned, and it is the "enlightened" North that is being gored. And they do not like it. Of course, they do not live in South Boston, but in lily-white suburbs. The point is that they are unwilling to tackle the white Bostonian with the zeal that they attacked the white southerner. Indeed, there is no perceptible attack at all. Silence reigns supreme in Cambridge and New Haven and on Park Avenue, as two groups of disadvantaged—the Irish and the blacks—battle it out. (The intellectuals in some respects resemble those pillars of Washington society who considered it high sport and *très amusant* to ride out to see men kill each other at Bull Run.)

This, of course, is not to condone the whites either in the South or in the North for their treatment of those citizens who had the lack of foresight not to be born with skins that shade of sallow pink so prized by the whites. The indecencies heaped upon the blacks, past and at the present, need no restatement here. They are too well known. My point is that most whites like it that way—and that is one of the principal, perhaps *the* principal, reason why judicial activism in racial matters, even when accompanied by political actions, is not prevailing in ways other than "tokenism" or cosmetic changes of no real substance. Despite Lerone Bennett's statement about "shattered community," America never has had "community" in any sense of full participation by the blacks. The "community" that was shattered was one with black Americans in a permanently subservient position. Outside of a handful in sports and entertainment and "tokenism," blacks are still second-class citizens. They have full legal rights but are not accepted into the mainstream of American life. Nor is there much evidence that they will be. The gap between the law in books and social practice, already frighteningly large, is growing. Law indeed has its limits, however promulgated. The "Negro problem," as Gunnar Myrdal said in 1944,[109] is really a problem in the hearts of white Americans. No one as yet knows how law can touch the hearts of anyone. If, as Pascal said, the heart has its reasons that Reason itself does not know, how is the putative rationality of the law to reach those reasons?

That bleak fact underlies the power questions of the judiciary. Americans are schizoid about the black citizenry. Judges and others verbalize or intellectualize ideas of freedom and equality, only to run hard against feelings—emotional responses—that cut through the putative rationality of the law and help to trigger hidden resentments and insecurity, because the beneficiaries take judicial rulings and American rhetoric seriously. No reasonably adequate resolution of the problem will take place unless and until the rational and irrational come together. If that does not happen, the law however articulated simply is not going to be much more than an exhortation to be good or to be better, rather like Sunday sermons or newspaper editorials. Judges, again speaking generally, have no way of imposing sanctions upon those who do not obey their decrees. Judge Garrity's order to put a Boston high school in "receivership" means at most that the schools will be run by federal courts, not by elected school boards; emphatically it does not mean that the social situation will change.

Would it make any difference if the American elites were to come out strongly for racial equality? Or, to put the question another way, is the apparent silence of most of the elite a tacit indication that the judges have lost, in some areas at least, a solid base of support in the community without which they cannot expect to be effective? Since the group theory of politics has, if not a dominant, at least a highly influential place in the thinking of political scientists, what are the consequences when a few federal judges are left to pursue their lonely way without the support, overt or tacit, of the most important groups? These questions must be answered if any comprehensive judgment is to be made upon judicial activism.

Professor Glazer suggests a partial answer: "Even the guardians of the 'guardian ethic'—the better educated, the establishment, the opinion-makers—are now doubtful of many of the rulings they urged when, unable to institute them through the elected representatives of the people, they made law through recourse to the courts." Glazer does not tell us in which way the guardians are doubtful; we are left to infer that it is either dislike of specific rulings or of a growing belief there indeed may be "limits to state action," as von Humboldt maintained.[110] Whatever the case, it is probable that if there are limits to governmental action, Americans must soon face one of the most potentially explosive social situations in their history. People in this country and elsewhere who have been taught to have expectations of personal betterment are now told, at times bluntly or even brutally, that it will not—it cannot—happen. When judges act in an "activist" way, they seem to be proceeding on an assumption that the limits of governmental action have not been reached. In this, they may be correct. No one knows the heights people may be able to reach. The judges may not prevail, but they should not be denigrated for trying to further the cause of human decency.

One important segment of the American elite was not listed among the "guardians" by Professor Glazer: the corporate and financial managers of the country's supercorporations and giant banking and other financial concerns. The Supreme Court, for most of its history, protected this group; it was in fact its ultimate guardian against a burgeoning majoritarianism. Since 1937, however, the Court no longer blocks socioeconomic programs on the basis of the Justices' notions of general principles which are common to our free institutions—and thus lost their strongest historical power base. The businessman turned from being highly favorable to being at least indifferent and perhaps even hostile to the judiciary. The result was the use of Congress as a "super court of appeals" by business enterprises,[111] accompanied by a lack of positive support for the judiciary. Other power groups—for example, the Roman Catholic church on the abortion and church-and-state issues—are similarly affected. Like the businessman, the attempt is to manipulate the political process, not the courts, as the way to achieve their ends.

This can be put another way. The judiciary, not the legislature nor the bureaucracy—for both are captives of interest groups[112]—has become the forum for furthering the rights of the unallied and the disadvantaged. It is, in many respects, a forlorn hope, a final desperate attempt to influence the organs of American constitutionalism without dropping into the abyss of violence. When the courts became the target of pressure from the black Americans, others on the lower scale of the social strata took hope that they, too, might get verbal and eventually emotional agreement with their demands. But these Americans—the poor, the black, the disadvantaged—by definition have insufficient political muscle adequate to alter public policy in fundamental ways. What they cannot do politically, it is doubtful that the courts can do for them. (The problems are multiplied when, as in South Boston, the disadvantaged are quarreling among themselves.)

The judges, for example, cannot mandate employment opportunities for the hard-core unemployed (at this writing some nine million workers are known to be out of work). To be sure, the Employment Act of 1946 makes it express government policy to take action to maximize employment opportunities for those desiring to work.[113] But even Professor Glazer's "imperial judiciary" is not likely to translate that statement of high policy into a requirement purportedly binding on Congress and the executive in fact to provide jobs, even though the need may be acute both in a personal and a societal sense. Tom Wicker, the columnist for the *New York Times,* said on December 14, 1975: "Leon Sullivan, a respected black leader from Philadelphia and a member of the board of General Motors, believes . . . that 'new seeds of insurrection are being sown in the cities of America' by the pervasive poverty to which unemployment rates contribute heavily, and that if nothing is done to move toward full employment 'within the next four years at most,' the resulting explosion will make the urban riots of the sixties 'look like little church meetings.' " [114] If there really were an imperial judiciary in the United States, then a constitutional right to a decent job could easily be found within the interstices of the due process and equal protection clauses.

The argument is easily made. A necessitous man is not a free man. Liberty is protected by due process of law; that clause, as Chief Justice Hughes said in 1937,[115] at times may *require* governmental action. Due process thus would become an affirmative command as well as a negative limitation.[116] The new judicial activism, noted above, in which affirmative duties are imposed upon government in certain situations could logically be extended to the economic sphere.

But that, as some English say, "ain't bloody likely." The judiciary is impotent to deal with such abrasive social problems; like the people in Kansas City, the judges have "gone about as fur as they can go" in intervening in the political process. Certainly they have gone as far as most of them *want* to go. Absent strong, yet subtle pressure from their peer groups, the judges will probably choose to remain silent—to exercise what Frankfurter thought was the supreme judicial virtue of self-restraint, save for an occasional maverick. Unless the elites get behind the courts and support them in all of their actions, little more can be expected of them.

CONCLUSION

The law, said Emerson, is but a memorandum. By and large he was correct, even though law, both judge-made and otherwise, may have a considerable educational impact. But a memorandum of what?

Government in the United States (and elsewhere) has always been and still is relative to circumstances. Judges know the limits of power. This does not mean that all will cease being activist—nor that they should stop intervening into abrasive human disputes. The judiciary, including the Supreme Court, *is* a part of government; it should be allowed to perform its lawful and constitutional role. No doubt many of its decisions will be disliked by segments, large or small, of the populace; but consensus or majoritarianism is not now, nor should it ever be, a test of what is right and proper for the judges. American constitutionalism will suffer—the American people will suffer—if the courts do not continue to act. By continuing to be activist, to protect the values of constitutionalism rather than of consensus, they can operate as a partial safety valve for bottled-up social protest; they can provide a breathing spell to enable slow-moving legislatures and executives to respond to reasonable expectations. With all of their failures and with their obvious shortcomings, Americans need them; the requirement is not to denigrate them for being "activist"—as was said above, that has always been true of judges—but to provide them with the necessary help and resources better to perform their important role.[117]

There are important, unmet needs in our scholarship (and social decisions) concerning the judiciary. One is this: What values should a judge further? If activist judges are considered to be doing "good" things today, will not others in the future do "bad" things? By what criteria is the good to be separated from the bad? And further: If the judiciary is to be a primary agency for social change, should not more attention be paid to the quality of the people now chosen to be judges? As Professor Kurland has said, "For the most part, judges are narrow-minded lawyers with little background for making social judgments." [118] On a more technical but still important level, are Judges Garrity and Johnson performing nonjudicial functions while sitting as Article III judges? [119] Finally: Is it not time to examine the adversary system as a means of setting public policy, in order to make sure that a system taken from feudal days and used for settling minor problems of *meum et teum* is in fact adequate to the needs of a highly industrialized, continental-sized nation with worldwide interests? [120] These, among other matters, must be provided if indeed the judiciary will be able both to remain activist and to perform in a reasonably adequate manner. The challenge stated by Alexander Pekelis has been met in part, but in so doing some flaws in the system have become apparent.

NOTES

1. A. Pekelis, *Law and Social Action,* pp. 1-41 (M. Konvitz, ed., 1950) (collection of essays).
2. *Morgan* v. *Kerrigan,* 388 F. Supp. 581 (D. Mass. 1975); affirmed, 530 F. 2d 401, 431 (1st Cir. 1976); cert. denied, sub nom., *White* v. *Morgan,* 426 U.S. 935 (1976). See also *Morgan* v. *Hennigan,* 379 U.S. 410 (D. Mass. 1974).
3. *Pugh* v. *Locke,* Civil Action No. 74-57-N, Jan. 13, 1976, U.S. District Ct. for Alabama (Middle District, Northern Division).
4. *Roe* v. *Wade,* 410 U.S. 113 (1973); *Doe* v. *Bolton,* 410 U.S. 179 (1973).
5. Discussed in, for example, W. Elliott, *The Rise of Guardian Democracy* (1974). *Baker* v. *Carr,* 369 U.S. 186 (1962) is the constitutional breakthrough.
6. *Miranda* v. *Arizona,* 384 U.S. 436 (1966).
7. *Perez* v. *United States,* 402 U.S. 146 (1971).
8. On the Positive State, see A. S. Miller, *The Supreme Court and American Capitalism* (1968); A. S. Miller, *The Modern Corporate State: Private Governments and the American Constitution* (1976).
9. For brief discussion, see Moynihan, "The American Experiment," *The Public Interest,* no. 41 (Fall 1975),; Wolin, "The New Conservatives," *New York Review of Books,* February 6, 1976, p. 6.
10. Glazer, "Towards an Imperial Judiciary?" *The Public Interest,* no. 41 (Fall 1975), 104.
11. Bell, "The End of American Exceptionalism," *The Public Interest,* no. 41 (Fall 1975), 193. See also Wheeler, "The Foundations of Constitutionalism," 8 *Loyola of Los Angeles L. Rev.* 507 (1975).
12. C. McIlwain, *Constitutionalism: Ancient and Modern,* rev. ed. (1947).
13. See Miller, "Supreme Court: Time for Reforms," *Washington Post,* January 11, 1976, p. F-1, for brief discussion. See also Miller and Barron, "The Supreme Court the Adversary System, and the Flow of

Information to the Justices: A Preliminary Inquiry," 61 *Va. L. Rev.*
1187 (1975).

14. Not one of the casebooks subjects the adversary system to critical,
searching analysis. Its premises are presumably taken as a given—
accepted, that is, as axiomatic—*for teaching purposes.* Even Thurman
Arnold, toward the end of his life, could maintain that the ideal of
dispassionate justice, though "unattainable," was of "tremendous
importance"; without it, "we would not have a civilized government."
Arnold, "Professor Hart's Theology," 73 *Harv. L. Rev.* 1298 (1960). But
Arnold can hardly be correct—although this is not the time to argue
the point. For brief rejoinder to Arnold, see Miller and Howell, "The
Myth of Neutrality in Constitutional Adjudication," 27 *Univ. of Chi. L.
Rev.* 661 (1960).

15. See Mishkin, "Foreword: The High Court, the Great Writ, and the
Due Process of Time and Law," 79 *Harv. L. Rev.* 56 (1965), criticized in
Miller and Scheflin, "The Power of the Supreme Court in the Age of
the Positive State: A Preliminary Excursus," (1967), *Duke L. J.,* 273,
522 (1967).

16. Said Warren: "We, of course, venerate the past, but our focus is on the
problems of the day and of the future as far as we can foresee it." He
went on to say that in one sense the Court was similar to the president,
for it had the awesome responsibility of at times speaking the last
word "in great governmental affairs" and of speaking for the public
generally. "It is a responsibility that is made more difficult in this
Court because we have no constituency. We serve no majority. We
serve no minority. We serve only the public interest as we see it,
guided only by the Constitution and our own consciences" (395 U.S.
vii [1969]).

17. See Miller and Sastri, "Secrecy and the Supreme Court: On the Need
for Piercing the Red Velour Curtain," 22 *Buffalo L. Rev.* 799 (1973).

18. See A. Berle, The Three Faces of Power (1967): "The danger is that
. . . the Supreme Court [could become] a variety of benevolent
dictator." This, he said, would eventually deaden the public to its
responsibilities. But, as was Berle's wont, this tends to be hyperbole; it
does not explore the complexities of the question.

19. See M. Rejai, *Democracy: The Contemporary Theories* (1967), for discussion. See also, E. Schattschneider, *The Semisovereign People,* pp. 130-31
(1960): "The great deficiency of American democracy is intellectual,
the lack of a good, usable definition." Professor Schattschneider
continues: "democracy [as "government by the people"] . . . is
something unattainable, . . . [but] it is one of the most emotion-
charged words in our civilization." And see Crick, Introduction to N.

Machiavelli, *The Discourses,* p. 27 (B. Crick, ed., 1970): "(. . . to call governments 'democratic' is always a misleading piece of propaganda. . . . It confuses doctrine with theory: we may want the democratic element in government to grow greater, but it is still only an element while it is government at all." In the judgment of the present writer, the word "democracy" is a slogan, a symbol which helps to organize the masses. To the extent that it connotes relative freedom of the individual vis-à-vis totalitarian nations, then it has some validity; but it has little if it means participation in government. See A. S. Miller, "For Reasons of State": Machiavellianism and the American Constitution (in process).

20. *Marbury* v. *Madison,* 5 U.S. 137 (1803). Chief Justice Marshall's statement about the role of the judiciary was quoted by Chief Justice Burger in *United States* v. *Nixon,* 418 U.S. 683 (1974).

21. See the candid comments of Judge Braxton Craven of the Court of Appeals for the Fourth Circuit, Craven, "Paean to Pragmatism," 50 *No. Car. L. Rev.* 977 (1972). Judge Craven maintains, rightly in my judgment, that all judges are "result oriented," the difference among them being that some know it but others do not. Furthermore, I believe that the history of American constitutional adjudication can and should be written around the theme of the Supreme Court being "result oriented." Surely *Marbury* v. *Madison* should be analyzed in that way.

22. M. Shapiro, *Law and Politics in the Supreme Court,* p. 332 (1964).

23. *Id.* at 31.

24. *Id.* at 27.

25. See *Miranda* v. *Arizona,* 384 U.S. 436, 531-32 (1966). This, to be sure, is no new insight, as Morris Raphael Cohen, among others, knew many years ago. See M. Cohen, *Law and the Social Order,* pp. 380-381 (1933) (collection of essays):

When I first published the foregoing views [on judicial legislation] in 1914, the deans of some of our law schools wrote me that while the contention that judges do have a share in making the law is unanswerable, it is still advisable to keep the fiction of the phonograph theory to prevent the law from becoming more fluid than it already is. But I have an abiding conviction that to recognize the truth and adjust oneself to it is in the end the easiest and most advisable course. The phonograph theory has bred the mistaken view that the law is a closed, independent system having nothing to do with economic, political, social, or philosophical science. If, however, we recognize that courts are constantly remaking the law, then it becomes of the utmost social importance that the law should be made in accordance with the best available information, which it is the object of science to supply.

26. L. Levy, *Against the Law: The Nixon Court and Criminal Justice,* p. xiv (1974): "My bias is in favor of well-wrought opinions that demand respect even from doubters who prefer different results. Regrettably, the judicial crusaders exert a greater influence than the judicial craftsmen. The public cares about results and has little patience for reasons." Professor Levy gives no examples of "well-wrought opinions."

27. The power of the judiciary is discussed on pp. 356-364 below.

28. *Glidden* v. *Zdanok,* 370 U.S. 530 (1962).

29. As Justice Douglas said in *Chandler* v. *Judicial Council of the Tenth Circuit of the United States,* 398 U.S. 74 (1970). The public, or at least the educated layman, has long known this, and lawyers so operate in their practice—when they go "judge-shopping," for example—but there is little exploration of the matter in the legal literature. As said *supra* note 14, the pretense that the Blackstone model of judicial decision-making is accurate is to this day assumed by those who publish teaching materials for law students.

30. *Cooper* v. *Aaron,* 358 U.S. 1 (1958).

31. Glazer makes no attempt to define the state. For discussion of some of the problems inherent therein, see A. d'Entreves, *The Notion of the State* (1967).

32. See cases cited *supra,* notes 20 and 30.

33. *Marbury* v. *Madison,* 5 U.S. 137 (1803); *Martin* v. *Hunter's Lessee,* 1 Wheat. 304 (1816); *McCulloch* v. *Maryland,* 17 U.S. 316 (1819); *Cohens* v. *Virginia,* 6 Wheat. 264 (1821); *Gibbons* v. *Ogden,* 22 U.S. 1 (1824).

34. *Fletcher* v. *Peck,* 10 U.S. 87 (1810); *Dartmouth College* v. *Woodward,* 17 U.S. 518 (1819).

35. Corwin, "The Basic Doctrine of American Constitutional Law," in *American Constitutional History: Essays by Edward S. Corwin,* p. 25 (A. Mason and G. Garvey, eds., 1964; essay first published in 1914).

36. W. Mendelson, *Capitalism, Democracy, and the Supreme Court,* p. 24 (1960).

37. Quoted in P. Magrath, *Yazoo: Law and Politics in the New Republic,* p. 150 (1966).

38. 10 U.S. 87 (1810).

39. *Ibid.*

40. 384 U.S. 436 (1966).

41. 410 U.S. 113, 179 (1973).

42. In *Santa Clara County* v. *Southern Pacific Railway Co.*, 118 U.S. 394 (1886).

43. See A. S. Miller, *The Modern Corporate State: Private Government and the American Constitution* (1976).

44. J. Commons, *Legal Foundations of Capitalism*, p. 7 (1924).

45. The quote is from Chief Justice Roger Taney's opinion in *Gordon* v. *United States*, 117 U.S. 697, 701 (1864).

46. 384 U.S. 436 (1966).

47. 410 U.S. 113, 179 (1973).

48. Ely, "The Wages of Crying Wolf—A Comment on Roe v. Wade," 82 *Yale L.J.* 920 (1973). In that statement, Professor Ely repudiates the growth of constitutional law through judicial decision-making as it has developed since the beginnings of the republic. One cannot believe that he really means what he said. But he said it.

49. See *Eisen* v. *Carlisle & Jacquelin*, 417 U.S. 156 (1974).

50. 391 U.S. 430 (1968), at 435, 437-438, and 492.

51. See, for general discussion, Miller "Toward a Concept of Constitutional Duty," 1968 *Sup. Ct. Rev.* 299 (1968).

52. As Professor Corwin predicted in 1949. See Corwin, "The Supreme Court as National School Board," 14 *Law & Contemp. Prob.* 3 (1949).

53. Judge Garrity's decision has been affirmed by the Court of Appeals for the First Circuit, and the Supreme Court denied certiorari. See *supra* note 2.

54. *Swann* v. *Charlotte-Mecklenburg Board of Education*, 402 U.S. 1 (1971); *Keyes* v. *School District*, 413 U.S. 189 (1973).

55. *Maryland* v. *Wirtz*, 392 U.S. 183 (1968); *Perez* v. *United States*, 402 U.S. 146 (1971).

56. *Kansas* v. *Colorado*, 206 U.S. 46 (1907). Perez, among other cases, squarely poses the question: When is a precedent binding on the Court? Answer: whenever a majority of the Justices so view it. There is no requirement to do so.

57. E.g., Professor John Ely of the Harvard Law School in his article cited *supra* note 48.

58. See F. O'Gorman, *Edmund Burke: His Political Philosophy* (1973). It is of more than passing interest to note that Burke is the patron saint of the present-day neoconservatives. In addition to the articles in the Fall 1975 issue of the *Public Interest*, no. 41, some of which have been cited *supra*, in notes 9, 10, 11, see A. Bickel, *The Morality of Consent* (1975) and Wolin, "The New Conservatives," *New York Rev.*, February 5, 1976, p. 6.

59. See O. Gierke, *Natural Law and the Theory of Society 1500 to 1800* (E. Barker, trans., 1934).

60. *Osborn* v. *Bank of the United States*, 22 U.S. 738 (1824).

61. 1 Blackstone, *Commentaries* * 69; Bacon, *Of Judicature.*

62. Glazer, note 10 *supra,* at 122.

63. Shapiro, note 22 *supra,* at 29 [emphasis added].

64. Traynor, "Badlands in an Appellate Judge's Realm of Reason," 7 *Utah L. Rev.* 157 (1960).

65. A. Bickel, *The Least Dangerous Branch—The Supreme Court at the Bar of Politics,* p. 229 (1962).

66. 165 F. 2d 152 (2d Cir. 1947). In 1956 Judge Frank said in *United States v. Flores-Rodriguez,* 237 F. 2d 405 (2d Cir. 1956): "I think it is a mistake for my colleagues to embark—without a pilot, rudder, compass or radar—on an amateur's voyage on the fog-enshrouded sea of psychiatry."

67. Frank, "The Lawyer's Role in Modern Society," 4 *J. Pub. L.* 8 (1955).

68. Cf. Howard, "On the Fluidity of Judicial Choice," 62 *Am. Pol. Sci. Rev.* 43 (1968); Shapiro, "Stability and Change in Judicial Decision-Making: Incrementalism or Stare Decisis?" 2 *Law in Transition Qtly.* 134 (1965). See Hand, *infra* note 87, at 36, in which Judge Hand discusses whether there is a common will. See also p. 74, in which he attributes notions of a common will to "the Hegelian State"—an organismic conception of the state.

69. So far as the private bureaucracies are concerned, see A. S. Miller, *supra* note 43—relying on Eugen Ehrlich's "living-law" theories to show that law is created by the interaction of the organs of public government and the institutions of the private governments of the nation.

70. *Northern Indiana Service Co.* v. *Izaak Walton League of America, Inc.,* 96 Sup. Ct. 172 (1975). The internal quote is from K. Davis, *Discretionary Justice: A Preliminary Inquiry* (1969).

71. Davis, *ibid.* See also K. Davis, *Police Discretion* (1975); Wright, "Beyond Discretionary Justice," 81 *Yale L.J.* 575 (1972).

72. There is little opposition, lay or intellectual, to the new role of the Supreme Court. See, for brief discussion of the general problem, P. Kurland, *Politics, the Constitution and the Warren Court,* pp. 170-206 (1970). Professor Kurland is one of the few scholars who have noted that the legitimacy of the Court promulgating general norms is a problem.

73. See cases cited in note 82, *infra.*

74. It is significant that what Professor Corwin called "the most influential treatise ever published on American constitutional law"—Thomas M. Cooley's *Constitutional Limitations*—was a long disquisition upon what government could not and indeed should not do. See E. Corwin, *Liberty Against Government,* pp. 116-153 (1948); B. Twiss, *Lawyers and the*

Constitution, pp. 18-41 (1942). It is only in recent years that the judges have begun to say what government must do, as distinguished from what they cannot do. See Miller, "Toward A Concept of Constitutional Duty, 1968 *Sup. Ct. Rev.* 299.

75. See Miller, "The Myth of Objectivity in Legal Research and Writing," 18 *Cath. U.L. Rev.* 290 (1969); Schubert, "Academic Ideology and the Study of Adjudication," 61 *Am. Pol. Sci. Rev.* 106 (1967). Professor Leonard Levy has said: "Much of the literature on the Supreme Court reflects the principle of the gored ox. Attitudes toward the Court quite often depend on whether its decisions are agreeable." Levy, "Judicial Review, History, and Democracy: An Introduction," in *Judicial Review and the Supreme Court,* p. 1 (L. Levy, ed. 1967).

76. E.g., G. Myrdal, *Value in Social Theory* (P. Streeten, ed., 1958). See also Engler, "Social Science and Social Consciousness," in *The Dissenting Academy,* p. 182 (T. Roszak, ed., 1968); *Ethics, Politics, and Social Research* (G. Sjoberg, ed., 1967).

77. In the interests of full disclosure, on which see Douglas, "Law Reviews and Full Disclosure," 40 *Wash. L. Rev.* 227 (1965), I say without hesitation that my personal values permit me to approve most of the Court's recent judicial activism. The problem, as I see it, lies not in the judiciary but in other societal institutions which have not responded and which do not attempt to make social reality catch up with the rhetoric about equality and democracy.

78. Since Oliver Wendell Holmes wrote in 1881 that the life of the law has not been logic but experience (see page 1 of *The Common Law*), we have known this, but for some reason still refuse to follow the logic of the Holmesian insight. Cf. Miller, "On the Choice of Major Premises in Supreme Court Opinions," 14 *J. Pub. L.* 251 (1965).

79. Craven, "Paean to Pragmatism," 50 *No. Car. L. Rev.* 977 (1972).

80. Y. Simon, *Philosophy of Democratic Government,* p. 123 (1951).

81. *Shapiro* v. *Thompson,* 394 U.S. 618 (1969); *Goldberg* v. *Kelly,* 397 U.S. 254 (1970); *Baker* v. *Carr,* 369 U.S. 186 (1962); *Perez* v. *United States,* 402 U.S. 146 (1971); *Boddie* v. *Connecticut,* 401 U.S. 371 (1971); *Reid* v. *Covert,* 351 U.S. 487 (1957).

82. *Miranda* v. *Arizona,* 384 U.S. 436 (1966); *Engel* v. *Vitale,* 370 U.S. 421 (1962); *Swann* v. *Charlotte-Mecklenburg Board of Education,* 402 U.S. (1971); *Roe* v. *Wade,* 410 U.S. 113 (1973); *Doe* v. *Bolton,* 410 U.S. 179 (1973).

83. E.g., in *Harris* v. *New York,* 401 U.S. 222 (1971). See Dershowitz and Ely, "*Harris* v. *New York:* Some Anxious Observations on the Candor and Logic of the Emerging Nixon Majority," 80 *Yale L.J.* 1198 (1971).

84. Glazer, *supra* note 10, at 123. Just why Professor Glazer singles out 1954 as the time that "the Court abandoned prudence" is completely mysterious, on two grounds: first, the Court had previously, in *Shelley* v. *Kraemer,* 334 U.S. 1 (1948), made what still could turn out to be an even more revolutionary ruling (in holding that judicial enforcement of private racial discrimination was invalid state action); and second, the Court in 1954 merely ruled on segregation in education; it took considerably more litigation for the *Brown* v. *Board of Education* principle to be extended to all areas of official action. See, for discussion and the cases, T. Emerson, D. Haber, and N. Dorsen, *Political and Civil Rights in the United States* (1966).

85. See L. Scarman, *English Law—The New Dimension* (1974); Miller, "Does Britain Need a Bill of Rights?" *The Guardian* (London), November 7, 1975, p. 15. It would be interesting to learn where the neoconservatives stand on the British effort: Would they support the judiciary over Parliament?

86. See W. Elliott, *The Rise of Guardian Democracy* (1974): Glazer, *supra* note 10.

87. Hand, "The Contribution of an Independent Judiciary to Civilization," in *The Spirit of Liberty: Papers and Addresses of Learned Hand,* 118, 125, I. Dilliard, ed. (paper edition, 1959):

> It is a condition upon the success of our system that the judges should be independent; and I do not believe that their independence should be impaired because of their constitutional function. But the price of this immunity, I insist, is that they should not have the last word in those basic conflicts of "right and wrong—between whose endless jar justice resides." You may ask what then will become of the fundamental principles of equity and fair play which our constitutions enshrine; and whether I seriously believe that unsupported they will serve merely as counsels of moderation. I do not think anyone can say what will be left of those principles; I do not know whether they will serve only as counsels; but this much I think I do know—that a society so riven that the spirit of moderation is gone, no court *can* save; that a society where that spirit flourishes, no court *need* save; that in a society which evades its responsibility by thrusting upon the courts the nurture of that spirit, that spirit in the end will perish.

88. In the *Steel Seizure* case, 343 U.S. 579 (1952).

89. Since the judiciary is not a self-starter, it is obvious that half of the litigants, speaking roughly, must always be pleased by the results of

the exercises of judicial power. One need not applaud everything the judges have done in recent years to say that Professor Glazer has little empirical evidence about general discontent among the American people on the conduct of the courts. See W. Watts and L. Free, *State of the Nation,* p. 72 (1974), indicating that, among governmental institutions, the courts are highest in esteem of the people.

90. See Downing, "Judicial Ethics and the Political Role of Courts," 35 *Law & Contemp. Prob.* 94, 106-107 (1970):

> The fact that the courts are the principal forum for resolving so many important political issues is indicative of serious default on the part of our legislative and executive institutions. So long as this default continues, and the courts are responsive to pleas for resolution of such issues, the judiciary (a most fragile institution in the halls of power politics) will continue to be buffeted by the full force of increasingly devastating political conflicts arising in the nation. . . .
>
> There appears to be little prospect that the legislative and executive processes can soon be transformed in such a way as to permit our political system to cope with society's deepest problems. . . .
>
> In short, while it is very doubtful that the courts can save the country, only they may be able to buy us the time necessary for revitalization of our other institutions.

In one of his last opinions, written after beset with the illness that forced his resignation, Justice Douglas said: "cases such as this one reflect festering sores in our society; and the American dream teaches that if one reaches high enough and persists there is a forum where justice is dispensed. I would lower the technical barriers and let the courts serve that ancient need. They can in time be curbed by legislative or constitutional restraints if an emergency arises. We are today far from facing an emergency. For in all frankness, no Justice of this Court need work more than four days a week to carry his burden. I have found it a comfortable burden even in my months of hospitalization" *(Warth* v. *Seldin,* 95 Sup. Ct. 2197, 2215 [1975] [dissenting opinion]). The majority denied standing to plaintiffs to contest zoning ordinances.

91. A. Bickel, *The Morality of Consent,* p. 123 (1975). I am not suggesting that the late Professor Bickel would have agreed with the thrust of the present paper. Quite the contrary: himself a self-acknowledged disciple of Edmund Burke, he may have found ways to agree with

Professor Glazer. Nevertheless, I am unable to understand what a "morality of process" means unless it means that citizens (plus the judges, of course) play the game according to the rules and abide by the results.

92. The question that must be answered by those who oppose Judge Garrity's action is this: Given the logic of the Swann case and the original busing order of Judge Garrity, what alternative did he have?
93. A. Berle, *The Three Faces of Power* (1967).
94. Kurland, Preface to *The Supreme Court and the Judicial Function,* p. ix (P. Kurland, ed., 1975).
95. C. Rossiter, *The American Presidency,* p. 28, Rev. ed. (1960); A. de Riencourt, *The Coming Caesars,* p. 330 (1957).
96. See Wilson, "The Rise of the Bureaucratic State," *Public Interest,* no. 41 (Fall 1975), 77. This is not to suggest that the departure of Richard Nixon from the White House means a diminution in the power of the presidency. Quite the contrary: despite Watergate, the presidency is and will be stronger than ever. Cf. Miller, "Implications of Watergate: Some Proposals for Cutting the Presidency Down to Size," 2 *Hastings Const. Law Qtly.,* 33 (1975).
97. In their introduction to H. Relyea, *A Brief History of Emergency Powers in the United States* (1974) (issued by the Senate's Special Committee on National Emergencies and Delegated Emergency Powers).
98. That a system of private governments exists in the United States is argued in A. S. Miller, *The Modern Corporate State: Private Governments and the American Constitution* (1976).
99. Discussed in *ibid.*
100. R. Merriam, *Public and Private Government,* 16 (1944).
101. See Miller, *supra* note 98.
102. *Ibid.*
103. Cf. Miller, "An Inquiry into the Relevance of the Intentions of the Founding Fathers, with Special Emphasis upon the Doctrine of Separation of Powers," 27 *Ark. L. Rev.* 583 (1974). See Watson, "Congress Steps Out: A Look at Congressional Control of the Executive," 63 *Calif. L. Rev.* 983 (1975), listing statutory provisions for legislative review or veto. However, the fact remains that the legislative veto, although possible (but perhaps, as Watson and others argue, unconstitutional), is seldom used.
104. *Report of the National Advisory Commission on Civil Disorders* (1968).
105. L. Bennett, *Confrontation: Black and White,* 3 (1965) (Penguin Edition, 1966). In many respects, the true "shattered community" is that of the poor and disadvantaged vis-à-vis the affluent. More and more it may be seen that the latter, relatively small group is at sharp odds with the

former, much larger group—which includes most blacks. The "shattered community" exists on a planetary scale (the Third World
nations vs. the "rich-man's club" of the North), as well as within the
United States.

106. *Shelley* v. *Kraemer,* 334 U.S. 1 (1948).

107. For example, A. Jensen, *Educability and Group Differences* (1973).

108. Cf. L. van der Post, *The Dark Eye in Africa* (1955).

109. G. Myrdal, *An American Dilemma* (1944).

110. W. von Humboldt, *The Limits of State Action* (J. Burrow, ed., 1969).

111. See Miller and Knapp, *Congress As a "Super Court of Appeals"* (to be
published in 1979).

112. See T. Lowi, *The End of Liberalism* (1969); G. McConnell, *Private Power
and American Democracy* (1966). On the judiciary as a target of interest
groups, see C. Vose, *Constitutional Change* (1972).

113. See, for discussion, the symposium in the December 1966 issue of the
George Washington Law Review, discussing the Employment Act.

114. *New York Times,* December 14, 1975, sec. 4, p. 15, col. 6.

115. *West Coast Hotel Co.* v. *Parrish,* 300 U.S. 379 (1937).

116. See Miller, "An Affirmative Thrust to Due Process of Law?" 30 *Geo.
Wash. L. Rev.* 399 (1962).

117. See Miller and Barron, "The Supreme Court, the Adversary System,
and the Flow of Information to the Justices: A Preliminary Inquiry,"
61 *Va. L. Rev.* 1187 (1975).

118. Quoted in Oster and Doane, "The Power of Our Judges," *U.S. News
& World Report,* January 19, 1976, p. 29.

119. See *Hobson* v. *Hansen,* 265 F. Supp. 902 (D.D.C. 1967), appeal
dismissed, 393 U.S. 801 (1968); cf. *Glidden Co.* v. *Zdanok,* 370 U.S. 530
(1962). For discussion and citation of cases of the problem of Article
III judges performing administrative functions, see Bator, Mishkin,
Shapiro, and Wechsler, *The Federal Courts and the Federal System,* pp.
237-238, 2d ed. (1973).

120. See Miller, "Supreme Court: Time for Reforms," *Washington Post,*
"Outlook," January 11, 1976; and Miller and Barron, "The Supreme
Court, the Adversary System and the Flow of Information to the
Justices: A Preliminary Inquiry," 61 *Va. L. Rev.* 1187 (1975).

EPILOGUE

J. ROLAND PENNOCK

When Mr. Justice McReynolds, nearly half a century ago, cried out from the Supreme bench, "The Constitution is gone!" it is unlikely that many people became exercised who were not already disturbed. But when a liberal and sober scholar like Edward S. Corwin, in a volume entitled *The Twilight of the Supreme Court,* argued that what had been considered the pillars of constitutionalism had been eroded almost to the vanishing point, the question of the future of constitutionalism became the subject of serious academic discussion.[1] Yet none of the papers prepared for this volume so much as raises the question (although Gordon Schochet, in his Introduction, points out that attacks on the idea of constitutionalism have become current in recent years). Apart from Schochet's paper, perhaps the closest approach to the subject is Arthur Miller's vigorous defense of the active role nowadays played by the courts in declaring and applying the restraints and commands of the Constitution. The reason for this neglect is not hard to find. After a period of quietism following the Court-packing threat of 1937, the Supreme Court embarked upon the most active period of its history. And, while constitutionalism and judicial activism are by no means synonymous, the fact is that a major part of this record has been directed toward upholding constitutional rights and duties.

But thirty years is a short period in the life of a nation—even of this "new nation." As Schochet has reminded us, recent years have witnessed a great deal of criticism of constitutionalism, along with pluralism and liberalism. The longing for a more virtuous republic has often led critics to argue as though we already had a virtuous citizenry, restrained only by the straitjacket of constitutionalism from the pursuit of justice and righteousness; although Watergate has placed something of a damper on their enthusiasm.

Of one thing we may be certain: no matter what may happen to the interpretation or even the existence of our Constitution, the issue of constitutionalism will never die. It was an issue in the days of "absolute" kings, as Nannerl Keohane has demonstrated, even as it was in the days of Aristotle. It is in fact the perennial question of rule ("the rule of law") versus discretion. Scholars will no doubt continue to argue about the meaning of each of these terms, as Hayek and Dworkin, Fuller and Hart, have done in our day. But, while they may argue about their meaning, and even about the role that each should play in a well-ordered society, none will deny the need for both rule and discretion, nor will any regime long persist that does not make use of both.

Although rule and discretion will always be with us, their relative importance and application in any given time and place will continue to be a matter of controversy, just as the role each plays will vary markedly with time and circumstance. In periods of revolutionary change, progressive or reactionary, the rule of law retreats into the shadows. In periods of great stability, it may cover so much of the legal landscape that stasis threatens to take over. As Sheldon Wolin has reminded us, in constitutional theory "we look in vain for any theory of political education, of political leadership, or, until recently, of social consensus." [2] Clearly, the tides of constitutionalism will continue to ebb and flow.

Precise definitions of constitutionalism have been avoided by most of our authors. In his Introduction, however, Schochet, distinguishing "modern" from "traditional" constitutionalism, says in effect that the former amounts to the proposition that the will of the people regarding the form of the society's political institutions and processes and concerning the standards for their evaluation should be formally enacted. And Thomas Grey carefully elucidates the concept and explores its numerous ramifications. I have no quarrel with either of these statements, but I would like to add a few words (as Supreme Court Justices sometimes say at the beginning of an exceptionally long concurring opinion). The essential notion of constitutionalism seems clearly to be that of restraint. (This is the obverse of Wolin's remark, quoted above.) Certain things, the doctrine holds, no government should be permitted to do—for example, punish a person for something that had not been publicly declared punishable when the act was committed. Moreover, government should not be permitted to act in an arbitrary manner. Arbitrary behavior is of two kinds. First, it is behavior that treats like cases differentially, or more broadly, treats some persons more or less favorably than others, without justification. Second, it is behavior for which it cannot be held to account. In a democracy, this means that it should be accountable to the adults of the society or their freely elected representatives. And to these ends such procedures should be provided for as will reduce to a minimum the likelihood of arbitrary governmental action.

This dependence upon forms and procedures suggests a nagging concern, one with which our authors have not much dealt. We live in an informal age. Perhaps this is a passing fad. On the other hand, it may be integrally related to democracy. Tocqueville warned us: "Men living in a democratic age do not readily comprehend the utility of forms: they feel an instinctive contempt for them. . . . Forms excite their contempt and often their hatred; as they commonly aspire to none but easy and present gratifications, they rush onwards to the object of their desires, and the slightest delay exasperates them. This same temper, carried with them into political life, renders them hostile to forms, which perpetually retard or arrest them in some of their projects." [3]

Before considering the question of whether Tocqueville's warning should be of concern to us today, it may be useful to note certain pairs of opposed concepts other than those of formalism and informalism. In moral philosophy, we find deontology opposed to consequentialism, classically expressed as Kant versus Hume or Bentham. In the English-speaking world at least, consequentialism, or, more specifically, utilitarianism, has for a long time predominated. But today, unless I mistake, the situation is reversed. It is the proponents of the right who tend to prevail over those who would measure everything by the good. Whether or not they agree with Dworkin, people are "taking rights seriously." Nowhere is this trend reflected more clearly than in the holdings of the United States Supreme Court. More strictly in the field of law, we have the warring schools of "conceptualists" (now qualified by a "neo-") and "legal realists." The latter apparently has turned out to be one of those short-lived but influential movements that has disappeared as a school but that has left its indelible marks. (One is reminded of behavioralism in political science, and Robert A. Dahl's "epitaph for a successful protest." [4]) Today's sophisticated neoconceptualists are far removed from mechanical jurisprudence (although Ronald Dworkin has been called a "Bealist"), but they (or at least some of them) are certainly seeking to place a limit on "result-oriented" decision-making (consequentialism) and trying to find principles and even rules to control discretion.

What these examples from the fields of philosophy and jurisprudence do, if nothing else, is to underline the point made above that the future, like the past, is likely to be characterized by continuing oscillations in the moving currents of thought and action rather than a complete and lasting victory for either side. Assuming this to be true, it may be worthwhile to survey some of the trends and forces that appear to threaten constitutionalism—or at least to diminish it to the extent that liberty and security are seriously abridged—and then to scan the landscape for signs of countervailing factors.

When Corwin described the erosion of American constitutionalism, he was identifying the latter with the power of the Supreme Court. But just as constitutionalism may exist without judicial review, so the attenuation of the Court's power in this country is not equivalent to the weakening of the Constitution. Thus, the demise of "dual federalism" has by no means abolished the states as checks upon the federal government. It is true that federal centralization has proceeded apace as Congress has utilized its powers, especially under the commerce clause, to regulate the American economy, and as, by its taxing and spending powers, it has largely displaced the states or reduced them to little more than administrative units for the federal government, in many areas of activity. But important qualifications must be made. A large part of the increase in federal functions has been accompanied by a similar growth of the activities of state and local governments, as the functions of government have increased relative to the private sector. Even more important, the states, with their own sources of patronage and control of distribution of funds, remain powerful political forces, as is reflected in the structure of the political parties and in the responses of Congress itself. True, the parties are more nationalized than they used to be, as well as being weaker forces in themselves; yet federalism remains a significant factor among the checks on national power.

As for the separation of powers, while its purity may have been polluted, its operation as a check on the powers of government has hardly been impaired. Jimmy Carter's ability to have his way with Congress does not compare with that of F.D.R. The Supreme Court itself, having recently played a key role in toppling a president and having throughout the postwar period played a vital part in the advancement of human rights, while enlarging its jurisdiction to cover areas, like that of legislative apportionment, long considered beyond its control, seems to have emerged from the "twilight" as from a passing cloud.

It is true that checks and balances, while operating to frustrate this or that branch of the government and this or that pressure group, do not necessarily insure the rule of law or otherwise protect the rights of individuals. The growth of overall governmental power, the multiplication of regulations, the invasion of areas once thought private and totally immune from government prying and intervention, while they do not necessarily lead to arbitrariness, certainly do increase the opportunities for departures from the rule of law and moreover often amount to the invasion of cherished rights. Nor does the increasing size and complexity of society hold out hope for a reversal of this trend. To this may be added that the "softening of power" by modern technology makes governmental invasion of private rights less obtrusive but no less obnoxious.

Historically the rights of property have constituted a major defense against the arbitrary actions of government. Today those rights are being progressively eroded, generally in the interest of equality or other laudable objective, but nonetheless diminished as an independent source of resistance against the always potentially

arbitrary power of the ever growing bureaucracy. Tocqueville's
"providential fact" of equality itself seems increasingly to lead to
invasion of those liberties that constitutionalism was designed to
protect.

Finally, the international situation. In a world in which isolation
is no longer possible, whether or not desirable, and in which
potential enemies are powerful, secretive, and expansive, often
flaunting human rights abroad as well as at home, how are we to
maintain our own security without resorting in some measure to the
same veil of secrecy and the same invasion of rights, even of our own
citizens, on which potential aggressors rely? Whatever the right
answer to this question, is not government—understandably biased
against taking chances with national security—bound to resolve all
doubts in favor of security measures and against individual claims
of right to liberty and privacy?

Do these various forms and tendencies foreshadow dark days for
American constitutionalism? Before reaching such a conclusion, one
should look for entries on the other side of the ledger. First, we
should note important elements in our tradition. They include a
hatred of tyranny and a suspicion of, indeed a contempt for,
government. The latter two may not be altogether admirable traits
in a people, but they can serve it in good stead when rights are
threatened. We should observe too the institution of judicial review
and the high regard Americans have for the Supreme Court. In
opinion polls, it regularly scores above the elective branches of the
government in public respect. Just what that tells us about
democracy is perhaps an open question; but, in this context, the fact
remains reassuring. It is true of course that judicial activism is not
always equivalent to constitutionalism. The rule of law may become
no more than the rule of lawyers. Government by judiciary is not
necessarily less arbitrary than is government by bureaucracy; but, for
numerous reasons that need not be recounted, it seems, in fact,
within its restricted ambit, to be so.

Just as "to every action there is an equal and opposite reaction,"
so it appears that whenever one of the branches of government gets
out of line in the use of its powers, a countermove sets in. The
"imperial presidency" appears to have been checked, by the
development of the congressional veto and by the enactment of the

War Powers Resolution of 1973, as well as by the precedent of President Nixon's forced resignation.

The American polity has long been subjected to attack for its vulnerability to pressure groups and, especially, for the fact that certain interests—notably consumer and general "public" interests— were notoriously ineffective in using this means for protecting their rights and advancing their interests. Today the rise of "consumerism" and "environmentalism" has cast a new light on this issue. Once people were aroused to what was needed and what could be done in these areas, our constitutional framework proved adequate to give it effective representation. Rights to pure air and water and rights to employment often conflict and will continue to do so. To the resultant controversies constitutionalism itself gives no definite answers. All it can do is to provide forums for their debate and ultimate resolution. But that contribution is not to be belittled, as George Kateb has made clear. The interesting and, I believe, constructive aspect of the way our constitutional system is dealing with such problems is the division of power, one might say the dialectic, between legislatures and courts in ongoing reflection, discussion, decision. We note here, not only the pitting of one abstract idea against another, but also the emergence of groups with recognized status and with an interest in protecting and advancing their claims of right. Thus, we see that while owners of property may be losing some ability to protect themselves against government, other people, or sometimes the same people differently organized, are gaining new protections. It is never safe to decry a loss at one point in the great conglomerate of society without taking careful look to see whether a compensating gain is not developing elsewhere.

It is interesting to note how, when it comes to action, the critics of proceduralism, who are more concerned, they say, with substantive results than with procedural mechanics, often try to amend the rules by adding *more* procedural devices. Many readers of this volume will have experienced this phenomenon in the politics and governance of academic institutions. More committees are established; members are elected rather than appointed; agendas must be voted on; and so on and so forth. Whether such constitutional devices are good or bad is not my present concern. I wish only to point out that

J. ROLAND PENNOCK

when it comes to a showdown the critics of constitutionalism often find that they are not critics of constitutionalism after all—they simply want a different set of rules.

A final point in this summary review. The Supreme Court itself has been busy for several decades, contrary to what the "threats" to constitutionalism discussed above might have led one to anticipate, extending certain old rights and creating new ones. This is not the place to elaborate on this theme—well known to the readers of *NOMOS*—but it will do no harm to remind the reader of four categories of such rights. The old common-law rights to privacy have been both expanded and raised to constitutional status since the famous article by Warren and Brandeis appeared in 1890. During the second half of this century the rights of the accused have been greatly expanded. Not surprisingly, the subject—involving the rights of the individual versus the rights of society—has proved highly controversial, and some backtracking has developed. But one part of it at least—the part designed to see to it that the right to have rights protected should not be denied because of indigency—seems destined to be of lasting effect. A third category comprises certain "fundamental" rights of uncertain provenance. The rights to travel and to procreate appear to be solid examples. Finally, in a series of areas where, for various reasons, constitutional rights have traditionally been held to be qualified or limited in favor of administrative or judicial discretion, a strong tendency to curtail discretion in favor of procedural due process now prevails. I have in mind the treatment of juveniles, of aliens, and of those who can claim title to any of all sorts of government benefits, most notably those providing for the economically disadvantaged, and also the field of sentencing and postsentencing treatment of the convicted.

Mr. Justice McReynolds was wrong. The Constitution is not "gone," nor does it appear to be going. It is continually evolving; but if limited government and nonarbitrary rule presents ever more difficult problems in a society in which the law plays a steadily growing role, it remains both here and abroad an ideal toward which the best efforts of legal craftsmen are seriously devoted, with results that bode well for the future of constitutionalism.

NOTES

1. *The Twilight of the Supreme Court, a History of Our Constitutional Theory* (New Haven, Conn.: Yale University Press, 1934).
2. *Politics and Vision, Continuity and Vision in Western Political Thought* (Boston, Mass.: Little, Brown, 1960).
3. Alexis de Tocqueville, *Democracy in America,* Bradley's edition of the Reeve translation (New York. Knopf, 1945), II, 325-326.
4. "The Behavioral Approach to Political Science—Epitaph for a Monument to a Successful Protest," *American Political Science Review,* 55 (1961), 763-772.

Index

Abortion issue, 334, 341, 343, 353, 356

Acceptance, 191; usage and, 204-5

Adams, John, 93, 109, 111, 212-13

Adegbenro, Premier, 169

Adversary system, 338, 348, 349

"Agrarian law," 104

Akintola, Premier, 169

Alien and Sedition Acts (1798), 145

"All-things-considered" as standard, 196

Amendment, provisions for: in Massachusetts constitution, 112-13, 115; in Pennsylvania constitution, 102, 105-6, 115; in U.S. Constitution, 146; in Virginia constitution, 115

American Society for Political and Legal Philosophy, vii

Anti-Federalists, 129, 133-34

Appian Alexandrin, 54, 57, 64

Aquinas, St. Thomas, 19, 25, 26, 28

Aristotle, 25, 26, 27, 55, 63, 76, 117, 310

Articles of Confederation, 143

Assemblée Casuelle, 68

Assemblée des Notables, 68

Association of American Law Schools, 269

Authority, 220; descending, 75; Seyssel's system of, 75-76

Awolowo, Chief, 169, 171

Azikiwe, Nnamdi, 166, 167

Bacon, Francis, 346

Bailyn, Bernard, 9